CCCC
CCCC**ONVIVIUM**PRESS
CCCC

Hosffman Ospino (ed.)

Hispanic Ministry in the 21st Century: Present and Future

El ministerio hispano en el siglo xxi: presente y futuro

CONVIVIUMPRESS

SERIES HISPANIA

2010

Hispanic Ministry in the 21st Century: Present and Future

El ministerio hispano en el siglo XXI: presente y futuro

http://www.conviviumpress.com
sales@conviviumpress.com
ventas@conviviumpress.com
convivium@conviviumpress.com

7661 NW 68th St, Suite 108,
Miami, Florida 33166. USA.
Phone: +1 (786) 8669718
Fax: +1 (305) 8875463

Edited by Hosffman Ospino *and* Rafael Luciani
Translated *by* Hosffman Ospino *in collaboration with* Carmen Aguinaco
Designed *by* Eduardo Chumaceiro d'E
Series: *Hispania*

ISBN: 978-1-934996-16-4

Printed in Colombia
Impreso en Colombia
D'VINNI, S.A.

Convivium Press
Miami 2010

THE «HISPANIA» SERIES
IS MADE POSSIBLE THROUGH THE
EDITORIAL COLLABORATION
OF THE INSTITUTE FOR HISPANIC/LATINO
THEOLOGY AND MINISTRY AT
BARRY UNIVERSITY

Hispanic Ministry in the 21ˢᵗ Century: Present and Future

El ministerio hispano en el siglo XXI: presente y futuro

Contents

APPENDIX 2

Symposium Participants by Study Areas PAGE *215*

Contenido

APÉNDICE 2

Participantes en el simposio <small>PÁGINA</small> *437*

1

Hispanic Ministry in the 21ˢᵗ Century: Present and Future

Acknowledgements

Every great project is possible thanks to people with creative minds, supporters, funders, companions, hard workers, inspirational persons, and those whom we have in mind as potential beneficiaries of our efforts. The 2009 *National Symposium on the Present and Future of Catholic Hispanic Ministry in the United States* without a doubt brought all these groups together. Thanks to everyone who made the symposium and this book possible.

Thanks to my colleagues at Boston College's School of Theology and Ministry (STM) who believed and embraced the idea of the symposium from the beginning. In particular I extend my heartfelt gratitude to Thomas H. Groome for his support, sincere mentorship, and inspiring vision; Richard Clifford, SJ, founding dean of the STM, for affirming the theological and ministerial formation of leaders for Hispanic ministry as a priority in our school; Nancy Pineda-Madrid and Roberto Goizueta for the blessing of friendship. Special thanks to Rebecca Camacho, graduate assistant for Hispanic ministry programs at Boston College in 2009, who along with Maura Colleary took care of perfectly-coordinated logistics during the symposium. I am also grateful to Katherine Klauser, graduate assistant for Hispanic ministry programs at Boston College in 2010, and to the STM graduate students who worked during the symposium. You are the best.

Thanks to the scholars and administrators from the academic institutions that accepted the invitation to partner with Boston College in the organization of the symposium: Barry University, Loyola Marymount University, and the Congar Institute for Ministry Development. Together we modeled that in which we believe: collaboration for the greater good of the Church and society. I was honored to work with you and I hope that our partnership continues to yield good fruits in the near future.

Thanks to the scholars and leaders who served as the main readers of these documents in their early drafts: Alejandro Aguilera-Titus, Ruth Bolarte, IHM, Cecilia González-Andrieu, Michael G. Lee, SJ, Nancy Pineda-Madrid, and Bill Rickle, SJ. A similar spirit of gratitude is extended to the scholars who accepted the invitation to write the essays in this collection. Your thoughts and observations are undoubtedly unique contributions to the contemporary reflection on the U.S. Catholic experience.

Thanks to the sponsoring publishing companies, organizations, and institutions —named and unnamed here— that made it possible that we had the appropriate resources to celebrate the symposium and publish this book: Claretian

Publications, Convivium Press, Harcourt Religion Publishers, Loyola Press, the Northeast Pastoral Center, Oregon Catholic Press, Our Sunday Visitor, Inc., RCL Benziger, Renew International, and William H. Sadlier, Inc. Thanks to the national organizations that endorsed the symposium and continue to advance the reflection about Hispanic ministry in the United States: Academy of Catholic Hispanic Theologians of the United States (ACHTUS), National Catholic Association of Diocesan Directors for Hispanic Ministry (NCADDHM), National Catholic Council for Hispanic Ministry (NCCHM), and the Secretariat of Cultural Diversity in the Church, Office of Hispanic Affairs at the United States Catholic Conference of Bishops.

And finally a profound word of thanks to the pioneers and giants of Hispanic ministry and theology in this country on whose shoulders we stand and to whom we owe admiration and praise for their abundant contributions; to the women and men who most recently have made the preferential option to serve Latinos/as as part of the Church's evangelizing mission in the United States; and to the participants in the 2009 National Symposium on the Present and Future of Catholic Hispanic Ministry in the United States. What an honor it is to walk with you at this time in history.

Introduction

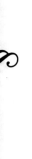

The u.s. Catholic experience in the twenty-first century is being significantly shaped by the presence and contributions of Hispanic[1] Catholics. As of 2010 it is estimated that Hispanics constitute nearly 40 percent of the whole u.s. Catholic population and within a few years the majority of Catholics in the country will be of Hispanic descent. Nationwide, Hispanics are 17 percent of the whole u.s. population and demographers estimate that by the middle of the century that number will rise to 25 percent. What does this mean for the Catholic Church in the United States and for Hispanic Catholics in particular?

Latino/a Catholics welcomed the twenty-first century aware of the wonderful legacy built throughout the centuries by countless generations of Catholic women and men living in the United States, many of them Hispanic. We acknowledge that to be u.s. Catholics means that we stand faithful to the principles of the Christian faith that nurtures and sustains our lives and summons us to participate in the building of a just and flourishing society. We know that our cultures, traditions, and convictions are important contributions to the tapestry of Catholic faith and life in this country. At the same time, we are aware that for a long time many of our contributions as a people have been relegated to the margins of the Church and society; often times our struggles have received little attention from our brothers and sisters who share our own faith and our voices have not always been fully heard. The twenty-first century is a unique opportunity for Catholics in the United States of every background to affirm the presence and contributions of Hispanic Catholics, to further the Catholic legacy in this country, and to forge a renewed experience of what it means to be u.s. Catholics in the culturally diverse context within which we witness our faith in the risen Christ. For many of us the arena where this happens is Hispanic ministry.

Hispanic ministry is the umbrella term for the Church's evangelizing activity with Latinos/as in the United States. Frequently Hispanic ministry is understood as a form of specialized ministry, mainly done by Hispanics with Hispanics. This is only half true. There are hundreds of non-Hispanic leaders fully committed to Hispanic ministry and hundreds of Hispanic leaders ministering beyond Latino circles. As the number of Hispanics increases in parishes and dioceses across the country the lines of differentiation are blurred. In many places

1 An important note on the use of language: the essays in this book use the terms Latino and Hispanic interchangeably. The presence of both terms along with the gender variations *Latino* and *Latina*, borrowed from Spanish, and the commonly used combination Latino/a, indicates that the conversation about which term is preferred when we refer to Hispanic-Latinos/as is still open. The use of one term by an author does not necessarily exclude the validity of others terms.

Hispanic ministry is simply *ministry* —and vice versa. Consequently, Hispanic ministry in the twenty-first century must be seen as a responsibility of the whole Church. It is the whole Church in the u.s. that is called to embrace and affirm the Latino Catholic experience in the context of ministry. On the one hand, this calling requires accompanying Latinos/as as we integrate our lives, visions, and hopes into the wider spectrum of the u.s. Catholic experience. On the other hand, all Latinos/as need to fully understand the magnitude of the evangelizing mission of the Church in this country and embrace with renewed spirit the possibilities that come with such mission. This will certainly lead to some significant transformations. It is a complex process that compels us to ask important questions such as: what do we bring to the table? How do we evangelize and educate in faith? How do we reflect theologically? How do we bring Christ to our youth? How do we celebrate and live our faith? How do we practice what we believe? How do we prepare our leaders?

To respond to these questions we look at the present as *lived experience*. This is not an abstract present in which things happen by chance or without consequences. The present is where we live, where we encounter God, where we enter into relationship with one another. For Hispanic Catholics in the United States the present is a privileged moment in history in which we discover the complexity of our diversity. Ours is a present in which we know that immigration, mestizaje, and globalization together have made us a new people, and thus as a new people we enter into dialogue with the Church in the United States, the larger society, and the Latin American communities where many of us still have deep roots. In the present we acknowledge that we have countless challenges that make our experience far from idyllic, yet we embrace them because those challenges constitute the kiln where the character of our communities and that of the new generations of u.s. Latino/a Catholics are strengthened. In this present we affirm our identity as missionary disciples of Jesus Christ who have in our hands the responsibility of building communities of faith and love where everyone can experience that God is real because God has been real to us. We look at the present as the *protagonistas* of a new time and a hopeful future.

We look at the future with *faithful hope*. As protagonists of a new moment in the history of u.s. Catholicism we are in a privileged, yet daunting position of proposing paths that lead to experiencing the Reign of God in both traditional and new ways. We cannot do this alone or afford to ignore the many other voices that accompany us in our faith communities. This is an opportunity for u.s. Hispanic Catholics to propose fresh models of pastoral action, theological reflection, and social commitment that respond to the changing times in which we live. As Christians we remain faithful to the call to be disciples of the Lord; we are hopeful because we trust in the God of Life whose presence accompanies us on our historical journey.

To speak of the present and envision the future of Catholic Hispanic ministry in the United States, however, would make little sense if we failed to honor our *memoria histórica*. That historical memory reminds us of the struggles and dreams of the many Latino/a Catholics in this land who celebrated their faith with conviction and raised their voices to advocate on behalf of their fellow sisters and brothers at various moments of a long history. This history antecedes the large migratory waves from Europe that profoundly shaped the ethos of our society; it antecedes the Civil War, the birth of the United States as a nation, the establishment of the first English colonies, and even the arrival of the Pilgrims in Plymouth, MA. Before all these important events took place, Hispanic Catholics were already *presente!*

Particularly in the twentieth century, Hispanic Catholics participated in the Civil Rights Movement and strengthened their voices in the Church and society. The rise of groups like PADRES and Las Hermanas and the establishment of institutions like the Mexican American Cultural Center were true signs of hope. The Secretariat for Hispanic Affairs at the Conference of Catholic Bishops at its various moments in history was an affirmation of the importance of the Hispanic presence in the Church at the institutional level. The consecration of Patricio Flores as the first Mexican American Catholic bishop in 1970 signaled a new moment in the world of ecclesial leadership followed by the consecration of a growing number of Hispanic bishops and the rise of more Latino/a Catholics to key leadership positions in the Church. In 2010 José H. Gómez was named Coadjutor Archbishop of Los Angeles, the largest archdiocese in the country, which opens the possibility for him to become the first Latino Cardinal in the history of U.S. Catholicism. The creation of national organizations, educational institutions, and various offices advocating for Hispanic ministry nationwide brought together the efforts of Hispanic Catholic leadership confirming that *trabajando en conjunto* (working together) we can accomplish more. The emergence of a growing body of U.S. Hispanic Catholic theologians has expanded the influence of our contributions beyond the borders of our faith communities into the world of the academy. Most Hispanic Catholic theologians are continuously involved in our faith communities not only sharing the insights gained in our reflections, but also being nurtured by the lived faith of the people. The number of Hispanic bishops, priests, permanent deacons, and vowed religious is growing, yet at a very slow pace compared to the rest of the larger Hispanic Catholic population. Latino/a lay ecclesial ministers continue to be the backbone of many of our faith communities. But perhaps no other set of events in our *memoria histórica* has had more impact in shaping the identity of Hispanic Catholic leadership than the Encuentro processes. The 1972, 1977, and 1985 National Encuentros for Hispanic Ministry (*Encuentros Nacionales Hispanos de Pastoral*), the 2000 Encuentro—which broadened the spirituality and dynamic of *Encuentro* to the larger Church in the United States under the prominent leadership of Hispanic Catholics— and more recently the 2006 First National Encounter for Hispanic Youth and Young Adult Ministry, together were spaces which, in their different stages, gave voice to hundreds of thousands of people, mostly Hispanic, at various levels of leadership in the Church to share their prophetic vision and hopes. These Encuentro processes were unique opportunities to affirm that our presence is neither temporary nor insignificant and that we accept the challenge of being protagonists of a common future with the larger, more diverse body of u.s. Catholics. In the spirit of these Encuentros, the Catholic bishops of the United States in 1987 presented a *National Pastoral Plan for Hispanic Ministry* and also have written several other documents reflecting on the Hispanic reality. Among these *Encuentro and Mission: A Renewed Pastoral Framework for Hispanic Ministry*, written in 2002, stands as particularly relevant for our contemporary reflections. It is imperative that we continue to learn and honor our *memoria histórica*; more so as we look at the present and future of Catholic Hispanic ministry in the twenty-first century. New generations of Catholic leaders are assuming ministerial responsibilities serving in communities where Latino/a Catholics are present and they will benefit from the wisdom of the people, the documents, and the movements that have informed Hispanic ministry during the last decades.

On June 8-10, 2009 sixty-two leaders from around the country met in Boston, MA to affirm the richness of our *memoria histórica*, analyze our present experience with critical eyes, and together envision the future of Hispanic ministry for the second decade of the twenty-first century. We gathered together for a *National Symposium on the Present and Future of Catholic Hispanic Ministry in the United States*. Bishops, theologians, scholars from various other fields, leaders from national offices, publishers, heads of major organizations advocating for Hispanic ministry, and practitioners working with Latino/a Catholics at different levels in the Church gathered to reflect on the challenges and promises of Hispanic ministry in the country. The symposium was organized by Boston

College in collaboration with Barry University in Miami, Loyola Marymount University in Los Angeles, and the Congar Institute for Ministry Development in San Antonio. Together these academic institutions provided a great model of collaboration that surely will shape the dynamic of reflection about Catholic ministry and theology in the coming years.

The collection of essays in this book brings together the revised study documents that inspired the conversation during the symposium. These essays are presented here as instruments for ongoing reflection among scholars, leaders, and practitioners working with Latino/a Catholics in ministry. In fact, the essays are valuable resources for anyone interested in the present and future of the overall u.s. Catholic experience—not just that of Hispanics.

In chapter 1 Timothy Matovina offers an analysis of Hispanic ministry in the larger context of u.s. Catholicism. He provides a historical overview of the emergence of ecclesial structures and ministries serving the Hispanic Catholic community in this country, assesses a number of contemporary approaches to the presence of Hispanic Catholics in the Church as we integrate in the larger u.s. Catholic context, and concludes by proposing a series of specific steps to continue the conversation as Latinos/as assume more leadership roles in the Church.

In chapter 2 Hosffman Ospino looks at evangelization and faith formation in the particular context of Hispanic ministry. He identifies some of the most pressing factors and situations shaping the present reality of Latino/a Catholics in this country and indicates how these need to be taken into careful consideration in the planning of every process of sharing faith with Latinos/as. He calls for the development of an analytical framework to guide major conversations about Catholic education, faith formation, and evangelization of Hispanic Catholics in the USA and proposes seven cornerstones to sustain such an important framework.

In chapter 3 Jorge Presmanes and Alicia Marill team up on a thought-provoking reflection about Hispanic ministry and theology. They draw from their personal experience serving Latinos/as in Catholic faith communities and that of their graduate students in ministry. The chapter argues that the lived experience of Latino/a Catholics in the particularity of our faith communities provides us with a unique ecclesiology that deeply shapes our theological reflection and ministerial praxis. The uniqueness of the Latino/a Catholic experience in the United States has been a rich source of theological categories that inform our theologies and our pastoral action; it is a rich source in the present, and will continue to be so in the foreseeable future.

In Chapter 4 Ken-Johnson-Mondragón brings together years of research and careful analysis of the reality of Hispanic youth and young adult ministry in the United States. Not only does he provide a complete reading of the current reality of Latino/a Catholic *jóvenes* in the country, but also he proposes helpful categories for ministers and educators to use in our work with this important sector of the Catholic population. This chapter carefully weaves the insights from recent studies on youth in the United States and introduces Hispanic ministry leaders to the conclusions of the 2006 First National Encounter for Hispanic Youth and Young Adult Ministry.

In chapter 5 Raúl Gómez-Ruíz reflects on the important relationship between liturgy and spirituality in Hispanic ministry. He invites us to enter deeper into the world of Hispanic Catholic spirituality, consistently expressed through popular Catholicism, and to discover its intimate connections to liturgical life. He looks closely at the categories of *mística* and sacramentality in the Latino/a Catholic experience in the United States and convincingly argues how these sustain the life of faith of our communities while leading to practical ministerial commitments.

In chapter 6 Arturo Chávez explores the connections between Hispanic ministry and social justice. He situates his reflection in the context of key conversations on issues such as economics, education, immigration, and human dignity, among others, which demand active engagement on the part of Hispanic Catholics. Pastoral discernment applied to issues of social justice, as Chavez suggests, has been integral to Hispanic ministry and thus must be seen as one of our key contributions to contemporary reflection on the u.s. Catholic experience. This is a time of opportunities for Hispanic Catholics and we must do our best in the midst of our present circumstances.

Lastly, in chapter 7 Hosffman Ospino and Elsie Miranda assess the possibilities and hopes of Latino/a Catholics increasingly assuming leadership roles in the life of the Church. The chapter offers a general overview of recent developments, documents, and conversations on formation of ecclesial leaders in the context of Hispanic ministry; it raises awareness about current trends and proposes some directions for further reflection in this area. The chapter concludes highlighting the need for inclusive theological reflection on ministry and leadership formation.

May this book spread among all its readers the energy and hope that we experienced during the national symposium in Boston and inspire many more conversations in the years to come.

Chapter 1

Hispanic Ministry and U.S. Catholicism

Timothy Matovina

Father José Antonio Díaz de León, the last Franciscan priest serving in Texas when it was still part of Mexico, died mysteriously in 1834 near the east Texas town of Nacogdoches. A judge exonerated an Anglo American accused of murdering Díaz de León amidst rumors that the priest's death of a gunshot wound was a suicide. Mexican Catholics decried this decision as a sham. How could their pastor, who had served faithfully on the Texas frontier for nearly all his years as a priest, have committed such a desperate act?

Seven years later, Vincentian priests John Timon and Jean Marie Odin made a pastoral visit to Nacogdoches. They deplored the conditions of Mexican Catholics, whom they said Anglo Americans had indiscriminately killed, driven away, and robbed of their lands. Father Odin also reported that Anglo Americans had burned the local Catholic church building to the ground. Yet these and other visitors observed that Mexican Catholic laity continued to gather in private homes for feast days and weekly worship services and celebrated rituals like funerals. Hispanic ministry in Nacogdoches remained almost entirely a lay-led effort until 1847 when (by then) Bishop Odin was finally able to appoint two priests to replace Father Díaz de León. The parishioners' eager reception of the sacraments from their new pastors testified to their enduring faith amidst a tumultuous period of social upheaval[1].

Efforts like those of the Nacogdoches faithful underscore the foundations of Hispanic ministry in local communities and initiatives. Spanish-speaking Catholics have been active in what is now the United States for twice as long as the nation has existed. The first diocese in the New World was established in 1511 at San Juan, Puerto Rico. Subjects of the Spanish crown founded the first permanent European settlement within the current borders of the fifty states at St. Augustine, Florida in 1565, four decades before the establishment of the first British colony at Jamestown. In 1598 at present-day El Paso, Texas, Spanish subjects established the permanent foundation of Catholicism in what is now the Southwest[2].

---

1 MATOVINA T., «Lay Initiatives in Worship on the Texas *Frontera*, 1830-1860» in *U.S. Catholic Historian* 12 (1994) 108-11.
2 General histories of U.S. Hispanic Catholicism include SANDOVAL M., *On the Move: A History of the Hispanic Church in the United States*, second edition, Orbis, Maryknoll, NY 1990, 2006; MATOVINA T. and POYO G.E. (eds.), *¡Presente! U.S. Latino Catholics from Colonial Origins to the Present*, Orbis, Maryknoll, NY 2000; BADILLO D.A., *Latinos and the New Immigrant Church*, Johns Hopkins University Press, Baltimore, MD 2006.

Though for much of u.s. Catholic history Hispanics have constituted a proportionately small and frequently overlooked group, since World War II their numbers and influence have increased dramatically. An influx of newcomers from diverse locales such as Puerto Rico, Cuba, the Dominican Republic, El Salvador, Guatemala, Nicaragua, Colombia, Peru, Ecuador, and Argentina, along with ongoing Mexican immigration, has added to the ranks of an established Hispanic population composed primarily of Catholics of Mexican descent. More important, Hispanic Catholic communities, previously concentrated in New York, the Southwest, and some Midwestern cities, now extend from Seattle to Boston, from Miami to Alaska.

As we approach the 500th anniversary of the (Arch)diocese of San Juan, a milestone that illuminates the longstanding Hispanic Catholic presence in territories now associated with the United States, Hispanic ministry is undergoing significant transitions in its support structures and in the approaches we employ in our ministries. Even as vibrant Spanish-language ministries flourish, bishops and other leaders call for greater integration of Hispanics into the wider u.s. Catholic Church. A future of mutual faith enrichment between Hispanics and their fellow Catholics holds bright promise. But if that promise is to be realized we must address the challenges of renewing our vision for Hispanic ministry, leadership parity, and fostering authentic Hispanic integration.

1

Structures and Ministies

Despite its longevity at the local level, a coordinated national effort in Hispanic ministry did not begin until 1945, when Archbishop Robert Lucey of San Antonio led the effort to found the Bishops' Committee for the Spanish Speaking. Leaders of the Committee labored to advance Hispanic ministry, especially through the establishment of diocesan Catholic councils for the Spanish speaking. In 1970 Pablo Sedillo became the new director of the initiative and its operation moved to the national offices of the Bishops' Conference in Washington, D.C. Finding he «had no easy access to the top administrative units, the secretariats» within the conference, Sedillo pushed for four years until the bishops granted the Hispanic office secretariat status. Leaders from the New York archdiocese such as Father Robert Stern and Encarnación Padilla de Armas, along with former staff member of the Latin American Episcopal Conference (CELAM) Edgard Beltrán, enhanced Sedillo's efforts and the national advancement of Hispanic ministry with their initiative to convene the First National Encuentro for Hispanic Ministry in 1972. Under Sedillo's guidance and that of his successor Ron Cruz, the Secretariat for Hispanic Affairs was a pivotal organizer for this and two subsequent national Encuentros for Hispanic Ministry in which Hispanic Catholics voiced their ministerial needs and vision, as well as numerous efforts to promote Hispanic leadership and ministry at the parish, diocesan, regional, and national levels. The Secretariat was also instrumental in the organization effort for Encuentro 2000, an initiative to unite leaders from the diverse racial and ethnic groups in u.s. Catholicism that culminated in a national summit entitled *Many Faces in God's House: A Catholic Vision for the Third Millennium*[3]. The bishops funded the Encuentros and supported them with directives such as a 1983 pastoral letter on Hispanic ministry, the 1987 *National Pastoral Plan for Hispanic Ministry*, and the 2002 document *Encuentro and Mission: A Renewed Pastoral Framework for Hispanic Ministry*[4].

Outside the Bishops' Conference, beginning with the 1969 founding of PADRES (*Padres Asociados por los Derechos Religiosos, Educativos, y Sociales*, or Priests Associated for Religious, Educational, and Social Rights) and the 1971 establishment of Las Hermanas («The Sisters»), regional and national initiatives in Hispanic ministry expanded rapidly. Over the following decades Latino Catholics established separate national organizations to support and advocate for Hispanic liturgical ministers, deacons, seminarians, catechists, theologians, Church historians, youth, and diocesan directors of Hispanic ministry. They also established pastoral institutes like the Mexican American Cultural Center

3 SANDOVAL M., «The Organization of a Hispanic Church» in DOLAN J.P. and FIGUEROA DECK A. (eds.), *Hispanic Catholic Culture in the u.s.: Issues and Concerns*, University of Notre Dame Press, Notre Dame, IN 1994, 131-65, at 139; STEVENS-ARROYO A.M., «The First Encounter» in *Prophets Denied Honor: An Anthology on the Hispano Church in the United States*, Orbis, Maryknoll, NY 1980, chapter 8; UNITED STATES CONFERENCE OF CATHOLIC BISHOPS, FAQS *About Many Faces in God's House:* Encuentro 2000, http://www.nccbuscc.org/encuentro2000/questions.htm (accessed May 2009).

4 NATIONAL CONFERENCE OF CATHOLIC BISHOPS (now the UNITED STATES CONFERENCE OF CATHOLIC BISHOPS), *The Hispanic Presence: Challenge and Commitment*, USCC, Washington, D.C. 1984; idem, *National Pastoral Plan for Hispanic Ministry*, USCC, Washington, D.C. 1988. Both documents are found in UNITED STATES CONFERENCE OF CATHOLIC BISHOPS, *Hispanic Ministry: Three Major Documents*, USCCB, Washington, D.C. 1995. UNITED STATES CONFERENCE OF CATHOLIC BISHOPS, *Encuentro and Mission: A Renewed Pastoral Framework for Hispanic Ministry*, USCCB, Washington, D.C. 2002. Quotations from these core documents are cited below in context.

(MACC, now the Mexican American Catholic College) in San Antonio, the Northeast Hispanic Catholic Center in New York, and the Southeast Pastoral Institute (SEPI) in Miami, which serve as centers for language and pastoral formation as well as advocates for Hispanic ministry and justice in church and society. In 1991 Jesuit priest Allan Figueroa Deck led the effort to found the National Catholic Council for Hispanic Ministry (NCCHM), an umbrella group of some 60 Hispanic Catholic organizations[5].

The 2007 restructuring of the United States Conference of Catholic Bishops (USCCB) established a new Secretariat of Cultural Diversity in the Church intended to nurture church unity and address the spiritual needs of Latinos, African Americans, Asian and Pacific Islanders, Native Americans, and migrants and refugees. In the process it also disbanded the Bishops' Committee on Hispanic Affairs and closed the Secretariat for Hispanic Affairs. One important goal of this restructuring is to integrate Hispanics and other historically-underrepresented groups more fully into the life and mission of the Church in the United States, including their participation in the five priority goals the USCCB identified: strengthen marriage; promote vocations to the Priesthood and Religious Life; enhance faith formation and sacramental practice; affirm life and the dignity of the human person; and appreciate cultural diversity with a special emphasis on Hispanic ministry in the spirit of Encuentro 2000[6].

A number of leaders in Hispanic ministry voiced their concern that in the USCCB restructuring they lost both important national support for their efforts and the most prominent symbol of Hispanic visibility within U.S. Catholicism. In August 2007 the NCCHM convened a symposium of key Hispanic ministry leaders who sent a statement of concerns and commitments to the Bishops' Committee on Hispanic Affairs (which was still active until its final meeting in November 2007). The statement thanked «the bishops who spoke out against the conference's decision to structurally subsume the Secretariat for Hispanic Affairs under a new Office [sic] for Cultural Diversity in the Church». It also

---

5   RODRÍGUEZ E., «The Hispanic Community and Church Movements: Schools of Leadership» in DOLAN J.P. and FIGUEROA DECK A. (eds.), *Hispanic Catholic Culture in the U.S.*, 206-39; MEDINA L., *Las Hermanas: Chicana/Latina Religious-Political Activism in the U.S. Catholic Church*, Temple University Press, Philadelphia 2004; MARTÍNEZ R.E., PADRES: *The National Chicano Priest Movement*, University of Texas Press, Austin 2005; BURGUÉS J.P., *SEPI 1978-2008: 30 Años de Evangelización en el Sureste y en la Nación*, Centro de Artes Gráficas, Miami 2008.

6   For an overview of the five priorities and the goals and objectives that the bishops established for each, see http://www.usccb.org/priorities/.

cautioned that «the restructuring plan may negatively impact the pastoral care and leadership formation of Hispanics» whose growing numbers and «unique challenges and opportunities… require resources and institutional support that may be diluted by grouping Hispanic ministry alongside other ethnic and racial ministries». The statement bemoaned that the plan for the new Secretariat of Cultural Diversity in the Church «structurally divides the Church into two groups —one for Catholics who are white and the other for Catholics who are not white according to the u.s. Census Bureau». It concluded with recommendations for addressing these concerns in the implementation of the five pastoral priorities and restructuring plan of the usccb, which despite their disagreements the Hispanic leaders of the ncchm firmly pledged to support[7].

The recent developments within the usccb reflect larger trends that are significantly reshaping support structures for Hispanic ministry. Funding has become alarmingly scarce. Groups like the National Organization for Catechesis with Hispanics (noch) have already disbanded and a number of others are in imminent danger of doing so. Several regional offices of Hispanic ministry created in the wake of the Second Encuentro of 1977 are now defunct and a number of national Hispanic organizations are weakened or undergoing transformation to a more self-sustaining model of operation. Some «dominant culture» national Catholic organizations evidence an encouraging desire to incorporate Hispanic leaders, such as the nccl Forum on Catechesis with Hispanics that Alex Sandoval, a young religious educator from Texas, helped inaugurate within the National Conference for Catechetical Leadership. Still, one crucial task for those of us committed to the future of Hispanic ministry is fostering those national organizations and institutes that are the most effective at coordinating and guiding our efforts. Thankfully Father Allan Figueroa Deck, whose appointment as executive director of the new Secretariat of Cultural Diversity in the Church was warmly endorsed by Hispanic leaders, has launched an initiative to create a national conversation with experienced leaders in Hispanic ministry aimed precisely at strengthening our national and regional structures.

Whatever success we might attain in revitalizing those structures, however, the daunting challenge is that the center of gravity for Hispanic ministry is more focused on local communities than it has been since World War ii, even as priestly vocations and resources in individual dioceses and parishes are stretched

---

7   NATIONAL CATHOLIC COUNCIL FOR HISPANIC MINISTRY, «Response to the usccb Reorganization» in *Origins* 37 (2008) 486-7.

thin. The graced opportunity is that, whether by necessity or design, Hispanic and other ministries flourish most when they are rooted in local initiatives, as was the case at Nacogdoches during those devastating years after Father José Antonio Díaz de León's assassination.

Much is in flux at the local level as well. Twenty years ago Father Allan Figueroa Deck identified three prominent models operative in Hispanic ministry: traditionalist, reformist, and transformationist[8]. Shifting ecclesial and social conditions ranging from church closings to immigrant controversies, along with the geographic dispersion of a growing Latino/a population across the United States, have altered the landscape of Hispanic ministry. The following four approaches collectively map the operative visions among many leaders currently engaged in ministry among Hispanics. They are not mutually exclusive options. Rather, they reflect divergent emphases and priorities. For each approach I offer a brief assessment of its weaknesses and strengths.

One approach could be deemed that of the «movimiento». The *veteranas* and *veteranos* who emphasize this approach helped create and develop Hispanic ministry over decades, some of them serving as leaders from the time of the First National Encuentro in 1972 and even before. They have long struggled to make Hispanics visible within u.s. Catholicism and to make Hispanic leadership and ministry a priority, in many instances applying lessons learned in social movements and community organizing to foster Hispanic concerns within the Catholic Church in the United States. According to *Encuentro and Mission*, such leaders helped develop a «*memoria histórica*» that illuminates the «unique identity» and «unique history of Hispanic Catholics in the United States» (n. 11). Members of this group are usually the most frustrated with recent transitions in the structures and general state of Hispanic ministry, changes which can appear to be a rejection or reversal of advances built on their own blood, sweat, and tears. They remind us that conversations about the future must stand on a critical understanding of the past. Their faithfulness, commitment to justice, experience, and wisdom are invaluable.

New immigrants comprise another major leadership group. Hispanic ministry initiatives in the u.s. Catholic Church tend to be strongest among immigrants: their traditional rituals and devotions, recognizable spiritual and material needs, preference for Spanish, and deep resonance with pastors who express

---

8 FIGUEROA DECK A., «Hispanic Ministry Comes of Age» in *America* 154 (1986) 400-02.

solidarity with them make them relatively easier to form into vibrant faith communities. The preponderance of foreign-born Latino clergy undergirds the prevalence of an immigrant-focused, Spanish-language approach in Hispanic ministry. One recent statistical analysis revealed that five of every six among the 2,900 Latino priests in the United States are foreign born[9]. Programs to orient these newcomers to the u.s. context include those at the Oblate School of Theology in San Antonio, Loyola Marymount University in Los Angeles, and St. Patrick's Seminary in Menlo Park, California, but unfortunately these programs do not reach all the émigré priests who come to serve in the United States[10]. Consequently new immigrant leaders often know little or nothing about the historical developments in Hispanic ministry summarized above. These leaders tend to equate Hispanic ministry with Spanish-language ministry, sometimes even judging as deficient Latinos/as who speak Spanish poorly or do not know and identify with their Hispanic cultural heritage. But such leaders also bring energy and spirit to parishes, apostolic movements, prayer groups, and the daily struggles of immigrants for dignity and survival. Their links to Latin America are vital for nurturing the sense of hemispheric communion and mission that Pope John Paul II called for in his 1999 apostolic exhortation *Ecclesia in America* and Pope Benedict XVI encouraged in his opening address for the Fifth General Conference of the Bishops of Latin America and the Caribbean in Aparecida, Brazil in 2007. Moreover, new immigrant leaders' dedication is essential for the Church's outreach to our émigré sisters and brothers who are among the most derided and vulnerable members of u.s. society.

A third leadership group is the integrationists, who accentuate the mandate to incorporate Latinos at all levels of Church and society. Many advocates for this approach serve the Church in the parishes and dioceses where a significant Hispanic presence has blossomed during the past two decades, a scenario in which Latinos/as typically are newcomers in established Euro-American congregations. In a growing number of instances a single Catholic parish serves more than two language groups, exacerbating the pragmatic challenge of ministering to such a diverse congregation, often with an overworked pastor. Intentionally or not, some integration efforts proceed at a pace and in a manner that

---

9 UNITED STATES CONFERENCE OF CATHOLIC BISHOPS, SECRETARIAT OF CULTURAL DIVERSITY IN THE CHURCH, HISPANIC AFFAIRS, «Remembering the Past with Gratitude», http://www.usccb. org/hispanicaffairs/rememberingpast.shtml (accessed January 9, 2010).

10 HOGE D.R. and OKURE A., *International Priests in America: Challenges and Opportunities*, Liturgical Press, Collegeville, MN 2006.

Hispanics perceive as an attempt at forced assimilation. Too often established parishioners rebuff Hispanic attempts to shape parish life with the claim that «our ancestors built this church» or «we were here first». Nonetheless, when enacted with mutual respect, integrationists' theological concerns about ecclesial unity and the need to work together to foster the life and mission of the Church are integral. Moreover, even from the narrower lens of Hispanic Catholicism, integrationists illuminate the pastoral reality of the massive generational transition in the U.S. Latino population: current trends indicate that over the next three decades the number of third-generation Latinos will triple, the second generation will double, and the overall percentage of first-generation immigrants will decline[11]. Integrationists remind us that the efforts of parents and pastoral leaders to form young Latinos in the Catholic faith, as well as the extent to which these young people practice the faith as they accommodate themselves within Church and society, will be decisive for the coming decades of U.S. Catholicism.

A fourth leadership group, youth and young adults, actually encompasses much from the other approaches, especially those of new immigrants and integrationists. Yet given their vision, their vitality, and their large number —Latinos comprise nearly half of U.S. Catholics under the age of twenty-five, and over three fourths of Catholics under eighteen in Texas, New Mexico, Arizona, and California— young Latino leaders merit their own category. Ken Johnson-Mondragón notes that Latino adolescents encompass four distinct pastoral categories: immigrant workers, identity seekers, mainstream movers, and gang members and high-risk teens. Further treatment of these groups and the leaders who serve them is available in the essay on Hispanic Ministry and *Pastoral Juvenil Hispana* in this volume. Suffice it to say here that, as Johnson-Mondragón's four categories imply, Latino youth face many challenges. Yet, as the conclusions of the 2006 First National Encounter for Hispanic Youth and Young Adult Ministry attest, «The new life young Hispanics are giving to our Church comes from the apostolic zeal of *jóvenes* who, having made Jesus the center of their lives, dedicate hours and hours to sharing and increasing the faith with other young people»[12]. While by no means limited to young Latinos, this «apos-

---

11 RODRÍGUEZ G., *Mongrels, Bastards, Orphans, and Vagabonds: Mexican Immigration and the Future of Race in America*, Pantheon, New York, NY 2007, 254.

12 JOHNSON-MONDRAGÓN K., «Socioreligious Demographics of Hispanic Teenagers» in JOHNSON-MONDRAGÓN K. (ed.), *Pathways of Hope and Faith Among Hispanic Teens: Pastoral Reflections and Strategies Inspired by the National Study of Youth and Religion*, Instituto Fe y Vida, Stockton,

tolic zeal» and its accompanying emphasis on vigorous evangelization are often deemed the most noteworthy element of the ministerial approach found in Hispanic youth and young adult ministries.

2
Incorporation

Ministerial approaches ranging from those of new immigrants to integrationists reflect a central and longstanding feature of u.s. Catholicism: the attempt to incorporate diverse groups and newcomers into a unified body of faith. A frequent point of contention is how to achieve the goal of incorporation. Many concerned Catholics broach the issue of Latino integration through the hotly-debated question of whether Latinos should retain the Spanish language and heritage as they adopt the dominant language and cultural ethos of the United States. Interviews of diocesan and parish leaders conducted for a 1999 report of the Bishops' Committee on Hispanic Affairs reveal disagreements among u.s. Catholics regarding the issue of «incorporation versus assimilation». The study report noted that «there is an on-going tension between those who propose that the best way to bring Hispanics into the Church is by assimilating them into mainstream Catholicism and culture in the United States as fast as possible and those who advocate that true incorporation requires that Hispanics be welcomed first on their own terms». One group contended that «forcing Hispanics to assimilate immediately only reproduces their subaltern status within the Church» and advocated for offering sacraments and other activities in Spanish, calling forth and nurturing Hispanic leaders, and, «once the Hispanic Catholic community has gained sufficient strength, then and only then» incorporating them more broadly into parish life. Another group held that such a «gradualist view» runs the «danger of making the same mistakes of the past, of producing exclusionary "mini national parishes" that divide the Church»[13].

CA 2007, 19-20, 33-9; NATIONAL CATHOLIC NETWORK DE PASTORAL JUVENIL HISPANA —LA RED, *Conclusiones: Primer Encuentro Nacional de Pastoral Juvenil Hispana*, PENPJH, USCCB, Washington, D.C. 2008, 12.

13 BISHOPS' COMMITTEE ON HISPANIC AFFAIRS, *Hispanic Ministry at the Turn of the New Millennium*, NCCB, Washington, D.C. 1999, On-Site Interview section, n. 2, http://www.nccbuscc.org/hispanicaffairs/study.shtml (accessed May 2009).

The integrative role of the ethnic or national parish for European Catholic immigrants is well known. Initially havens where émigrés nurtured their faith and felt a sense of ownership and belonging in a strange new land, over time national parishes enabled the descendants of immigrants to integrate into u.s. society and ecclesial life from a position of strength[14]. Today the stated norm in most dioceses is for integrated or multicultural parishes, though in fact many such congregations could more accurately be deemed «Americanizing» parishes that promote the assimilation of newcomers or, conversely, «segmented» parishes in which two or more groups share the same church facilities but remain substantially isolated from one another[15]. Historically the reasons for the shift in pastoral strategy away from national parishes include the depleted congregations and aging church buildings of previous immigrant groups, the loss of faith among some immigrant descendants who identify Catholicism with the «archaic» practices of their national parish community, increasing shortages of priests and fiscal resources, and the contention that national parishes lead to fragmentation in the body of Christ.

Encuentro and Mission expressed reservations about a «"multicultural" model» that frequently «dilutes the identity and vision of Hispanic ministry» and excludes «Hispanic ministry staff from the decision-making process» (n. 69). The bishops noted that «the commitment of Hispanics to become active participants and to offer their unique contributions in the life of the Church and society —versus *being assimilated*— has been a key value and principle for Hispanics in ministry» (n. 14, emphasis in original). One Hispanic lay leader bemoaned, «I am discouraged by the fact that we, Hispanics, don't count here in this parish. We come to Mass in great numbers and our Masses are really filled with the spirit. But all the power is in the hands of a small group of (non-Hispanic) old-timers who contribute a lot of money to the Church»[16].

---

14 Silvano Tomasi's landmark study of Italian immigrants in New York is a frequently cited work on this influential thesis. TOMASI S.M., *Piety and Power: The Role of Italian Parishes in the New York Metropolitan Area, 1880-1930*, Center for Migration Studies, Staten Island, NY 1975.

15 JOHNSON-MONDRAGÓN K., «Ministry in Multicultural and National/Ethnic Parishes: Evaluating the Findings of the Emerging Models of Pastoral Leadership Project», report and presentation to the National Ministry Summit: Emerging Models of Pastoral Leadership conference, April 2008, 9-10, http://www.emergingmodels.org/doc/Multicultural%20Report%20(2).pdf (accessed June 2009).

16 BISHOPS' COMMITTEE ON HISPANIC AFFAIRS, *Hispanic Ministry at the Turn of the New Millennium*, on-site interview section, n. 8.

Hispanics frequently respond to integrated parishes with what could be deemed the «national parish dynamic», which is arguably the most significant lesson to be learned from the history of Hispanic ministry over the past half century. Consciously or not, like European immigrants who built national parishes, Latinos attempt to establish and nurture feast-day celebrations, renewal movements, pious organizations, and other structures of Catholic life that enable them to move from at best feeling hospitality in someone else's church to a sense of homecoming in a faith community that is their own. Theologically, Latinos' considerable ecclesial activism over the past half century echoes the same core conviction of millions of other newcomers throughout the long saga of u.s. Catholicism: God's house is not holy just because all are welcome; God's house is holy because all belong as valued members of the household.

Yet, pastoral leaders are deeply concerned about the dynamics of Latino incorporation into u.s. Catholicism and the wider society. As our bishops noted in *Encuentro and Mission*: «[Hispanic] ministry must be seen as an integral part of the life and mission of the Church in this country. We must be relentless in seeking ways to promote and facilitate the full incorporation of Hispanic Catholics into the life of the Church and its mission» (n. 60). Such statements avow that Hispanic ministry is not solely or even primarily about Hispanics, but about the Catholicity of the entire Church in the United States.

Many church leaders are particularly attentive to what the dynamics of integration portend for the vitality of Latino allegiance to the Church and for the unity of the growing number of multiethnic u.s. parishes. Most Latinos —some 60 percent, according to the u.s. Census Bureau— are not immigrants. The linguistic impact of u.s. birth and residence is substantial: while more than half of Latino adults speak exclusively or primarily Spanish in their home, two thirds of Latino teens speak exclusively or primarily English among their friends[17]. Latino leaders plead for greater initiatives in ministry among u.s.-born Latino youth, a need clearly articulated in the First National Encounter for Hispanic Youth and Young Adult Ministry. Bishops, pastors, and diocesan directors increasingly express the expectation that Hispanic ministry leaders not only provide excellent pastoral service in Hispanic communities but also serve as «gente puente», a bridge-building source of unity between Latinos and their coreligionists[18].

17 JOHNSON-MONDRAGÓN K., «Socioreligious Demographics of Hispanic Teenagers», 24.
18 GURZA A., «*Ni Aquí* Nor There» in *u.s. Catholic* 73 (2008) 12-17.

What is most distinctive about Latinos as a group within u.s. Catholicism is that, while they evidence both the national parish dynamic and the tendency to integrate as did European Catholics, in their case *both* dynamics are taking place concurrently over a more extended period of time. No previous group has encompassed such an expansive population of immigrants and their descendants, English-speakers and those who speak another tongue, newcomers and established residents as do today's Latinos. A 2000 national poll confirmed that Latinos value both their ethnic heritage and their life in the United States: while 89 percent of Latinos surveyed agreed that it is important «for Latinos to maintain their distinct cultures», 84 percent of the same group also said that it is important «for Latinos to change so that they blend into the larger society as in the idea of the melting pot». The conclusions of the First National Encounter for Hispanic Youth and Young Adult Ministry included the Latino youth delegates' joint declaration that «We aspire to be a part of the society in the United States, without losing our identity and cultural roots»[19].

The *simultaneity* of ethnic solidarity and ongoing immigration, *along with* generational transition into u.s. Church and society, which has been evident among the children of Latino Catholic immigrants since at least the 1920s, frequently remains unacknowledged among Hispanic and other Catholics. On the one hand, one often hears statements like: «They'll assimilate in another generation or so anyway. By offering services in Spanish, you're just holding them back. Other immigrant groups also felt "put upon" when they first got here. This is just one more group going through the adjustment to American life. This too will pass». Such statements ignore realities like the continuing arrival of new immigrants, the influence that proximity to the border has on language and cultural retention, the power of the mass media in Spanish, the resilience of many u.s.-born Latinos in preserving their customs and their Spanish-speaking ability, and Church teaching on respect for a group's faith traditions and heritage. On the other hand, some Hispanic ministry leaders focus on these same realities and proceed to underestimate or discount the considerable number of Latinos who are monolingual English speakers, have weakened ties to their Hispanic heritage, worship in largely non-Latino parishes, or even have switched from Catholicism to another denomination or to no religion at all. The vibrant

---

19 GOLDSTEIN A. and SURO R., «A Journey in Stages: Assimilation's Pull Is Still Strong, But Its Pace Varies» in *Washington Post*, January 16, 2000, A1; NATIONAL CATHOLIC NETWORK DE PASTORAL JUVENIL HISPANA —LA RED, *Conclusiones: Primer Encuentro*, 51.

faith among Hispanic immigrants in many Catholic parishes feeds the misconception that the vast majority of Hispanics will retain indefinitely their cultural ties and Spanish-language ability. Unilateral pastoral approaches are inadequate in this context, both those that solely emphasize rapid assimilation and exclusive English-language use *and* those that promote prolonged ethnic separatism and monolingual Spanish ministries.

When vital Hispanic ministries are integrated into the wider Church, they enable Latinos to both receive from and contribute to u.s. Catholicism. The zeal and organizational genius of Catholics in the United States enabled them to build the largest private educational, health care, and social service systems in the world. Despite profound fiscal and personnel challenges that must be addressed to expand Latino access where available —sadly only 3 percent of Hispanic children are enrolled in Catholic elementary and secondary schools[20]— Catholic schools in particular are among the most effective pathways for Latino parents to give their children faith formation and a brighter future. The emphasis in the United States on the parish as the heart of Catholic life encourages Latinos to strengthen their cultural and familial Catholic traditions with a deeper commitment to the Church as a sacramental community united in common faith and mission. Numerous faith and leadership formation programs urge Latinos to expand their knowledge of their Catholic faith and live it as catechists, youth ministers, deacons, and more. Permanent diaconate programs, for example, are relatively rare in Latin America but thriving in many u.s. dioceses. Nationally the number of Hispanic permanent deacons rivals the number of Hispanic priests. The vast array of ethnic and racial groups in the u.s. Catholic Church, which is the most diverse national institution in the world, invites Latinos and their coreligionists to embrace the unity rooted in faith and baptism that exceeds all human divisions.

For their part, Latinos have much to offer u.s. Catholicism and the wider society, particularly their Catholic traditions and faith and their propensity to engage their faith in struggles for justice. As our bishops noted in their 1983 pastoral letter on Hispanic ministry, Latinos have salutary values such as respect for the dignity of each person, profound love for family life, a deep sense of com-

---

20 See THE NOTRE DAME TASK FORCE ON THE PARTICIPATION OF LATINO CHILDREN AND FAMILIES IN CATHOLIC SCHOOLS, *To Nurture the Soul of a Nation: Latino Families, Catholic Schools, and Educational Opportunity,* University of Notre Dame, December 12, 2009, http://catholicschool advantage.nd.edu/assets/19176/nd_ltf_report_final_english_12.2.pdf (accessed January 8, 2010).

munity, an appreciation of life as a precious gift from God, and pervasive and authentic devotion to Mary, the mother of God (n. 3). Echoing their pastoral letter, in *Encuentro and Mission* the bishops stated that «Hispanic Catholics are a blessing from God and a prophetic presence that has transformed many dioceses and parishes into more welcoming, vibrant, and evangelizing faith communities» (n. 6).

To cite just one example, Hispanics bring renewed life to the public presence of u.s. Catholicism, along with a style of engagement that transcends a singular focus on public policy lobbying efforts. The late Cardinal Avery Dulles avowed that «the immigration flows from culturally Catholic areas such as Latin America… have the potential for increasing the church's influence on American culture»[21]. This influence encompasses public religious expressions such as devotion to the crucified Jesus and his suffering mother on Good Friday. Patricia, a leader in the Way of the Cross through Chicago's Pilsen neighborhood, summed up the power of these events: «Christ suffered way back two thousand years ago, but he's still suffering now. His people are suffering. We're lamenting and wailing. And also we are a joyful people at the same time… So this is not a story, this is not a fairy tale. It happened, and it's happening now». For such participants the power of the ritual is its capacity to mediate an encounter with God that transcends limiting distinctions like those between Pilsen and Calvary Hill, Chicago and Jerusalem, our «secular» age and the «sacred» time of Jesus. They engage religious traditions not merely as pious reenactments but as holy events integrated with the everyday world that animates devotees to struggle for the transformation of their personal and collective lives. Sociologist of religion Stephen Warner, who is Lutheran, commented after his first experience of Good Friday processions organized by the San Fernando Cathedral congregation through the streets of downtown San Antonio: «Many of these rituals were foreign to me… Right in front of us we saw realistically reenacted the suffering and death of Jesus, the cruelty of his tormentors, and the grief of his mother. There was nothing metaphorical, nothing merely figurative, nothing generic about these rites. Yet, as an Anglo, I did not feel excluded». Echoing such insights, former San Fernando rector, Father Virgilio Elizondo, contends that «Latinos' love

---

21 DULLES A., «The Impact of the Catholic Church on American Culture» address at the John Paul II Cultural Center, Washington, D.C., November 13, 2001, as reported in *America* 185 (2001) 5. See also DULLES A., «The Impact of the Catholic Church on American Culture» in RAUSCH T.P., (ed.), *Evangelizing America*, Paulist Press, Mahwah, NJ 2004, 11-27, esp. 23-4.

for public ritual is a contribution we make to American society. I think there is a hunger for it in American life. It lets you enter into the power of a collective experience»[22].

3
Future

ℭ∕∕𝕆

We face at least three formidable challenges if we are to realize the potential for mutual enrichment between Latinos and their fellow Catholics. One regards shrewdly renewing our vision for Hispanic ministry. On the national and regional levels, we must be astute enough to recognize that, barring an unexpected windfall or act of divine providence, in the current climate the weakening of some of the structures so many of us labored to construct is irreversible. The most pressing challenge is how to refashion our efforts so they are more effective than ever in promoting ministries at the local level of the diocese and the parish. In order to do this we need to have a frank discussion about which of our current national and regional structures are most essential for sustaining local ministries. Should we focus on organizations with a renowned track record of success as a catalyst in a region, such as SEPI has been in the Southeast? Should we consider the vital links that particular organizations have to local churches, such as the National Catholic Association of Diocesan Directors for Hispanic Ministry (NCADDHM), whose members each have direct influence in the dioceses where they serve? Should we work strategically within extant «dominant culture» organizations as is the case with the NCCL Forum on Catechesis with Hispanics established after the demise of NOCH? These criteria are sound priorities from which to begin a forthright conversation. The greatest tragedy will be if we engage in this discernment with the narrow parochialism of defending our own turf and allow our national and regional organizations to be restructured merely according to the survival of the fittest.

---

22 DAVALOS K.M., «"The Real Way of Praying": The Via Crucis, *Mexicano* Sacred Space, and the Architecture of Domination» in MATOVINA T. and RIEBE-ESTRELLA G. (eds.), *Horizons of the Sacred: Mexican Traditions in U.S. Catholicism*, Cornell, Ithaca, NY 2002, 60; WARNER R.S., «Elizondo's Pastoral Theology in Action: An Inductive Appreciation» in MATOVINA T. (ed.), *Beyond Borders: Writings of Virgilio Elizondo and Friends*, Orbis, Maryknoll, NY 2000, 50; ROURKE M., «A Return to Ritual» in *Los Angeles Times*, March 28, 1997, E8.

In parishes and dioceses, the primary locus for Hispanic ministry, we need further analyses of the four approaches outlined above, along with others that might be articulated. The purpose of such conversations is not to argue that one approach is superior to the others. Indeed, the discernment of which approach to emphasize should not be based principally on the preferences of a pastoral leader, but on the needs of the faith community he or she serves. Many of our pastoral leaders wisely combine elements from more than one approach. Identifying one's own core vision for Hispanic ministry —a set of perceptions and priorities we many times adhere to unconsciously— is an important first step for critical self-examination regarding our varied approaches to ministry and how we can more effectively place ourselves at the service of Christ and the Church.

As we discern the renewal of Hispanic ministry so that it addresses young and old, immigrant newcomers and established residents, and the tremendous diversity among Hispanic Catholics, a second important challenge we face is leadership parity at all levels of the Church. To do this we must recognize who we are. The u.s. Catholic Church is no longer an overwhelmingly immigrant church, as it was a century ago, nor is it solely an «Americanized» church as is often presumed. Rather, it is a church whose leaders at every level are largely European-descent Catholics but whose members encompass growing numbers of Latino, Asian, and African immigrants, along with sizeable contingents of native-born Latino and African American Catholics and some Native Americans. Our ancestors in the faith teach us that the most effective strategy for building a diverse but united Church is calling forth and forming leaders from all the groups that make up our Church, making deliberate efforts to ensure that leaders from each group actively participate in the decisions that affect us all. We must learn from the wisdom of the twelve apostles, who called seven Greeks to leadership as deacons in response to complaints that Greek widows received treatment unequal to their Hebrew counterparts (Acts 6:1-6), resolving a pastoral difficulty between ethnic groups while simultaneously enriching the Church with new leaders.

The formation of Hispanic pastoral leaders receives frequent emphasis from Hispanic Catholics. It was listed as a «high priority» in the 2006 Study on Best Practices for Diocesan Ministry among Hispanics/Latinos[23] and was one of the

---

23 UNITED STATES CONFERENCE OF CATHOLIC BISHOPS COMMITTEE ON HISPANIC AFFAIRS, *Study on Best Practices for Diocesan Ministry among Hispanics/Latinos*, Washington, D.C. 2006, 4, http://www.usccb.org/hispanicaffairs/BestPractices2.pdf (accessed June 2009).

four specific dimensions of the *National Pastoral Plan for Hispanic Ministry*. Promoting leadership formation and parity will stimulate a domino effect with regard to other concerns for Hispanic ministry, such as the sounder pastoral planning, evangelization, and missionary outreach also called for in the *National Pastoral Plan*. How can we operate in such a way that our pool of effective Hispanic ministers increases? One way is to evaluate diocesan and parochial ministry activity by asking, «How will this activity enable more effective leadership to emerge?» To cite one example, a program for baptismal preparation would be deemed most effective if it not only provided engaging catechesis, but also identified, called forth, and trained new leaders to participate in giving that catechesis. Since many couples and godparents who attend baptismal preparation classes have marginal relations with their parish, one effective strategy is to carefully select couples whose Catholic faith was rejuvenated as they baptized their child, then invite and prepare these couples to give a witness talk to other parents. This «peer-to-peer» witness can be a powerful means for the Holy Spirit to work in the lives of others who seek baptism for their children and who need a similar revitalization of their practice of the faith.

The formation of leaders cannot be limited to liturgical ministries, however, nor can it be confined to an «old guard» or some other privileged group. Often new leaders do not come forth until diocesan personnel, pastors, or other church leaders personally invite them. The gradually increasing number of more formally educated and middle-class Latinos, a number of whom relate to the Church only peripherally or not at all, are a frequently untapped resource. Discussion of whom to invite for formation and specific ministries should be a consistent agenda item for parish organizations and staff and pastoral planning meetings.

One of the gravest needs is for Hispanic vocations to the priesthood and religious life. European immigrants regularly had pastoral service from vowed religious and priests of their own background, who in turn often provided access to Church authorities and decision-making processes. No previous group has had a dearth of religious vocations relative to its size as do Latinos. The ratio of Hispanic priests to Hispanic laity in u.s. Catholicism is approximately 1 to 10,000, roughly ten times more lay persons per priest than the overall ratio for the rest of the u.s. Catholic population[24]. Permanent deacons, women religious,

---

24 UNITED STATES CONFERENCE OF CATHOLIC BISHOPS, UNITED STATES CONFERENCE OF CATHOLIC BISHOPS, SECRETARIAT OF CULTURAL DIVERSITY IN THE CHURCH, HISPANIC AFFAIRS, «Remembering the Past with Gratitude».

and dedicated non-Latino pastoral leaders have helped fill the gap, but only partially. Explanations for the lack of Hispanic vocations are varied, but many Latino leaders point to a history of scant educational opportunities, ethnic prejudice in seminaries, strong kinship ties among Hispanics that deter prospective candidates from leaving the family circle, and cultural norms that conflict with the requirement of mandatory celibacy. Today some seminaries, bishops, and other leaders have initiated efforts to increase Hispanic vocations to the priesthood, such as those in the archdiocese of San Antonio, which in 2009 ordained its largest group of priests since 1930, more than half of them Hispanic. Nationally, however, Hispanics comprise only 12 percent of priests ordained in 2009[25]. In particular, the relatively minute number of u.s.-born Hispanic priests and vowed religious diminishes role models and the development of ministries that engage younger generations and other Latinos as they adapt to life in the United States. Prayer, encouragement, and support of religious vocations are priorities we have long known but cannot waiver in promoting.

A third major challenge is living out an ecclesial vision of integration rooted in the Gospel and in two thousand years of development in the Church's tradition. One pitfall to be avoided is equating unity with uniformity. The expectation that Hispanics, even recent immigrants, participate in English-language Masses and parish events for the sake of «unity» often provides a superficial harmony at best. At worst it causes frustration, resentment, and a tragic choice of Hispanics to vote with their feet and abandon participation in Catholic parish life. It is helpful to bear in mind that European immigrant Catholics tended to integrate fully over three generations, during which time, due to both choice and circumstance, many of them congregated in national parishes. In retrospect their gradual incorporation was prudent, allowing both for the practice of their Catholic faith and for European ethnic unity in u.s. parishes to emerge. Similar prudence and focus on gradual progress would alleviate the tensions that often accompany parishes and dioceses undergoing an influx of Hispanic newcomers.

Authentic incorporation involves mutual respect, listening to others and allowing their insights to shape my own. It entails not only Hispanic participation in parishes and dioceses, but also considering Hispanic perspectives in

---

25 UNITED STATES CONFERENCE OF CATHOLIC BISHOPS News Release, «Ordination Class 2009 Has Many Asian-Born, Despite Low Percentage of Asian Catholics in the United States», April 20, 2009, http://www.usccb.org/comm/archives/2009/09-083.shtml (accessed May 2009).

wider conversations and decision-making processes that shape Catholicism in the United States. These perspectives reveal a fundamental gap between many Hispanic Catholics and their coreligionists of European descent. Over the past four decades, Euro-American Catholics have tended to give most attention to the internal dynamics of the Church: liturgical reform, the voice and role of the laity, dissent or obedience to sexual ethics and other Church teaching, the proper exercise of authority, the question of who is called to ordination. The focus on these issues tends to produce debates along a liberal-conservative continuum, an approach so familiar that its application to public discourse about events such as the clergy sex abuse crisis or the selection of a new pope is as much reflex as it is a conscious choice. Media outlets reinforce this dialectical approach with their tendency to cover nearly all stories that deal with the Catholic Church with comments from Catholics on the «right» and the «left», but rarely from Hispanics, whom we are left to presume fit into one camp or the other, or soon will.

Hispanics have been more inclined in recent decades to accentuate the mission of the Church, frequently calling for more funding for Hispanic ministry offices, youth initiatives, outreach efforts, and leadership training and formation programs, as well as an increase in Spanish Masses, Hispanic bishops, celebrations of feast days that are part of their Hispanic traditions, and culturally sensitive formation programs for seminarians and other Hispanic leaders. While these efforts encompass and reflect attempts at internal reform in areas like liturgy and participation in ecclesial leadership, they are primarily directed at the larger concern of equipping the Church to serve and accompany its Hispanic members in their faith and daily struggles.

In a word, while Hispanic Catholic leaders frequently perceive the Catholic Church in the United States as a significant institution that could do much to uplift their suffering sisters and brothers, American Catholic leaders of European origin or descent tend to be more concerned with democratization and the adaptation of the Church to the u.s. milieu or, conversely, with the alarming worry that u.s. Catholicism has in fact already progressed much too far along the road to becoming more American than Catholic. One of the most hopeful possibilities of incorporating Hispanics into the u.s. Catholic Church is their potential to help transcend that impasse. From local parishes to national organizations, the Hispanic tendency to focus on the mission of the Church reminds us that, as the saying goes, it is not so much that the Church has a mission, but that the evangelizing mission of Jesus Christ calls forth the Church. Engaging Hispanics in decision-making requires breaking old habits of assuming their views are subsumed in existing perspectives and paradigms. We will know Hispanic incorporation has taken deep roots when, however faintly or loudly articulated in the channels of Catholic opinion-making, Hispanic leaders' insights and intuitions become a central part of our collective deliberations as a faith community. This is not merely a pragmatic challenge to ensure we will retain Hispanic members, nor a sociological strategy for group cohesion. More fundamentally, it is an ecclesial challenge to be the Church of all God's people that the Gospel calls us to be.

Hispanic Ministry, Evangelization, and Faith Formation

HOSFFMAN OSPINO

It is not a secret that people involved in Hispanic ministry in Catholic communities throughout the United States invest most of their time, energy, and creativity in furthering the evangelizing mission of the Church, particularly through processes of faith formation[1]. Such is the experience of many of the ecclesial leaders —ordained, vowed religious, and lay— working with u.s. Latino/a Catholics whom I have met throughout the years and from whom I continue to learn. Evangelization and faith formation were precisely the two not-so-small tasks that summarized the job description that I received when I responded to the call to serve as a lay ecclesial minister leading Hispanic ministry at St. Patrick Parish in Lawrence, MA about ten years ago. I worked —and continue to do so though with a different level of commitment— with Spanish-speaking Catholics in this parish, the vast majority recent immigrants from Caribbean countries. Three responsibilities defined Hispanic ministry at that moment: design programs of religious education and sacramental preparation in Spanish for children and adults in parallel to what already existed for English-speaking parishioners; make sure that there were enough opportunities for spiritual growth for Spanish-speaking Latinos/as, including the planning of liturgical celebrations; take care of the administrative responsibilities that involved working with Latinos/as.

Hispanic ministry, a pastoral unit with unique character in the structure of the parish, rapidly developed. Crucial questions began to emerge which, coupled with questions that I read or heard from different sources, led me to further study of very important issues: what do we do with our Hispanic children who asked for religious instruction in English yet attended services in Spanish with their families? How do we involve Hispanic parents in the processes of faith formation of their children? What does it mean to form Hispanic youth in the faith? How effective are religious educators and administrators who do not speak Spanish, know little or nothing about Hispanic culture, and cannot communicate well with Hispanic parents? How effective are those who only speak Spanish in contexts where English is highly needed? What kind of formation

---

1 Two initial observations: 1) in this essay I refer to evangelization and faith formation as parallel processes in the life of the Church. Though both are intimately related, they are not exactly the same and thus one should not be subsumed into the other. Evangelization is broader than faith formation. Cfr. PAUL VI, *Evangelii Nuntiandi*, n. 22; JOHN PAUL II, *Catechesi Tradendae*, n. 18. 2) I use «faith formation» as a general term to refer to all processes that aim at educating in the faith women and men of all ages in different contexts. From this perspective, faith formation makes reference to catechesis, religious education, and to some extent Catholic education.

programs did dioceses offer to prepare DREs and catechists to work in culturally diverse contexts? Did they have any? Were seminarians and priests adequately prepared to work in these contexts? What religious education materials were more appropriate for bilingual children? How many of these materials were simply translations from resources originally written English? How good were the translations? How many of these materials sincerely incorporated the richness of Hispanic culture and faith traditions? Are there any good materials for Hispanic adult faith formation that truly reflected the experience of Latino/a Catholics in the United States? Did any of the Bible study courses available in the market actually offer culturally sensitive materials to be used with Hispanic Catholics? How do religious education, Catholic school curricula, and catechist training programs help *all* Catholics in the U.S. to understand what it means to live as Christians in culturally diverse contexts? Why did Hispanic

ministry not always involve being part of major conversations related to Catholic schools? Why were so many Catholic schools closing their doors, particularly in inner-city contexts, at a time when the Hispanic Catholic presence was exponentially growing around them? Can Hispanics afford the current costs of Catholic education? Will Catholic schools in two decades be an available resource to the new generations of Catholics in the United States, particularly Hispanics? Without a doubt all these are key concerns within Hispanic ministry and they needed some answers.

A few years later I reentered the conversation as a professor of theology and religious education at Boston College. My research and teaching have led me to further explore many of the questions listed above and I must confess that the findings are a mix of good and not-so-good news. Besides my research work, I have been privileged to lecture, present and teach in several parts of the country, opportunities that I have used to inquire about how Hispanic Catholics in the United States are responding to the same questions in their communities. I started with four working hypotheses:

1) Hispanic Catholics in the Southwest, a region where the Hispanic presence goes back several centuries, must have already taken significant steps in addressing some of the challenges faced by other Latinos/as in other parts of the country whose presence is comparatively more recent. Their models of faith formation and evangelization can be used by other Hispanics Catholics elsewhere though adapting them to their local needs.

2) Hispanic Catholic religious educators and ministers are very familiar with the Encuentro processes and conclusions, the various documents by the U.S. bishops on Hispanic ministry, and other ecclesial resources on faith formation guiding the conversation in various forums throughout the country.

3) Considering that Hispanic Catholics constitute nearly half of all Church members in the United States, in some places more, all processes of reflection on faith formation, evangelization, leadership formation, Catholic education, and development of materials for religious education at all levels in the life of the Church involve and affirm the leadership of a significant number of Hispanic voices.

4) Non-Hispanic Catholics would not initiate major process of reflection in the areas just listed in the previous hypothesis without first engaging in conversation with Hispanic leaders and experts and thus make sure that the complexity of the Hispanic experience is fully addressed.

Was it naiveté, wishful thinking or plain hope? Not sure, but that was how my pastoral sense perceived the ideal order of things. In fact, this is what I hear many Hispanic Catholic leaders hope to achieve. Years of investigation, praxis, and conversations continue to reveal that the situation is much more complex than initially assessed. Factors such as the constant migration flow from Latin America, the rather small number of Hispanic leaders in positions of leadership at all levels in the Church, the failure to make Hispanic ministry everyone's concern, the unwillingness to change the status quo in some quarters, racial and cultural biases, the expectation that Hispanic Catholics will eventually «adjust» (read assimilate) to models of ministry considered normative, the limitation of resources to execute creative initiatives, the weak implementation of policies and plans, and the inability to comprehensively grasp the complexity of the Hispanic experience on the part of many Hispanic and non-Hispanic Catholic leaders, among others, constantly take the attention in too many directions making it difficult for everyone to advance a sustained conversation.

The main challenge is not necessarily a lack of vision or desire to make things work for the good of all. As a matter of fact, there are many visions, lots of good intentions, and great energy around issues related to evangelization and faith formation among Hispanic Catholics. However, at this historical point it is urgent that these efforts be interpreted in light of an analytical framework that helps all Catholics, Hispanic and non-Hispanic, to properly read our present experience and propose practical strategies to better address the needs of faith formation among Hispanic Catholics. In 2002 the Catholic bishops of the United States published a very important pastoral statement entitled *Encuentro and Mission: A Renewed Pastoral Framework for Hispanic Ministry*[2]. In this document the bishops, in conversation with Hispanic leaders from around the country, proposed a fresher vision for Hispanic ministry at the beginning of the new millennium, which built on the insights and experiences gained after several decades of reflection on the u.s. Hispanic Catholic reality. *Encuentro and Mission* remains a valid framework within which other frameworks such as the one I call for in this essay should be designed.

This essay is an exercise of practical reflection that aims at providing some directions toward the formulation of an analytical framework for evangelization and faith formation among Hispanic Catholics in the United States. Such framework calls for a major overhaul of how we do ministry, how we evangelize, how we educate Christians in our communities, how we develop materials for faith formation, and how we prepare the next generation of leaders to serve Catholics in our country. To do this, we must *look at the context* where these activities take place, *evaluate* what works and what does not work well, and *envision* fresher directions that lead us to advance effectively the mission of educating Hispanic Catholics in the faith[3].

1

The State of Affairs

ℭℐℴ

The Church's evangelizing mission in the United States is currently being shaped by unique circumstances that call for systematic analyses and the proposal of effective strategies. At the beginning of the twenty-first century we find ourselves facing urgent challenges such as low church attendance, scarcity of clergy, secularizing currents, massive leadership transition, indifference about organized religion, widespread illiteracy in matters of faith, increasing pluralism, painful

---

2 UNITED STATES CONFERENCE OF CATHOLIC BISHOPS, *Encuentro and Mission: A Renewed Pastoral Framework for Hispanic Ministry*, USCCB, Washington, D.C. 2002, http://www.usccb.org/hispanicaffairs/encuentromission.shtml.

3 The basic *see-judge-act* method of pastoral reflection is integrated in various forms in this essay. The method, in all its variations, has been particularly useful in many processes of pastoral study and consultation among Hispanic Catholics in the United States such as the National Encuentros, pastoral planning, small faith communities, and u.s. Latino/a Catholic theology. Cfr. *Encuentro and Mission*, n. 21.

generational divides, and —still— little idea about how to strategically respond to the presence of millions of Catholic immigrants from all over the world, to mention only a few. The rapid growth of Hispanic Catholics in the United States, currently 40 percent of the whole Catholic population in the country, is happening in the midst of this context. Not only Hispanic Catholics must worry about the challenges just mentioned, but also we must face others that are unique to our own socio-cultural reality: high levels of poverty, weak presence in positions of leadership in society and the Church, undocumented immigration, overall low educational attainment, not enough attention to our youth and young adults, significant defection from Catholicism, and lack of resources for organized evangelization, among others[4].

All these challenges deeply affect the *what* and the *how* of faith formation in communities serving Hispanic Catholics. In terms of the *what*, there is no doubt that Catholic educators are aware of the basic elements of the faith that need to be shared. For this we count on excellent resources such as the Scriptures, the Catechism of the Catholic Church, the General and National Directories for Catechesis, religious education guides, and many other resources prepared by publishers, educators and theologians. These resources remind us that there are central convictions that all Catholic Christians must know, yet they also indicate that there are different ways of getting to know those convictions. Religious educators working in Hispanic contexts must be able to discern what elements of the Christian tradition relate more directly to the experience of Latinos/as who come to learn about God and deepen their Christian convictions. Such elements will serve as the gates that will lead Hispanic women and men into the wider tradition and thus help them to appreciate the harmony of truths that constitute our Christian faith. The common experience that determines the starting point for faith formation in the various Latino communities may not always be the same. In some cases, that common experience is immigration; in others, exile; in others, to live as Hispanic women raising families in this country; in others, some form of marginalization; in others, the search for one's identity in a culturally diverse society —and the Church. Consequently, two questions that religious education leaders must ask when defining the curriculum, that is to say the *what* in processes of faith formation among Latino/a Catholics are: 1) how does what we share connect with the actual experience of

4 Cfr. *Encuentro and Mission,* n. 63-75.

the Latinos/as who come to learn about God and deepen their faith convictions? 2) What elements of the Christian tradition must first be presented in light of that experience in order to lead to a better appreciation of the central tenets of our faith?

In terms of the *how*, we venture into the realm of pedagogies and strategies of faith formation. In the last decades, Catholics in the United States have been blessed by the development of various models of faith formation that seek to respond to the mature analysis of what it means to be a Christian in this society. Some of these approaches have emerged in dialogue with the social sciences, others with the human sciences; others have explored a more political dimension of faith formation[5]. Some approaches have retrieved models of faith formation that served in the past and are perceived as helpful in today's context (e.g. the kerygmatic movement[6], the catechumenate[7]). Some focus on whole community dynamics[8]. Some rely on the use of catechisms; others on the Scriptures. U.S. Latino/a Catholics for the most part have participated, and continue to participate, in processes of faith formation that use these widely accepted models. Nonetheless, we must ask the following question: *do these models of faith formation truly respond to the complex experience of being Hispanic Catholics in the United States?*

To answer this question we must consider at least three factors:

First, many of these pedagogical models are implemented in institutional contexts: schools, universities, parish programs of faith formation. However, Hispanics are severely underrepresented as a group in these settings[9]. Not all

---

5 Cfr. O'HARE P. (ed.), *Foundations of Religious Education*, Paulist Press, New York, NY 1978; GROOME T.H., *Christian Religious Education: Sharing Our Story and Vision*, Jossey-Bass Publishers, San Francisco, CA 1980.

6 See JUNGMANN J.A., *The Good News Yesterday and Today*, translated (abridged) and edited by William A. Huesman, William H. Sadlier, New York, NY 1962.

7 *Rite of Christian Initiation of Adults*, Liturgical Press, Collegeville, MN 1988, approved for use in the dioceses of the United States of America by the National Conference of Catholic Bishops and confirmed by the Apostolic See; UNITED STATES CONFERENCE OF CATHOLIC BISHOPS, *Our Hearts Were Burning within Us: A Pastoral Plan for Adult Faith Formation in the United States*, USCCB, Washington, D.C. 1999.

8 See HUEBSCH B., *Whole Community Catechesis in Plain English*, Twenty-Third Publications, Mystic, CT 2002; Generations of Faith Project, http://www.generationsoffaith.org/

9 In 2000 only 10.7 percent of all students in Catholics schools (elementary and secondary) were Hispanic. In the same year, only 8.2 percent of all students enrolled in 260 Catholic colleges and universities in the country were Hispanic. Only half of all Catholic school-age children participate in parish-based programs of religious education. Cfr. FROEHLE B.T. and GAUTIER M.L., *Catholicism USA: A Portrait of the Catholic Church in the United States*, Center for Applied Research in the Apostolate [CARA], Washington, D.C. 2000, 63-86, cited in UNITED STATES CONFERENCE OF CATHOLIC

parishes serving Latinos/as have programs for Hispanic youth. Not all young Hispanics find the standard youth group dynamic with its traditional divisions —junior, youth, young adult— attractive or even inviting to participate in the life of the Church[10]. Not all Hispanics find the schooling system characteristic of most religious education programs in parishes helpful for their children; many do not understand it. Hundreds of thousands of Hispanic Catholic families do not attend any formal program of faith formation at all.

Second, a number of these approaches rely on cultural models of reflection and interaction that often times appear unfamiliar to many Hispanic Catholics, particularly recent immigrants. Occasionally such models of faith formation require participants to invest significant amounts of time and resources. Such expectation often times is more consistent with the experience of more established Catholics who seem to have the luxury of both, time and resources, yet little takes into consideration the wide range of limitations of the vast majority of Hispanic families. Hispanics in the United States as a body confront urgent problems such as high levels of poverty: «[w]hile the poverty rate for non-Hispanic whites is 8 percent, the rate for African Americans is 24.1 percent, for Hispanics, 21.8 percent, and for Native Americans, 23.2 percent»[11]. Low levels of educational attainment among Hispanics are troubling: about 30 percent of the Latino population in secondary educational levels drop out of school (immigrants being the most affected group), not counting the nearly 15 percent of Latino/a students who do not make it to high school[12]; only 54 percent of Lati-

BISHOPS, *National Directory for Catechesis,* USCCB, Washington, D.C. 2005, *C,* 4A, note 25; McGRATH R.J., «Students in Catholic Schools» in HUNT T.C., JOSEPH E.A., and NUZZI R.J. (eds.), *Catholic Schools Still Make a Difference: Ten Years of Research, 1991-2000,* second edition, National Catholic Educational Association, Washington, D.C. 2004, 84; PETTIT J., *Enrollment in Catholic Higher Education in the United States: 1980 to 2000,* Catholic Higher Education Research Cooperative, Rockville Centre, NY 2004, 5, http://www3.villanova.edu/cherc/research/pdf_j_pettit_enrollment.pdf (accessed January 15, 2010).

10 Cfr. CERVANTES C.M. and JOHNSON-MONDRAGÓN K., «Pastoral Juvenil Hispana, Youth Ministry, and Young Adult Ministry: An Updated Perspective on Three Different Pastoral Realities» in *Perspectives on Hispanic Youth and Young Adult Ministry,* Publication 3, Instituto Fe y Vida, Stockton, CA 2007; *Encuentro and Mission,* n. 70.

11 CATHOLIC CHARITIES USA, «Poverty and Racism: Overlapping Threats to the Common Good» in *Origins* 37, n. 34 (2008) 539. As of January 2010, due to the current economic crisis affecting the United States, the overall poverty level among U.S. Hispanics increased to 23.2 percent.

12 Cfr. GÁNDARA P. and CONTRERAS F., *The Latino Education Crisis: The Consequences of Failed Social Policies,* Harvard University Press, Cambridge, MA 2009, 22-23; CARGER C.L., «Dropout Rates» in DIAZ L. (ed.), *Latino Education in the U.S.,* Rowman & Littlefield Education, Lanham, MD 2008, 106-108; see also VÉLEZ W., «The Educational Experience of Latinos in the United States» in RODRÍGUEZ H., SÁENZ R., and MENJÍVAR C. (eds.), *Latinas/os in the United States: Changing the Face of America,* Springer, New York, NY 2008, 129-148.

nos/as who graduate from High School move on to college and from this group half go to two-year institutions, the majority of whom never continue their education to earn a bachelor's degree[13]. Some studies indicate that overall Hispanic Catholics are poorer and less educated than Hispanic Protestants[14]. Though Catholics schools have proven to be great resources to secure high levels of graduation and educational achievement among ethnic minorities, only 3 percent of Latinos/as attend Catholic schools in this country[15]. Poverty and low educational attainment thus place Hispanic Catholics in positions of disadvantage that seriously affect their processes of faith formation[16]. Under these circumstances, millions neither have the time nor the resources nor the cultural background to bring about necessary transformations in their faith communities and in society.

Third, faith formation processes in the United States heavily rely on the materials produced by publishers, theologians, and other professionals. The industry of textbooks, pedagogical resources, guides, scholarly works, electronic media, and other resources that support the formation of Catholics in this country is perhaps one of the most significant achievements of u.s. Catholicism —yet it can become its own Achilles' heel if it fails to understand in time the changing demographics that are transforming our faith communities. In general the publishing industry serves primarily English-speaking Catholics, especially those who can be said to identify with mainstream Catholicism. Nonetheless, we must commend companies that have responded to the challenge of publishing materials that are bilingual (English and Spanish), in Spanish, and in English incorporating Latino/a perspectives. We see the path and we must move forward. To meet the most immediate faith formation needs of the growing Latino population, some Hispanics leaders have opted for importing books from Latin America or Spain. However, while useful in many ways many of these materials do not reflect the experience of being Hispanic Catholic in the United States and, frankly, do not help Latinos/as develop an identity as mem-

---

13 Cfr. GÁNDARA P. and CONTRERAS F., *The Latino Education Crisis*, 24.

14 Cfr. DAVIS K.G., HERNÁNDEZ A., and LAMPE P.E., «Hispanic Catholic Leadership: Key to the Future» in HERNÁNDEZ E.I., PEÑA M., DAVIS K.G., and STATION E. (eds.), *Emerging Voices, Urgent Choices: Essays on Latino/a Religious Leadership*, Brill, Boston, MA 2006, 40-45.

15 See THE NOTRE DAME TASK FORCE ON THE PARTICIPATION OF LATINO CHILDREN AND FAMILIES IN CATHOLIC SCHOOLS, *To Nurture the Soul of a Nation: Latino Families, Catholic Schools, and Educational Opportunity*, University of Notre Dame, December 12, 2009, http://catholicschooladvantage.nd.edu/assets/19176/nd_ltf_report_final_english_12.2.pdf (accessed January 8, 2010).

16 Cfr. UNITED STATES CONFERENCE OF CATHOLIC BISHOPS, *National Directory for Catechesis*, Introduction, 4C.

bers of the Church in this country. Some leaders and publishers turn to the practice of translating books and other resources from English into Spanish. Again, many of these translations are useful but fail to utilize the potential of Latino/a trained theologians, religious educators and other professionals in the country who could produce original materials, in English and Spanish, reflecting the depth and richness of the u.s. Hispanic Catholic experience.

Many contemporary models of faith formation in the United States do have an impact on the development of the Hispanic Catholic experience, yet fall short of responding to some of the critical dimensions of such experience. Often times such models serve Latinos/as who are considered to be more «Americanized», by birth or acculturation, and those who accommodate more easily to mainstream standards. Some creative religious educators and pastoral leaders do a great job adapting these models to the needs of Hispanic communities. But there is still a large number of Hispanics who are not being served in our faith communities and their faith formation is in peril because of the lack of fresher models and creative resources that meet their particular needs. It is imperative that Church leaders, scholars, religious educators, publishers, and all who are involved in processes of evangelization and faith formation understand the multiple contexts in which Catholics in our culturally diverse Church live. On the one hand, we must understand the complexity of the experience of being Hispanic Catholics in the United States. On the other hand, we must take advantage of the spaces for faith formation and gifts that Hispanic Catholics offer in light of their own cultural and religious experiences.

As we begin the second decade of the twenty-first century, traditional models of faith formation, developed within particular historical and cultural contexts, must be reassessed in light of our present Catholic experience. We need renewed frameworks for faith formation among Hispanic Catholics —and ultimately for all Catholics in the United States.

2

Shared Reality, Everyone's Concern

The effectiveness of our conversations about evangelization and faith formation among Hispanic Catholics depends on the depth of our understanding of the overall Catholic experience in the United States. At the same time, in order to develop models of evangelization and faith formation for Catholics in the United States we must continuously build on the experience of Latinos/as and those of the other groups that constitute our culturally diverse Church[17].

I propose to focus on five major situations that shape our present reality. First, we began the twenty-first century reclaiming the sense of the religious and the spiritual. Contrary to predictions of widespread secularism and the end of organized religion, we presently witness an amazing renewal of the search for God and the desire to belong to communities of faith[18]. What is different at this time is that the so called historical churches are not perceived as the exclusive sources of answers in that search for God and meaning —not even among Catholics. We witness women and men making their own decisions about their religious associations; they choose which beliefs to accept and which to set aside; they want to have a voice in setting the criteria and the standards of religious fulfillment. This is a phenomenon widely common among the younger generations[19]. Vast numbers of Catholics do not attend church yet still identify with this religious tradition and want their children baptized; many integrate non-Christian practices into their spiritual lives; many have multiple church affiliations. Some scholars identify this as a postmodern attitude; others dismiss the phenomenon as pure relativism. What is of interest to us is that we are at a time in history when people are thirsty for God in the midst of a pluralistic context. If the Church does not find creative and appropriate ways to meet contemporary women and men in their search for God and speak a language that these people can understand, they will go somewhere else[20].

---

17 Given the significant shifts in demographics in thousands of Catholic communities across the nation, to speak of Hispanic ministry literally means to speak of Catholic ministry in general —and vice versa. In other words, researchers, pastoral leaders, and organizations concerned about issues of evangelization and faith formation in the u.s. must not treat the Hispanic experience as an isolated phenomenon, much less as an addendum or simply a concern that only affects Hispanics.

18 Cfr. UNITED STATES CONFERENCE OF CATHOLIC BISHOPS, *National Directory for Catechesis*, n. 11B; CELAM, *Aparecida: v Conferencia General del Episcopado Latinoamericano y del Caribe: Documento Conclusivo*, CELAM, Bogotá, Colombia 2007, n. 52.

19 HORELL H.D., «Cultural Postmodernity and Christian Faith Formation» in GROOME T.H. and HORELL H.D. (eds.), *Horizons and Hopes: The Future of Religious Education*, ed., Paulist Press, New York, NY 2003, 83-89.

20 The number of Christians in the United States abandoning their traditional historical churches and changing religious affiliation has rapidly increased in the last two decades. Because of the continuous flow of immigrants from Latin America, mostly Catholics, u.s. Catholicism's growth has remained steady. However, if we bracketed the Hispanic phenomenon for a moment, we would see a dramatic decline. Cfr. KOSMIN B.A., and KEYSAR A., *ARIS 2008: Summary Report*, Institute for the Study of Secularism in Society and Culture, Trinity College, Harford, CT 2008, http://livinginliminality.files.wordpress.com/2009/03/aris_report_2008.pdf (accessed April 15, 2009).

Second, U.S. Catholicism is undergoing a process of multiple transitions: from a Euro-American dominant way of being Catholic to one that is more culturally diverse, with a stronger influence of Hispanic cultural and religious traditions. From a middle-class Catholicism to one that is rapidly growing roots in the barrios and large urban centers. From mainstream Catholicism to a Catholicism that is largely defined by immigrant and marginal experiences. From models of leadership that rely primarily on professionally trained personnel to models of charismatic leadership that thrive at the grassroots yet need appropriate formation to exert significant impact in the larger ecclesial and social structures. From leadership perspectives that focused mostly on «the local» to perspectives that pay serious attention to «the global» because of the new expressions of transnational Catholicism. All these transitions call for a new analytical framework that preserves the best insights on faith formation and leadership that U.S. Catholics have developed until now, yet creatively incorporates the new perspectives and voices that are emerging in every corner of the Church in the United States. Failure to do this will leave us with anachronistic and unresponsive models that eventually will undermine the overall process of faith formation of Catholics in the country.

Third, to be Catholic in the United States is to experience «Catholicity» at its best, particularly as expressed in the richness of the Church's cultural diversity[21]. U.S. Catholicism is a rich mix of cultural, linguistic and religious traditions. Indeed, this is not a new phenomenon in an ecclesial body that from the very beginning has been constituted by immigrants from all parts of the world. Yet, at various points in history U.S. Catholics have settled with the idea of a standard, mainstream experience that often neglects voices, practices, and perspectives that do not conform to constructs perceived as normative. But these diverse voices, practices, and perspectives, often thriving in the margins of Church and society, have never stopped shaping the U.S. Catholic experience. Today we are more aware of their presence and their contributions because ironically they are becoming, without losing the vibrancy of their diversity, the new mainstream.

Even though Hispanic Catholics constitute the largest ethnic body within the Church in this country, we must be careful not to treat the Hispanic experience as a homogeneous phenomenon. There are in our midst many Hispanic experiences each shaped by unique cultural, linguistic, historical, and religious

---

21 On the concept of «Catholicity» see SCHREITER R., *The New Catholicity: Theology between the Global and the Local*, Orbis Books, Maryknoll, NY 1997.

particularities. Among these, perhaps the most significant challenge for religious educators and pastoral leaders working with Hispanic Catholics is the multi-generational reality of our people. The ministerial needs of the first and second generations of Hispanics are very distinct, though not completely unrelated, to those of the fourth, fifth, and further generations. Issues such as language, so-cialization, historical perspectives, intergenerational communication, and cul-tural identity, among others, play important roles that require the development of multiple approaches to evangelization as well as engagement of different ques-tions depending on the group with which one works. An analytical framework for faith formation among Hispanic Catholics must embrace the diversity that characterizes the various coexisting experiences in our Latino communities and facilitate the development of pedagogies that build on those experiences.

Fourth, low levels of religious literacy in the United States should be a mat-ter of concern to religious educators and pastoral agents of every religious tra-dition[22]. Unfortunately I was not able to find scientific data on the levels of reli-gious literacy among Catholics, but we can assume that it is a major problem in our ranks as well. The *National Directory for Catechesis* observes that nearly half, perhaps more, of all Catholic children and most young Catholics in this coun-try do not receive formal religious education:

> Presently in the United States, 52 percent of all Catholic school-age children are en-rolled in parish-based catechetical programs; and 16 percent of Catholic elementary school-age children are enrolled in Catholic schools. Perhaps 2 percent are being home-schooled, and the percentage of Catholic young people of high school age who re-ceive no systematic catechesis is generally much higher[23].

Furthermore, many Catholics do not actively practice their faith and have no full clarity as to how to integrate basic Christian values into their lives. His-panic Catholics are not necessarily the exception. Nevertheless, Hispanic Catholics in general baptize their children in large numbers, share a strong sense of the sacred, and their spirituality is continuously sustained by practices of popular Catholicism. Consequently, the limitations and consequences of religious illit-

---

22 See PROTHERO S., *Religious Literacy: What Every American Needs to Know—and Doesn't*, Harper San Francisco, San Francisco, CA 2007.

23 FROEHLE B.T. and GAUTIER M.L., *Catholicism USA*, in UNITED STATES CONFERENCE OF CATHOLIC BISHOPS, *National Directory for Catechesis*, n. 4A, note 25.

eracy must be analyzed alongside the lived faith of the people. Both perspectives must be present as we set the foundations for an analytical framework for faith formation developed within the context of the New Evangelization[24].

Fifth, the success of the evangelizing mission of the Church as well as that of its processes of faith formation largely depends on the leaders advancing them. The Catholic Church in the United States has been blessed with abundant vocations to ordained ministry, vowed religious life, and lay ecclesial ministry. Despite the declining number of priests and vowed religious, new forms of leadership continue to emerge[25]. However, the numbers of Hispanic leaders well prepared to evangelize and educate in the faith have not kept up with the rapid growth of Hispanic Catholics in the pews during the second part of the twentieth century and first decade of the twenty-first. It is imperative to foster more vocations to ecclesial leadership among Latinos/as and expand their access to academic formation at the level of universities and seminaries in order to better serve their communities. Furthermore, in a culturally diverse Church like ours in the United States, all ministers from all ethnic backgrounds must be trained with the appropriate cultural competencies and sensibilities to serve the rich diversity that we encounter in our communities. This certainly requires a good understanding of the reality where we evangelize and educate in faith as well as a firm commitment to engaging all the voices that constitute the Church in the United States.

These five situations are indicative of how complex is the reality where we are called to evangelize and educate Hispanic Catholics in the faith. Certainly the list could be longer. We share this common reality with all Catholics in the country and, to some extent, all Catholics in the continent[26]. The development of reflections and resources for evangelization and faith formation among Hispanic Catholics must continuously respond to the challenges of our context but we must do this building on the strengths of our communities.

---

24 This is the proposal of *Encuentro and Mission*. Cfr. *Encuentro and Mission*, n. 25-28.
25 Cfr. DeLAMBO D., *Lay Parish Ministers: A Study of Emerging Leadership*, National Pastoral Life Center, New York, NY 2005.
26 Cfr. *Aparecida*, n. 33-59; 98-100.

Evangelization and Faith Formation among Hispanic Catholics: Cornerstones

∞

The previous observations provide the background to better understand where we currently stand in terms of the Catholic experience in the United States. They are helpful to identify the most pressing issues that require our attention as we develop pedagogies, programs, and materials for evangelization and faith formation among Hispanic Catholics.

Now we turn our attention to seven *cornerstones* that are constitutive to the experience of most Hispanic Catholics in this country and must be integrated in any analytical framework for faith formation and evangelization. Major documents and conversations on Hispanic ministry have already identified the centrality of these cornerstones[27]. It is imperative that we revisit and assess them regularly with the purpose of checking whether they are really present in our methodologies and resources for evangelization and faith formation among Hispanics.

---

27 Of particular interest is the *National Pastoral Plan for Hispanic Ministry*, published in 1988. See UNITED STATES CONFERENCE OF CATHOLIC BISHOPS, *Hispanic Ministry: Three Major Documents*, USCCB, Washington, D.C. 1995, 59-98. See also *Encuentro and Mission*. For religious educators, the *National Directory for Catechesis* is an invaluable resource. In the development of these reflections I incorporate several insights gained from the conclusions and reports of three resent important gatherings in which I participated: 1) Symposium on Faith Formation among Catholic Hispanic/Latinos/as organized by the Secretariat of Cultural Diversity in the Church, Baltimore, December 5, 2008; 2) NCCHM Symposium on Paradigmatic Changes in National Catholic Hispanic Ministry, San Antonio, TX, August 28-29, 2007; 3) National Consultation *Soy Catequista: the Dignity, Vocation, and Mission of the Catechist*, University of Notre Dame, South Bend, IN, November 7-9, 2006.

Most Latinos/as in the United States identify themselves as Catholic[28]. However, not all Hispanic Catholics actively practice their faith[29]. The majority of u.s. Latino/a Catholics share a cultural Catholicism (not to be confused with nominal Catholicism[30], though sometimes both coincide) that permeates our worldview and our understanding of God, humanity, nature, and life. This cultural Catholicism is rooted in the strong influence of Catholic institutions in the social, political and cultural structures of Latin American societies since colonial times. Catholicism, whether in a strict or loose sense, is continuously handed on through culture. Moreover, despite the fact that most Hispanic Catholics were born and raised in the United States, cultural Catholicism continues to be a deep marker of Latino identity, even among Hispanic Protestants[31]. Church leaders, scholars, organizations, religious educators, and pastoral agents cannot assume the costs of hastily dismissing this important reality.

Furthermore, cultural Catholicism in the u.s. Hispanic experience is not necessarily an indicator of religious homogeneity. The Hispanic experience as a whole can be described as a coexistence of different ways of being Catholic sustained by common faith convictions, yet shaped by multiple historical, cultural and ecclesial experiences[32]. Approaches and resources for evangelization and

28 It is difficult to establish an exact number. In 2007 The Pew Forum on Religion and Public Life released the results of a study on Hispanics and religion. The study estimates that 68 percent of all Latinos/as are Catholic, though affiliation may vary according to several factors such as age, education, and socio-economic status. See THE PEW FORUM ON RELIGION AND PUBLIC LIFE, *Changing Faiths: Latinos and the Transformation of American Religion*, Pew Hispanic Center, Washington, D.C. 2007, 6, http://pewforum.org/newassets/surveys/hispanic/hispanics-religion-07-final-mar08.pdf (accessed March 30, 2009). The *American Religious Identification Survey* (*ARIS 2008*) released in March of 2009 indicates that 59 percent of Hispanics identified themselves as Catholics. It is interesting to observe that such number still reflects a decline in self-identification compared to a similar survey in 1990 where 66 percent of Hispanics said to be Catholic. See KOSMIN B.A. and KEYSAR A., *ARIS 2008*, 14.

29 It is estimated that 42 percent of Hispanic Catholics attend Sunday Mass at least weekly. Cfr. THE PEW FORUM ON RELIGION AND PUBLIC LIFE, *Changing Faiths*, 16. I personally believe that this number is much lower than what the study indicates. A few years ago the Office of Hispanic Apostolate of the Archdiocese of Boston reported that about 13 percent of Hispanic Catholics attended Mass on a regular Sunday. This number seems to reflect more the reality that leaders observe in their communities on a weekly basis.

30 I borrow the categories «nominal» and «cultural» Catholicism from the work of sociologist Allen Spitzer in his essay «The Culture Organization of Catholicism» in *The American Catholic Sociological Review* 19, n.1 (1958) 2-3.

31 Cfr. GONZÁLEZ J.L., *Mañana: Christian Theology from a Theological Perspective*, Abingdon Press, Nashville, TN 1990, 66.

32 Though experiences such as crossing the border in search of better opportunities, living in exile, and escaping violent circumstances may have elements in common, each leads to a different

faith formation among Hispanic Catholics must incorporate as many of these experiences as possible and yet remain open to be adjusted to the experiences of each group. The idea that «one-size-fits-all» may yield immediate, temporary results but in the end it proves to be methodologically ineffective.

3.2. FAMILY AND COMMUNITY

Hispanic Catholicism is often described as a socio-religious experience strongly rooted in traditional values of family and community[33]. Once again, we can affirm that this dimension is another manifestation of the influence of Catholic evangelization on the overall Latino cultural experience. It is in the family and the community where Hispanic Catholics primarily develop our cultural and ecclesial identity[34], indeed a countercultural conviction in a society in which focus on the individual tends to prevail[35]. The family plays a very important role in the development of human relations and the stability of the community. While the concept of traditional family —father, mother, and children— is central to the experience of community among Hispanics, *familia* more frequently includes other immediate blood relatives, in-laws, *padrinos, madrinas, compadres* and close friends. Consequently, evangelization efforts and processes of faith formation among Hispanics will be enhanced by building on models that fully integrate the experience of family and community. For instance, the model of small ecclesial communities is well-known among Hispanic Catholics[36]. These communities are flexible, empowering, and participative. Along with the small ecclesial communities we must highlight the evangelizing impact and dynamism of the apostolic movements as well as their ability to foster the communal dimension of people's religious experience. It is estimated that 54 percent of Hispanic Catholics who attend church identify themselves as having some association with the Catholic Charismatic Renewal[37]. Religious educators and pastoral agents need

---

reading of history and of God's presence in the Latino communities formed by people who experience them.

33 See for instance the pastoral letter published by the bishops of the United States in January 1984, «The Hispanic Presence: Challenge and Commitment» in UNITED STATES CONFERENCE OF CATHOLIC BISHOPS, *Hispanic Ministry: Three Major Documents*, 3; *Encuentro and Mission*, n. 15; 56.2.

34 See GOIZUETA R., *Caminemos con Jesús: Toward a Hispanic/Latino Theology of Accompaniment*, Orbis Books, Maryknoll, NY 1995, 47-53.

35 Cfr. GOIZUETA R., *Caminemos con Jesús: Toward a Hispanic/Latino Theology of Accompaniment*, 53-65.

36 Cfr. UNITED STATES CONFERENCE OF CATHOLIC BISHOPS, *National Pastoral Plan for Hispanic Ministry*, 37-38; *Encuentro and Mission*, n. 40-42.

37 Cfr. THE PEW FORUM ON RELIGION AND PUBLIC LIFE, *Changing Faiths*, 29-38.

to work closely with the apostolic movements to facilitate processes of faith formation that strengthen the unity of the ecclesial communities where they are present.

At the same time, a «taken-for-granted» Latino sense of family and community needs some critical analysis. Church leaders, scholars, and religious educators cannot fall into the temptation of idealizing these dimensions of the Hispanic Catholic experience. It is true that Latino/a Catholics in principle value the ideal of family, yet Latino families in the United States are in the midst of a serious crisis in which they are not alone[38]. 42 percent of Hispanic children were born out-of-wedlock in 2006; half of all births to native-born Hispanic women and 35 percent to immigrant Hispanic women were to single mothers[39]. Hispanic immigrant couples have a lower divorce rate than native couples, yet their children born and raised in the United States tend to replicate the exact patterns of the larger population: about 50 percent of marriages in this country end in divorce[40]. Thousands of Hispanic families are fragmented because of transnational separation, long work hours, and struggles to adapt to the new culture. In this context, evangelization efforts and faith formation initiatives must embrace a twofold approach: on the one hand, they must affirm the positive images of family and community ingrained in the Latino worldview; on the other hand, they must directly address the challenges that Hispanic families face and lead to healing processes.

3.3. THE FAITH OF THE PEOPLE: POPULAR CATHOLICISM

Catholicism's rich spiritual and theological traditions are fully expressed through the power of the liturgy, the Church's greatest expression of Christian worship that leads to a deep experience of the Paschal Mystery[41]. While the liturgy retains its primacy over any other form of worship in the life of the Church, it does not diminish or negate the value of other expressions of spirituality such as popular Catholicism: «the Liturgy and popular piety are two forms of worship which are in mutual and fruitful relationship with each other»[42].

---

38 Cfr. *Encuentro and Mission*, n. 56.2.

39 GONZÁLEZ F., *Hispanic Women in the United States*, Pew Hispanic Center, Washington, D.C. 2007, revised May 14, 2008, 9, http://pewhispanic.org/files/factsheets/42.pdf (accessed April 15, 2009).

40 Cfr. CHERLIN A.J., *The Marriage-Go-Round: The State of Marriage and the Family in America Today*, Alfred A. Knopf, New York, NY 2009, 4; 180.

41 Cfr. *Sacrosanctum Concilium*, n. 10, 61, in FLANNERY A. (ed.), *Vatican Council II: Constitutions, Decrees and Declarations*, Costello Publishing Company, Northport, NY 1996. See also Raúl Gómez-Ruíz's essay in this book.

42 Cfr. CONGREGATION FOR DIVINE WORSHIP AND THE DISCIPLINE OF THE SACRAMENTS, *Directory on Popular Piety and the Liturgy: Principles and Guidelines*, Vatican City 2001, n. 58, http://www.

Practices of popular Catholicism play an important role in the mediation of the relationship between God and humanity in the everyday[43]. Many u.s. Latino/a Catholic theologians and Church leaders have seen in popular Catholicism an immensely valuable source of insights that continuously helps Hispanics to understand what it means to be human in relationship with the God of Revelation in the particularity of our history. Popular Catholicism empowers women and men to deepen into the mysteries of the faith already celebrated in the liturgy; sometimes it is the only language that the dispossessed have available to articulate their experience of God[44]; it sustains the life of faith beyond the context of liturgical celebrations and reveals the love of God who becomes accessible to women and men in their *experiencias cotidianas* (everyday experiences)[45].

The pedagogical potential of popular Catholicism is evident when we look at the widespread practice of these expressions in the life of many communities throughout the country: processions, devotions, Marian celebrations, veneration of saints, novenas, etc. Latino/a Catholics have brought awareness about practices very particular to our own cultural experiences such as *las posadas*, *quinceañeras*, and *altarcitos*, among others. The power of popular Catholicism to facilitate processes of evangelization and faith formation is then unique. Programs and resources for faith formation among Hispanics should strategically pay attention to these expressions and integrate them as content and method in every possible way. Even in situations when these expressions are the only form of Christian ritual that people practice with regularity, religious educators and pastoral agents have the responsibility to draw attention to the appropriate relationship between popular Catholicism and liturgical life[46]. Excesses or deviations must not become an excuse to ignore the potential of these practices to mediate pedagogies of faith[47].

vatican.va/roman_curia/congregations/ccdds/documents/rc_con_ccdds_doc_20020513_vers
-direttorio_en.html (accessed March 16, 2009).

43 Cfr. GOIZUETA R., *Caminemos con Jesús*, 26-29.

44 Cfr. GONZÁLEZ J.L., *Mañana*, 61.

45 See OSPINO H., «Unveiling the Human and the Divine: The Revelatory Power of Popular Religiosity Narratives in Christian Education» in *Religious Education* 102, n.3 (2007) 328-339.

46 Cfr. CONGREGATION FOR DIVINE WORSHIP AND THE DISCIPLINE OF THE SACRAMENTS, *Directory on Popular Piety and the Liturgy*, n. 59.

47 Cfr. CONGREGATION FOR DIVINE WORSHIP AND THE DISCIPLINE OF THE SACRAMENTS, *Directory on Popular Piety and the Liturgy*, n. 57.

Catholic Social Teaching principles are not a secret when faith communities constantly confront situations that demand immediate reflection and action in light of the best insights of the Christian tradition. Hispanic Catholics in the United States face significant challenges that require continuous reflection about what it means to be a Christian in the midst of adverse conditions such as poverty, racism, exploitation, marginalization, etc. In many dioceses and parishes across the country, Hispanic ministry operates in direct collaboration with offices for social concern and departments of social justice. To do Hispanic ministry constantly requires involvement in issues of advocacy, conflict resolution, and social justice.

Evangelization and faith formation initiatives among Hispanics will reach a level of completion and effectiveness when they lead to a clear understanding that we are a Church in solidarity with those who are most in need. In the words of Pope Paul VI:

Chapter 2

75

> ...evangelization would not be complete if it did not take account of the unceasing interplay of the Gospel and of man's [*sic*] concrete life, both personal and social. This is why evangelization involves an explicit message, adapted to the different situations constantly being realized, about the rights and duties of every human being, about family life without which personal growth and development is hardly possible, about life in society, about international life, peace, justice and development —a message especially energetic today about liberation[48].

To educate Latino/a Catholics in the faith must be a permanent call to make the preferential option for the poor and for those, Hispanic and non-Hispanic, who live under circumstances in which their human dignity is not fully affirmed. Resources and pedagogies of faith formation in this context must address the root causes of social injustice that have an impact in the lives of millions of Latinos/as as well as others in our society. To speak of Catholic Social Teaching and Christian solidarity and to affirm that living our faith in the everyday has social implications will have no effect in the processes of religious education and Hispanic ministry unless those actions address directly the specific conditions that define the *vida cotidiana* of millions of Latinos/as in the United States.

---

48 PAUL VI, *Evangelii Nuntiandi*, n. 29.

Closely related to the previous cornerstone, immigration emerges as one of the most urgent issues to be addressed in any process of evangelization and faith formation among Hispanic Catholics in the United States today. Most U.S. Latinos/as are immigrants or children of immigrants who have arrived in the country in the last five decades. Consequently, matters of immigration have a unique place in every reflection about Latino/a identity. Immigration is a complex phenomenon that affects multiple areas of the U.S. Hispanic experience: culture, family relationships, international law, politics, the economy, access to education, and religion, to mention only a few[49].

An analytical framework for faith formation among Hispanics must place immigration at the center of the conversation. One of its most important goals should be to help all Catholics in the country to better understand not only the complexity of the issues involved in this phenomenon, but also the negative implications of positions such as indifference or anti-immigrant activism. Religious education resources need to mediate a better understanding of how immigration directly touches the lives of almost half the Catholics in the country (and indirectly the lives of the other half), what are the best insights from our Christian tradition to reflect upon this reality, how the Catholic experience in the United States has been transformed through immigration at different moments in our short history, and why it is important that all Catholics, not just Hispanics, become familiar with the Church's teaching on migration.

3.6.   NEW EVANGELIZATION, MISSIONARY DISCIPLESHIP, AND PERMANENT MISSION

Encuentro and Mission proposed the New Evangelization as the overarching dimension grounding all commitments to ministry with Latino/a Catholics in the United States[50]. Such concern for evangelization is also significantly present in other key documents such as the *National Pastoral Plan for Hispanic Ministry* and the conclusions of the various Encuentros[51]. At the heart of evangelization

---

49 For a good overview of the complexity of immigration in the lives of Catholics in the United States, Hispanic and non-Hispanic, see the project Justice for Immigrants sponsored by the U.S. Catholic Bishops: http://www.justiceforimmigrants.org/

50 See *Encuentro and Mission*, n. 25-34.

51 Cfr. *National Pastoral Plan for Hispanic Ministry*, 37-50; Prophetic Voices: Document on the Process of the Third Encuentro Nacional Hispano de Pastoral, section IV, published by the bishops of the United States in August 1986, in UNITED STATES CONFERENCE OF CATHOLIC BISHOPS, *Hispanic Ministry: Three Major Documents*, 34-35.

is the conviction that the Church is in a state of permanent mission whose ultimate goal is to lead women and men to a transforming encounter with Jesus Christ. Thus, *Encuentro and Mission* reminds us that Hispanic Catholics in the United States have repeatedly opted for a style of evangelization marked by a strong missionary character[52]. Such missionary option guarantees the vibrancy of a ministry that hopes to permeate every structure in the life of the Church and society.

In the context of the New Evangelization, discipleship and the missionary option emerge as two essential notions. This is confirmed by the spirit of the Fifth General Conference of the Bishops of Latin America and the Caribbean in Aparecida, Brazil in 2007. There the Latin American bishops proposed that evangelization today must be understood in terms of forming missionary disciples of Jesus Christ[53] in a Church that is in a permanent state of mission[54]. These two powerful images bring together a long tradition of reflection on discipleship and missionary option that has permeated conversations among Latin American Catholics and Hispanic Catholics in the United States for several decades. In light of the conclusions of Aparecida, the Latin American bishops launched a continental mission (*misión continental*) whose goal is to stimulate the missionary vocation of all Christians, strengthening the roots of their faith and awakening their responsibility so that all Christian communities enter into a state of permanent mission. It is about arousing in all Christians the enthusiasm and fruitfulness of being disciples of Jesus Christ, to celebrate with true joy «being with him» and «loving like he does» as we are sent into the mission… We need a new Pentecost! We need to reach out to women and men, families, communities, and all sectors of society to communicate and share with them the gift of encountering Christ. He gives our lives a «sense» of truth and love, joy and hope! Thus, to be in mission is to live the encounter with Jesus as a dynamic of personal, pastoral and ecclesial conversion. Such dynamic has the power to lead the baptized toward holiness and service; it invites those who have abandoned the Church, those whose lives are not permeated by the Gospel, and those who have not experienced the gift of faith to come to the Lord[55].

---

52 Cfr. *Encuentro and Mission*, n. 56-57.
53 Cfr. *Aparecida*, n. 129-153.
54 Cfr. *Aparecida*, n. 151.
55 CELAM, *La Misión Continental para una Iglesia Misionera: Orientaciones*, CELAM, Bogotá, Colombia, 2008, #2, http://www.celam.org/principal/index.php?module=PostWrap&page=Mision_Home (accessed March 25, 2009), my translation.

Faith formation frameworks only make full sense when understood as part of the larger context of evangelization. Thus, processes, pedagogies, and resources of faith formation among Hispanic Catholics in the United States must be crafted within the spirit of the New Evangelization and lead to the formation of missionary disciples. Catholicism in the continent is in a state of permanent mission. This requires that faith formation initiatives clearly explain what this mission is, its content, and its goals. It is imperative that present and future generations of religious educators prepare to work collaboratively in this common mission. In the context of a culturally diverse Church, to be missionary disciples of Jesus Christ means to remain aware of the many experiences that shape the identity of our faith communities, to cherish the richness of our Christian tradition mediated through centuries of reflection across cultures, and to be in solidarity with women and men beyond our comfort zones and borders. u.s. Catholics, Hispanic and non-Hispanic, have the responsibility of joining the continental mission with the best of our resources, contributions, and insights.

3.7. PUBLIC CATHOLICISM

The Hispanic Catholic presence in the United States is constitutive to the identity of the Church and society in this part of the world. Every day Hispanic Catholics become increasingly involved in major public conversations that call for the wisdom of Christian Catholicism at all levels. We enter these conversations both as u.s. Catholics and as u.s. Hispanics. At the same time, the growing presence of Hispanic Catholics in the Church and society has served as an opportunity to raise awareness about unique concerns that are intimately linked to the Hispanic experience (e.g. biculturalism, relationship with Latin America, Latino intellectual and religious traditions).

Faith formation and evangelization initiatives among Hispanic Catholics must prepare Latinos/as to properly respond to the challenges of entering the various public conversations taking place in the Church and in the wider society. It would be a serious mistake to consider Hispanic Catholics as passive spectators in these major conversations or to ignore our contributions. Faith formation programs and resources used in Hispanic communities must provide sound introductions to the major issues that affect our lives in our context. They must prepare Latino/a Catholics to become fully familiar with the richness of our Christian tradition, the genesis of the questions that concern women and men in our society, and the most adequate ways to develop a public voice.

This requires the embrace, and development when necessary, of pedagogies of faith formation that empower Hispanics to appropriate our faith in critical ways in order to speak publicly. Though this should be the goal at all levels of faith formation, it is imperative to focus on programs of adult faith formation among Hispanic Catholics that lead to a better understanding of the public dimensions of Catholicism.

4
Looking at the Future

We do not know exactly what the future of Catholic Hispanic ministry in the United States will be like. However, we can imagine the future that we want for our communities and thus start setting the foundations for it here and now. For decades Hispanic Catholic leaders at all levels have worked intensely in offices, organizations, academic institutions, and in processes such as the Encuentros to get to where we are in our reflection today. In 2002 *Encuentro and Mission*, building on the insights gained from the processes that led to the *National Pastoral Plan for Hispanic Ministry*, the *Plan* itself, and other documents, proposed a renewed pastoral framework that is still valid for our ministry at the beginning of the second decade of the twenty-first century. However, more than an end in itself *Encuentro and Mission* was rather a fresh beginning. I propose the reflections in this essay as a step forward in the formulation of an analytical framework for evangelization and faith formation among U.S. Catholics, with particular focus on Latinos/as.

The four working hypotheses at the beginning of this essay consequently remain as a hope for Hispanic ministry in general and faith formation and evangelization processes among Hispanic Catholics in particular:

1) We need to creatively articulate models and resources for faith formation and evangelization that can be shared among the different communities serving U.S. Hispanic Catholics. They must reflect the uniqueness of our experience as Latinos/as in this country. Though these models and resources will necessarily have to be adjusted according to the particular socio-cultural and religious circumstances of each community, they should serve as helpful starting points for new communities working with Hispanic Catholics.

2) Hispanic Catholic religious educators and ministers must become very familiar with the Encuentro processes and conclusions, the various documents on Hispanic ministry sponsored or written by the u.s. bishops on Hispanic ministry, the works of u.s. Catholic theologians, and other ecclesial resources on faith formation guiding the conversation in various forums throughout the country.

3) Hispanic Catholics must continue the effort to participate in all processes of reflection on faith formation, evangelization, leadership formation, Catholic education, and development of materials for religious education at all levels in the life of the Church —and increase such participation wherever necessary.

4) Non-Hispanic Catholics working in organizations and institutions that develop resources and initiatives for faith formation and evangelization in the Church in the United States will work with Hispanic leaders and experts in various fields as part of their creative teams. These leaders and experts will bring their professional expertise and perspectives and raise awareness about the complexity, challenges, and contributions of the Hispanic Catholic experience to the larger Church and the rest of society.

Hispanic Ministry and Theology

Jorge Presmanes *and* Alicia Marill

1

Introduction

«All politics is local» is an often used axiom coined by the late Thomas «Tip» O'Neill who was the Speaker of the House of Representatives for many years. His adage continues to remind elected officials to be ever-attentive to the day in and day out needs faced by their constituents at the grass-roots level; otherwise their political careers might be short-lived. Borrowing from the former Speaker, the ministerial hermeneutic that underlies this reflection is that «all theology is local». Better phrased, «all theology must be local» lest it becomes disconnected from the ecclesial context and social location of the faithful and thus irrelevant to those outside of our academic institutions. This is the challenge posed to us by our ministry students whose entry point into theological discourse is their concrete ministerial framework.

The relationship between Hispanic Ministries and theology addressed in the pages to follow finds its source in the concrete pastoral praxis of our Latino/a ministry students both in our English language Master of Arts degree in Practical Theology and Doctor of Ministry degree programs on our main campus and our Spanish language Master of Arts in Pastoral Ministry for Hispanics degree at the Southeast Pastoral Institute. While most of our students are lay ecclesial ministers from the Catholic Church, our student body is also composed of Catholic priests and religious as well as ordained Protestant ministers. Each of these ministers engages the work of the theological academy from their unique ecclesial and ministerial context with the hope of better responding to the particular pastoral needs of their constituents. Given the diversity of ministerial contexts and functions of our students we pose that «Hispanic ministry» in the singular is an abstraction. There is no «Hispanic ministry» but rather there are Hispanic ministries that are defined by the pastoral, religious, cultural, social, economic, political, geographical, and historical specificity of each ecclesial and ministerial context.

For the sake of this essay, we suggest that the contemporary subject area known as *practical theology* helps to provide a theoretical basis for this project. Practical theology is an expanding sub-discipline within theological studies that operates out of a *praxis—theory—praxis* modality. Without supplanting the need for theology to be grounded in historical and systematic research, practical theologians re-orient the theological task so that its reflection both begins and ends with the ministerial context of theology. The in-depth examination of where theologians begin their reflection is necessary for the theological task to arise out of communities' practice of the faith. Accordingly all theology begins with «thick description» of «theory-laden practice»[1]. A comprehensive description of biases and presuppositions inherent to theological reflection and ministry frees theology from masking those presuppositions.

Finally we claim that what have grounded Hispanic/Latino/a theological reflection in the United States over the last 30 years are its praxis-based methodologies. The exigency of the rapidly developing Hispanic communities in the United States has focused the work of the Academy of Catholic Hispanic Theologians of the United States (ACHTUS). Moreover the concerns of organizations like the National Catholic Council for Hispanic Ministry (NCCHM) overtly have employed practical approaches to its work. Therefore practical theology and U.S. Hispanic/Latino/a theology are natural dialogue partners. In this essay the insights of both contributions are utilized.

Therefore from the prism of our students' social location, our own ministerial practice, and practical theology, this reflection will respond to the two questions assigned to us: first, *what questions for theology emerge out of the current experience of Hispanic ministry in the United States?* And second, *how does Hispanic ministry benefit from the current theological research in this country, with special attention to u.s. Latino/a Catholic theology?* While the scope of these questions is quite broad and can be approached in many ways, we will limit our response to the exploration of three areas of pastoral practice: inculturation and interculturality, ministerial praxis, and ecclesiology. We are aware that adequate reflection upon each of these theological realities and their corresponding pastoral praxis would require a platform much larger than this analysis. However, we consider that the following can begin a more comprehensive engagement of the relationship between theology and ministry in the context of the u.s. Hispanic Catholic experience today.

---

1 BROWNING D., *Fundamental Practical Theology: Descriptive and Strategic Proposals*, University of Chicago Press, Chicago 1996, 1-12; 75-93.

2
Inculturation and Interculturality

For decades leaders in our community have challenged those in positions of power in the U.S. church to embrace an inculturated approach to ministry. This method in ministry is rooted in the certainty that culture is not only the epistemological key that opens the door to the understanding of a particular human group or society[2], but also, in the context of the Church's evangelizing mission, the gateway through which the Good News of the Gospel can be effectively communicated[3].

Much too often, and to the detriment of an effective ministerial praxis, the prevalent cultural-specific approach to pastoral action is adaptation instead of inculturation. Adaptation is a term that was employed in ecclesial documents when addressing the issue of trans-cultural evangelization. Robert Schreiter argues that adaptation is a classification that was widely used in missiological circles in the period between the two World Wars and continued to be extensively used until the Synod on Evangelization held in Rome in 1974[4]. This missiological method was understood as a process through which «the faith» was adapted or accommodated to a very limited degree in order to communicate the Gospel message in a given cultural context. Schreiter holds that adaptation as a ministerial practice is «inadequate because of its simplistic and too static understanding of culture —as if a culture can be so easily read that an adaptation can be readily prescribed, and that this process takes place once and for all in an unchanging culture»[5].

Inculturation is the word most widely utilized in Roman Catholic circles to describe the proper relationship between faith and culture[6]. In the Protestant tradition the term that is often used is contextualization and hence these two

Chapter 3

85

---

2 ESPÍN O., «Grace and Humanness: A Hispanic Perspective» in *Journal of Hispanic/Latino Studies* 2, n.2 (1994) 134-135.
3 FIGUEROA DECK A., «A Latino Practical Theology: Mapping the Road Ahead» in *Theological Studies* 65 (2004) 292-293.
4 SCHREITER R., «Faith and Cultures: Challenges to a World Church» in *Theological Studies* 50 (1989) 746.
5 SCHREITER R., «Faith and Cultures: Challenges to a World Church» in *Theological Studies* 50 (1989) 746.
6 SCHREITER R., «Faith and Cultures: Challenges to a World Church» in *Theological Studies* 50 (1989) 747.

terms are often utilized interchangeably in current scholarship on the subject. The word «contextualization» was first used by a study group commissioned by the Fund for Theological Education in 1972 while the term «inculturation» was being used in the Roman Catholic tradition as early as the 1960's to refer to the dialogue between the Christian faith and the world's cultures within the Church's evangelizing praxis[7].

In an article entitled «Christianity as Faith and Culture», Yves Congar demonstrates that inculturation, when seen as the principle of correlation between faith and culture, is at the very core of the Christian mission. Congar defines faith as the human response to God's call to right relationship with God and God's people. This call can only reach the person in his or her own cultural particularity but at the same time it «transcends this particularity»[8]. «Whenever man [*sic*], through faith», writes Congar, «enters into the sharing of the life of Jesus Christ, he [*sic*] lives within the limits and the particular forms of his [*sic*] given situation, a concrete, unique mystery of absolutely universal value»[9]. For Congar, faith is the «internal principle» of catholic unity. It is locus of unity because faith is necessarily historically and culturally bound. Congar elaborates further here:

> The revealing initiatives of God on the one hand, and the faith which responds to them on the other do not exist except concretely, and thus they exist at the meeting points of time and place, of social context, of expression. The response of faith is not the response of someone, of a concrete human subject, unless it is given, lived, expressed in the flesh of a concrete humanity. Thus revelation and the Church are catholic only in some particular. «Particular» is opposed to «general» but not to «catholic». The particular realizations or expressions of the Catholic Faith are *«pars pro toto»*, *«totum in parte»*[10].

Ministry as inculturation is thus the process through which the universality of the Gospel message is preached by the Church and the faithful respond in the concreteness of time and in the particularity of culture. As a result, the key to

7 SCHREITER R., «Faith and Cultures: Challenges to a World Church» in *Theological Studies* 50 (1989) 747.

8 CONGAR Y., «Christianity as Faith and Culture» in *East Asian Pastoral Review* 18, n. 4 (1981) 304.

9 CONGAR Y., «Christianity as Faith and Culture» in *East Asian Pastoral Review* 18, n. 4 (1981) 305.

10 CONGAR Y., «Christianity as Faith and Culture» in *East Asian Pastoral Review* 18, n. 4 (1981) 305.

inculturation lies in the Church's capacity to discover a unity of faith diversely expressed through the symbolic structures and social practices of a specific culture.

Unlike adaptation, an inculturated approach to ministry does not make absolute those elements of the tradition that were modeled in one culture and then are translated into another. Instead, in the process of inculturation faith and culture are placed in a relationship of open Intercultural dialogue whose outcome is the enrichment and conversion of both the community of culture and the tradition of faith. Unfortunately, what is most often defined as «inculturation» is «adaptation» in its practice. Because inculturation as a method in ministry is too often stripped of its intercultural core, we suggest that an alternative term to refer to the Church's missiological praxis may be «interculturation».

Intercultural theology is an emerging theological movement which «consciously opts for interculturality as [its] central methodological axis»[11]. Building on the philosophical work of Raúl Fornet-Betancourt, María Pilar Aquino argues that intercultural theology challenges a polycentric Christian identity that manifests itself in the «excessive monocultural character of Western Christianity»[12]. «Interculturation» as a method in ministry may be a more appropriate term than «inculturation» because interculturality more clearly points to the interaction between faith and culture that is at the heart of the ministerial project of the Latino/a community. As we see it, the pastoral agent in the Latino/a community is called to do more than «adapt» the Christian message to Hispanic cultures or translate an «Anglo» understanding of the tradition into Spanish as a method in ministry. Rather, the starting point of evangelization as interculturation begins with a critical understanding of the «historical context of each people and each culture» that are present in the faith community in which the ministerial praxis is enveloped[13]. This intercultural approach is essential to ministry in the Latino/a context because of the multicultural character of the u.s. Hispanic community.

11 AQUINO M.P., «Theological Method in u.s. Latino/a Theology: Toward an Intercultural Theology for the Third Millennium» in ESPÍN O. and DÍAZ M. (eds.), *From the Heart of Our People: Latino/a Explorations in Catholic Systematic Theology*, Orbis, Maryknoll, NY 1999, 35.

12 AQUINO M.P., «Theological Method in u.s. Latino/a Theology: Toward an Intercultual Theology for the Third Millennium» in ESPÍN O. and DÍAZ M. (eds.), *From the Heart of Our People: Latino/a Explorations in Catholic Systematic Theology*, Orbis, Maryknoll, NY 1999, 35.

13 AQUINO M.P., «Feminist Intercultural Theology: Toward a Shared Future of Justice» in AQUINO M.P. and ROSADO-NUÑEZ M.J. (eds.), *Feminist Intercultural Theology: Latina Explorations for a Just World*, Orbis, Maryknoll, NY 2007, 14.

For over twenty years the evangelizing mission of the Church in the u.s. Hispanic community has significantly benefited from the Latino/a theological academy's systematic reflection on the faith experience of the Mexican-American community which represents approximately 64 percent of our people[14]. For example, the work of Virgilio Elizondo, Allan Figueroa Deck, Roberto Goizueta, Arturo Bañuelas, Timothy Matovina, Orlando Espín, and Nancy Pineda-Madrid among many others, have made important contributions to theology from the context of the Mexican-American experience. To a lesser degree the same can be said of the theological reflection on the Cuban-American religious experience. Here, the research done by Miguel Díaz, Michelle González, Fernando Segovia, Ada María Isasi-Díaz, and others, has greatly advanced theological discourse from the social location of Cuban-Americans. We believe that it is crucial to continue to theologize not only from the social location of these communities, but also from the cultural context of other Hispanic cultures present among our numbers. Such research will facilitate ministry as interculturation within the u.s. Hispanic community.

Throughout the history of Christian missiological praxis numerous paradigms of evangelization have been developed in order to respond to specific cultural and historical contexts[15]. The evolution of methods of interculturation is crucial to the effectiveness of culture-specific ministry because culture is a dynamic and ever changing reality[16]. Thus it is incumbent on pastoral agents and on theologians to be attentive to the dynamism of culture and to continually seek new methods of interculturation. In his book, *La Cosecha: Harvesting Contemporary United States Hispanic Theology (1972-1998)*, Eduardo Fernández correlates u.s. Hispanic theology to Stephen Bevans' models of contextual theology and in so doing has advanced the study of the relationship between faith and culture from the prism of the u.s. Hispanic context and assisted ministers in the Latino/a community to broaden the methods of interculturation that they employ in their pastoral work[17]. We believe that Hispanic ministry can greatly

---

14 U.S. CENSUS BUREAU, «Facts for Features: Hispanic Heritage Month 2009, Sept 15 - Oct 15», http://www.census.gov/Press-Release/www/releases/archives/facts_for_features_special_editions/013984.html (accessed January 12, 2009).

15 BOSCH D., *Transforming Mission: Paradigm Shifts in Theology of Mission*, Orbis Books, Maryknoll, NY 1991, 181-182.

16 SCHREITER R., «Faith and Cultures: Challenges to a World Church», 746.

17 FERNÁNDEZ E., *La Cosecha: Harvesting Contemporary United States Hispanic Theology 1972-1998*, Liturgical Press, Collegeville 2000. See also BEVANS S., *Models of Contextual Theology*, Orbis Books, Maryknoll, NY 1992.

benefit from the further development of models and methods of interculturation in the context of the varying cultures present among u.s. Hispanics. Such theological research will significantly enhance much needed cross-cultural competencies in our ministers.

3
Ministerial Praxis

Most of us who have labored in Hispanic ministry for decades at the diocesan, regional, and national levels have participated in and benefitted from the Encuentro processes. And yet many of those engaged in Hispanic ministry today have very little knowledge of the Encuentro movement and the other historical developments of pastoral ministries in the Latino/a community. Too often contemporary ministers remain ignorant of the foundational initiatives and important historical accomplishments that their predecessors achieved as they established culture-specific pastoral ministries among Hispanics. In order to remedy this lacuna, those who are engaged in the formation of pastoral agents in the Hispanic community must instruct them in the area of u.s. Latino/a church history. For these purposes, the now classic, *Fronteras: A History of the Latin American Church in the usa Since 1513* edited by Moises Sandoval is an invaluable resource for the historical education of our ministry students[18]. A more contemporary history of the Latino church in the u.s., written from the context of four urban localities (San Antonio, New York City, Miami, and Chicago), is David Badillo's *Latinos and the New Immigrant Church*[19]. Even though these historical works are invaluable to theology and ministry, further historical research on the faith and ecclesial experience of u.s. Hispanics remains needed.

u.s. Hispanic history emphasizes that many aspects of the ministerial context of the Latino/a community have changed considerably since coordinated pastoral ministry for Hispanics at the national level was officially established. Nevertheless, the grassroots method for pastoral planning that was developed through the Encuentro processes can be considered to be as relevant today as it

18 SANDOVAL M. (ed.), *Fronteras: A History of the Latin American Church in the usa Since 1513*, MACC, San Antonio, TX 1983.
19 BADILLO D.A., *Latinos and the New Immigrant Church*, Johns Hopkins University Press, Baltimore, MD 2006.

was then prophetic[20]. From its emergent stages, the primary concern of the Encuentro processes and of the methodology of Hispanic pastoral planning was that the ministries respond directly to the concrete reality of Latinos/as and that the participation of *la base* (the grassroots) in the pastoral planning process be prioritized.

The methodological cornerstone of the Encuentro processes saw praxis as both its initial and final reflection; it establishes a practical theology done from the underside of history and human experience. This methodology remains a «pastoral discernment that focuses on the needs and aspiration of the faithful, judges that reality in light of the Scriptures and Tradition, and moves into transforming action»[21]. Popularly referred to as *ver-juzgar-actuar-evaluar* (see-judge-act-evaluate), this process continues to be the pastoral planning method of choice of many u.s. Hispanic leaders in the Church.

Our engagement with ministry students points to a need for further practical theological reflection that is framed by the praxis of the Hispanic community. Thus, we think it helpful to further develop praxis-based theological research in Hispanic theological scholarship. While we support the efforts of contemporary Latino/a theologians who establish philosophical correlation between Hispanic experience and emergent thought-forms, we stress that the practical starting point for Latino/a theologies must not be left behind. A renewed commitment to praxis-based theological reflection is instrumental for bridging the gap that often exists between theological theory and the lived experience of faith at the level of *la base*.

We suggest that the area in which there is the greatest disconnect between the work of the Latino/a theological academy and ministry is in the area of ministerial faith formation. On a consistent basis, ministerial faith formation from *la base* remains the primary concern of the pastoral ministers in our theology and ministry programs. While some efforts at ministerial faith formation are being made at the local and diocesan levels, these programs continue to attract small numbers when compared to the over-all membership of the Latino/a population in the Church. Moreover, that formation is often devoid of much of the reflection that arises in the u.s. Hispanic/Latino/a theological academy.

---

20 SOUTHEAST PASTORAL INSTITUTE, *Memoria Histórica Común: Proceso Pastoral Hispano en los EE.UU.*, SEPI, Miami, FL 2004.

21 UNITED STATES CONFERENCE OF CATHOLIC BISHOPS, *Encuentro and Mission: A Renewed Pastoral Framework for Hispanic Ministry*, USCCB, Washington, D.C. 2002, n. 21, http://www.usccb.org/hispanicaffairs/encuentromission.shtml.

For the overwhelming majority of Latinos/as, ministerial faith formation takes place in the context of the parish, its liturgy, and in the varying ecclesial movements that sustain our communities. Too often in-depth theological reflection and analysis fails to inform these settings. For example, there is a chasm between scholarly theological discourse and Christologies that operate at the level of *la base*. Reinforced by liturgical preaching and other praxes that underlie popular church movements, many christologies of *la base* continue to emphasize a triumphal imperial Christ that is distant and removed from human experience and tend to overly center on the divinity of Jesus to the neglect of his humanity. While the work of Virgilio Elizondo in *Galilean Journey* and of Roberto Goizueta in *Caminemos Con Jesús: Toward a Hispanic/Latino Theology of Accompaniment* accentuate a historical Jesus who suffers because of his liberating solidarity with the poor, the christologies that often prevail at the grassroots are those that are more focused on the legitimization of suffering as the will of God imposed on humanity rather than one that empowers the faithful to be authors of their own history and destiny[22]. Moreover, if taken to the extreme, such christologies manifested in our communities can promote a contemporary docetism whereby the humanity of Christ is so de-emphasized that it is really subverted altogether. Thus, we believe that Hispanic ministries can benefit from further research on New Testament christologies sensitive to Latino/a cultures in the U.S. that speak to liberating interpretations of Jesus. We also encourage the development of soteriologies that correspond to such Christological research. Finally, we infer that this Christological/soteriological reflection will also influence theologies of God operative in the U.S. Hispanic ministerial context.

Another example of the chasm between the work of the Hispanic academy and ministerial faith formation is in the area of moral theology. Our experience, like that of our students, points to the regrettable fact that the preaching and sacramental catechesis in our communities are rooted in a highly individualist view of the moral life. Such moral understanding promotes spiritualities that focus solely on the interior life and limit and obscure the social justice de-

---

22 ELIZONDO V., *Galilean Journey: The Mexican-American Promise*, Orbis Books, Maryknoll, NY 1983; GOIZUETA R., *Caminemos Con Jesús: Toward a Hispanic/Latino Theology of Accompaniment*, Orbis Books, Maryknoll, NY 1995.

mands of the Gospel[23]. We contend that the overly individualistic ethics that often prevails in many of our communities supplants the demand to transform social structures that perpetuate the oppression of u.s. Latinos/as[24]. While much has been written by Latino/a theologians on issues of justice, Hispanic ministries need to benefit more from the development of moral theologies reflective of the social location of u.s. Hispanics. This ethical concern promotes an approach to the moral life which underscores the social ethical reflection that educates against forces that marginalize and oppress Hispanics in the United States.

4
Ecclesiology

Highly influenced by the base ecclesial community movements in Latin America, the Encuentro processes arose from community-based methodologies of ecclesial reflection. At the heart of the ecclesiology of the Encuentros, and subsequently in the *National Pastoral Plan for Hispanic Ministry* was a theology of baptism which called for the involvement of the baptized in a full and comprehensive fashion in the mission of the Church. To this end, the model of Church of the Encuentros was one that radiated around the concepts of *comunión y participación* (*communion* in one faith in Jesus Christ and in his mission, and *participation* in the building up of the Kingdom of God)[25]. In his book, *Basic Ecclesial Communities in Brazil,* Marcello Azevedo points to the interrelationship between communion and participation as crucial to the ecclesiology and theology that became an integral element of the model of church embraced by the *National Pastoral Plan*:

> Communion (*koinonia*) is essential for effectiveness and credibility of the faith-community, whose life is to profess and bear witness, announce and denounce, and establish love and justice among human beings in the framework of truth and freedom. Participation is the commitment of all, with their differing personalities and voca-

23 GONZÁLEZ J. and GONZÁLEZ C., *Liberation Preaching: The Pulpit and the Oppressed,* Avingdon Press, Nashville 1980, 23.
24 DE LA TORRE M., *Doing Christian Ethics from the Margins,* Orbis Books, Maryknoll, NY 2004, 56.
25 *Encuentro and Mission,* n. 37-39.

tions, to build and serve the community (*diakonia*) and to construct a society that dovetails with the postulates of faith in all their reach[26].

The ecclesiology of *comunión y participación* underlying the *National Pastoral Plan* was a welcomed fit for u.s. Latino/a Catholics given the dwindling numbers of priests and religious serving it and the fact that Latinos/as had been excluded from the decision making process within ecclesial structures[27]. As a result, the model of Church embraced by the Latino/a community in the Encuentro processes challenged an ecclesial praxis of privilege which limits or absolutizes power for an elite few, be they priests, religious, or lay leaders. In the framework of this Latino/a ecclesiology, all of the members of the community are recognized as equal and all share in the mission of Jesus Christ. To say that all members are equally responsible in carrying out the Church's mission does not mean that there are no differences among the community's membership. There are differences, but differences are meant to serve the community. In other words, the different roles enable a diversity of functions to be realized. All of the baptized, religious and ordained have the same charismatic foundational function which is the building up of the church community[28].

This egalitarian model of church of co-responsibility continues to recognize the differences between those ordered to ministry and those who are not. The ecclesiology forged by the Encuentro processes was not one that deconstructed ecclesial structures as its agenda. On the contrary, ordination remains integral to a Latino/a view of Church which sees it as necessary for the governance and pastoral direction of the community[29]. The Latino/a model of Church called for the ordained and other ecclesial forms of leadership to subsist within the assembly and to assume their place within the community.

26 AZEVEDO M., *Basic Ecclesial Communities in Brazil*, Georgetown University Press, Washington, D.C. 1987, 194. For a brief history of the development of communion ecclesiology see GAIL-LARDETZ R., *Ecclesiology for a Global Church: A People Called and Sent*, Orbis Books, Maryknoll, NY 2008, 85-131.
27 NATIONAL CONFERENCE OF CATHOLIC BISHOPS, *National Pastoral Plan for Hispanic Ministry*, USCC, Washington, D.C. 1987, n. 67, in UNITED STATES CONFERENCE OF CATHOLIC BISHOPS, *Hispanic Ministry: Three Major Documents*, USCCB, Washington, D.C. 1995.
28 AZEVEDO M., *Basic Ecclesial Communities*, 201-202.
29 FIGUEROA DECK A., «A Pox on Both Your Houses: A View of Catholic Conservative-Liberal Polarities from the Hispanic Margin» in WEAVER M.J. and APPLEBY R.S. (eds.), *Being Right: Conservative Catholics in America*, Indiana University Press, Bloomington, IN 1995, 101.

Our experience indicates that there are numerous ecclesiologies that are operative in our Hispanic communities today. Many, we regret, fail to reflect the prophetic model of Church that underlies the Encuentro processes. While the ecclesiology of the Encuentros flows out of baptismal dignity manifested in *comunión y participación*, the ecclesiology of many of our communities continues to be characterized by patriarchal structures that absolutize the power of the clergy. This ecclesial dynamic is attributed to historical, social and cultural factors beyond the scope of this reflection. Nevertheless the Latino/a population in the United States has increased substantially in numbers since the writing of *The National Pastoral Plan*. And yet most Latinos/as still find themselves at the margins of ecclesial power structures at all levels. For these reasons the ecclesiology of *comunión y participación* remains more vital than ever to affect and empower the evangelizing mission of the Church in the Hispanic community.

A significant correlate to the ecclesiology of *comunión y participación* is the u.s. bishops' more recent document on lay ecclesial ministry *Co-Workers in the Vineyard of the Lord: A Resource for Guiding the Development of Lay Ecclesial Ministry*. *Co-Workers* presents a valuable contemporary reflection on lay ecclesial ministry, the formation of lay ecclesial ministers, and the pastoral implications of the ministry of the baptized. Richard Gaillardetz's claim that the role, function and responsibilities of lay ecclesial ministers demand further ecclesial, liturgical and sacramental reflection is an appropriate extension of the ecclesiology of *communion y participación*[30]. Gaillardetz's theological challenge is of great importance to Latino/a theologians given the need to reflect on the key concepts that sustain *Co-Workers in the Vineyard* from a Hispanic perspective.

Our Hispanic lay ministry students argue that an important issue that needs to be developed in a theology of ministry is the relationship between lay ministers and clergy in the United States. Again, Gaillardetz sheds light on this situation through the lens of the expanding role of lay ministers in the Church in this country:

> The North American church has struggled [to] find a theology of ministry capable of doing justice to this new ministerial situation. Many American clergy have felt threatened by the growing number of ministries now undertaken by the laity. Some critics see lay ecclesial ministry as a distraction from the council's teaching that the proper

---

30 GAILLARDETZ R., *Ecclesiology for a Global Church*, 147.

sphere of lay activity is in the world. A significant number of lay ministers have themselves complained about being treated as ministerial auxiliaries by the clergy[31].

The dynamic of conflict between lay ministers and clergy impedes the model of the Church *comunión y participación* of the Encuentro processes. Furthermore, what Gaillardetz claims needs to be addressed by contemporary theologies of ministry is complicated in the Hispanic community because of the presence of foreign born and trained clergy from Latin America who often remain apprehensive about the expanding role of the laity in the North American context. This dynamic, exacerbated by the lack of indigenous U.S. Hispanic clerical vocations, also can be attributed in some part to the fact that «only in North America did the renewal of parish life envisioned by Vatican II ever really take place»[32]. Thus, foreign born and trained clergy often have little understanding of the role of the lay minister in the context of the postconciliar church in the United States and how the growth in lay ministries has been instrumental in the revitalization of parish life[33]. Another reason that contributes to the conflicting relationship between U.S. Latino/a lay ministers and foreign born and trained clergy from Latin America is the fact that these clergy did not participate in Encuentro processes and thus failed to gain exposure to the model of Church that was forged by these processes.

In light of these ecclesiological and ministerial challenges faced by the Latino/a community in the U.S., we pose that Hispanic ministries will benefit from further research into five important ecclesiological elements. First, there is a need for the development of Latino/a theologies of baptism that attend to the priesthood of the faithful[34]. Second, Hispanic ministries will be enhanced by the articulation of theologies of ministry that address the often conflicting ecclesial dynamic between the clergy and lay ministers in our communities. Third, the development of Latino/a lay theologies and their corresponding spiritualities will advance the ministerial and spiritual growth of the laity in the Hispanic community. Fourth, further ecclesiological research is needed on the role, function and responsibilities of the laity for a renewed ecclesiology of *comunión y participación*. Fifth, given the multicultural reality of the Church in the United

31 GAILLARDETZ R., *Ecclesiology for a Global Church*, 148.
32 GAILLARDETZ R., *Ecclesiology for a Global Church*, 148.
33 GAILLARDETZ R., *Ecclesiology for a Global Church*, 148.
34 See WOODS S. (ed.), *Ordering the Baptismal Priesthood*, Liturgical Press, Collegeville, MN 2003. See also PHILLIBERT P., *The Priesthood of the Faithful: Key to a Living Church*, Liturgical Press, Collegeville, MN 2005.

States, we look to the theological academy to develop much needed intercultural ecclesiologies that will enable an experience of Church where «there is a place for all peoples and where human dignity and human rights become possible»[35].

5
Conclusion

For the last 30 years Latino/a theology and ministry have needed their own unique reflection in order to generate foundational and systematic categories that correlate our experience to the theological tradition. In so doing, the scholarly corpus generated by Latino/a Catholic theologians has broadened the horizon of theological discourse to the benefit of not only Hispanic ministries, but also to the enrichment of the larger theological community. Given that much of these theologians' work has been culture-specific theological reflection, their insights have provided our students with a very beneficial perspective on their own faith experience as well as that of the varying cultures that make up the U.S. Hispanic community. Such research has provided Latino/a ministers in theological formation with methods for reflection that enable them to approach their ministries as a *locus theologicus* of practical theology.

An invaluable contribution to ministry in Latino/a contexts has been ACHTUS' extensive theological reflection on the popular religious practices of Hispanics in the United States. Such analyses have provided not only a greater appreciation of the praxis of popular devotions as a revelatory source and theological text[36], but they have also provided methodological models for theological research from the particularity of culture and social location[37]. From the prism of ministry at the grassroots level, we think that it is important to develop practical theologies that use popular religiosity as an instrument of evangelization and yet at the same time challenge the devotions that are inconsistent with the tradition in terms of both orthodoxy and orthopraxis[38].

---

35 AQUINO M.P., «Feminist Intercultural Theology», 16.
36 For a comprehensive reading of the *sensus fidelium* as revelatory source in U.S. Hispanic popular religiosity see ESPÍN O., *The Faith of the People: Theological Reflections on Popular Catholicism*, Orbis Books, Maryknoll, NY 1997.
37 GOIZUETA R., *Caminemos con Jesús*, 20.
38 ESPÍN O., «Tradition and Popular Religion: An Understanding of the Sensus Fidelium» in FIGUEROA DECK A. (ed.), *Frontiers of Hispanic Theology in the United States*, Orbis Books, Maryknoll, NY 1992, 65-66.

The Academy of Catholic Hispanic Theologians of the United States has been an instrument of *concientización* for the u.s. Latino/a community in terms of justice as it relates to issues of poverty and the preferential option for the poor, human dignity, the often dislocating experience of *mestizaje* and exile of Latinos/as, and the marginalization of Latinas. What is often overlooked however is that the body of work produced by ACHTUS members has modeled a liberative praxis giving voice to a people who in many occasions has been systematically silenced by the dominant u.s. culture, some sectors of the Church in North America, and in scholarly theological discourse.

Our students refer to Hispanic/Latino/a theology as a hidden treasure that needs to be further revealed to the greater Hispanic community. To this end we believe that strategies must be developed for such revelation. We affirm the efforts that are being made to translate the work of Latino/a theologians into Spanish for students in both the u.s. and Latin American contexts. We also encourage the further dialogue between theologians and pastoral agents and for the development of theological materials accessible at the level of *la base*. As we look at the future of Hispanic ministry in the United States, we believe that the insights and challenges of our students highlighted in this essay will help to inform a broader reflection on the relationship between Hispanic ministries and contemporary Latino/a theological discourse in this country.

Hispanic Youth and Young Adult Ministry

KEN JOHNSON-MONDRAGÓN

We, the Catholic Latino young people
who participate in Hispanic youth and young adult ministry,
feel called and committed to the mission of the Church,
to wholly form and prepare ourselves through pastoral action,
and to lovingly evangelize other young Hispanics
according to their own situation and experience.

We strive to offer immigrants and citizens alike,
the ever new and joyous truth of the Gospel,
highlighting gospel values,
and making an effort to reach
those who need the Good News the most,
who do not know God,
or who have strayed from the way of Jesus.

We propose to carry out this mission
through the testimony of our lives
and our prophetic leadership among our peers,
investing our gifts and talents
in evangelizing and missionary efforts
rooted in the places where they live, work, study, and have fun,
always following the example of Jesus,
and strengthening ourselves in the Eucharist[1].

The above *Mission Statement of Hispanic Youth and Young Adult Ministry* was developed and approved by the 1,680 young adult delegates to the First National Encounter for Hispanic Youth and Young Adult Ministry (Encuentro or PENPJH for its initials in Spanish) in 2006. These delegates represented more than 40,000 young Latino/as who participated in the parish, diocesan, and regional encuentros across the country. This articulation is a milestone achievement in the history of Hispanic ministry in the United States because in these words, the Encuentro delegates indicated that they:

---

1   NATIONAL CATHOLIC NETWORK DE PASTORAL JUVENIL HISPANA —LA RED, *Conclusions: First National Encounter for Hispanic Youth and Young Adult Ministry*, USCCB, Washington, D.C. 2008, 54.

- are critically aware of their own identity as a nationwide community that is young, Latino, and Catholic
- wholeheartedly embrace the mission of the Church as their own
- are protagonists in their mission as disciples of Jesus, not dependent on the initiative of adult leaders to get them started
- need the assistance of the Church for proper formation, guidance in following the example of Jesus, and full participation in the Eucharist.

The maturation of *Pastoral juvenil hispana* (PJH — Hispanic youth and young adult ministry) as a ministry with its own principles, vision, and leadership structures at the national, regional, and local levels sets the context for any discussion of Hispanic youth and young adult ministry in the 21ˢᵗ century. Nevertheless, this ministry does not exist apart from the young Latino/a men and women who are called to exercise leadership in it. In other words, it is a ministry rooted in the languages and cultures of Hispanic young people; it is animated by their prophetic zeal for evangelization and holiness as a response to baptism; it responds to the pastoral circumstances of the young people involved, especially the obstacles and challenges of daily life; and it forms young Latino/as in the Catholic faith for the building of God's Kingdom.

This description of Hispanic youth and young adult ministry may appear very straightforward, but it raises a number of important questions. What are the obstacles and challenges young Hispanics face in their daily lives? How do culture and language shape their experience and understanding of the Catholic faith? What formation do our ministry leaders have, and what pastoral and catechetical resources are available to assist them in their ministry? How is the Church as a whole responding to its young Latino/a members? What is the current state of religious formation among young Hispanics?

This essay responds to the various questions stated above in three sections. Section 1 presents the contemporary context of PJH in the U.S.; section 2 offers an overview of PJH in the United States today; and section 3 offers some reflections on current efforts and areas for growth in the field.

1

The Contemporary Context of Pastoral Juvenil Hispana *in the U.S.*

The *Conclusions of the* PENPJH provide a brief history of *PJH* in the United States that describes its roots in Latin America, its development through the process of the three National Encuentros for Hispanic Ministry, its relationship to mainstream youth and young adult ministry, and its recent growth[2]. Although it will not be repeated here, this historical context frames the discussion that follows.

In 2002, Instituto Fe y Vida published an assessment of the state of ministry with young Hispanics, providing clear evidence of the pervasive material and spiritual challenges facing young Hispanics. Despite the U.S. Catholic bishops' commitment to a preferential missionary option in favor of service to the poor and the young in Hispanic ministry[3], the report found that «most mainstream Catholic youth ministry programs in the U.S. are reaching only a small segment of young Hispanic Catholics, while programs directed specifically to Hispanic *jóvenes* are both few in number and limited in scope and depth»[4].

In the years since that preliminary assessment was made, the PENPJH process (2005-2006) has stimulated efforts in parishes and dioceses to improve and expand the pastoral care and accompaniment of Hispanic youth and young adults. In addition, the groundbreaking insights of the National Study of Youth and Religion (NSYR, 2003-2008) have shed light on the current state of religious formation —as well as the numerous pastoral challenges that stem from differences of language, culture, and socioeconomic status— among Hispanic adolescents. Given the breadth of information now available from these and other sources, it is an opportune moment to assess once again where we stand in our ministry «to and with young Hispanics, from their lived reality»[5].

2 NATIONAL CATHOLIC NETWORK DE PASTORAL JUVENIL HISPANA —LA RED, *Conclusions: First National Encounter for Hispanic Youth and Young Adult Ministry*, 19-22.

3 NATIONAL CONFERENCE OF CATHOLIC BISHOPS, *National Pastoral Plan for Hispanic Ministry*, USCC, Washington, D.C. 1987, n. 51-56; 64-66, in UNITED STATES CONFERENCE OF CATHOLIC BISHOPS, *Hispanic Ministry: Three Major Documents*, USCCB, Washington, D.C. 1995.

4 JOHNSON-MONDRAGÓN K., *The Status of Hispanic Youth and Young Adult Ministry in the United States: A Preliminary Study*, Instituto Fe y Vida, Stockton, CA 2002, 30.

5 This phrase is taken from Specific Objective #3 of the PENPJH, *Conclusions*, 28. In many ways, it is a poor translation of the original Spanish, «la pastoral con, hacia y desde la juventud hispana». The Spanish captures the essence of evangelizing action in *PJH* as it has come to be articulated in Latin America—a ministry that is carried out «desde la juventud» is one that is informed by and responds to the immediate and global context of the young people's lives, while relying on

As shown in Figure 1 below, Latino/a children are already about half of all Catholics under age 18 in the United States, and Latino/as are poised to become the majority of all Catholics in less than 40 years. Thus, the pastoral work of our Church in this century will be shaped by a tremendous demographic shift to a majority Hispanic population. In this context, we must ask ourselves: is our Church prepared to address this change constructively through leadership development and pastoral services that meet the needs of the whole Catholic community?

FIGURE 1

u.s. Catholic Population Projections by Age, Race/Ethnicity and Year

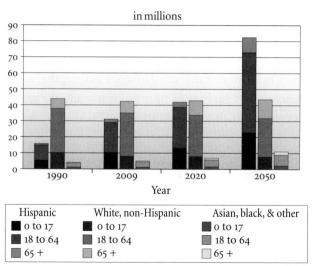

Based on: RSL 2007, ICR Omnibus 2008, NSRI 1990, LNPS 1990, Census 1990, u.s. Census Bureau national population estimates 2009 & Pew Hispanic Center projections

Due to the steep increase in the number of Latino/a immigrants between ages 20 and 25, as shown in Figure 2, nearly half of our young adult Hispanic Catholics today are foreign-born. Furthermore, the youngest Latino/as in the u.s. today are mostly the children of immigrants. As a result, it should be ex-

the giftedness of the same *jóvenes* to develop and implement the pastoral response. A full description of the Latin American articulation of this ministry can be found in CONSEJO EPISCOPAL LATINOAMERICANO, *Civilización del Amor: Tarea y Esperanza*, CELAM, Sección de Juventud, Santa Fé de Bogotá, Colombia 1995, 2ª Parte, Sección III, n. 2.1-2.2.

pected that their experience of growing up between two cultures will have a great impact on the life of our Church as they mature into young adulthood and eventually take their place among our leaders —or not— depending on the quality of leadership training and faith formation they receive.

FIGURE 2

Hispanics in the United States in 2009 by Age and Generation

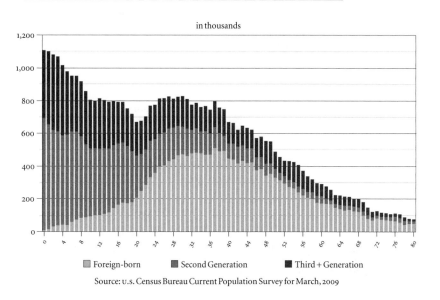

in thousands

Foreign-born · Second Generation · Third + Generation

Source: u.s. Census Bureau Current Population Survey for March, 2009

As a final indication of the demographic reality of youth and young adult ministry in the Catholic Church today, Figure 3 divides the overall population of Catholic adolescents and young adults into its ethnic, racial, and generational segments. This comparison clearly shows that immigrants form the largest group of young adult Latino/a Catholics, while it is the children of immigrants who predominate among the teens. It is also significant to note that Hispanics have now surpassed the whites as the largest segment of the high school-age Catholic population in the United States according to Instituto Fe y Vida's estimates.

FIGURE 3

Estimated Catholic Youth and Young Adults in the u.s. by Age Group, Race/Ethnicity, and Generation in 2009

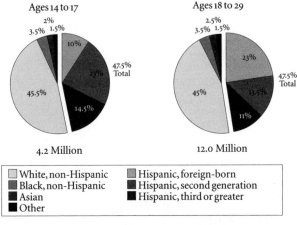

Based on: RSL 2007, ICR Omnibus 2008, and U.S. Census Bureau national population estimates for July 1, 2009

1.2. KEY ASPECTS OF THE SOCIOCULTURAL CONTEXT

To help situate the lived experience of Latino/a young people in the United States, it is helpful to highlight some of the significant differences between Hispanic and white youth and young adults in general, and to contrast the reality of Hispanic and white *Catholic* youth and young adults whenever the data are available. The research findings reported here come from various sources, collected and published by Instituto Fe y Vida[6].

1.2.1. *LANGUAGE*

- 58 percent of Hispanic teens speak at least as much Spanish as they do English at home, including 47 percent of u.s.-born Hispanic teens.
- 62 percent of Latino/a young adults (ages 18 to 29) said they do not speak English «well».

These statistics reflect the proportion of immigrants and children of immigrants shown in Figure 2 above. Pastorally, the language spoken at home tends to be the preferred language of prayer and faith for most people.

6 INSTITUTO FE Y VIDA, «Hispanic Youth and Young Adult Ministry: Recent Findings» in *Perspectives on Hispanic Youth and Young Adult Ministry* 4, Instituto Fe y Vida Stockton, CA 2007, available online, http://www.feyvida.org/research/researchpubs.html

1.2.2. *IMMIGRATION STATUS*

- Although the Census Bureau does not track immigration status, current estimates suggest that as many as half of the *immigrant* Latino/a youth and young adults are undocumented.
- Combined with the Census data behind Figure 3, this means that about 80 percent of the Hispanic youth and young adults in the u.s. overall are citizens or legal residents[7].

1.2.3. *EDUCATION*

- More than 30 percent of Hispanics in their 20s in 2007 had not completed high school, compared to only 7 percent of their white counterparts.
- By the age of 25 to 29, only 15 percent of Hispanics had completed a bachelor's degree or higher, compared to 34 percent of their white peers.
- The differences for Catholics are even greater: among the parents of Catholic adolescents in the nsyr survey, 38 percent of the white fathers and 39 percent of the white mothers had at least a bachelor's degree, compared to 8 percent and 12 percent of their respective Hispanic peers[8].

1.2.4. *HOUSEHOLD FINANCES*

Not surprisingly, these differences are also reflected in household income and assets:

- 26 percent of the Hispanic Catholic households in the nsyr survey had an annual income of less than $20,000 and only 14 percent had more than $60,000; this compares to 4 percent and 52 percent respectively for white Catholic households.
- Similarly, 75 percent of the Hispanic Catholic parents said they were in debt or just breaking even, and only 1 percent said they had «a lot» of savings and assets; among the white Catholic parents, only 41 percent were in debt or just breaking even, and 13 percent had «a lot» of savings and assets.

---

7 INSTITUTO FE Y VIDA, «Hispanic Youth and Young Adult Ministry: Recent Findings» in *Perspectives on Hispanic Youth and Young Adult Ministry* 3, 5.
8 INSTITUTO FE Y VIDA, «Hispanic Youth and Young Adult Ministry: Recent Findings» in *Perspectives on Hispanic Youth and Young Adult Ministry* 3, 5. In this section, only white and Hispanic results from the National Study of Youth and Religion (nsyr) are mentioned because the survey sample did not include sufficient Catholic respondents among the black, Asian, Native American, and other groups to provide statistically meaningful comparisons.

- The white Catholic parents were also nearly twice as likely to say they own their home (82 percent vs. 46 percent) as their Hispanic counterparts[9].

1.2.5. *MARRIAGE AND CHILDREN*

- 49 percent of all Latinas ages 16 to 30 are raising a child or children, and 19 percent of all Latinas in this age group are single mothers; this compares to 27 percent and 10 percent respectively for all other women combined[10].
- Hispanics also tend to marry earlier than non-Hispanics. Among Hispanics ages 16 to 30, 31 percent were married or had been married, compared to 25 percent of their non-Hispanic peers[11].
- 62 percent of Hispanic Catholic teens have married parents, compared to 76 percent of their white peers[12].

108 1.2.6. *RISKY AND CRIMINAL BEHAVIOR*

Hispanic youth and young adults demonstrate significantly higher rates of risky and criminal behavior than their white peers:

- Hispanic youths are 50 percent more likely to attempt suicide; nearly three times as likely to become incarcerated; more than three times as likely to get pregnant or get someone pregnant as adolescents; and roughly 30 times as likely to be active members of a gang[13].
- The exception to this pattern was regarding substance abuse: Hispanic and white Catholic teens reported similar levels of marijuana use, and the white Catholic teens were actually 33 percent more likely to have gotten drunk in the last year than their Hispanic counterparts[14].

These risk factors correlate to increased exposure to violence and abuse at home, at school, and in their neighborhoods; less parental supervision and guidance; and experiences of discrimination and negative stereotypes.

9 INSTITUTO FE Y VIDA, «Hispanic Youth and Young Adult Ministry: Recent Findings» in *Perspectives on Hispanic Youth and Young Adult Ministry*, 4.
10 U.S. CENSUS BUREAU, *Current Population Survey* for March, 2009.
11 U.S. CENSUS BUREAU, *Current Population Survey* for March, 2009.
12 JOHNSON-MONDRAGÓN K., «Youth Ministry and the Socioreligious Lives of Hispanic and White Catholic Teens in the U.S.» in INSTITUTO FE Y VIDA, *Perspectives on Hispanic Youth and Young Adult Ministry* 2, Instituto Fe y Vida, Stockton, CA 2005, 3.
13 INSTITUTO FE Y VIDA, «Hispanic Youth and Young Adult Ministry: Recent Findings», 5.
14 JOHNSON-MONDRAGÓN K., «Youth Ministry and the Socioreligious Lives of Hispanic and White Catholic Teens in the U.S.», 22.

Overview of Pastoral Juvenil Hispana *in the United States Today*

∾

The previous section of this essay demonstrated that the Hispanic segment of the Catholic youth and young adult population is growing far more rapidly than the overall young Catholic population, and it is marked by significant sociocultural differences with respect to other young Catholics. Undoubtedly, many of these differences impact the spiritual, emotional, intellectual, and physical well-being of young Hispanic Catholics. Indeed, the data demonstrate that too many of our Latino/a young people are making poor decisions with terrible consequences for themselves, their children, our Church, and society at large. With that in mind, this section examines the state of faith formation and pastoral care among Hispanic youth and young adults.

Chapter 4

109

2.1. RELIGIOUS IDENTITY, FAITH FORMATION, AND RELIGIOUS PRACTICE

The phenomenon of Hispanics leaving the Catholic Church for evangelical and Pentecostal communities continues to be widely discussed and analyzed[15], yet a more fundamental issue is whether young Latino/a Catholics are being effectively formed in their faith in the first place. Many of the Hispanic Catholic teens interviewed for the NSYR spoke in very strong terms about their Catholic identity, but their professed commitment to the faith was only weakly reflected in their religious practices and their ability to speak about what they believe. In general, the Hispanic Catholic teens practiced more personal and family-based religious devotions, while their white peers were much more likely to be involved in parish-based activities[16]. Even so, both groups tended to describe their faith as a form of «moralistic therapeutic deism» (MTD)[17], rather than accurately reflecting Church teachings.

---

15 For a recent analysis of this phenomenon see THE PEW FORUM ON RELIGION AND PUBLIC LIFE, *Changing Faiths: Latinos and the Transformation of American Religion,* Pew Hispanic Center, Washington, D.C. 2007, 41-48, http://pewforum.org/newassets/surveys/hispanic/hispanics-religion-07-final-mar08.pdf (accessed January 11, 2010).

16 JOHNSON-MONDRAGÓN K., (ed.), *Pathways of Hope and Faith Among Hispanic Teens: Pastoral Reflections and Strategies Inspired by the National Study of Youth and Religion,* Instituto Fe y Vida, Stockton, CA 2007, 97-100; 324.

17 Moralistic Therapeutic Deism is a term developed by Christian Smith, the principal investigator of the NSYR, to describe the «benign whateverism» that characterizes the religious faith of most

What is of great pastoral concern is that even the Latino Catholic parents who are very committed to their faith and involved in their parish are struggling to pass their faith to their adolescent children, in sharp contrast to the experience of their religiously committed white Catholic peers. The NSYR analysis described this reality in the following passage:

«The Hispanic children of religiously "committed" Catholic parents in the NSYR sample are less than half as likely as their white counterparts to attend weekly Mass, about one-third as likely to participate in a church youth group, about one-fourth as likely to attend a Catholic school, about one-fifth as likely to be a youth group leader, and one-sixth or less as likely to have attended a religious retreat or summer camp»[18].

The reasons for the religious disconnect between Latino parents and teens are complex and vary from family to family and parish to parish, but two factors stand out: 1) many u.s.-born Hispanic youth do not easily relate to the faith expressions and traditions of their immigrant parents because of the overarching cultural divide they experience with their parents[19]; and 2) the differences of language, culture, and social class that many Latino/a Catholic teens experience with other youth or adult leaders in their parish often lead them to opt out of participation in parish youth and young adult ministry programs, especially when the parish provides just one youth ministry program[20].

2.2.   VOCATIONS TO ECCLESIAL MINISTRY

In many ways, the greater disengagement of Latino Catholic teens from parish life is a reflection of the neglect, and in some cases outright racism, with which the institutional Catholic Church in the u.s. has responded to the pastoral needs of its Hispanic members of all ages over the years[21]. The consequences of this

---

adolescents in the u.s. today. For a full description of this term as it relates to Hispanic teens see JOHNSON-MONDRAGÓN K., (ed.), *Pathways of Hope and Faith Among Hispanic Teens*, 72-74; 324.

18 JOHNSON-MONDRAGÓN K., (ed.), *Pathways of Hope and Faith Among Hispanic Teens*, 100; 324. INSTITUTO FE Y VIDA, «Hispanic Youth and Young Adult Ministry: Recent Findings», 6-7.

19 See CERVANTES C. and JOHNSON-MONDRAGÓN K., «The Dynamics of Culture, Faith, and Family in the Lives of Hispanic Teens, and their Implications for Youth Ministry» in INSTITUTO FE Y VIDA, *Perspectives on Hispanic Youth and Young Adult Ministry* 5, INSTITUTO FE Y VIDA, Stockton, CA 2008, available online, http://www.feyvida.org/research/researchpubs.html.

20 NATIONAL CATHOLIC NETWORK DE PASTORAL JUVENIL HISPANA —LA RED, *Conclusions*, 33.

21 JOHNSON-MONDRAGÓN K., (ed.), *Pathways of Hope and Faith Among Hispanic Teens*, 326-329.

neglect are nowhere more evident than in the statistics about religious and ministerial vocations:

- 11 percent of U.S. Catholic deacons are Hispanic
- 9 percent of U.S. Catholic bishops are Hispanic
- 6 percent of U.S. Catholic priests are Hispanic, and 83 percent of them are foreign-born
- 4 percent of U.S. lay ecclesial ministers are Hispanic
- 2 percent of U.S. vowed religious (men and women) are Hispanic
- 1 percent of U.S.-born priests are Hispanic[22].

From another perspective, the ratio of laity to priests can be seen as one measure of institutional identity and commitment in the Catholic community. There are currently about 1,900 Catholic lay people for every Catholic priest in the United States. In contrast, there are roughly 10,000 lay Latino Catholics for every Latino priest, and the ratio jumps to nearly 30,000 U.S.-born lay Hispanic Catholics for every U.S.-born Hispanic priest[23]. Perhaps this should come as no surprise, since it is difficult to elicit a lifelong commitment among young Latino/as to an institution with a mediocre and uneven record of reciprocating that commitment in Hispanic communities, despite the high ideals articulated by the U.S. bishops in the *National Pastoral Plan for Hispanic Ministry* and other Hispanic ministry documents.

2.3. PASTORAL CATEGORIES OF LATINO/A YOUTH
       AND YOUNG ADULTS

Bringing forth a commitment to the Church among young Latino/as will require a systematic effort to create welcoming programs that address their concerns and pastoral needs. In this regard, the alienating effects of linguistic, cultural, and social differences among youth ministry participants are often overlooked. The variety of pastoral circumstances found among just the young *Hispanics* (not to mention young Catholics of other racial/ethnic backgrounds) calls for ministry settings and programs targeted to particular segments. The NSYR describes four distinct pastoral categories of young Hispanics to assist youth ministry leaders in recognizing this diversity[24]. That information will not be repeated in detail here, but it is summarized in the following tables:

22 INSTITUTO FE Y VIDA, «Hispanic Youth and Young Adult Ministry: Recent Findings», 8.
23 INSTITUTO FE Y VIDA, «Hispanic Youth and Young Adult Ministry: Recent Findings», 8.
24 JOHNSON-MONDRAGÓN K., (ed.), *Pathways of Hope and Faith Among Hispanic Teens*, 33-39.

TABLE 1
Pastoral Categories of Young Hispanics

Immigrant Workers	
· Mostly Spanish-speaking	· Little formal education
· Mostly of Mexican origin	· Tend to have large families
· Many are undocumented	· Motivated and hopeful
· About 74% are Catholic	· Willing to work hard
· Many seek moral and spiritual support from the church	
· Mostly at the lower end of the economic spectrum	
· Interested in forming peer groups and communities	

Identity Seekers	
· Mostly bilingual	· Few will go to college
· Mostly born in the U.S.	· Low self-esteem
· Children of immigrants	· Unmotivated / apathetic
· Some struggle to stay in high school and graduate	
· May find hope in work or family relationships	
· Some seek refuge in alcohol, drugs, or sexual promiscuity	
· Mostly in lower-middle part of the economic spectrum	

Mainstream Movers	
· Mostly English-speaking	· Motivated and hopeful
· Mostly born in the U.S.	· Willing to work hard
· Will likely go to college, and some attend private schools	
· Do not associate much with lower-income Hispanics	
· More likely than other Hispanics to leave Catholic Church	
· May look down on other categories of Hispanics	
· Mostly in middle-upper part of economic spectrum	

Gang Members and High-Risk Youth	
· Limited bilingual abilities	· Little formal education
· Mostly born in the U.S.	· Anger towards society
· Many live in inner cities	· Experience despair
· Most are unemployed	· Many are incarcerated
· May become habitual drug users / sellers	
· Mostly at the lower end of the economic spectrum	
· Will only get involved at church in specialized programs	

TABLE 2
Pastoral Needs of Young Hispanics by Category

	Immigrant Workers	Identity Seekers	Mainstream Movers	Gang Members and High-Risk Youth
Spiritual life	Need to form faith-based communities grounded in their culture of origin	Need mentoring to integrate faith and life amid cultural transition	Need guidance to overcome individualism and consumerism, and to value Hispanic spirituality	Need faith to heal and move from anger / hatred to forgiveness
Intellectual development	Need an accessible alternative system of education	Need encouragement to finish high school and set goals for higher education	Need financial aid and help understanding U.S. system of higher education	Need an accessible alternative system of education
Affective maturity and socialization	Need a healthy environment for developing relationships	Need assistance to develop self-esteem and faith in themselves	Need positive role models of social and cultural integration	Need a peer group and a safe place to belong with positive role models
Acquisition of human virtues	Need help to avoid the pitfalls of vice and addictions	Need guidance and direction in life	Need to value community service and social justice	Need counseling to overcome bad habits and attitudes
Percent of Hispanic young adults / teens	25% to 45% / 10% to 20%	25% to 45% / 40% to 50%	15% to 25% / 20% to 30%	10% to 15% / 10% to 15%

Of course, the relative proportion of young Latino/as in each category will vary from place to place. Nevertheless, the pastoral needs of each category are so distinct that it is difficult to imagine a single program or group that could effectively address the needs of all. Thus, Hispanic youth and young adult ministry is most successful when it provides a differentiated pastoral response through a variety of structures, programs, events, and activities designed to serve particular segments of the young people in the parish or diocese, each according to their needs. The more programs and activities a parish offers, the more likely it will be that the young Catholics in the community will find a spiritual home and community in which to grow in faith.

It is also important to recognize that not all young Catholics are ready to engage in an intensive program of catechesis and faith formation. The home and social environments of many Latino/a youth and young adults are often dominated by values contrary to the Gospel, such as:

- Consumerism that values individuals according to what they buy
- Peer pressure to seek immediate gratification in sex, drugs, and other risky behaviors
- Extreme individualism that sees others as objects to be used for personal gain or pleasure
- Secularism that marginalizes religious beliefs and values
- Experiences of domination, violence, racism, sexism, abuse, and discrimination as «normal» aspects of their world about which nothing can be done
- Impaired moral reasoning due to addictions

In these environments, effective ministry may require a period of pre-evangelization composed of activities designed to win the trust of the participants without making them feel judged, while providing them with safe and constructive activities to orient their lives. The loving commitment, the personal faith witness, and the probing questions of the adult and youth leaders will gradually draw these young people into a desire for greater understanding of the faith, conversion, and a deeper spirituality —when they are ready. It may also be necessary to catechize the larger community on how to welcome and accept young people as they are, in order to minimize the common experience of being judged or rejected by adults in the parish community for not having the «look» of proper young Catholics.

2.4. DEVELOPMENT AND ORGANIZATION OF THREE COMPLEMENTARY PASTORAL RESPONSES

While it cannot yet be said that the Church consistently offers a comprehensive response to the pastoral needs of all four categories of young Latino/as in all parishes, there are three existing ministries that each provide at least a partial response: youth ministry, young adult ministry, and *pastoral juvenil hispana*. As already mentioned, key aspects of the development of p*astoral juvenil hispana*, including its roots in Latin America and a brief outline of its historical process of inculturation in the Catholic Church in this country, can be found in the *Con-*

clusions of the PENPJH[25]. Mainstream youth ministry and young adult ministry also have their particular history and development as distinct pastoral efforts in the United States.

One commonality is that each ministry has developed its own set of operating principles and national organizations to support leaders at the diocesan and parish levels:

- Mainstream youth ministry has *Renewing the Vision: A Framework for Catholic Youth Ministry* (from USCCB Publishing), the National Federation for Catholic Youth Ministry (NFCYM), and the National Association of Catholic Youth Ministry Leaders (NACYML).
- Mainstream young adult ministry has *Sons and Daughters of the Light: A Pastoral Plan for Ministry with Young Adults* (from USCCB Publishing), the National Catholic Young Adult Ministry Association (NCYAMA), the Catholic Campus Ministry Association (CCMA), and the National Association of Diocesan Directors of Campus Ministry (NADDCM).
- *Pastoral juvenil hispana* has *Civilización del Amor: Tarea y Esperanza* (from the Consejo Episcopal Latinoamericano, Sección de Juventud), the *Conclusions of the* PENPJH (from USCCB Publishing), and the National Catholic Network de Pastoral Juvenil Hispana —La Red.

Despite the best efforts of the national organizations and the ministries they represent, many Hispanic youth and young adults continue to fall through the cracks. The high risk Latino/a youth and young adults seldom benefit from an organized pastoral effort to reach them, and the vast majority of Hispanic identity seekers do not feel at home in either the mainstream youth and young adult ministries or PJH (assuming their parish is one of the few that offers a choice), so they simply opt out. These «culturally squeezed» young people are among the most likely to lose their Catholic faith and identity in adulthood, often stemming from an initial rejection of their parents' culture that extends over time to their religious faith as well[26].

114

---

25 NATIONAL CATHOLIC NETWORK DE PASTORAL JUVENIL HISPANA —LA RED, *Conclusions*, 19-22.
26 For a description of the most common patterns of cultural adaptation between immigrant parents and their u.s.-born children, see CERVANTES C. and JOHNSON-MONDRAGÓN K., «The Dynamics of Culture, Faith, and Family in the Lives of Hispanic Teens, and their Implications for Youth Ministry», 3-5.

5. DISTINCT PASTORAL APPROACHES AND THE PROTECTION OF ADOLESCENTS

It is important at this point to recognize some of the key differences in pastoral approach between mainstream youth ministry and *pastoral juvenil hispana*. First of all, although mainstream youth ministry is described as a ministry to, with, by, and for adolescents[27], in the U.S. context it is assumed that the teens will only exercise leadership under the direction of adult leaders —paid or volunteer— who are responsible for everything that goes on in the ministry. There are limits on what leaders can and cannot do according to their age, even for adult leaders between 18 and 25 years of age. In addition, since the sexual abuse scandals at the beginning of this century, the bishops have implemented a *Charter for the Protection of Children and Young People,* and its requirements are enforced in nearly all youth ministry programs.

In contrast, *pastoral juvenil* in Latin America is understood as a peer ministry —a ministry *of* the young people to their peers— generally without a paid staff person or even an adult volunteer appointed to be in charge of the gatherings[28]. In the U.S., *La Red* has defined PJH as a peer ministry serving single Hispanics between the ages of 16 and 30[29], although examples of groups serving a broader range of ages can still be found in many places. With the arrival of the bishops' *Charter,* diocesan and parish pastoral leaders have had to face the issue of how to ensure that PJH provides a safe environment for its participants under age 18. This is especially problematic considering that many of the young adult leaders and participants may be undocumented, so they are fearful of undergoing a criminal background check. As a result, some parishes and dioceses have opted to separate the ages, while others have designated the groups as «intergenerational ministries» with screened and trained leaders assigned to supervise the adolescents during small group activities[30].

---

27 UNITED STATES CATHOLIC CONFERENCE, DEPARTMENT OF EDUCATION, *A Vision of Youth Ministry: Edición Bilingüe,* Washington, D.C., USCC 1986, 6-7.

28 CERVANTES C. and JOHNSON-MONDRAGÓN K., «Pastoral Juvenil Hispana, Youth Ministry, and Young Adult Ministry: An Updated Perspective on Three Different Pastoral Realities» in INSTITUTO FE Y VIDA, *Perspectives on Hispanic Youth and Young Adult Ministry* 3, Instituto Fe y Vida, Stockton, CA 2007, 3.

29 NATIONAL CATHOLIC NETWORK DE PASTORAL JUVENIL HISPANA —LA RED, *Conclusions,* 23.

30 For a discussion of the pros and cons of keeping the mixed-age groups together versus separating them, see JOHNSON-MONDRAGÓN K., (ed.), *Pathways of Hope and Faith Among Hispanic Teens,* 342-344.

While each diocese has appointed someone to hold the parishes accountable to the requirements of the *Charter,* it is important to acknowledge that there are many apostolic movements in the Church that serve Hispanic youth and young adults, often with little oversight from the parish or diocese. The diocesan encuentros conducted as a preparation for the PENPJH included representatives from more than 60 distinct movements, 67 percent of whom reported that they serve youth and young adults together[31], and in most dioceses there are no clear structures of accountability to ensure that their leaders are prepared to provide the protections required in the bishops' *Charter.* In fact, anecdotal feedback from the field suggests that leaders in a significant number of mixed-age groups are not even aware that this is an issue that needs to be addressed —in some cases due to an unspoken decision by the diocesan staff to allow the ministries to continue as they always have, rather than impose regulations that would be pastorally difficult to meet.

2.6. OTHER IMPORTANT DIFFERENCES WITH MAINSTREAM YOUTH MINISTRY

In addition to their distinct age groupings, PJH and mainstream youth ministry rely on different forms of leadership, face different challenges, and employ different approaches in key dimensions of Church's pastoral care and accompaniment of the young. When these differences are not understood by pastors and diocesan leaders, it often happens that one ministry is simply canceled in favor of the other. Thus, it is important to recognize the complementarity of their respective approaches in order to expand ministry to and with young Latino/as in parishes and dioceses. Listed below are some of the key differences between these two ministries:

- Leadership structures. As a peer ministry, PJH is organized with shared leadership structures in which leadership roles are periodically rotated based on the gifts and availability of the individual, so that all participants may have opportunities to develop their leadership skills irrespective of their chronological age[32]. Also, the leadership team for PJH seldom includes a paid professional coordinator —a position that is increasingly common in main-

31 JOHNSON-MONDRAGÓN K., (ed.), *Pathways of Hope and Faith Among Hispanic Teens,* 99.
32 NATIONAL CATHOLIC NETWORK DE PASTORAL JUVENIL HISPANA —LA RED, *Conclusions,* 57.

stream youth ministry, especially in wealthier parishes[33]. Instead, the young adult leadership teams in PJH require guidance and oversight from an adult adviser (i.e. a priest, spiritual director, member of the parish pastoral staff, or the diocesan coordinator of *pastoral juvenil*) who usually is not present at the regularly scheduled gatherings of the group, community, or movement.

· Parish staffing and leadership formation. Ideally, every parish that serves a significant Latino population should have an adult adviser for PJH on staff. This would provide stability and continuity to the ministry during times of transition or crisis, as well as continuous mentorship and leadership development. However, few immigrant Latino parishes have the economic resources to hire a full-time professional for this ministry, and there is a critical lack of adult leaders with the training in PJH, the academic credentials for ministry, and the linguistic and cultural skills required to exercise this role —even among the priests and parish directors of religious education. As a result, entire ministries are often dismantled when there is a change of leadership in the parish, while other ministries are vulnerable to the inexperience of their leadership team, or to the changes that occur when life circumstances require established leaders to step down.

· Diocesan coordination and support. In this context, one of the most effective structures to support PJH in parishes and movements has proven to be the trained professional coordinator of *pastoral juvenil* at the diocesan level. In contrast to the work of most diocesan directors of *youth ministry* —whose ministry consists largely of supporting, resourcing, and training the parish youth ministry leaders— diocesan coordinators of PJH have to be much more hands-on with the ministries they support.

In parishes where PJH does not yet exist, they may be asked to assist the pastoral staff in identifying, inviting, motivating, and training a team of volunteer leaders to establish a ministry. Advocating for the ministry with parish pastoral leaders who do not fully understand the model, or who are determined to have a single parish youth ministry program «for everyone», is also a major component of the coordinator's outreach. Furthermore, it is practically impossible for parishes on their own to provide intermediate and advanced levels of pastoral-theological and leadership training for this min-

33 The NSYR found that white Catholic teens were nearly 50 percent more likely to have a full-time paid youth minister in their parish than their Hispanic counterparts. See JOHNSON-MONDRAGÓN K., (ed.), *Pathways of Hope and Faith Among Hispanic Teens,* 90-92.

istry, so the formation and support of volunteer leaders in parishes and movements is a critical component of the diocesan coordinator's ministry.

- *Pastoral de conjunto. Pastoral juvenil hispana* also differs from mainstream youth and young adult ministry in its emphasis on a *pastoral de conjunto* —a ministry concept that has no exact equivalent in English, but is often translated loosely as «communion in mission». One dimension of this approach to ministry occurs when various groups and movements collaborate for large-group events and celebrations. Due to the strong communitarian dimension of Latino cultures, PJH thrives when regular group meetings are supplemented with periodic experiences of larger gatherings. This is one of the most effective ways to engage newcomers to the ministry, maintain the energy and commitment of those already involved, and develop new leaders through a process of formation-in-action. The Latin American bishops' pastoral letter on *pastoral juvenil* emphasizes that networking, gathering, and collaborating among groups should occur at multiple levels: intra-parish, inter-parish, diocesan-wide, regional, national, and international[34].

- A differentiated ministry. Another aspect of *pastoral de conjunto* that is highlighted by the Latin American bishops is the importance of coordinating the pastoral efforts of various ministries, such as: mainstream youth and young adult ministry, detention ministry, Hispanic ministry, gang outreach, PJH, family ministry, ministry to the sick and disabled, migrant ministry, campus ministry, and others[35]. It is only through the coordination of such efforts that young people of diverse backgrounds and needs will be guaranteed access to faith formation, pastoral care, accompaniment, and opportunities to participate in the life and mission of the Church.

- Approaches to evangelization and vocation. Because PJH is articulated as a peer ministry, it places great importance on the protagonism of the young in the work of evangelization[36]. Drawing from the mission of the Church[37], PJH understands the proclamation and inculturation[38] of the Gospel to be

---

34 CONSEJO EPISCOPAL LATINOAMERICANO, *Civilización del Amor*, 3ª Parte, n. 4.1 - 4.2.

35 CONSEJO EPISCOPAL LATINOAMERICANO, *Civilización del Amor*, 3ª Parte, n. 3.2 - 3.4.

36 NATIONAL CATHOLIC NETWORK DE PASTORAL JUVENIL HISPANA —LA RED, *Conclusions*, 54-55 and 57, especially PJ-22, #3. See also CONSEJO EPISCOPAL LATINOAMERICANO, *Civilización del Amor*, 2ª Parte, Sección I, n. 1.2 and Sección III, n. 2.2.

37 See PAUL VI, *Evangelii Nuntiandi*, n. 14, 17-18, 22, and 29.

38 A deeper explanation of inculturation and its application in youth ministry can be found in CERVANTES C. and JOHNSON-MONDRAGÓN K., «The Dynamics of Culture, Faith, and Family in the Lives of Hispanic Teens, and their Implications for Youth Ministry», 5-10.

the task of all young Catholics in response to their baptism[39]. Indeed, evangelization is not complete until the evangelized take up this mission as evangelizers[40]. Similarly, the discernment of a vocation rooted in our common baptismal call —a «*proyecto de vida*» (life project) as it is referred to in Spanish— is at the heart of *PJH* because it defines who we are as followers of Christ[41].

In contrast, the theory and practice of u.s. mainstream youth ministry provide Catholic teens with little preparation to participate in the evangelizing mission of the Church by reaching out to their peers with a word of Good News. Instead, the work of evangelizing the young is visualized primarily as a task for the adults in the community —especially those adults engaged as youth ministry leaders[42]. Also, while it is true that vocational resources for youth ministry exist, they are mostly targeted to high school seniors, and the vocational orientation of the ministry as a whole is nearly absent.

3
Assessing the Journey

Given the social and pastoral challenges described in the foregoing sections, the faith-filled and visionary mission statement articulated by the young Encuentro delegates (see page 1) becomes even more remarkable. Nevertheless, the pastoral reality begs the question of whether this statement accurately reflects the collective intentions and self-understanding of *all* Hispanic Catholic youth and young adults in the United States. The short answer to the question is: no, it does not —at least not for the vast majority of them.

---

39 NATIONAL CATHOLIC NETWORK DE PASTORAL JUVENIL HISPANA —LA RED, *Conclusions*, 13-15, 54, and 60-61.

40 *Evangelii Nuntiandi*, n. 24.

41 Cfr. CONSEJO EPISCOPAL LATINOAMERICANO, *Civilización del Amor*, 2ª Parte, Sección I, n. 2.3.1. The phrase «*proyecto de vida*» appears 35 times throughout the document.

42 UNITED STATES CONFERENCE OF CATHOLIC BISHOPS, *Renewing the Vision: A Framework for Catholic Youth Ministry*, USCCB, Washington, D.C. 1997, 36-37.

However, the general description of the pastoral context hides another truth: ministry to and with Latino/a Catholic youth and young adults, from their lived reality, has made great strides in the years since Fe y Vida's preliminary study in 2002, even though there have been setbacks in some places and there is certainly much work yet to be done. The following list briefly describes some of the significant advances in the field over the last seven years.

a) Development of diocesan and national leadership for Hispanic youth and young adult ministry. Thanks in large part to the work of *La Red* in leading the Encuentro process, more dioceses now have personnel dedicated to ministry with Hispanic youth and/or young adults. A hopeful sign is that some dioceses have begun to hire bilingual directors of youth and young adult ministry who are given responsibility for these ministries in both English and Spanish, but qualified and experienced bilingual/bicultural leaders to fill these positions remain scarce.

b) Growing role of *La Red* as an important partner to other national ministry organizations. The prominence of *La Red* is especially evident in its continuing partnership with the NFCYM and the U.S. Bishops' Secretariat of Laity, Marriage, Family Life & Youth. This partnership is helping to make the work of the NFCYM more inclusive, and it is bearing fruit in the development of a *Five-Year Strategic Plan for Pastoral Juvenil Hispana* as a follow-up to the Encuentro[43].

c) Completion of the First National Encuentro for Hispanic Youth and Young Adult Ministry, and its documentation in the *Conclusions*. The successes and limitations of the Encuentro provide a baseline account of where the Church stands in its outreach to Latino/a youth and young adults. Furthermore, in the *Conclusions* document, we now have in one place a bilingual account of the history, theological and pastoral context, vision, principles, pastoral needs, and best practices and models as articulated by the young people themselves, with the endorsement and support of the U.S. bishops.

d) Solid sociological research on the religious reality of Latino/a youth and young adults. The nationally representative sample of adolescents and early young adults surveyed and interviewed in the National Study of Youth and Religion (NSYR) provides a reliable account of the religious beliefs and practices of adolescents in the United States today. In *Pathways of Hope and Faith*

---

43 The full text of the *Five-Year Strategic Plan for PJH* is available online at http://www.laredpjh.org.

Among Hispanic Teens, a multidisciplinary team of nine writers contributed to the analysis of the NSYR's Latino/a respondents from a variety of perspectives, making it an invaluable resource for anyone preparing for or engaging in ministry with young Latino/a Catholics.

e) Wide availability of formation programs for *pastoral juvenil hispana.* The Southeast Pastoral Institute (SEPI) and several dioceses across the country have developed formation programs for leaders and advisers in PJH. In addition, Instituto Fe y Vida has a mobile pastoral team that is able to provide formation at a variety of levels in any diocese in the country on request, and it offers an annual week-long intensive formation program (*Programa Nacional de Verano*) to make formation available even to leaders whose dioceses do not yet offer a formation option. Finally, numerous apostolic movements have developed their own programs and resources for leadership formation.

f) Increasing human resources in the Catholic community—among both Hispanics and non-Hispanics alike. Through the Encuentro process and in its aftermath, many more mainstream youth ministry directors, coordinators, and leaders have become aware of the need to increase their capacity to serve Hispanic teens. In addition, the Encuentro process itself was designed as a formation-in-action process that has forged a new generation of young Latino/a leaders for PJH and youth ministry in Latino communities.

.2. AREAS FOR FURTHER DEVELOPMENT

Achieving these advances has only been possible through the coordinated efforts of thousands of leaders in Catholic youth ministry, young adult ministry, and p*astoral juvenil hispana.* Nevertheless, the pastoral reality as presented in the first part of this essay reveals that there is much more that needs to be done. That information will not be summarized here; rather, this section will focus on the structural developments that need to occur in order to facilitate a comprehensive response to the pastoral needs of Latino/a youth and young adults at the local, diocesan, regional, and national levels.

a) Develop a comprehensive pastoral plan at the national level that brings together the various ministries and ministry organizations for the pastoral care and accompaniment of *all* Catholic youth and young adults. This pastoral plan needs to be expressed as a response to the social, cultural, linguistic, educational, and spiritual reality of Catholic youth and young adults today, of whom Hispanics now make up nearly half. When assessing this reality, special attention must be given to the living situation of the families, as well as to the ability of parents to serve as role models and reliable guides in the formation of their children's faith. In addition, there ought to be tools to assist diocesan and parish pastoral leaders in conducting an analysis of the local reality, so they can develop pastoral plans that respond to their own needs.

It will be critical to empower leaders to see the full gamut of needs the young people in their pastoral care may have —especially those of the vast majority that is not currently participating in youth and young adult ministry programs— and propose a differentiated approach to address the diverse pastoral needs in the parish through a variety of programs, groups, movements, events, activities, and services. The plan should provide guidance for the development of evangelization and outreach efforts in which the young people themselves are the primary agents, as well as criteria to discern in what circumstances pre-evangelization efforts should be the most immediate response. Finally, pastoral and theological criteria should be presented to help leaders identify the urgent and fundamental needs that should be addressed as priorities in their ministry.

b) Structure parish youth and young adult ministry on an ecclesiology of the parish as a community of communities. Far too often, parish youth ministry programs are limited due to an erroneous theological conviction that the multiplication of youth and young adult ministry programs would divide the parish[44]. In this regard, the *Conclusions of the* PENPJH are quite clear:

> «The leaders in *Pastoral Juvenil,* Hispanic ministry, and mainstream youth and young adult ministry are increasingly aware that the programs and activities of the mainstream culture do not attract the full participation of Hispanic adolescents and *jóvenes,* even though they may speak English. This occurs due to economic, cultural, educational, geographic, and linguistic differences between the young people, especially when the parish ministry is limited to a single youth group» (emphasis added)[45].

---

[44] For a fuller discussion of the cultural and pastoral circumstances that may contribute to this erroneous pastoral vision, and an articulation of the «community of communities» approach, see JOHNSON-MONDRAGÓN K., (ed.), *Pathways of Hope and Faith Among Hispanic Teens,* 332-339; 345-352.

[45] NATIONAL CATHOLIC NETWORK DE PASTORAL JUVENIL HISPANA —LA RED, *Conclusions,* 33.

As a response, parishes in the United States would do well to take a tip from the Fifth General Conference of the Bishops of Latin America and the Caribbean in Aparecida, Brazil:

> «At the beginning of the third millennium, the renewal of the parish requires the reformulation of its structures, so that it may become a network of communities and groups capable of entering into relationship with one another in such a way that their members feel and really become disciples and missionaries of Jesus Christ in communion with one another»[46].

c) Increase collaboration and dialogue with partners in Latin America. The quote above is a clear response to Pope John Paul II's call for parishes to become a «community of communities and movements» in *Ecclesia in America*[47]. It also underscores his hope that the Church on the American continent would begin to see itself as a single continental Church with meaningful collaboration between the countries of the North and South. As this essay has already demonstrated, the practice of Catholic youth and young adult ministry in the United States would benefit from a greater consideration of the guidelines in *Civilización del Amor: Tarea y Esperanza*, as well as the pastoral priorities of the *Documento de Aparecida*. Such an exchange of ideas and practices would be the first step toward developing a genuine *pastoral de conjunto* between North and South.

d) Increase collaboration and dialogue with partners in mainstream Catholic ministry in the United States. Given the size of the young Hispanic Catholic population, it is no longer acceptable (if it ever was) for major documents to be written for the whole U.S. Church, or for ministerial initiatives with implications for all —especially in the areas of youth and young adults— to be undertaken without a meaningful representation of Latino/as at the decision-making and editorial tables. Significant initiatives are already underway to develop guidelines and criteria for the future of adolescent catechesis, evangelization, Catholic education, lay ministry formation, and the promotion of vocations to ecclesial ministry. PJH has much to contribute in

---

46 CELAM, *Aparecida: V Conferencia General del Episcopado Latinoamericano y del Caribe: Documento Conclusivo*, CELAM, Bogotá, Colombia 2007, n. 172, my translation.
47 JOHN PAUL II, *Ecclesia in America*, n. 41.

all of these areas, and *La Red* ought to be both a conversation partner and a prime mover in these efforts.

e) Develop strategies and responses to overcome the structural obstacles to PJH. Some of the major challenges currently encountered in the field include:

• *Pastoral formation and theological reflection.* Too few diocesan leaders, priests, and youth ministers have an adequate understanding of the needs, vision, mission, principles, and history of PJH. As a consequence, their misguided pastoral convictions often prevent them from providing effective support to this ministry, and in many cases lead them to shut the ministry down or prevent its inception in the parish or diocese[48]. Furthermore, the limited pastoral and theological formation of many young adult peer leaders in PJH continues to diminish their capacity to form and sustain the ministries with which they are entrusted. Unfortunately, the lack of attention to the pastoral care of Latino/a youth and *jóvenes* is also evident in Hispanic ministry formation programs and among Hispanic/Latino/a theologians. The result is that even our best-prepared leaders in Hispanic ministry are often ill-equipped to support and advocate for PJH.

• *Academic education.* The low educational attainment of young Latino/a immigrant workers and high drop-out rates among U.S.-born Hispanic teens conspire to limit the pool of Latino/a leaders qualified to begin academic studies for ministry or to secure a paid pastoral position in the Church. At the same time, hundreds of Catholic elementary and secondary schools are in danger of being closed, while millions of low-income Catholic families are not having their educational needs met by underperforming public schools. This calls for a national initiative to improve the education of Catholic immigrants, their children, and other underserved racial/ethnic groups, both in Catholic and public schools.

• *Immigration issues.* The undocumented status of many young immigrants, which limits their access to scholarships, leadership positions in ministry with adolescents, and generally increases the instability in their lives, makes it difficult to realize a return on the investment in their formation for PJH and/or youth ministry. The U.S. bishops have already made advocacy for immigrants a priority, but this has not yet translated into many parishes or

---

48 Chapter 10 of JOHNSON-MONDRAGÓN K., (ed.), *Pathways of Hope and Faith Among Hispanic Teens* describes ten factors that need to be addressed in our Church in order for ministry with Hispanic youth to gain greater traction. See pages 321-359.

Catholic political action groups joining local and national efforts for comprehensive immigration reform grounded in the principles of Catholic Social Teaching.

- *Pastoral de conjunto.* The lack of coordination between mainstream youth and young adult ministry and PJH has contributed to the low participation rates among the vast majority of u.s.-born Hispanic youth and young adults, who are primarily English-speaking and not college-educated or college-bound. An effective outreach to these young people will require collaboration and shared oversight between Hispanic ministry, youth and young adult ministry, p*astoral juvenil hispana,* and the apostolic movements.

f) Increase the human, financial, and programmatic resources for PJH. This will require a significant investment in leadership formation at all levels —in both English and Spanish— so that mainstream youth ministry leaders can improve and expand their ministry while immigrant young adult leaders of PJH are doing the same. Perhaps the most cost-effective and practical first step would be to hire a diocesan coordinator for PJH. This person would be responsible for spearheading the formation of the leaders in parishes and apostolic movements, providing continuous support to their ministerial efforts, and engaging them in processes of formation-in-action and a *pastoral de conjunto.*

On another note, there are few programmatic materials or multimedia resources available to support PJH. Equally hard to find are bilingual resources to assist Hispanic parents in overcoming the linguistic and cultural conflicts they often experience with their children, in order to fulfill their role as their primary educators in the faith. Unfortunately, most of the resources developed for mainstream youth and young adult ministry or Latin American *pastoral juvenil* do not translate well to the u.s. Latino context. It will require a significant investment from the Church as a whole, and Catholic publishers in particular, to develop the capacity of Latino/a youth and young adult ministers and artists to create resources to support these ministries.

Finally, creative and effective models for financing these efforts need to be developed at the local and diocesan levels, and shared nationally. The role of *La Red* in the support and continued development of PJH at the national level has become indispensable, yet it continues to operate with only volunteer leaders and without a central office for records and communication. Considering that *La Red* is charged with advocating for half of all young

Catholics in the United States, there ought to be greater institutional and philanthropic support for its ministry.

g) Create certification standards for coordinators of youth ministry and PJH designed to equip both mainstream and Latino/a ministers for effective ministry to and with Hispanic youth and young adults, from their lived reality. Five national ministry organizations are currently revising the *National Certification Standards for Lay Ecclesial Ministry*. Given the size and geographic extension of the Hispanic Catholic population, the general standards should reflect the competencies and methodologies required for ministry in Hispanic communities. Furthermore, the specific standards for youth ministers should include competencies based on the vision, needs, and principles for ministry with Hispanic adolescents described in the *Conclusions of the* PENPJH. *La Red* should also participate in the revision process, developing specific standards for the certification of leaders, coordinators, and advisers of PJH.

4

Conclusion

The pastoral challenges facing Hispanic youth and young adults in the United States are immense, and they undoubtedly contribute to the conclusion of the NSYR that «Latino/a teens as a group are even more religiously inarticulate and disengaged than other Catholic teens, despite the fact that their parents demonstrate greater commitment to their faith than do the white Catholic parents»[49]. Indeed, their needs are so diverse, and their presence so pervasive in Catholic communities throughout the country, that it will take a coordinated effort of the whole Church to adequately provide them with pastoral care, faith formation, and an invitation into the life and mission of the Church.

The good news is that our Catholic community is already blessed with thousands of immigrant young adult leaders of PJH and thousands more directors and coordinators of youth ministry in parishes and apostolic movements across the country. In addition we have a blueprint for how to serve and empower Hispanic youth and young adults in the *Conclusions of the* PENPJH and the *Five-Year Strategic Plan for* PJH. All that is required at this point is for our Church to

---

49 JOHNSON-MONDRAGÓN K., (ed.), *Pathways of Hope and Faith Among Hispanic Teens*, 324.

muster the institutional will to implement this plan by means of a genuine *pastoral de conjunto* in parishes and dioceses throughout the country. In carrying out this process, the fields of Catholic youth ministry, young adult ministry, and *PJH* will set the example for bridging Hispanic and mainstream ministry to forge the Church anew in 21st century America.

Hispanic Ministry, Liturgy and Spirituality

Raúl Gómez-Ruíz

1

Introduction

As evening fell, participants in the first Raíces y Alas Conference (1992) gathered in Loyola-Marymount University's chapel to celebrate the opening prayer[1]. The members of the Instituto de Liturgia Hispana[2] were asked by the organizers to plan the prayers and Eucharists of the Conference and I as a member was to coordinate this prayer. The *ordo* for 14 August 1992 showed that traditionally Vespers on this date was prayed in honor of the Dormition of the Virgin. This was our starting point: we used the skeleton of the liturgy but added Hispanic devotional elements to give it life. We asked participants of both genders to volunteer as presider, reader, homilist, etc. To begin, a woman silently entered the aisle from the back carrying a smoking incense pot. She led in four men carrying a bier with a recumbent image of the Virgin Mary covered with a sheer cloth. Candle bearers accompanied the bier followed by the prayer leaders. The men carried the image to the side of the altar and then the woman incensed it. The participants were startled to see this but their engagement in the silent procession was palpable. Vespers continued as usual, Hymn, Psalms and Canticle, Reading, Reflection, Magnificat, Intercessions, and then something inserted: all were invited to come forward to place flowers on the recumbent image and offer a silent prayer in memory of the deceased. Soft music accompanied this act adding to the solemnity and beauty. Returning to their pews many were moved to tears. All who desired placed a flower on the image of the Virgin and the prayer ended as usual with blessing and dismissal. The image was left at the side of the altar for those who wished to return later and pray. Some of the people who were present told me that they had never been so moved by a liturgical celebration like this and that they were amazed at how just a few touches of Hispanic[3] devotional

1   This first gathering of leaders of organizations involved in Hispanic ministry in the United States was convened by the National Catholic Council for Hispanic Ministry (NCCHM) and took place on the campus of Loyola-Marymount University, Los Angeles, 14-17 August 1992.
2   The Instituto as it is known, now goes by Instituto Nacional Hispano de Liturgia or the National Hispanic Institute of Liturgy and is housed at The Catholic University of America, Washington, D.C.
3   The term «Hispanic» has been favored to name the pastoral efforts towards the Spanish-speaking in the United States. Though overly broad due to the lack of homogeneity among those identified as such, from my perspective it describes the peoples in the world who share history and familial connections derived from Spain. In this regard see GRACIA J., *Hispanic/Latino Identity: A Philosophical Perspective*, Blackwell, Malden, MA 2000.

piety could have so much power while still respecting the integrity of Vespers. Tapping into Hispanic devotion to the Virgin, acknowledging the sorrow of death, being accompanied by ministers in bilingual prayer, using flowers, candles, incense, and music, all worked together to inculturate the liturgy and help participants see the link between it and their expressions of spirituality or *mística*[4].

The liturgy as the foundation of Hispanic *mística* and thus the starting point of ministry among Hispanics in the United States has yet to be fully examined and appreciated. Instead popular religiosity has been the primary focus of pastoral efforts and theological reflection among Hispanics and others involved in Hispanic ministry[5]. In Catholic circles, these expressions of spirituality are often marked by attitudes and practices reflecting the adoption and adaption of theological, liturgical, and spiritual elements that can be called popular Catholicism.

Acknowledging the role of popular Catholicism in Hispanic spirituality, the u.s. bishops in their 1984 pastoral letter *The Hispanic Presence: Challenge and Commitment* noted that «Hispanic spirituality is an example of how deeply Christianity can permeate the roots of a culture»[6]. Being cognizant of the centrality of the liturgy the bishops called for a bridge between popular religiosity and liturgy. In this essay I explore some reasons why Hispanic popular religiosity has been at the center of ministerial and theological reflection, then give some reasons why liturgy's role as the foundation of Hispanic spirituality and ministry has to be more fully examined and appreciated, and conclude with some suggestions for further reflection and dialogue in this regard.

---

4 The *National Pastoral Plan for Hispanic Ministry* (published in 1988; hereafter NPPHM defines *mística* as «the series of motivations and deep values which enliven the process of the people and create experiences of faith, producing a spirituality that encourages life and pastoral work». See NPPHM, «D. Terminology» in UNITED STATES CONFERENCE OF CATHOLIC BISHOPS, *Hispanic Ministry: Three Major Documents*, USCCB, Washington, D.C. 1995, 96. It is important to note that this definition appears in the NPPHM after the Third Encuentro and the follow up theological reflection events that took place; they used this term prior to any clear definition as to what it meant. Consequently my use of «expressions of spirituality» is drawn from the documents including the NPPHM.

5 I use the term «popular religiosity» purposefully to encompass the expressions of spirituality that some call popular religion, piety, or devotional practices. All are attempts to describe a complex reality: the experience of or faith in a transcendent reality and its incorporation into everyday life, especially by those who are not religious elites. For an extensive discussion of this see GÓMEZ-RUÍZ R., *Mozarabs, Hispanics, & the Cross*, Orbis Books, Maryknoll, NY 2007, 166-169.

6 NATIONAL CONFERENCE OF CATHOLIC BISHOPS, *The Hispanic Presence: Challenge and Commitment*, USCC, Washington, D.C. 1984, n. 12, 0, in UNITED STATES CONFERENCE OF CATHOLIC BISHOPS, *Hispanic Ministry*, 15.

Reasons for the primary focus on Hispanic popular religiosity

The Third Encuentro Nacional Hispano de Pastoral (Third Encuentro) celebrated in 1985 was a defining moment in the recent history of Hispanic ministry[7]. A major aspect of the Third Encuentro was its *mística* or «expression of spirituality». Two subsequent pastoral theological reflection events after the Third Encuentro helped identify what this meant[8] and expressed it primarily in a *Credo*.

The spirituality identified through the Third Encuentro process is embedded in the eighth and final major section of the *Credo* developed there. The first part reads: «We believe in Mary, our Mother, who has taken our Hispanic culture under her protection, and who has accompanied us and will accompany us always in our journey as she works to carry the message of Jesus to the whole world»[9]. The second part continues «We believe in the intercession of our beloved Mother and in her example of humility, simplicity, and availability, which form the basis of our Hispanic culture». Therefore, the spirituality that emerges from the *Credo* is primarily Marian, devotional, and popular in nature. Missing in this is the influence that the Charismatic Movement has had among Hispanics with its stress on affective experiences of the Spirit and on Scripture.

Even in the second major section of the *Credo* in which belief in Christ is expressed, the stress is placed on identification with the suffering Christ. This section, divided into five declarations, starts by stating «We believe in our identification with Christ, as the suffering people we are. We believe, even as he did, in the divinity of all human beings and in their liberation through love»[10]. Though both of these examples from the *Credo* indicate a liberationist bent to the spirituality identified through pastoral theological reflection, they build on what I identify as the cultural roots of Hispanic spirituality.

7   The methodology and resulting commitments were published in *Prophetic Voices: Document on the Process of the III Encuentro Nacional Hispano de Pastoral*, USCC, Washington, D.C., 1986, in UNITED STATES CONFERENCE OF CATHOLIC BISHOPS, *Hispanic Ministry*.

8   These took place in Seattle involving 35 Hispanic Pastoral Ministers in October 1985 and in Tucson involving 17 bishops of the former NCCB Ad Hoc Committee for Hispanic Affairs in January 1986. See also note 4 above.

9   This and the following quote are found in *Prophetic Voices* 48.

10   *Prophetic Voices*, 47.

Significantly neither the *Credo* nor the follow-up pastoral theological reflections identify the liturgy as a major factor in Hispanic *mística*[11]. This despite the fact that the liturgy was instrumental in providing a *mística* for the Third Encuentro and the bishops' call in *The Hispanic Presence* to pay attention to liturgy albeit by «making provision for Spanish and bilingual worship according to the traditions and customs of the people being served». They go on to state: «We are thus challenged to greater study of Hispanic prayer forms» especially those emerging from Hispanic homes since «the home has traditionally been for them the center of faith and worship». Thus, «the celebration of traditional feasts and special occasions in the home should therefore be valued and encouraged»[12]. This suggests that Hispanic *mística* at its roots is devotional and popular rather than primarily liturgical. It also points to a certain romanticizing tendency that calls for further reflection.

Stress on popular devotional practices is reiterated in the *National Pastoral Plan for Hispanic Ministry*. The NPPHM declares that «the spirituality or *mística* of the Hispanic people springs from their faith and relationship with God … Since spirituality penetrates the totality of life, it is likewise made manifest in a multitude of expressions»[13]. This affirmation of popular religiosity is an affirmation of Hispanic culture which unmistakably has been marked by a rich devotional life both at home, as evidenced by *altarcitos*, and in the streets as seen in the frequent processions and pilgrimages involving large segments of the community.

This stress was probably needed at the time since the dominant voices in the Church in the United States were communicating an antipathy to popular religious practices. This «mixed feeling» about popular religiosity has continued to persist despite affirmations of it by the u.s. bishops and even the Holy See[14]. I encountered it in a study conducted of Hispanic ministry in 1998-1999. Manuel

---

11 Juan Sosa, a member of the study group that discussed the relationship between Hispanic Ministry, Liturgy, and Spirituality at the 2009 National Symposium and a participant at the Third Encuentro, noted that the Credo did not share the *mística* generated by the liturgical aspect of the Encuentro and instead ignored it. Thus the framers of the Credo did not capture the entirety of what they experienced. In his estimation this is because Hispanic Catholic leadership does not always articulate liturgy as an important component of Hispanic spirituality.

12 *The Hispanic Presence*, n. 12a.

13 UNITED STATES CONFERENCE OF CATHOLIC BISHOPS, *National Pastoral Plan for Hispanic Ministry*, 16.

14 UNITED STATES CONFERENCE OF CATHOLIC BISHOPS, *Popular Devotional Practices: Basic Questions and Answers*, USCCB, Washington, D.C. 2003; CONGREGATION FOR DIVINE WORSHIP AND THE DISCIPLINE OF THE SACRAMENTS, *Directory on Popular Piety and the Liturgy: Principles and Guidelines*, North American edition, Pauline Books and Media, Boston 2002.

Vásquez and I were commissioned by the former Bishops' Committee on Hispanic Affairs to provide qualitative information on Hispanic ministry. One of the eleven Key Issues and Challenges we identified in our 1999 report highlighted tension between popular religiosity and evangelization. We noted that «in the eyes of some pastors, popular devotions are nothing more than "a Catholicism of a day" which focus on rituals and symbols, stressing great but isolated moments of fervor, yet failing to translate into deep and lasting spiritual transformation and sustained participation in the life of the Church»[15]. We found that some pastors sought to eliminate popular devotional practices while others saw them only as stepping stones to a «greater faith maturity» that should be dropped once that maturity was attained. The 1999 study shows that where the celebration of the sacraments has been the primary pastoral approach in ministry among Hispanics, it has tended to be a celebration with little catechesis and attention to the ethical dimension of the sacramental life[16]. Thus, at times parishes have become «sacrament mills».

Certainly popular religiosity is a notable trait of Hispanic spirituality. It has been well studied by Hispanic theologians, promoted by Hispanic pastoralists, and affirmed by the Church's hierarchy. Many have written how Hispanic devotional practices have sustained Catholic faith even when the Church seemed to devalue Hispanics. However, I hold that one reason why popular religiosity has been such a sustaining force is because it has emerged and been fostered in a cultural context that has heretofore been primarily Catholic and thus where all the sacramental dimensions of its drama and beauty could be unleashed. Specifically, Latin America has been imbued with a cultural Catholicism that is periodically reinforced through public displays of faith highly devotional in character[17]. Holy Week processions, *fiestas patronales*, and periodic pilgrimages have served to instill in the populace a sense of the sacred and of Catholicism's belief system. Marked by ritual, color, music, and incorporation of large numbers of people (even if only as spectators) Hispanic popular religiosity has been capable of capturing the senses and imagination of its practitioners not only as an

---

15 UNITED STATES CONFERENCE OF CATHOLIC BISHOPS, SECRETARIAT FOR HIPANIC AFFAIRS, *Hispanic Ministry Study*, USCCB, Washington, D.C. 1999, section III, 6, www.usccb.org/hispanic affairs/studygomez.shtml.

16 UNITED STATES CONFERENCE OF CATHOLIC BISHOPS, SECRETARIAT FOR HIPANIC AFFAIRS, *Hispanic Ministry Study*, USCCB, Washington, D.C. 1999, III. 7.

17 This is not to diminish the longstanding but isolated occurrences of this phenomenon in the Southwest.

expression of faith but also often as a means to differentiate identity and manifest national pride[18]. Thus it stands to reason that this should be valued and sought to be recreated in the u.s. cultural context. This was also done in earlier waves of immigration by other cultural groups imbued with Catholicism such as the Italians, the Polish, and the Irish in their first generations in the United States, and fostered by Church leaders[19].

Stress on popular Catholicism is reinforced by the pastoral efforts characteristic of Hispanic ministry in the United States. Since the early 1970s its focus and thus its beneficiaries have been recent Latin American immigrants who have come from that Catholic cultural context. In Latin America liturgy has often been the realm of the clergy and popular religion the realm of the people[20]. Consequently liturgy has been seen as less important by those ministering to Hispanics in the United States because of the notion that it is for specialists, that is, those trained, educated and selected for this task. Though essential, liturgy has often been judged staid, formal, and restrictive and so has little to do with the «real» pastoral needs of the people. Thus the dichotomizing of Hispanic *mística* as popular religiosity over and against liturgy has been inadvertently reinforced over the course of the Encuentro processes. Laudably, the notion of Hispanic *mística* as encompassing both has begun to emerge. This is an important

---

18 This insight draws on the personal response from Cecilia González-Andrieu to this essay as part of her participation in the 2009 National Symposium for which it was written. In her comments she rightly notes: «This lack of homogeneity while at the same time sharing the characteristic of "other" makes what have traditionally been religious practices ways to resist assimilation, underscore national identity, and reinforce community. I think the cultural and political need to be acknowledged as possibly being the driving force behind the preservation of many religious practices. This does not mean that these have lost their religious significance, but rather invite us to look more closely at the role of religious ritual, sacramentality and spirituality in the preservation of identity and the strategy of resistance». See also GÓMEZ-RUÍZ R., *Mozarabs, Hispanics, & the Cross,* introduction and chapter 1, 8-9.

19 See among others TAVES A., *The Household of Faith: Roman Catholic Devotions in Mid-Nineteenth-Century America,* University of Notre Dame Press, Notre Dame, IN 1986. Unfortunately many jettisoned their cultural faith practices once they assimilated or became upwardly mobile—something that seems to be occurring also among many Hispanics.

20 There are many historical, cultural, and pastoral reasons why liturgy became the realm of the clergy and popular religious practices the realm of the laity, much of which was encouraged by the clergy. Especially during the conquest and subsequent evangelization of the Americas, Franciscans, Dominicans, Augustinians and others used popular religious practices as a way to interpret the liturgy and catechize and draw people to Catholicism. See among others LARA J., «Visual Preaching: The Witness of Our Latin Eyes» in DAVIS K.G. and PRESMANES J. (eds.), *Preaching and Culture in Latino Congregations,* Liturgy Training Publications, Chicago 2000, 75-92; idem, «The Liturgical Roots of Hispanic Popular Religiosity» in DAVIS K.G., OFM, Conv. (ed.), *Misa, Mesa y Musa,* second edition, World Library Publications, Schiller Park, IL 1997, 2004, 25-32.

step since both popular religiosity and the liturgy are encounters with God that capture, imbue, and give life to the faithful providing them with avenues to express their response to that encounter both formally and informally, officially and unofficially, as both resistance and adherence to what it means to be Catholic. Even so, the role of popular religiosity as an encounter with God has to be more fully examined by all Catholics and the liturgy's role in this needs further attention particularly by all Hispanics.

3
Reasons why the liturgy needs to be more fully examined and appreciated

ơౖౖ

When I began doctoral studies in Liturgy in 1994, I was aware that a major focus of Hispanic theology at the time was popular religiosity. Though it continues to be a primary focus for Hispanic theologians, at that time it seemed to be the only focus. I was concerned because when liturgy was mentioned, my heroes within the Academy tended to dismiss it saying that «liturgy is too important to be left to the liturgists». I am not sure what that exactly means but in some sense I agree that many voices besides those of liturgists need to be heard when it comes to reflection on the liturgy. Nonetheless, the expression says that some way is needed to talk about the link between popular religion and liturgy, especially in our u.s. Hispanic context. This is also the concern of the bishops as expressed in 2002 in *Encuentro and Mission: A Renewed Pastoral Framework for Hispanic Ministry*[21]. Moreover, unlike other Spanish-speaking countries around the world, the main contact our people have with their Catholic faith in the United States is at the Mass in their local parishes and not the streets filled with numerous periodic devotional events.

Some factors identified in the study of Hispanic ministry indicated that a major shift has been occurring among Hispanic Catholics. It confirmed that the bulk of Hispanic ministry efforts were geared toward the recent immigrant. To a large extent this made sense in the 1970s through the mid-1990s as large numbers of immigrants were still arriving primarily from Mexico as well as an increasing number from Central and South America. Mexicans were especially

---

21 UNITED STATES CONFERENCE OF CATHOLIC BISHOPS, *Encuentro and Mission: A Renewed Pastoral Framework for Hispanic Ministry*, usccb, Washington, d.c. 2002, n. 34, 58.1, 58.2 and 58.4, www.usccb.org/hispanicaffairs/encuentromission.shtml.

bringing with them a strong sense of Catholic identity and were turning to their local parishes for help. Dioceses responded by establishing Hispanic ministry offices and many began to take the NPPHM as a model for diocesan plans. Along with assistance in terms of housing, jobs, and immigration, pastoralists identified the need for basic catechesis and instruction in doctrine.

Lost in this effort were the pastoral needs of already established Hispanics many of which were second, third, and even fourth generation. Whereas the recent immigrants were primarily Spanish-speaking and often looked for the traditional forms of religious practice that they had enjoyed in their home countries, more established Hispanics had become accustomed to liturgy in English and the more privatized approach to the devotional life which generally marks Catholicism in the United States. Along with this factor, a troublesome trait we identified was that of the «second generation syndrome»[22]. In relation to this issue, the pastoralists we interviewed expressed being at a loss as to how to minister to the growing number of Hispanics who speak no Spanish, tend to drop out of school, have poor self-esteem, and/or feel uncertain about their identity. Additionally, they raised concerns about conflict among the different generations of Hispanics, including different immigrant waves and nationalities. These concerns have continued to persist. Unfortunately since 1999, many diocesan offices of Hispanic ministry have closed or merged into a «multicultural ministries office». This also occurred at the national level with the 2008 reorganization of the U.S. Catholic Conference of Bishops and the establishment of the new Secretariat of Cultural Diversity in the Church[23]. Such changes have a significant impact on the ability to minister both to first generation Hispanics and those already established.

Another factor is that despite efforts to try to recreate traditional devotional practices and to celebrate the sacraments as in Latin America, conflicts have arisen among national groups and even within the same group due to marked differences in how certain sacraments and rites are celebrated[24]. Especially il-

22 UNITED STATES CONFERENCE OF CATHOLIC BISHOPS, SECRETARIAT FOR HISPANIC AFFAIRS, *Hispanic Ministry Study*, section II, paragraph 4. Regarding Hispanics and liturgy see http://cara.georgetown.edu/Symposium.html.

23 See http://www.usccb.org/hispanicaffairs/index.shtml. Also for a critique of this trend see CASARELLA P., «Recognizing Diversity after Multiculturalism» in *New Theology Review* 21, 4 (2008) 17.

24 An important caution as well is that not all Latin Americans participate in popular religious practices since there these appear to be associated mostly with the poor or poorly educated, who unfortunately are the vast majority of the population. Therefore, immigrants to the United

lustrative of this conflict has to do with which advocation(s) of Mary to honor and how to celebrate them. Competition among the groups and limited resources tend to create factions and resentments in this regard.

Most important in my opinion, however, is a factor that has to do with how one fosters and maintains Catholic identity. In Latin America one can imbibe Catholicism from the environment without having to go to Church due to the public displays of faith and the periodic rites of passage that draw one to Church occasionally such as baptisms, first communions, *quince años* celebrations, marriages and funerals. These events, imbued with the power of symbol and marking ordinary life, do not require much involvement in liturgy and so parish involvement does not seem as important. No wonder liturgy is seen as the realm of the clergy! Nonetheless, in much of the u.s. context the parish and its activities are basically all many Hispanic Catholics have available[25].

If one wants to touch base with one's identity as a Hispanic Catholic or deepen one's faith in the u.s. context, one generally must go to Mass. One reason for this, I propose, has something to do with the concept of separation of Church and State that has led to the restriction of public displays of faith. This has promoted the privatization of faith and been reinforced by such things as the need for parade permits and fees if a religious group wants to organize processions or pilgrimages. In effect these traditional public displays of religious fervor are curtailed and even discouraged unless some economic benefit to the city can be shown such as an increase in tourism; a prime example of this is Holy Week in San Antonio[26]. Even if permits are easily attained, the weather in most of the United States is not conducive to things such as elaborate, days-long Holy Week processions. In Milwaukee where I minister, Holy Week often is marked

States from the upper classes may be expected to participate in activities to which they never ascribed and this can also be a source of conflict. The identification of popular religiosity with the poor in some Latin American cultures also means that «upward mobility» and «assimilation» into the u.s. mainstream is regarded as necessitating the repudiation of devotional practices and in some cases of Catholicism itself.

25 Pedro Rubalcava, a participant in the study group that discussed the relationship between Hispanic Ministry, Liturgy, and Spirituality at the 2009 National Symposium, noted that there are some notable exceptions to this depending on the area of the country asserting that popular Catholicism continues to exercise power over the religious imagination of Hispanics in various generations.

26 In 1998 I was a consultant as part of a study group that observed, analyzed and reflected upon the events organized by the staff at San Fernando Cathedral, San Antonio, tx; the Study was funded by the Lilly Foundation and the Mexican American Cultural Center; our input was later published in various sources.

by cold temperatures and either rain or snow. It seems that the environment conspires to restrain and limit public displays of faith that could foster Catholic identity and periodic renewal in Catholic spirituality outside of the liturgy. Furthermore, most parishes focus on religious formation programs more than on fostering a rich devotional life centered on the parish.

Despite these factors, we found in the 1999 study that Hispanics are at the center of a revival in many parishes abandoned by earlier immigrants of other ethnicities. We found evidence of vibrant parishes marked by rich devotional practices adapted to the conditions as well as a rich liturgical life. The Spanish-language formation and ministerial programs promoted by Hispanic ministry offices have also drawn Hispanics and tapped into a great thirst for knowledge of the Bible and of what it means to be Catholic. It seems that this thirst has increased because people have had to attend the liturgy in order to sustain or enliven their faith, spirituality, and identity[27]. As people have come to listen to the readings and homilies explaining the Scriptures and what Catholics believe, and as they have been encouraged to take roles in the liturgy, many have responded by wanting to learn more not only about the Bible but also about the liturgy.

One great example is the case of Juan and Martha Andrade[28]. I have come to know this couple very well over the last twenty years as I have celebrated the Eucharist and other sacraments at St. Hyacinth's parish on the Southside of Milwaukee. Juan and Martha are first generation immigrants. They came to the United States as young adults and met in Chicago. Juan, the oldest of several brothers and sisters who have followed him to Milwaukee, dreamt of saving money for a business back home. Martha, among the middle cohort of her siblings, went to Chicago with the dream of improving herself through education. They met at a dance, fell in love, got married, and moved to Milwaukee, where their three grown children were born, raised, and educated.

Seeking to maintain their Catholic identity, the Andrades went to St. Hyacinth's since it was close to their dwelling at the time. This was originally a parish for Polish immigrants. As their economic situation improved, Martha earned an undergraduate business degree at a local Catholic women's college and became a financial advisor, developing clientele among Hispanics in Mil-

---

27 This is of course in the best case scenarios. Unfortunately too often Hispanics have found a lack of welcome and have left Catholicism for other denominations or have stopped identifying with any church at all.

28 Their names and story are used with permission.

waukee's Southside. But Martha wanted more than just attending Mass. She began as a reader and then a Eucharistic minister, drawing in Juan with her. At the same time she got involved in the parish festival committee and with time asked the pastor if she could start a Hispanic «parish council» to help organize Hispanic celebrations, such as the Feasts of Our Lady of Guadalupe and of *la Purísima* as well as to address other pastoral needs of the Spanish-speaking community. In time she also involved her sisters-in-law and their families in different activities. Martha eventually got the parish council to become «bilingual» and afterward became one of its lay leaders. Now she is one of three parish trustees.

Martha attributes her involvement in the parish to the liturgy. She has worked to improve its celebration and attends diocesan-sponsored formation programs in liturgy. She has invited relatives and friends to get involved in the religious education programs of the parish and has helped to introduce certain devotional practices that Hispanics have maintained in their homes heretofore. They pray the Posadas *novenario* in the church rather than going through the streets, including the rosary and a *convivencia* afterwards. She has encouraged others to develop their talents and bring them to bear on the liturgy and surrounding celebrations like teaching children how to do traditional dances to honor the Virgin. Martha also sees her work of advising others on their finances as a ministry imbued by the values she has imbibed from the liturgy. Manuel Vásquez and I found in our study that in many places «the Hispanic community has led to a renewal of devotional practices and to an increase in parish activities centered on spiritual development»[29]. This is true for St. Hyacinth's. It is due not only to Martha's efforts but to those like her who have found the liturgy empowering. It has inspired them to combine forces and develop ways to renew and reinterpret their devotional practices for the context in which they live and worship.

As seen in the example of Juan and Martha, Hispanics themselves are building bridges between popular religion and liturgy. They have also attracted Hispanics from earlier and later generations. For this reason alone, it is important for leaders who engage in and reflect on Hispanic ministry to take the liturgy more seriously than has been the case. It is not about diminishing the importance of popular religiosity but to about seeing that the liturgy is not only the

---

29 UNITED STATES CONFERENCE OF CATHOLIC BISHOPS, SECRETARIAT FOR HIPANIC AFFAIRS, *Hispanic Ministry Study,* section II, paragraph 5.

realm of the clergy and a few experts. A way to build the required bridges is to look at what both popular religious practices and liturgy have in common, the sense of God's presence enlivening, healing, accompanying, and sanctifying their practitioners through an encounter with Christ. We call this sacramentality.

4

Sacramentality as the key to understanding Hispanic mística

Sacramentality has to do partially with religious experience and its formalization through specific rituals and celebrations that foster and extend this experience. This means that in this event, comprised of sign and symbol, we participate in an encounter with Christ which is transformative and life-giving. We are divinized in this sacred exchange where God enters into our reality that we might participate in God's. Or as the prayer at the mixing of the water and wine during the Eucharistic celebration says: «By the mystery of this water and wine may we come to share in the divinity of Christ, who humbled himself to share in our humanity»[30]. In a certain way all those experiences we have of encountering Christ in our lives are thematized and ritualized so that we may continue to encounter Christ in our lives and find our lives in Christ.

Because the encounter with Christ is so central to our identity as Catholics, sacramental theologians have been examining what sacraments are, how they work, and what they mean[31]. To a certain extent, sacraments are incarnational —they make present Christ's saving activity in our flesh, in our humanity. An important facet to note was introduced by St. Isidore of Seville (d. 636) who stressed the *remembrance aspect* of the sacramental rituals[32]. Thus, sacramentality has something to do with anamnesis and incarnation. And these notions trade in the concepts of sign and symbol. As members of the Academy of Catholic Hispanic Theologians of the United States (ACHTUS) have noted, popular religiosity is chock full of signs and symbols as well as rituals and actions through which we encounter the sacred.

---

30 From *The Sacramentary*, Catholic Book Publishing Company, New York, NY 1985, 370.

31 For a premier text on the history of sacraments see MARTOS J., *Doors to the Sacred: A Historical Introduction to Sacraments in the Catholic Church*, revised and updated edition, Liguori/Triumph, Liguori, MO 2001.

32 See OSBORNE K.B., OFM, *Sacramental Theology: A General Introduction*, Paulist Press, New York/Mahwah 1988, 23-24. Osborne makes reference to Isidore's *Etymologia*.

For that reason, sacramentality is an area that merits further study. It is a complex and extensive conversation in which Hispanic theologians and pastoralists have yet to fully participate[33]. In my judgment the conversation is poorer without our distinctive voice. We need to speak more about sacramentality from the Hispanic viewpoint. Though sacramentality for us is rooted in the sacraments, it goes beyond them. Deeply embedded in the Hispanic worldview is the sense that God's action and grace abound around, above, below and through us[34]. Sacramentality is the experience of encountering something holy, significant, and transforming; it is the desire to repeat that experience through actions and to hold onto it through objects that participate in the experience and extend it into one's life. This is what sacraments and sacramentals do. Moreover, sacramentality is a relational term: it implies encounter, response, and transformation. It is a dynamism that generates and reverberates and courses through the sacraments and sacramentals which we call grace. Sacramentality is also found in various events and situations in *lo cotidiano* that transform one's life and draw one to an encounter with Christ if one but has eyes to see and ears to hear. The devotional practices associated by Hispanics with the sacraments and the use of sacramentals such as blessings and blessed objects point to this encounter and response to God's action, God's grace in one's life, and the desire to prolong that experience in a relationship marked by rituals, practices, and objects that help one re-enter into that experience. In some cases, the transformation that occurs because of the event requires that it be symbolized by a variety of objects and actions that reinforce the change in relationship with the sacred and results in a new identity. In the case of baptism, some Hispanics symbolize with the *bolo*

33 Other members of ACHTUS and of the Instituto Nacional Hispano de Liturgia have addressed sacramentality as part of their works. For example see DÍAZ M.H., *On Being Human: U.S. Hispanic and Rahnerian Perspectives,* Orbis Books, Maryknoll, NY 2001, particularly chapter 3; MATOVINA T. and RIEBE-ESTRELLA G. (eds.), *Horizons of the Sacred: Mexican Traditions in U.S. Catholicism,* Cornell, Ithaca, NY 2002; GARCÍA-RIVERA A. «Community and Communion: The Language of the Sacraments» in GÓMEZ-RUÍZ R., SDS (ed.), *Languages of Worship/El Lenguaje de la Liturgia,* Liturgy Training Publications, Chicago 2004; DAVIS K.G., OFM, Conv. (ed.), *Misa, Mesa y Musa,* second edition, World Library Publications, Schiller Park, IL 1997; DAVIS K.G., OFM, Conv. (ed.), *Misa, Mesa, y Musa, Vol 2: Liturgy in the U.S. Hispanic Church,* World Library Publications, Franklin Park, IL 2008. The following two works address the issue of sacramentality from a post-modern and a theological aesthetics approach respectively: EMPEREUR J. and FERNÁNDEZ E., *La Vida Sacra: Contemporary Hispanic Sacramental Theology,* Rowman & Littlefield, Lanham, MD 2006; GARCÍA-RIVERA A. and SCIRGHI T., *Living Beauty: The Art of Liturgy,* Rowman & Littlefield, Lanham, MD 2007.
34 I address this topic in great detail in GÓMEZ R., SDS, «Preaching the Ritual Masses among Latinos» in DAVIS K.G. and PRESMANES J. (eds.), *Preaching and Culture in Latino Congregations,* 103-119. The same article appears in *Chicago Studies* 39, 3 (2000) 295-311.

(the coins thrown in the air by the *padrino*) that there is a new Christian filled with the abundance of grace; in the case of the *quinceañera*, she is now a woman of faith who gives thanks for it publicly; in the case of marriage, a *lazo* (a cord tied around the couple at their wedding) symbolizes that the couple is inextricably linked for life. How do we bridge the gap then between popular religiosity and liturgy so that Hispanic *mística* is more fully grasped and reflected upon as force for the future of Hispanic ministry in the United States?

5

Suggestions for further reflection and dialogue

I offer four suggestions that can help bridge the gap between popular religiosity and the liturgy in an effort to advance Hispanic ministry. They concern reflecting more on sacramentality as the basis of Hispanic *mística*, tapping into the power of liturgy and of popular religiosity as a tool for its inculturation, identifying and empowering leaders in the community in these efforts, and making explicit links between Hispanic *mística* and the dominant Catholic approach to liturgy and spirituality in the United States.

1) *Reflect more on sacramentality.* Reflection on how sacramentality is expressed among Hispanics will help us to promote the building of bridges and attend to the pastoral needs of Hispanics of various generations in the United States. The revision of the sacramental rites of the Roman Catholic Church has given rise to a vibrant sacramental theology. A result of this reflection is the contemplation of sacramentality as part of the liturgical life of the Church, *el culto*, and a richer appreciation of the liturgy as the expression of participation in sacramentality by means of the sacraments[35].

We can especially contribute to the conversation on sacramentality by using the category of relationship. Roberto Goizueta has noted that our identity as Hispanics is clearly linked to our interconnectedness in what we call «familia» or «comunidad»[36]. We exist in relationship, that is, our identity as individuals is

---

35 This is reflected in the *Catechism of the Catholic Church*, second edition 1997; the entire discussion of the sacraments is found in the section on the liturgy, Part Two: The Celebration of the Christian Mystery.

36 See GOIZUETA R.S., «The Symbolic World of Mexican American Religion» in MATOVINA T. and RIEBE-ESTRELLA G. (eds.), *Horizons of the Sacred,* 121; idem, «The Symbolic Realism of U.S. Latino/a Popular Catholicism» in *Theological Studies* 65, 2 (2004) 258.

linked to the group that grounds us. For Hispanics this is fruit of our history as a mixture of races, languages and cultures —our *mestizaje* and *mulatez*— that have helped us to open ourselves up to others, to take in the stranger, and incorporate a variety of customs and perspectives. Dora Tobar affirms that this trait provides a principle of communion and a profound encounter which the liturgy ought to and can celebrate[37]. This principle of communion is at work in our attempt to do *teología en conjunto*. To reflect together theologically also implies a principle of reconciliation as we expose our innermost thoughts and try to reconcile or unite many points of view. We do this in order to uncover who God is and who we are in relation to God and to one another.

Hispanic relational terms have a richness that can uncover for us ways to speak about and understand sacramentality as an encounter with Christ that is transformative and meaningful, that is found in *lo cotidiano* and in *el culto*. I refer to terms that name and draw out the array of relationships that go unnamed or are not particularly reflected upon in English. These are terms of *compadrazgo* such as *padrino* and *madrina* and their corresponding *ahijado* and *ahijada*. *Padrinos* are not really godparents, they are another set of parents; *ahijados* are not godchildren, they are affiliates or members of one's progeny not by blood but by spirit[38]. *Tocayos* and *tocayas, primo hermano, prima hermana, tío abuelo, tía abuela, comadre* and *compadre* are only the beginning of the ways through which we create, name, and foster a web of relationships with and within our communities. It is primarily in relationships that we encounter life as meaningful, life as blessed, life as sacred. To be out of or alienated from relationships is to be among the living dead.

We exist in relationships. By engaging in relationship we enter into the vortex of a force that pulls us beyond ourselves to a place where one learns to negotiate and to take a stand, to enter into mutuality and commitment, to form bonds of friendship and love as well as to repair them when needed. In that place we are moved to live with demands on our time, emotions, and independence so as to learn how to trust and let go, to give and to take. In short, through the tug and pull of relationship we become fully human. The sacramentality of relationship

---

37 TOBAR D.E., «El Lenguaje de la cultura hispana y la liturgia» in GÓMEZ R., SDS (ed.), *Languages of Worship/El Lenguaje de la Liturgia*, 71. My paraphrase and translation of «Aquí hay por tanto un principio de comunión y de encuentro profundo que la liturgia debe y puede celebrar», citing Puebla 409.

38 The root word for *affiliates* is the Latin *affilii*, adopted sons/daughters. See «Affiliate» in: *Webster's New Universal Unabridged Dictionary*, Barnes & Noble 1992.

has to do with recognizing we are incomplete without the other. As we seek completeness with and in the other, both God and human beings, we encounter the fullness of life into which God has loved us and draws us deeper. We become who God has created us to be in this dynamic but also we share in the cross of Christ as we die to ourselves and become a source of new life for the other. In other words, relationship bears what is sacred and divine for us. Relationship is sacramental.

In relationship as experienced by Hispanics I often see that Christ is central, albeit as the one who is weak and small either at the beginning of his life or at its end, but dependent on us and echoed in the attitudes that we have toward the innocent and the elderly[39]. I see the importance of the incarnation, the sacramental event of human and divine integration where God and human beings dwell together; it provides the sense that God is found in everyday affairs, *lo cotidiano*. Our religious attitudes and practices draw us into the life of the Trinity

which reinforces our emphasis on family, the activity of accompanying those who suffer, and the need to celebrate the *fiesta* that brings all of life together. Spanish with its God-talk found in our sayings, expressions, and music mediates for us what is meaningful and gives us a sense that being God's people is integral to our identity. Seemingly ordinary objects, like *milagritos* shaped in the form of human body parts, and ordinary events like self-sacrifice and *juramentos* mediate an encounter with God that can lead to ethical action. Is that not what *mandas* and *promesas* are really all about? I see that ritualizations like our distinctive way of making the sign of the cross, the role of suffering, and the role of the feminine, especially of Mary, in our spirituality also mediate an encounter with Christ that enlivens us, transforms us, and completes us. Our *mística* is truly powerful.

2) *Tap into the power of liturgy and of popular religiosity as a tool for its inculturation.* At liturgy we mark relationships through *bautizos, primeras comuniones, quince años, bodas,* and even *sepelios*. We also mark them with the saints and the divine through *fiestas patronales* and a whole array of religious practices which have acquired their symbols from the liturgy such as *altarcitos* and *veladoras,*

---

39 «Weak» here refers to the estimation by others of Jesus' physical condition in these situations. As Cecilia González-Andrieu rightly notes «Christ is not weak on the way to cavalry, nor is he weak on the cross as he dies a horrible death for us —I think Hispanic religiosity recognizes in Christ indomitable strength, profound strength to withstand and keep going, to persevere in faith against all odds. I especially see this when I compare some art pieces from Latin America with similar ones from a European context —Christ is powerful in his suffering and his death in the Latin American context. I think this also translates to the Christ of other suffering communities, such as Africans» (personal communication with the author via e-mail, 16 July 2009).

despojos and *ensalmes, procesiones* and *cofradías*. In this way the main sacramental events identified by the Church are prolonged by collateral celebrations we have developed over time. This is where *lo cotidiano* meets *el culto* and viceversa. It is here where Hispanics can make a great contribution to the liturgy by building on this relationship.

Through liturgy individuals are called into an assembly, into a relationship of individuals convoked to be formed into the People of God. They become the Body of Christ and the Temple of the Holy Spirit, i.e., the Church, because of the work of the Spirit. The church building is a symbol of this, it has an evangelizing role. Therefore, the building itself is to be dignified and beautiful so that those who gather there feel that they are in God's house. Sacred images found in churches in a Hispanic context draw people to them through their design: they are to be clothed, articulated, movable, taken out in procession so that people are drawn to them. They evoke the person imaged and act as three-dimensional icons. As they go out in procession they call attention, draw people and bring them back to the church thereby enacting the dictum that the liturgy is the source and summit of the Church's activity (i.e. life). In a sense they become instruments of the Holy Spirit for convoking the Church[40]. Just as popular Catholicism has been able to employ ritual, symbol, environment and the full array of senses so must the liturgy if it is to have force beyond the confines of church walls. Thus, we must pay attention to ritual, symbol, image, and environment and all those elements that are related to them, just as popular religious practices do. This is part of the bridge that can be built between them.

The pastoral statement *Encuentro and Mission* affirms that the bishops see popular religiosity as key to the inculturation of the liturgy, which is to be the summit and source of Christian life. For this to occur the bishops insist that «[a]ll are invited to share ways of prayer that reflect their different cultural values and traditions and welcome their talents» (*Encuentro and Mission* 34). One way to do this is to accept the liturgy for what it is: the official prayer of the Church. An important maxim in this regard is *lex orandi, lex credendi,* or basi-

---

40 However, Eduardo Fernández, a member of the study group discussing the relationship between Hispanic Ministry, Liturgy, and Spirituality at the 2009 National Symposium, cautioned that it is also important to be aware of popular Catholicism's dark side, such as his grandmother's blaming San Lorenzo for burning her family farm because a promise to the saint was not fulfilled. Nonetheless, Robert Hurteau, a member of the study group as well, noted that such observation points to the ethical dimensions of popular Catholicism.

cally we pray what we believe[41]. What we believe as a Church is partly comprised of what we believe as individuals as well and some of both aspects can be discerned in popular Catholicism. Catholic theologian Cecilia González-Andrieu rightly points out that popular religion makes visible a deep longing for further participation in the official life of the Church, and we can see this through the appropriation of symbols stemming from the liturgy[42]. The liturgical norms in the General Instructions found in liturgical books as well as «rubrics» give ample room for incorporating elements that help bridge individual and communal, private and public faith expressed in both the liturgy and popular religiosity. They provide hints that help approach liturgy as a skeleton to be enfleshed through options, actions, symbols, and the use of cultural expressions of spirituality like our *mística*[43]. This means eliminating the barriers of paternalism that have kept the faithful from taking a more active and fuller role in the liturgy.

148

3) *Identify and empower leaders in the community.* This is the principal way in which paternalism can be overcome. The NPPHM gives nine prophetic pastoral guidelines from the Third Encuentro (see n. 16). Particularly, objective «B. Evangelization» sees pastoral leaders as bridges between the «marginalized and the Church», appreciative of the value of popular religiosity[44]. Still one notes a significant shift in the same objective where it calls for the acquisition of «basic knowledge of the liturgy and its relationship to private prayer»[45]. This is further reiterated in objective «D. Formation» which calls for «seminars/study sessions of reflection for pastoral specialists in the different areas of liturgy, catechesis, theology, and evangelization»[46]. Notice however, that it is directed to «pastoral specialists» and not the faithful in general. Nevertheless, a greater understand-

---

41 This maxim is the shortened form of Prosper of Aquitaine's (d.c. 460): *legem credendi lex statuat supplicandi.*

42 Cecilia González-Andrieu's personal response to this essay in communication with the author.

43 Guidelines, suggestions, and principles for adapting the liturgy can be found in CONGREGATION FOR DIVINE WORSHIP AND THE DISCIPLINE OF THE SACRAMENTS, *Directory on Popular Piety and the Liturgy;* FRANCIS M.R., *Multicultural Celebrations/Celebraciones Multiculturales,* Federation of Diocesan Liturgical Commissions Publications, Washington, D.C. 2000; SOSA J.J. *One Voice, Many Rhythms,* Oregon Catholic Press, Portland, OR 2009; idem, *Manual para entender y participar en la misa,* Liguori Publications, Liguori, MO 2009. Furthermore, *Sacrosanctum Concilium,* n. 37 states: «Even in the liturgy, the Church has no wish to impose a rigid uniformity in matters which do not implicate the faith or the good of the whole community; rather does she respect and foster the genius and talents of the various races and peoples».

44 See NPPHM 48 (4), in UNITED STATES CONFERENCE OF CATHOLIC BISHOPS, *Hispanic Ministry,* 78.

45 NPPHM 48 (4), in UNITED STATES CONFERENCE OF CATHOLIC BISHOPS, *Hispanic Ministry,* 78.

46 NPPHM 48 (4), in UNITED STATES CONFERENCE OF CATHOLIC BISHOPS, *Hispanic Ministry,* 71 (2), in UNITED STATES CONFERENCE OF CATHOLIC BISHOPS, *Hispanic Ministry,* 83.

ing of the role that sacramentality plays in liturgy and popular religiosity can help us further experience both as significant encounters with Christ. This needs to be done through catechesis and preaching as well as seminars and study sessions for everyone interested, not just specialists. It is imperative to identify the natural leaders in the parish, engage them in a two-way conversation, ask their advice and use it, and empower them to bring to bear the Hispanic *mística* on the liturgy to make this dynamic an even more powerful force for Hispanic pastoral ministry across the generations.

Leaders can be found in movements such as Cursillo and the Charismatic Renewal, among others, or vibrant associations like the National Catholic Network de Pastoral Juvenil Hispana - La Red. By building bridges with these movements and their leaders the link to the liturgy can be greatly strengthened. To achieve this it is important to go back to what has been done in order that new people can enter the *memoria histórica*, understand it, and build on it[47]. Also, by seeing liturgy as broader than the Eucharistic celebration, that is, including the Liturgy of the Hours and blessings, the large number of women who have leadership roles in these movements can be prepared to preside at these events as envisioned by the liturgical norms related to these types of liturgy. By taking on these liturgical roles lay presiders come to know Christ in a different way that can also empower them to call the community to the *encuentro* that leads to living more fully in the presence of God and to the evangelization of the world all Christians are called to as disciples. Furthermore, it lifts up the ecclesiology Hispanics are offering the Church, one marked by a spirit of hospitality and a struggle for justice as well as a *pastoral de conjunto* and a *teología en conjunto* in their different forms as highlighted by different voices participating in the National Symposium on the Present and Future of Catholic Hispanic Ministry in the United States at Boston College in 2009.

4) *Make explicit connections between Hispanic mística and the dominant Catholic approach to liturgy and spirituality in the United States.* It is possible that because liturgical celebrations happen every day, they can be taken for granted. González-Andrieu suggests that a coherent aesthetic theory could be helpful in order to

---

47 Alejandro López-Cardinale, a member of the study group discussing the relationship between Hispanic Ministry, Liturgy, and Spirituality at the 2009 National Symposium, noted the importance of not losing the memory of what has been accomplished so that new leaders and recent arrivals see the basis for why things are as they are and they can build on it to advance what has been gained and to leave behind what is no longer needed.

take what is familiar, make it unfamiliar and then bring it back again for greater understanding of what is taking place in popular Catholicism and making links to liturgy. We Hispanics also have to build bridges with other Catholics and their faith expressions. One way to do this is to tap into what Andrew Greeley calls the «Catholic imagination»[48]. It is interesting to read the jacket of his book which declares: «Catholics live in an enchanted world: a world of statues and holy water, stained glass and votive candles, saints and religious medals, rosary beads and holy pictures. But these Catholic paraphernalia are merely hints of a deeper and more pervasive religious sensibility that inclines Catholics to see the Holy lurking in creation. The world of the Catholic is haunted by a sense that the objects, events, and persons of daily life are revelations of Grace». Clearly expressions like «lurking» and «haunted by» are marketing terms intended to create interest in the topic but they betray a certain bias found in the dominant U.S. culture against the mysterious or religious[49].

The tendency to privatize faith has had an impact on later generations of Catholics of all groups. This is expressed as resistance to public displays of faith and a stress on individual salvation[50]. On the one hand, Hispanics are called to embrace the great variety of expressions of spirituality that non-Hispanic Catholics offer to us. On the other hand, Hispanic Catholic spirituality is a reminder that faith is also communal and public. In fact some of this influence can be seen in emerging religious practices being embraced by members of the dominant culture such as *ofrendas* (Day of the Dead altars) and *descansos* (crosses on roadways marking deadly car accidents of loved ones). These show that despite the tendency to privatize faith, the Hispanic Catholic imagination can be adapted and transmitted to others. Part of the reason is that for the Hispanic Catholic, the world is indeed «enchanted» in the sense that it is an astonishing and wonder-filled place, overflowing with signs of God's presence and grace. As awesome as this can be, it inspires wonderment and humility rather than the fright that words like «lurking» and «haunted by» imply. Sacramentality *a la*

---

48 GREELEY A., *The Catholic Imagination*, University of California Press, Berkeley, CA 2000.
49 Though this is certainly not Greeley's perspective personally, this bias is often communicated by the dominant media in particular.
50 Some surveys indicate growing numbers who call themselves Christians are either self-identifying as Evangelicals or as generic Christians both of which tend to be marked by a personal or privatized faith. See for example the *American Religious Identification Survey (ARIS 2008)* released in March of 2009, http://www.americanreligionsurvey-aris.org/2009/03/catholics_on_the_move_non-religious_on_the_rise.html (accessed January 3, 2010).

Latina is not filled with troubled feelings or eeriness, strangeness or oddness but consolation, peace, and well-being, things at once familiar and recognizable as well as mysterious yet decipherable, memorable yet ephemeral. For many Hispanics, God is a member of the family: the Father is «Tata Dios» (Grandfather God); Jesus, while clearly Lord and Savior, is «el niño Dios» (the child God), innocent and inspiring affection, or «el Nazareno» (the Nazarene or suffering Lord) who elicits sorrow and disquiet. Both of these aspects of Jesus draw one out of one's self to respond to the other in need. The Spirit, far from a ghost, is Holy and life-giving, able to console, comfort, gladden and guide in good times and in bad. And so, Hispanics look for ways to cultivate their «sacramental imagination» and enter into and prolong the religious sensibility that is sacramentality and that grounds their *mística* both in the forms of popular religiosity and liturgy. The first generation of Hispanic immigrants carries much of this with it innately; our challenge is to transmit this to the following generations and to share it with the rest of our Catholic brothers and sisters in the United States. I agree with González-Andrieu who notes that Hispanic popular religiosity, as a holder of the wisdom of the community, «in some ways…may have safeguarded the church's sacramental imagination, keeping it alive against the forces that would have radically removed them. This is important, it allows for continuity and intelligibility with past generations of Catholics (and indeed the whole history of the Church) and also has the potential for creating bridges to other highly imaginative Catholic communities especially those of Africa and Asia»[51].

6

Conclusion

Here we are at the beginning of the second decade of the twenty-first century considering the present and the future of Hispanic ministry in the United States. Many Hispanic ministry offices have either been closed or combined with other ethnic ministry offices. The Secretariat for Hispanic Affairs at the USCCB closed its doors. Many institutes dedicated to leadership formation for Hispanic ministry are struggling for funding. In terms of the «Present and Future of Hispanic

---

51 Cecilia González-Andrieu's personal response to this essay.

Ministry, Liturgy and Spirituality in the United States», the *Instituto Nacional Hispano de Liturgia*, the only institute dedicated to the formation and promotion of good liturgical celebrations among the diverse Hispanic communities in the country is in danger of disappearing altogether due to lack of resources[52]. What will help us move forward?

The experience of the Andrades is instructive. The present and future depends on people like them who are finding ways to bridge liturgy and popular religion and are taking on the pastoral work of the Church. They also depend on us, people dedicated to reflection on the Hispanic reality to help name, guide, and articulate what is taking place. Perhaps Hispanic faith, already vibrant in this land before it became the United States of America, can now become a force to help enliven, transform, and complete the many and varied faces of the United States so that we give better credence to being the People of God, the Body of Christ, and the Temple of the Holy Spirit as our sacraments *qua* liturgy invite us to be. To do so, our *mística* must be theologically articulated in ways which perhaps only u.s. Hispanics can. Drawing on the rich array of relationships we foster through *familia, comunidad, mestizaje, teología en conjunto,* etc., we can sacramentalize not only the mixture of water and wine at Eucharist, but also the ethnic, political, and theological streams of water and wine offered by all people of faith so that we can all come to truly celebrate and live the Eucharist together and thus share in the divinity of Christ we encounter there.

152

---

52 See *Amén,* Newsletter of the Instituto Nacional Hispano de Liturgia, Spring 2008: «What About the Instituto?» in the News-Noticias section, http://liturgia.cua.edu/newsletter/Amen Spring 2008.pdf (accessed January 5, 2010).

Hispanic Ministry and Social Justice

ARTURO CHÁVEZ

«*La bendición del Padre, la bendición del Hijo, la bendición del Espíritu Santo...y la mía que te acompañe*». With this blessing, my *abuelita* would send me off to journeys near and far. Long after the warmth of her embrace faded, I felt her love and prayers —her *acompañamiento*— as I faced the joys and pains of my journeys. In her simple way of love, my grandmother passed on to me a deep faith in the Trinitarian God whose very essence is loving relationship. Similarly, the elders of Hispanic ministry have blessed the Church with a historical memory of our struggles for justice in society and a place of belonging in the Church. This *testimonio* has been preserved orally and in documents that emerged in the seventies and eighties from the historic Encuentros, culminating in 1987 with the *National Pastoral Plan for Hispanic Ministry*, unanimously adopted by the National Conference of Catholic Bishops (NCCB, later USCCB), that calls Catholics to live and promote... by means of a *pastoral de conjunto*, a model of Church that is: communitarian, evangelizing, and missionary, incarnate in the reality of the Hispanic people and open to the diversity of cultures, a promoter and example of justice... that develops leadership through integral education... that is leaven for the Kingdom of God in society[1].

This mission statement for Hispanic ministry, pregnant with theological meaning, inspired years of deep reflection, lively debates, and new scholarly works that gave birth to what we now refer to as Latino/a contextual theology and spirituality[2]. On the whole, the discourse was fruitful not only in the academy but as the rationale for establishing diocesan offices for Hispanic ministry throughout the country and for empowering a new ecclesial leadership —Hispanic bishops and clerics, religious, and lay ministers. The mission statement also served as the impetus for social action, especially at the parish level, using the principles of Catholic Social Teaching and the organizing tactics and networks of the times[3]. Hispanic ministry, thus, became inseparably linked with social justice and firmly established in many dioceses and parishes.

1   NATIONAL CONFERENCE OF CATHOLIC BISHOPS, *The Hispanic Presence: Challenge and Commitment*, USCC, Washington, D.C. 1984, in UNITED STATES CONFERENCE OF CATHOLIC BISHOPS, *Hispanic Ministry: Three Major Documents*, USCCB, Washington, D.C. 1995, 71.
2   For a comprehensive review of Hispanic contributions to theology see FERNÁNDEZ E., *La Cosecha: Harvesting Contemporary United States Hispanic Theology 1972-1998*, The Liturgical Press, Collegeville 2000.
3   Many of the pioneers of Hispanic Ministry had also been actively involved in the struggles for civil rights, the «Better World Movement», labor organizing, immigration reform, and the Sanctuary Movement.

The trajectory for implementing the *National Pastoral Plan* consistently throughout the country, however, was unfortunately miscarried. Rather than building a strong, national network, Hispanic ministry splintered into various special interest groups in the 1990's competing for the same, diminishing resources[4] of a Church facing multiple challenges. Externally, the tragic events of September 11, 2001, the Iraq War, the growing anti-immigrant climate, and the global economic crisis have further hindered the implementation of the *National Pastoral Plan for Hispanic Ministry*, even after the USCCB reaffirmed it in their 2002 document, *Encuentro and Mission*. While the pastoral care of Hispanics continues throughout many of our dioceses, the more important but less urgent goals of integral education, leadership formation, social justice, and systemic change have been placed on the back burner. We are left disoriented in both Church and society, even as we refer to the maps that once guided and inspired our journey. The invaluable *bendiciones* we received from our elders still accompany us, but the path has now become an eight-lane highway, with a myriad of under and over passes, during rush hour! The signs are clearly marked, and now we even have our fancy GPS gadgets and «smart phones» but we are moving too fast and too isolated in our individual vehicles to accurately see the rapidly changing landscape for what it is and thus adjust our vision accordingly.

1

Without a Vision, the People Perish

Pope Benedict XVI in his recently released encyclical *Caritas in Veritate* affirms that the whole Church is at a crossroads. The new complexities and challenges of the twenty-first century —culminating in the global economic crisis— are the new «signs of our times» that must be seen through the lens of our fundamental, Catholic values. He calls us to a profound cultural renewal that is fueled by a confident hope and tempered with a «realistic attitude»[5]. His exhortation is especially pertinent to our efforts in Hispanic ministry to promote social justice. Heeding his call, we must «re-plan our journey» as we chart a new course that builds on all the positive experiences and rejects the negative ones that have led

4   CHAVEZ A., «Diversity: Barriers Blown Away» in *CHURCH Magazine* 24, 8 (2008).
5   BENEDICT XVI, *Caritas in Veritate*, n. 21.

us astray. The Holy Father assures us that only then, can the crisis become «*an opportunity for discernment, in which to shape a new vision for the future*»[6].

A vision for Hispanic ministry in the twenty-first century must be realistic and still compelling enough to inspire a renewed commitment to *pastoral de conjunto.* This theologically rich term describes not only the mechanics of a collaborative ministry —communication, consensus, shared planning— but also the spirit of harmony among diverse instruments that complement rather than compete for the sake of the common good. It calls us to pray together and to share our resources. Communion in mission requires a sustained investment of spiritual, financial, institutional, and human resources. This is indeed a challenge when so many diocesan offices for Hispanic ministry are being closed, merged with other ministries, or asked to do more with less.

The demographics are very clear; the future of the Catholic Church in the United States is directly related to how effectively it responds to the spiritual, educational, and social justice issues of Hispanics today[7]. We must therefore be more astute and creative. We cannot do everything. However, we must prioritize our agenda and do what is ours to do with such hope that our enthusiasm for the future will contagiously enlist the help of the whole Church and of new *protagonistas* —Hispanic professionals, intellectuals, politicians, business owners, active voters, artists, philanthropists, and especially our youth. They are mostly Catholic but have not been part of our journey to date. Often, they are neglected by or estranged from the Church. Even so, they are seeking spiritual meaning in their lives. They have a passion for social justice and want to invest in a better future for Hispanics and for the whole country.

---

6 BENEDICT XVI, *Caritas in Veritate,* n. 21, original italics.
7 For a comprehensive look at the dramatic changes of Hispanic demographics see THE PEW FORUM ON RELIGION AND PUBLIC LIFE, *Changing Faiths: Latinos and the Transformation of American Religion,* Pew Hispanic Center, Washington, D.C. 2007, http://pewforum.org/newassets/surveys/hispanic/hispanics-religion-07-final-mar08.pdf (accessed January 4, 2010).

Making the Most of Opportunities

Setting priorities implies discernment. In our quest for social justice, it is essential to distinguish between a social problem and an issue. While they are certainly interrelated, no progress on addressing poverty, racism, sexism, violence, or other social problems can be accomplished without carefully discerning the interrelated issues they spawn. For example, the persistent problem of poverty among Hispanic children is directly related to the specific issues they face: limited access to quality education, family violence, healthcare, etc. Yet, after a careful discernment of the problems and issues, prioritizing the «win-able» issues in the ever-changing political landscape can be even more challenging. Timing is everything when it comes to politics where there are never permanent allies or enemies. As Catholics, our principles for social action go beyond politics and particular ideologies; however, our strategies must include working and negotiating with «the powers that be» at any given time, without compromising integrity in both the ends and the means of our action.

Hispanic voters in the last two presidential elections have demonstrated the growing, political power that we have. It is not surprising that President Barack Obama has appointed more Latinos to his administration during his first few months in office than any of his predecessors, including the high profile appointments of Sonia Sotomayor to the Supreme Court and theologian Miguel H. Díaz as the new u.s. ambassador to the Holy See. What are the opportunities and the challenges of this historic moment? How do we seize the opportunities of our new-found power without compromising our values? For me, personally, this is no longer an abstract debate but a daily examination of conscience. In early February 2009, I was contacted by the Obama administration to gauge my willingness to serve as a member of the White House Advisory Council for Faith Based and Neighborhood Partnerships. After consulting with my own spiritual advisors, I agreed to serve as a way of bringing the concerns and values of the Catholic Church and the critical needs in Hispanic communities to the agenda of the new administration.

Since then, I have been working with 24 other leaders from various religious and cultural backgrounds to advise the White House on the most effective ways for the government to partner with faith communities and nonprofit organizations on the following areas of concern: the economic recovery of our country; effectively responding to the basic human needs of people who are poor especially women and children who are among the most vulnerable in our society; preventing teenage pregnancy and reducing the number of abortions; promoting responsible fatherhood and healthy families; and fostering interfaith dialogue around the world as a means of building global peace and cooperation. This is truly an ambitious agenda, one that we must fully engage with the best of our abilities and resources.

Following the example of our bishops[8], we must work with the new administration to enact social policy that is just and responds to the needs of the most vulnerable and frail. We can work together to heal the divisions in our country and our world by finding common ground instead of polarization. Above all, we must stand with our bishops in defense and support of the life and dignity of every human person «from womb to tomb». They have set a pattern we can follow as they strongly oppose the positions of the Obama administration regarding stem cell research and abortion. At the same time they have affirmed the positions of the administration that are congruent with Catholic Social and Moral Teaching, e.g. forbidding the use of torture, ending the war in Iraq responsibly, caring for the environment, nuclear disarmament, a two state solution in the Holy Land, and many of the initiatives included in the Recovery Act that will directly benefit people who are poor and vulnerable. The USCCB is also actively engaged in upholding our Catholic Social Teaching as the heated debates continue on healthcare and immigration reform. Careful discernment and making the most of the opportunities of these upcoming years are essential if we are to bring the principles of Catholic Social Teaching to the decision-making table.

---

8 In a November 4, 2008 congratulatory letter to then President-elect Barack Obama, Cardinal Francis George of Chicago, president of the USCCB, offered the bishops' support and prayers while still challenging him to uphold the central tenet of Catholic Social Teaching, the defense and support of the life and dignity of every human person. More recently, on September 17, 2009 Archbishop José Gómez of San Antonio led a delegation of Hispanic bishops to meet with democratic and republican legislators on four areas of deep concern: a broken immigration policy, lack of access to quality education, adequate medical care and economic opportunities. See www.usccb.org for more timely information on the bishops stances on a variety of social issues.

Ongoing Pastoral Discernment

In Hispanic ministry, the tried and true method of *ver, juzgar,* and *actuar* has served to mobilize our people «from pews to shoes»[9], through effective social action guided by the light of the Gospel and our «best kept secret»[10]—the numerous documents, encyclicals, and pastoral letters of the Magisterium on Catholic Social Teaching. Over the decades, we have incorporated the additional steps of celebrating our accomplishments *(celebrar)* and evaluating their impact *(evaluar)*. The unique pedagogical approach of *Instituto Fe y Vida* has also introduced the dimension of *«ser»* to the hermeneutical circle to emphasize that education and the call to justice are intrinsic to the nature of the human person.

More recently, the post-synodal Apostolic Exhortation *Ecclesia in America* and Pope Benedict's statements at the Fifth General Conference of the Bishops of Latin America and the Caribbean in Aparecida, Brazil exhort the whole Church to contextualize discernment for social action within the call to discipleship flowing from an encounter with Jesus Christ, the Risen Lord. This leads us to a deeper conversion, a closer communion, and a courageous commitment in solidarity with those who are poor and suffering. The Holy Spirit continues to guide our plans for social action by opening our eyes to see with the eyes of Jesus and to judge these realities with the mind of Christ. This is, of course, nothing new to Hispanic ministry. However, it is possible that our implicit assumption of this essential element for true discernment has opened the door to ideologies and methods of social analysis that are incompatible with the Gospel. The fundamental error of Marxist materialism is only one example and perhaps the easiest to contest. The fatal flaws of capitalism, reductionism, and the relativism of postmodernity are closer to home and therefore more insidious.

The most important reason, however, to begin our analysis of social issues with *creer,* is for the sake of a whole new generation of Latinos/as who have never received a systematic catechesis in the fundamental tenets of our faith, nor experienced the richness of our Catholic culture. It is incumbent upon us as leaders

---

9 NATIONAL CONFERENCE OF CATHOLIC BISHOPS, *National Pastoral Plan for Hispanic Ministry,* dimension C, 79.

10 DEBERRI E.P., HUG J.E., with HENRIOT P.J. and SCHULTEIS M.J., *Catholic Social Teaching: Our Best Kept Secret,* fourth revised and expanded edition, Orbis Books, New York, NY 2003.

in Hispanic ministry to explicitly root the communal processes and methods for discerning, planning, and implementing social action in the ontological dignity of the human person *(ser)* and the primordial call to holiness through faith *(creer)*. This way we can ensure that the following five phases of pastoral discernment are rooted in an overall understanding and faithfulness to the rich deposit of our apostolic faith:

«Cycle of Pastoral Discernment»

   Along with this familiar method for discernment, we need to be clear on the fundamental principles that should guide the goals and strategies of our social action. The remainder of this essay will outline some of the central themes of Catholic Social Teaching with a few suggestions for action on issues that are central to Hispanic ministry.

3.1. THE RIGHT TO LIFE

The foundation of Catholic Social Teaching is a deep, uncompromising respect for life. Pope Benedict makes this point exceedingly clear as he exhorts Catholics to put first things first[11]. We cannot plan an agenda for social justice ignoring or having a fragmented knowledge of the Church's teachings; rather, we begin our discernment and plan our social action from this fundamental truth to ensure we are faithfully guarding the whole of the Church's seamless teaching on the dignity of human life. This includes the Church's countercultural teachings on sexuality and the sanctity of marriage as the union between one man and one woman.

---

11 *Caritas in Veritate*, n. 67.

There is a major disconnect, however, between the clarity of the Church's teachings and the ambiguity of so many Catholics on artificial contraception and abortion. This is a growing issue among Hispanics where cultural attitudes towards sex and gender roles (e.g. machismo) further exasperate the problem. Recent statistics indicate that approximately 53 percent Latinas become pregnant at some point between the ages of 15 and 19, about twice the national average[12]. Over 40 percent of these pregnancies are unintended. The rate of Hispanic women, particularly teens, who have abortions is climbing and they are becoming the most likely to contract sexually transmitted diseases, including HIV. Often, their decisions are severely restricted by abusive spouses and sexual partners with little regard for their dignity and health.

How do we address these complex life-and-death issues in the language of ordinary Hispanics, especially teenagers and pre-teens who are barraged by the media's messages on sex? This is particularly pernicious in the Spanish language media venues such as television, radio, music, and cinema. The reason many «abstinence only» programs are not working is their failure to give teenagers viable and well-communicated alternatives to which they can say yes. How can we develop educational materials that teach the Catholic theology of the body in ways that are accessible to non-theologians? How do we make education on sexuality culturally relevant while still being counter-cultural? How do we work to reduce the number of abortions through political engagement and still be faithful to the Church's teachings?[13]

3.2. THE ECONOMIC SYSTEM

Social systems are a necessary part of our life together as human beings. Political, economic, educational, and other social systems can bring order and stability to society. However, Catholic Social Teaching reminds us that there are no perfect systems. Christians and people of good will must work together to ensure that systems are just and responsive to the needs of all people without discrimination. The principle of subsidiarity holds that systems should never get too big because this inevitably leads to unresponsiveness to the «lived realities» of people. Human needs are best met through systems at their simplest level.

12 BASU M., «Survey delves into high birth rate for young Latinas» in *ccnHealth.com*, May 19, 2009, http://www.cnn.com/2009/HEALTH/05/19/latinas.pregnancy.rate/index.html (accessed January 4, 2010).
13 See JOHN PAUL II, *Evangelium Vitae*, n. 73.

Utmost in everyone's mind these days is the current economic downturn. The underlying corruption and blatant manifestation of greed in the global economic system have been revealed. Bishop Michael Pfeifer of San Angelo, Texas aptly put it in an article published recently: «It is not just the bank balances that are in the red; it is not just the global economic system that has been rocked; our religious equilibrium and moral direction has also slipped out of control»[14]. We are in a state of panic as the temporal sources of our security slip away. Millions have lost their jobs, homes, and savings and, experts warn, this is just the beginning.

How does this affect Hispanic ministry? Undoubtedly, the rate of poverty among Hispanics, already estimated at 23.2 percent, will continue to grow especially among women, children, and the elderly. In December 2009 the u.s. Department of Labor reported that the unemployment rate in the country remained at 10 percent, yet for Hispanics it was 12.9 percent[15]. This obviously does not include the vast number of day laborers and undocumented workers who can no longer find work. With unemployment comes the loss of healthcare benefits and homeownership, a central part of achieving the «American Dream». 30.7 percent of Hispanics in the United States are uninsured[16]. While national foreclosure statistics are not reported by ethnicity or race, there is ample evidence that Hispanic homeowners have been disproportionately affected by the current wave of foreclosures especially in California, Nevada, and Florida. The Pew Research Center found that nearly one-in-ten (9 percent) Hispanic homeowners say they have missed a mortgage payment in the past year, and 3 percent have received a foreclosure notice. Sadly, more than one-third (36 percent) of Latino homeowners fear they will likely face foreclosure in the next twelve months[17].

14 BISHOP MICHAEL PFEIFER, OMI, «Economic Crisis Fueled by Greed» in *West Texas Angelus*, 39, 5 (2009) 17, http://www.talleypress.com/angelus/wta0509.pdf (accessed January 8, 2010).

15 U.S. DEPARTMENT OF LABOR, «The Employment Situation — December 2009», news release, January 8, 2010, http://www.bls.gov/news.release/pdf/empsit.pdf (accessed January 8, 2010).

16 U.S. CENSUS BUREAU, «Income, Poverty, and Health Insurance Coverage in the United States: 2008», report released in September 2009, http://www.census.gov/prod/2009pubs/p60-236.pdf (accessed January 8, 2010).

17 KOCHHAR R., GONZÁLEZ-BARRERA A., and DOCKTERMAN D., «Through Boom and Bust: Minorities, Immigrants and Homeownership» in *Pew Research Center Publications*, May 12, 2009, online resource, http://pewresearch.org/pubs/1220/home-ownership-trends-blacks-hispanics (accessed January 8, 2010).

Our agenda for social action in the area of the economic system must answer the poignant questions raised by the u.s. bishops in their prophetic pastoral letter *Economic Justice for All*:

> Every perspective on economic life that is human, moral, and Christian must be shaped by three questions: What does the economy do for people? What does it do to people? And how do people participate in it?[18].

These are not easy questions to answer, especially because the economic systems of our times are inseparably linked to other powerful social systems, primarily political, that provide privilege to some groups and individuals while others are disenfranchised.

164   3.3.   POVERTY AND EDUCATION

Although difficult to track accurately, the high school drop out rates among Hispanic youth are consistently higher than those of their white counterparts; in many states they are twice as high. This has serious implications for higher education. An update to the 2000 u.s. Census reports that only about 13 percent of adult Hispanics hold a BA degree, compared with 19 percent of African Americans, and 32 percent of whites. Even our Catholic educational system has failed to provide access to quality education to Latinos. Currently only 3 percent of Latino school-age children attend Catholic schools in the United States[19]. This is particularly alarming because Latinos are already the majority of u.s. Catholics under the age of 18 and are more likely than their white counterparts to remain Catholic[20].

Catholic schools serve low income minority students, especially Latinos, far more effectively than comparable public school options. Hispanic students in Catholic high schools are 42 percent more likely to graduate and 2½ times more

---

18 NATIONAL CONFERENCE OF CATHOLIC BISHOPS, *Economic Justice for All: Pastoral Letter on Catholic Social Teaching and the u.s. Economy*, USCC, Washington, D.C. 1986, n. 1.

19 Cfr. THE NOTRE DAME TASK FORCE ON THE PARTICIPATION OF LATINO CHILDREN AND FAMILIES IN CATHOLIC SCHOOLS, *To Nurture the Soul of a Nation: Latino Families, Catholic Schools, and Educational Opportunity*, University of Notre Dame, December 12, 2009, available online http://catholicschooladvantage.nd.edu/assets/19176/nd_ltf_report_final_english_12.2.pdf (accessed January 8, 2010).

20 See Ken Johnson-Mondragón's essay on Hispanic Ministry, Youth and Young Adult Ministry in this book.

likely to go to college than Hispanic students in public schools[21]. Catholic schools continue to be the most effective means of passing on the faith in the Church in the u.s. as many studies demonstrate. Despite what would seem to be a compelling value proposition for Latino families, the percentage of Hispanic children in Catholic schools is extremely small (3 percent). It is imperative to ask why the number of Hispanic children is no higher in our Catholic Schools. A common argument is that Catholic education is too expensive for Latino families who are disproportionately represented among the working poor and cannot afford it. However, research indicates that money is not the only barrier[22]. So we must ask: what are the systemic barriers and cultural mindsets that keep Latino children underrepresented in our Catholic Schools?

The 2009 report from The Notre Dame Task Force on the Participation of Latino Children and Families in Catholic Schools proposes a national strategy to encourage participation and ownership of Catholic schools among Latinos/as nationwide. The report is an invitation to make Catholic schools more welcoming and accessible to Hispanic children and families and to improve their capacity to effectively serve Latino/a children. The Task Force has set the ambitious but realistic goal of doubling the percentage of Hispanic children enrolled in Catholic schools by 2020. In light of projected population growth, this will mean bringing the number of Hispanic children in Catholic schools from 290,000 today to over 1,000,000 by 2020[23]. Leaders involved in Hispanic ministry must prioritize this issue in our social justice agenda. This will truly make a profound impact on the Hispanic community in the United States.

3.4. OPTION FOR THE POOR: CHARITY AND JUSTICE

The preferential option for people who are poor is one of the cornerstones of Catholic Social Teaching and is central to Hispanic ministry. The strength of a society is measured by how it treats its most vulnerable members. The Church's option for the poor is not meant to create a division between social classes; rather, it is based on the scriptural mandate to always ask how social policies and practices affect the poorest of God's children. Everyone is precious to God and de-

---

21 Cfr. THE NOTRE DAME TASK FORCE ON THE PARTICIPATION OF LATINO CHILDREN AND FAMILIES IN CATHOLIC SCHOOLS, *To Nurture the Soul of a Nation.*
22 Cfr. THE NOTRE DAME TASK FORCE ON THE PARTICIPATION OF LATINO CHILDREN AND FAMILIES IN CATHOLIC SCHOOLS, *To Nurture the Soul of a Nation.*
23 Cfr. THE NOTRE DAME TASK FORCE ON THE PARTICIPATION OF LATINO CHILDREN AND FAMILIES IN CATHOLIC SCHOOLS, *To Nurture the Soul of a Nation.*

serves a just share of this world's goods. The Church's preferential option for the poor goes beyond national borders and calls for global solidarity to end hunger and poverty throughout the world caused by misuse of the earth's natural resources and irresponsible development.

What does this option mean today as the number of people living in poverty dramatically increases in this country and around the world? Certainly, it means an even greater generosity in charitable giving and increasing Catholic charitable services and relief efforts. This includes strengthening and expanding safety nets for people who are poor to provide services such as: transitional housing for the increasing number of homeless people, expanding healthcare coverage for children, providing for the basic nutritional needs of families through school based programs, and other direct service programs and resources that can be delivered to people in need at the most effective level: person to person, one family at a time, one child at a time.

Catholic Social Thought clearly teaches that we must also strive to discern the root causes of poverty and courageously work for systemic change on behalf of and alongside people who are poor. Given the present realities resulting from the collapse of the economic system, our agenda for social action and advocacy must include innovative approaches to address the root causes of poverty, especially in understanding the relationship between formal education and equitable economic opportunity. This agenda must include: reinvestment in our inner cities through an increase for community development funds, fiscal integrity at all levels of government and public corporations, access to financing and homeownership, access to early and ongoing education, especially bi-literate programs, and, ideally, Catholic education that is affordable for poor families. This can happen with initiatives such as the passage of voucher programs that give parents viable choices for their children's education. Accessible and affordable college education must also be considered a basic right for all people in today's competitive job market. Effective job training programs and childcare for single parents must be part of the equation for success, especially among Hispanics.

3.5. IMMIGRATION, RACISM, AND WORKERS' RIGHTS

The Catholic Church has a long tradition of upholding the fundamental right to meaningful labor in conditions that are safe and respect human dignity. Workers have the right to fair wages and to organize unions[24]. In general, the

24 LEO XIII, *Rerum Novarum*, n. 49.

Church upholds the rights of individuals to hold private property and to exercise economic initiative. These rights however must be balanced with a proper understanding of principles related to justice, the common good, and the careful stewardship of God's creation. Economic systems exist to serve people, not the other way around. These teachings are important for Hispanic workers in the United States, particularly when most are employed as blue-collar and service industry workers. Just labors laws and the right to unionize are essential for these workers.

For Hispanics, issues related to workers' rights are significantly linked to immigration policies. Sadly, many of these policies reflect that intrinsic evils such as racism still persist in the social fabric of the United States and that of the Latin American countries where the majority of immigrant workers originate. Despite the fact that migration is primarily fueled by economic forces, governments have consistently refused to address this issue with any substance in negotiating treaties and agreements for trade and investment like the North American Free Trade Agreement (NAFTA). The pacts, for the most part, only open the doors for the unrestricted movement of capital, materials, and products beyond national borders. Multinational corporations now yield more political power than Nation States and are constantly reinventing themselves through subsidiary entities in countries where people are desperately poor and willing to work for pittance. They operate above the laws of the state, weakening not only its political power but eventually eroding all aspects of its civil society. This is the new colonialism that continues to rob developing countries of their raw materials and their brightest and most determined citizens[25]. This «New World Order», recently called into question by Pope Benedict XVI, imposes legally binding pacts among powerless nations to ensure the free movement of capital and products and at the same time restricting the movement of laborers from these impoverished countries. When money and things have more rights than human beings, we can truly say, «this is not Catholic!»

These free trade agreements, corporate tax breaks, and economic policies have generated great wealth for less than a fourth of the world's population. For the other three-fourths of the world, however, the unrestricted economic «rights» of corporations and the severely restricted economic rights of workers have triggered compulsory mass migrations. For every person who benefits from

25 *Caritas in Veritate*, n. 32-33.

the present economic and political order, thousands upon thousands are forced to choose between poverty in their homelands or the possibility of a better life for themselves and their families elsewhere. Migration is a fundamental right and Catholic Social Teaching affirms it.

By means of their recent joint pastoral letter *Strangers No Longer: Together on the Journey of Hope*[26] and the *Justice for Immigrants* campaign[27], the u.s. Catholic bishops have sought to courageously uphold the basic human rights of migrants and called on Catholics to actively welcome the «stranger in our midst» and also to push for comprehensive immigration reform. More recently, the bishops have offered practical policy solutions to the Obama administration proposing compelling moral arguments for bringing the estimated 12 million undocumented immigrants in the United States out of the shadows. Hispanic and non-Hispanic bishops together are lobbying Congress to fix our broken immigration system and denounce the rising tide of dehumanizing rhetoric that demonizes immigrants as «aliens». The Catholic vision for a humane immigration reform system is not only rooted in appeals to justice and morality, practical arguments are also critical. During the last two decades the federal government has allocated about 10 billion dollars to reinforce security along the u.s.-Mexican border. Migrants have responded by finding new and more dangerous routes into the United States. There is no wall high enough to deter the dreams of those seeking a better life.

Stopping migration's socioeconomic engine and the negative consequences for the real people whose lives are negatively affected by imperfect policies requires more than tough talk from finger-wagging politicians or the cowboy antics of local sheriffs. It requires a systematic response that rejects false choices. We can protect our borders and uphold human dignity. Comprehensive immigration reform would include an earned path to citizenship, appropriate worker protections, and policies that keep families from being separated. This is not amnesty or a handout. It's a sensible solution to a system where employers and u.s. consumers benefit from the labor of undocumented workers and millions of immigrants in general have no protection from exploitation. The failure of Congress to pass reform legislation has forced states to enact a hodgepodge of

---

26 UNITED STATES CONFERENCE OF CATHOLIC BISHOPS, *Strangers No Longer: Together on the Journey of Hope: A Pastoral Letter Concerning Migration*, USCCB, Washington, D.C. 2003, available online, http://www.usccb.org/mrs/stranger.shtml.

27 http://www.justiceforimmigrants.org/

punitive local ordinances. The National Council of La Raza and the Urban Institute report that two-thirds of children separated from their parents during immigration raids are u.s. citizens. This is shameful. If we hope to move beyond simplistic solutions and the hateful rhetoric that define our polarized immigration debate, we need deeper conversations and bold Hispanic leadership in both Church and society.

We in Hispanic ministry must support our bishops in continuing to lift their voices and advocate on this critical issue. We have an opportunity, perhaps sooner than we thought possible, to be instrumental in enacting laws that can begin to reform the racist and broken immigration system. As bridge-builders, an even more important role will be to find ways to «reframe» the heated discourse on immigration reform in our country: from debate to dialogue; from problem to opportunity; from symptoms to causes; and from unilateral action to innovative, multinational collaboration. We cannot do this alone or only at the parish level; we must breathe new life into our national and international networks. Migration is a global phenomenon that calls for global solidarity. Cardinal Óscar Andrés Rodríguez Madariaga of Honduras reminds us: «the first way to globalize solidarity is to globalize respect for life…every life»[28].

At a minimum, the leadership in Hispanic ministry must work together to advocate for the following:

1) Provisions to ensure that recently arrived immigrants become integrated, educated, healthy and law abiding residents who are licensed to drive, insured as motorists, with good access to credit, banking, and education;

2) Improved border management to protect people most affected by the violence and drug trafficking along the border instead of building costly and ineffective walls;

3) Bilateral cooperation on economic, labor, health, education, social, environment and infrastructure issues;

4) A temporary workers' program that is focused on and monitored by workers, employers, and independent human rights organizations or NGO's

5) A reasonable path to earned citizenship for those immigrants who want to become part of the u.s. society;

28 RODRÍGUEZ MADARIAGA O.A., «The Catholic Church and the Globalization of Solidarity» in *Caritas.org*, July 7, 2003, http://www.caritas.org/activities/economic_justice/the_catholic_church_and_the_globalization_of_solidarity.html (accessed January 8, 2010).

6) Protection and assistance for the most vulnerable —women, children, elderly, and those who are sick or physically handicapped; and,

7) Laws and policies that strengthen and reunite immigrant families.

Finally, we must also work together to make college possible for young Latino/a immigrants who, through no fault of their own, lack the proper documentation to access higher education. This is the time when legislation like the DREAM Act can become a reality.

4

Conclusion

This essay calls for a unified effort by the leaders in Hispanic ministry to develop a compelling vision for how we can collaboratively meet the critical signs of our times with creative innovation and by partnering with new protagonists in the struggle for justice. It has offered suggestions for enhancing the pastoral discernment method of *ver, juzgar,* and *actuar* with an emphasis on *creer.* Most urgently, it has identified key social justice agenda items for a unified, national plan of action that upholds the whole range of life issues. These include responsible sexuality and affirming the sacredness of marriage and family, economic justice that flows for a preferential option for people who are poor, equitable access to education, especially Catholic education, and a summary of what comprehensive immigration reform should include to truly benefit Hispanic workers. Most importantly, this essay is a call to all leaders in Hispanic ministry to renew our commitment to be instruments of peace.

We have experienced the good news of the Gospel and have preserved *las bendiciones* of our elders in Hispanic ministry. Through their struggles for justice in society and a place of belonging in the Church, we believe that we have a unique gift of leadership to offer to the whole world community, especially the poor and suffering. We rejoice in our culture and in our Catholic faith that was first proclaimed in this hemisphere by our ancestors. We seek to share this faith by responding generously to the call for a New Evangelization directed especially to people who are disinherited, uneducated, sick and suffering, and all those who yearn to know Jesus. In our national networks we have pledged to grow in faith and knowledge. We are working to breathe new life into these necessary national organizations through a communal plan of action propelled by a vision that is becoming clearer each time we gather to listen and speak as the Holy Spirit guides. We accompany each other as we learn to trust again, as we risk again, as we boldly envision new dreams for our world today and confidently claim the promise of our loving God: « For I know well the plans I have in mind for you… to give you a future full of hope» (Jer 29:11).

Hispanic Ministry and Leadership Formation

Hosffman Ospino *and* Elsie Miranda

We, as Hispanic people, commit ourselves to participate in planning and decision making and in assuming positions of responsibility in the Church at all levels (national, regional, diocesan, parochial)[1].

u.s. Hispanic Catholics for decades have affirmed the commitment to developing strong structures of ministerial leadership. Such commitment emerges from the conviction that Latino/a voices and perspectives are integral to the life of the Church in the United States, particularly in the culturally diverse context in which we live and celebrate our faith. At the beginning of the second decade of the 21st century, when Hispanic Catholics constitute nearly 40 percent of the entire u.s. Catholic population, this commitment acquires renewed life. As practical theologians who have been involved in various processes of reflection on Hispanic Ministry, it is our conviction that a clear reflection about leadership formation is necessary to strengthen the work of evangelization among Latinos/as in the United States. This is the task to which we turn our attention in the following pages.

In this essay we look at the present and future of Hispanic leadership formation in the United States. This reflection builds on our personal experience, our study of this reality, and in great part the insights gained from our participation in the 2009 National Symposium on the Present and Future of Catholic Hispanic Ministry in the United States at Boston College. Considering the abundance of resources in this area, we deliberately narrow our analysis to key developments and conversations taking place during the first decade of the 21st century with a look at the most immediate future. It is important to note, however, that any reflection on Hispanic ministry must honor our *memoria histórica* (historical memory): the insights, movements, and achievements of u.s. Hispanic Catholics in previous decades that forged the way for the organized forms of Hispanic ministry that exist today. Some articulations of this historical memory are already available to us[2]. However, we echo the call of many Hispanic leaders to further interpret and share such tradition[3].

---

1 *Prophetic Voices: Document on the Process of the III Encuentro Nacional Hispano de Pastoral,* USCC, Washington, D.C. 1986, n. 40, in UNITED STATES CONFERENCE OF CATHOLIC BISHOPS, *Hispanic Ministry: Three Major Documents,* USCCB, Washington, D.C. 1995, 43.

2 See DOLAN J.P. and FIGUEROA-DECK A. (eds.), *Hispanic Catholic Culture in the u.s.: Issues and Concerns,* University of Notre Dame Press, Notre Dame, IN 1994; MATOVINA T. and POYO G.E. (eds.), *Presente!: u.s. Latino Catholics from Colonial Origins to the Present,* Orbis Books, Maryknoll, NY 2000; SANDOVAL M., *On the Move: A History of the Hispanic Church in the United States,* revised 2nd edition, Orbis Books, Maryknoll, NY 2006.

3 Members of the study group reflecting about the relationship between Hispanic ministry and leadership formation during the symposium called for more resources and scholarship explor-

The national Encuentros for Hispanic ministry (1972, 1977, 1985) have been perhaps the most significant instances in the history of u.s. Catholicism where Hispanic Catholic leaders voiced their thoughts about the importance of the Latino/a presence in the life of the Church in the United States and thus envisioned the type of leadership needed to affirm such presence[4]. The communal, prophetic voices of Latino/a leaders have called for reflection about what it means to minister in a church where Hispanics are present in large numbers, often times as a numeric majority that is perceived as a socio-political «minority», and thus develop the appropriate strategies to form leaders who can pastorally meet the spiritual needs and expectations of the Church *here* and *now*. Echoes of these voices are available to us through the records from the Encuentros, numerous symposia, leadership gatherings, Hispanic Ministry meetings, and statements from the United States Catholic Conference of Bishops (usccb) on Hispanic Catholicism[5].

Hispanic Catholics welcomed the 21ˢᵗ century with renewed hope and heightened awareness about the many challenges that the Church faces in the United States today. Among these we highlight the increasingly diverse makeup of parochial and diocesan communities, the «hispanization» of considerable geographical and ecclesiastical regions around the country, the large number of advanced age clergy and vowed religious, the scarcity of vocations to replace them, the small numbers of clergy adequately prepared to work with Hispanic Catholics, and a steady process of re-urbanization of Catholicism. Furthermore, in the new century two more challenges have led u.s. Catholics to rethink long standing attitudes and practices: the scandals related to sexual abuse of children in the Church and the recent financial recession. Both realities have forced major processes of institutional reorganization and massive relocation of resources.

---

ing the contributions of Latino/a Catholic leaders during the 20ᵗʰ century. It is imperative that new generations of leaders, Hispanic and non-Hispanic, learn *about* and *from* the wisdom of the many Latino/a Catholics and our movements advocating for better leadership structures in the Church and in the larger society. The *memoria histórica* of u.s. Hispanic Catholics must become available to everyone involved in ministry in the Church and be named as a central contribution to the historical experience of u.s. Catholicism.

4 See NATIONAL CONFERENCE OF CATHOLIC BISHOPS, *Conclusiones: Primer Encuentro Nacional Hispano de Pastoral*, United States Catholic Conference, Washington, D.C. 1972; GASTÓN M.L. (ed.), *Proceedings of the II Encuentro Nacional Hispano de Pastoral*, NATIONAL CONFERENCE OF CATHOLIC BISHOPS, SECRETARIAT FOR HISPANIC AFFAIRS, USCC, Washington, D.C. 1978; *Prophetic Voices: Document on the Process of the III Encuentro Nacional Hispano de Pastoral*.

5 There is an urgent need that such records be systematically collected, organized, and made available to the new generations of leaders in the Church, preferably in electronic format.

Fully aware of the above challenges and their direct impact on Hispanic ministry, Latino/a pastoral leaders are committed to being part of the collaborative processes that will lead to addressing them. We believe that this century is a time for Hispanic Catholics to further share our ministerial gifts, imaginations and full participation with the larger Church and to lead the way creatively into the next phase of the history of the u.s. Catholic experience.

In the previous decade Church leaders, Hispanic and non-Hispanic, gathered together on several occasions to be part of several conversations about ministry and leadership formation in the context of Hispanic ministry. These meetings highlighted many of the concerns and hopes repeatedly identified during the second part of the 20th century and were successful in continuing to develop a more national awareness about these areas. No credible conversation today about the life of the Church in the United States can afford to ignore the reality of u.s. Hispanic Catholicism. Nearly every discussion about lay ecclesial ministry, youth ministry, parish reconfigurations, episcopal appointments, priestly and diaconal formation, theological education, etc., has involved some reflection about the growing presence of u.s. Latino/a Catholics in the Church and the questions related to such presence. However, to adequately address the relationship between u.s. Hispanic ministry and leadership formation in the Church, an honest commitment to be inclusive and collaborative must be set in motion by *all* pastoral leaders. Aware that this is truly a vast and complex task, we propose to focus on two major areas of concern: effective leadership and support structures for Hispanic ministry and leadership formation.

1

Effective Leadership

The effectiveness of pastoral initiatives in Hispanic communities does and will largely depend on the quality of the leaders advancing them. It is important to note that leadership in Hispanic ministry is not exclusively of Latinos/as nor is it focused only on the concerns of Catholics of Hispanic background. The complexity of the Catholic experience in the United States is rather an invitation to leaders of all ethnicities and cultural backgrounds to work and serve the needs of a pluralistic population in general and to participate in the richness of the Hispanic Catholic experience in particular.

In 2002 the Catholic bishops of the United States presented their pastoral statement *Encuentro and Mission* to all Catholics in the country. The document was written to « affirm those pastoral efforts of Hispanic ministry that promote the general objective and the specific dimensions of the 1987 National Pastoral Plan for Hispanic Ministry» and provide «basic pastoral principles, priorities, and suggested actions to develop efforts in Hispanic ministry while strengthening the unity of the Church in the United States»[6]. *Encuentro and Mission* is a pastoral framework that provides a compelling vision for Catholic ministry in the new century with particular attention to the Hispanic experience. The document captures well the spirit of previous reflections on Hispanic Catholicism envisioning the kind of leadership that the Church in the United States needs at this historical moment. Four key themes about effective leadership emerge in the document: the New Evangelization, *pastoral de conjunto*, leaders who are *gente puente*, and the centrality of social justice.

First, *Encuentro and Mission* clearly proposed the New Evangelization as the lens through which ministry ought to be interpreted and done in the new century[7]. Hispanic ministry leaders must be true witnesses of the encounter with the living Christ, builders of the ecclesial community, and active participants of the mission of the Church[8]. All expressions of our ministry must reflect this triple relationship with Christ, the Church, and evangelization.

Second, the Church needs women and men who understand and are willing to embrace the model of *pastoral de conjunto* (communion in mission)[9], which given the particular circumstances of our ecclesial context requires «the close collaboration in ministry among all ethnic and cultural groups»[10]. Such model of leadership, rooted in the shared wisdom of Hispanic leaders in Latin America and the United States, requires the affirmation of processes of participation

---

6 UNITED STATES CONFERENCE OF CATHOLIC BISHOPS, *Encuentro and Mission: A Renewed Pastoral Framework for Hispanic Ministry*, USCCB, Washington, D.C. 2002, n. 1, http://www.usccb.org/hispanicaffairs/encuentromission.shtml.

7 Cfr. UNITED STATES CONFERENCE OF CATHOLIC BISHOPS, *Encuentro and Mission: A Renewed Pastoral Framework for Hispanic Ministry*, n. 27.

8 Cfr. UNITED STATES CONFERENCE OF CATHOLIC BISHOPS, *Encuentro and Mission: A Renewed Pastoral Framework for Hispanic Ministry*, n. 25-29.

9 Cfr. UNITED STATES CONFERENCE OF CATHOLIC BISHOPS, *Encuentro and Mission: A Renewed Pastoral Framework for Hispanic Ministry*, n. 19.

10 UNITED STATES CONFERENCE OF CATHOLIC BISHOPS, *Encuentro and Mission: A Renewed Pastoral Framework for Hispanic Ministry*, n. 33.

and consultation, particularly at the grassroots levels, in «collaboration with clergy, religious, and lay people»[11]. Such was the spirit of the Encuentro processes that led to the proposal of pastoral and planning practices «conducted with the people, not for the people»[12].

Third, there is an urgent need for leaders who are *gente puente*, bridge-builders[13]. The complexity of our communities can seem overwhelming to anyone involved in ministry in the u.s. pluralistic context. Such complexity is often times exacerbated by the multiple factors that coincide in the lives of Latinos/as: different generations, multiple origins, different histories, many languages, distinct social locations, and even a variety of interpretations of the Catholic experience. It would be rather naïve to expect that all leaders address every dimension of the life and faith of our diverse communities and be all for all. Yet, *Encuentro and Mission* suggests that ministry leaders should be —or at least aspire to be— bridge-builders, women and men who embody an openness to «embracing people from different cultures, a flexibility for working and journeying with them, and an understanding of the broader Church… [with] a commitment to serve all Catholics… [They need to be] excellent listeners and have great sensitivity to and interest in people's lives, needs, aspirations, and ideas. They need to believe in and be models of service, with a profound commitment to solidarity with the most vulnerable… [and be] pioneers in opening doors to self and to others»[14].

Fourth, *Encuentro and Mission* called for pastoral leaders in the United States, and more particularly those in Hispanic ministry, to be sincerely committed to issues of social justice. The Hispanic Catholic experience in the United States unfolds in the midst of challenging circumstances such as widespread poverty, social biases like racism, classism, homophobia, and dehumanizing sexism against Latinas, as well as shocking neglect of Hispanic youth at every level. It is not enough to name such issues and do little or nothing about them; neither is it enough to simply hope for the best. Ministerial leaders of all ethnicities working in Hispanic ministry must be proactive in educating «Hispanic Catholics

---

11 UNITED STATES CONFERENCE OF CATHOLIC BISHOPS, *Encuentro and Mission: A Renewed Pastoral Framework for Hispanic Ministry*, n. 44.

12 UNITED STATES CONFERENCE OF CATHOLIC BISHOPS, *Encuentro and Mission: A Renewed Pastoral Framework for Hispanic Ministry*, n. 44.

13 Cfr. UNITED STATES CONFERENCE OF CATHOLIC BISHOPS, *Encuentro and Mission: A Renewed Pastoral Framework for Hispanic Ministry*, n. 46.

14 UNITED STATES CONFERENCE OF CATHOLIC BISHOPS, *Encuentro and Mission: A Renewed Pastoral Framework for Hispanic Ministry*, n. 46.

about public policy issues and processes as well as basic community organizing skills»[15] that will be transformative for the community. Current conversations about immigration reform, adequate access to health care, quality education, and workers' rights, to mention only a few, require the participation of Church leaders that are knowledgeable about the Church's teachings on these issues, denouncing with prophetic voice that which is unjust, and guiding the reflection about these issues in their communities. The woes of Latinos/as in the United States are the woes of the whole ecclesial body and those who carry these burdens must be offered the balm of compassionate and caring action as modeled by Jesus' life and ministry.

1.2. CHALLENGES

In 1999 a study on pastoral leadership among Latinos/as in five states with high concentrations of Hispanic population revealed that approximately 70 percent of Latinas and Latinos actively involved in Catholic ministry were first generation immigrants[16]. This number highly contrasts with the fact that the majority of Latinos/as living in the United States, a decade ago and today, were born in the country. That first-generation Hispanic leaders are involved in ministerial leadership in such large numbers speaks well of their zeal and willingness to serve in our diverse communities, many of which are sustained primarily by these women and men. Nevertheless, the work of these leaders is often times constrained by their own limitations: many speak only Spanish and unintentionally perpetuate the segregation of their communities, particularly in parishes where there is more than one language group. Many do not know how «the system» works and thus lack the basic knowledge to network within their dioceses, parishes, and other ecclesial and social organizations. Even though most are well-intentioned in their hopes to implement models of ministry that worked well in their home countries, they become frustrated because such models «do not work» in the United States. Furthermore, many are unaware of the *memoria histórica* of the Hispanic Catholic community in the United States and fall into the tempta-

15 UNITED STATES CONFERENCE OF CATHOLIC BISHOPS, *Encuentro and Mission: A Renewed Pastoral Framework for Hispanic Ministry*, n. 57.4.c.
16 Cfr. DAVIS K.G., HERNÁNDEZ A. and LAMPE P.E., «Hispanic Catholic Leadership: Key to the Future» in HERNÁNDEZ E.I., PEÑA M., DAVIS K., and STATION E. (eds.), *Emerging Voices, Urgent Choices: Essays on Latino/a Religious Leadership*, Brill, Boston, MA 2006, 55. The number is based on the findings from the 1999 survey run by the National Community on Latino/a Leadership (NCLL) in California, Texas, New York, Florida and Illinois, commissioned by the National Catholic Council for Hispanic Ministry (NCCHM).

tion of continuously starting from zero. Some of the essays in this book raise awareness about the fact that many first-generation leaders are priests from Latin America[17] who, because of their ordained status, are almost immediately placed in charge of entire communities. Their ministerial impact on these ecclesial communities is obviously very significant, yet such communities have the potential to grow or stall depending on how these ordained leaders respond to the issues just delineated and on their capacity to work collaboratively with (instead of estranging) the lay leaders already there. This reality calls for serious reflection about the «skipped» generation (our term) of potential leaders from second and third generations, especially children of immigrants who are rapidly integrating into mainstream culture and do not feel compelled to serve in their ecclesial communities. The failure to engage these generations has created a huge vacuum that requires the Church to address internal issues such as just wages for lay workers, institutional sexism, lack of effective and inclusive leadership, and limited opportunities for collaboration. Ironically, many of these Latinas and Latinos often serve the community as bicultural and bilingual leaders in contexts that are unrelated to the Church. What must the Church do to offer them a home and a viable alternative for their openness to serve?

A second major challenge that Latinos/as must frequently address is the educational level of our leaders. Currently, the majority of Latinos/as in the United States have very low levels of formal educational attainment, a situation that puts them in positions of extreme disadvantage in a context that values education as a status symbol. By and large education is the single most significant factor that facilitates social mobility in our society and u.s. Latinos/as lag behind most groups in this regard[18]. This raises serious concerns when we reflect about pastoral leadership in the Church. Ministry in the United States is often defined in terms of professional standards not only for the clergy and vowed religious, but also for the thousands of women and men who work as lay ecclesial ministers throughout the country. With low levels of educational attainment and less than 15 percent of adults having obtained a bachelor's degree, the number of Latinos/as who can respond to the call to ministry within the current ecclesial

---

17 Approximately eighty-three percent of Latino priests ministering in the United States are foreign-born. Cfr. INSTITUTO FE Y VIDA, «Hispanic Youth and Young Adult Ministry: Recent Findings» in *Perspectives on Hispanic Youth and Young Adult Ministry* 4, Instituto Fe y Vida, Stockton, CA 2007, 8, available online, http://www.feyvida.org/research/researchpubs.html.

18 See Hosffman Ospino's essay on Hispanic Ministry, Evangelization, and Faith Formation in this book.

structures and actually succeed is very small. In 2005 the bishops of the United States in a document on lay ecclesial ministry, *Co-Workers in the Vineyard of the Lord*, indicated that «[i]nadequate and faulty formation harms rather than helps the mission of the Church. Usually, a master's degree, or at least a bachelor's degree, in an appropriate field of study is preferable»[19]. On the one hand, one could not agree more with this recommendation and the hope to achieve it is a benchmark that would require the Church as a whole to value and invest in the education and formation of its lay ecclesial leaders like it values and invests in the education and formation of those seeking ordination. On the other hand, making the completion of a degree program a requirement for lay ecclesial ministry under the present circumstances would lead to the exclusion of many Latinos/as from ministry and widen the vacuum in ecclesial leadership[20]. Furthermore, it is important to observe that low educational attainment, particularly at the level of seminaries and universities, does not necessarily constitute an indicator of lack of leadership. Thousands of Latinos/as serve pastorally in different capacities in the life of the Church, many of them voluntarily exercising functions that are similar —in some cases more complex and more time consuming— to those of hired ministers. This situation reveals two anomalies: first, the work of many Latino/a ministers is not being fully acknowledged nor adequately remunerated under the guise of lack of educational credentials, thus bypassing already established standards that supposedly apply to all ministers. When this becomes a deliberate practice, the issue must be judged under the parameters of labor justice —not to mention basic Christian moral praxis[21]. Second, Latinos/as are implementing models of creative leadership in their communities as part of their involvement in ecclesial movements and small ecclesial communities that need

---

19 UNITED STATES CONFERENCE OF CATHOLIC BISHOPS, *Co-Workers in the Vineyard of the Lord: A Resource for Guiding the Development of Lay Ecclesial Ministry*, USCCB, Washington, D.C. 2005, 34, also available online at http://www.usccb.org/laity/laymin/co-workers.pdf. The document also provides some important statistics that point to the high educational level of Catholic lay ecclesial ministers in the United States: «In 2005, 48.1 percent of lay ecclesial ministers hold a master's degree or better, 51.4 percent of these in a pastoral/theological field. More than half of the lay ecclesial ministers employed by parishes have completed a ministry formation program, 64.3 percent of which were sponsored by the diocese».

20 Cfr. 2007 National Symposium on Lay Ecclesial Ministry: *Executive Summary*, 3, http://www1.csbsju.edu/SOT/Symposium/documents/ExecutiveSummary.pdf (accessed March 19, 2010).

21 One helpful resource in this regard is the 2007 statement «Working in the Vineyard: A Position Statement on Employment Practices for Lay Ecclesial Ministers» written by the National Association for Lay Ministry (NALM). The document is available online at http://www.nalm.org/mc/page.do?sitePageId=45861&orgId=nalm (accessed March 16, 2010).

to be studied and recognized as forms of lay ecclesial ministry, even if the potential outcome would challenge the dominant understanding of professional ministry. Thus an important question emerges: are all members of the Church in the United States ready and willing to have an open, honest, and truly inclusive conversation in regard to the education and formation of Latino/a lay ecclesial ministers?[22]

One last major challenge facing the Catholic Church in the United States in terms of training pastoral leaders is the slow pace at which programs of ministerial formation integrate strategies to prepare women and men to effectively serve Latinos/as —and other non-dominant Catholic communities. In many institutions for ministry formation such programs do not even exist, even when large percentages of Latinos/as live in the geographical areas they purport to serve. *Encuentro and Mission* summarizes well the major hopes about leadership formation for ministry that Hispanic leaders have articulated throughout various deliberative processes:

- «Develop and support programs designed to help Hispanic lay people attain degrees for Church ministry»[23]
- Establish partnerships between ecclesial structures and academic institutions such as universities, seminaries, and institutes[24]
- Affirm the value of certification programs[25]
- Foster collaboration between offices for Hispanic ministry and formation programs for ordained, religious, and lay ecclesial ministers[26]
- «Incorporate Hispanic ministry, culture, and language into programs in offices of evangelization, religious education, and formation, as well as in seminaries»[27]

---

22 Cfr. BURGALETA C., «A Latino/a Perspective on Co-Workers» (unpublished essay). We are grateful to Rev. Claudio Burgaleta, s.j. for sharing with us this essay first presented at a conference on lay ecclesial ministry at Fordham University on September 25, 2009.

23 UNITED STATES CONFERENCE OF CATHOLIC BISHOPS, *Encuentro and Mission: A Renewed Pastoral Framework for Hispanic Ministry*, n. 55.1.a.

24 Cfr. UNITED STATES CONFERENCE OF CATHOLIC BISHOPS, *Encuentro and Mission: A Renewed Pastoral Framework for Hispanic Ministry*, n. 55.1.a.

25 Cfr. UNITED STATES CONFERENCE OF CATHOLIC BISHOPS, *Encuentro and Mission: A Renewed Pastoral Framework for Hispanic Ministry*, n. 55.1.c.

26 Cfr. UNITED STATES CONFERENCE OF CATHOLIC BISHOPS, *Encuentro and Mission: A Renewed Pastoral Framework for Hispanic Ministry*, n. 55.2.a.

27 UNITED STATES CONFERENCE OF CATHOLIC BISHOPS, *Encuentro and Mission: A Renewed Pastoral Framework for Hispanic Ministry*, n. 55.2.c.

- Form ministers able to serve in culturally diverse contexts[28]
- «Support young Hispanics on their educational attainment efforts, catechetical formation, and human and leadership development»[29]
- «Develop Hispanic leaders able to minister in the context of a culturally diverse and pluralistic society while strengthening their Hispanic cultural and ministerial identity»[30]
- «Promote the involvement of Hispanic church professionals as leaders and experts in different ministries and disciplines, not only in Hispanic ministry issues»[31].

Most of these points were also addressed in the study area exploring the relationship between Hispanic ministry and leadership formation at the 2009 National Symposium. It would take more than this essay to adequately reflect on each one of them. Nevertheless, we believe that it is imperative that any conversation about leadership formation of pastoral leaders preparing to minister in u.s. ecclesial communities, and particularly in contexts where Latinos/as are present, begin by attentively studying these points and integrating them in their guidelines, curricula, and programs of ministerial formation. We commend the work of the universities, seminaries, pastoral institutes and diocesan programs that are already incorporating these points in their educational practices. However, these few institutions continue to be exceptions. The effectiveness of ministry in the 21st century will significantly depend on the ability of ecclesial and academic institutions to offer ministerial and theological formation that not only attracts Latinos/as, but also intentionally addresses the questions that culturally diverse communities are asking. In what ways will institutions of ministerial formation intentionally adopt a stance of cultural plurality and consider the implications of diversity for their programs? How open will the sectors of the Church that currently hold the decision-making power be to non-dominant voices? How much access will be given to Hispanic leaders who have pioneered initiatives to shape curriculum, methodologies, and programs?

---

28 Cfr. UNITED STATES CONFERENCE OF CATHOLIC BISHOPS, *Encuentro and Mission: A Renewed Pastoral Framework for Hispanic Ministry*, n. 55.3.b.

29 UNITED STATES CONFERENCE OF CATHOLIC BISHOPS, *Encuentro and Mission: A Renewed Pastoral Framework for Hispanic Ministry*, n. 55.4.a.

30 UNITED STATES CONFERENCE OF CATHOLIC BISHOPS, *Encuentro and Mission: A Renewed Pastoral Framework for Hispanic Ministry*, n. 57.4.a.

31 UNITED STATES CONFERENCE OF CATHOLIC BISHOPS, *Encuentro and Mission: A Renewed Pastoral Framework for Hispanic Ministry*, n. 57.4.b.

Support Structures for Hispanic Ministry and Leadership Formation

cᵔᵖᵕ

The Church's evangelizing mission also requires adequate structures and re-sources for its effectiveness. Without these the mission can only achieve limited results. It is clear that the evangelizing mission among u.s. Latino/a Catholics has benefitted from the creation of offices, networks, and movements at differ-ent levels: national, regional, diocesan, and parochial. These structures have been instrumental in advocating for issues related to u.s. Latinos/as in the Church and in the larger society. While some of these offices, organizations, and move-ments continue to contribute to the reflection about what it means to be His-panic and Catholic in the United States today, a number of them seem to be grad-ually giving way to new efforts and initiatives[32]. Whether they remain strong or disappear will significantly shape the present and future of Hispanic ministry and any initiatives of leadership formation among Hispanic Catholics.

1. THE VISION

The first decade of the 21st century provided several occasions for Latino/a Catholic leaders to reflect upon key questions about Hispanic leadership and ministerial formation. These moments of self-reflection were opportunities to assess the work that has been done and to envision potential changes to be implemented at various levels in the life of the Church.

The history of u.s. Hispanic Catholicism attests to the power of Hispanic ministry movements, gatherings, and meetings shaping the imagination of gen-erations of Latino/a leaders at different moments. Each series of events has con-tributed to the development of a common language, visions, and pastoral models that have influenced major shifts in Hispanic ministry during the last half a century. They responded to the particularity of the historical circumstances in which they occurred. Today we must discern what kind of initiatives will be most effective to bring Catholic Hispanic leaders together, what questions they need to discuss, and under what circumstances they need to meet. For instance, the process leading to the First National Encounter for Hispanic Youth and Young Adult Ministry in 2006 mobilized more than 40,000 young Latinos/as from

---

32 See Timothy Matovina's essay on Hispanic Ministry and u.s. Catholicism in this book.

around the country. This process simultaneously served as an opportunity to form young Latino/a leaders —an effort that is already yielding fruits in dioceses and parishes nationwide— and to provide Hispanic ministry with a new generation of allies and resources. The newness of this National Encounter resides in the kind of the leaders it involved, the particular goals it sought to accomplish, and the historical moment in which it occurred when 50 percent of all u.s. Catholics under the age of 18 are Hispanic[33].

Only forty years ago the Mexican American Cultural Center (MACC, now the Mexican American Catholic College) was technically the only pastoral institute training ministers of all cultural backgrounds to serve Latinos/as in the United States. Today, nearly twenty pastoral institutes associated in the *Federación de Institutos Pastorales* (FIP) serve in the process of ministerial formation of Spanish-speaking leaders alongside dozens of diocesan institutes of leadership formation, biblical institutes, and online programs in Spanish[34]. An increasing number of universities and seminaries are developing academic programs that integrate courses and initiatives in Hispanic theology and ministry, some of them in Spanish. The u.s. Catholic Bishops' fifth edition of the *Program of Priestly Formation* (2006) repeatedly recommends that seminarians learn Spanish —or another language depending on the pastoral needs of the local communities where the future priests will minister— and become familiar with Hispanic cultures[35]. In the words of *Encuentro and Mission*, «[t]his is no longer an option —it is a need»[36]. The emergence of national organizations like the National Catholic Council for Hispanic Ministry (NCCHM), the National Catholic Association of Diocesan Directors for Hispanic Ministry (NCADDHM), the Academy of Catholic Hispanic Theologians of the United States (ACHTUS), the National Association of Hispanic Priests (ANSH, Spanish acronym), and the National Catholic Network de Pastoral Juvenil Hispana – La Red was instrumental in

---

33 See Ken Johnson-Mondragón's essay on Hispanic Ministry, Youth and Young Adult Ministry in this book. Also, Cfr. NATIONAL CATHOLIC NETWORK DE PASTORAL JUVENIL HISPANA —LA RED, *Conclusions: First National Encounter for Hispanic Youth and Young Adult Ministry*, USCCB, Washington, D.C. 2008.

34 Cfr. CENTER FOR APPLIED RESEARCH IN THE APOSTOLATE (CARA), *Catholic Ministry Formation Enrollments: Statistical Overview for 2008-2009*, Washington, D.C. 2009, 30, http://cara.georgetown.edu/pubs/Overview200809.pdf (accessed March 19, 2010). See also http://www.fipusa.com/.

35 Cfr. UNITED STATES CONFERENCE OF CATHOLIC BISHOPS, *Program of Priestly Formation*, 5th edition, USCCB, Washington, D.C. 2006, n. 162, 172, 182, 228.

36 UNITED STATES CONFERENCE OF CATHOLIC BISHOPS, *Encuentro and Mission: A Renewed Pastoral Framework for Hispanic Ministry*, n. 55.2.c.

bringing together the voices of Latino/a leaders from around the country to plan major projects with a common vision[37]. The growth of the structural organization of Hispanic Catholicism in the second part of the 20th century was indeed remarkable.

Aware of such growth, diversity, and potential to form Hispanic ministry leaders, *Encuentro and Mission* recommended the affirmation and strengthening of these organizations and institutions. The document invited Hispanic ministry organizations and institutions to develop ties of mutual collaboration and work closely with ecclesial structures at different levels[38]. It is imperative that these organizations propose pathways for Latinos/as to move from basic levels of leadership in parishes and ecclesial movements to higher level education programs in institutes, universities and seminaries[39]. They must take advantage of their unique position to incorporate Hispanic ministry, theology, culture, and language in all instances of leadership formation in the life of the Church[40]. In doing so, they fulfill the double responsibility of forming Latinos/as to work with everyone in the Church as well as non-Hispanics to be more effective in Latino/a ecclesial contexts[41]. These are the organizations and institutions that Catholic Hispanic professionals will seek for guidance on how to better use their gifts in the Church[42]. Taking a prophetic stance, *Encuentro and Mission* clearly articulated that inter-dependent organizations and institutions in the Church had to assume the responsibility of providing culturally pluralistic education and formation to ministers working in Hispanic contexts.

---

37 NCCHM has successfully organized three major convocations of Catholic Hispanic leaders from around the country under the name *Raíces y Alas* (1992, 1996, 2003) to discuss and reflect on urgent issues related to Hispanic Ministry in the United States. A fourth convocation is being planned for the year 2010. Every year ACHTUS brings together dozens of Catholic U.S. Latino/a theologians during its annual Colloquium. In 2006 the National Catholic Network de Pastoral Juvenil Hispana –La Red organized the First National Encounter for Hispanic Youth and Young Adult Ministry.

38 Cfr. UNITED STATES CONFERENCE OF CATHOLIC BISHOPS, *Encuentro and Mission: A Renewed Pastoral Framework for Hispanic Ministry*, n. 48.

39 Cfr. UNITED STATES CONFERENCE OF CATHOLIC BISHOPS, *Encuentro and Mission: A Renewed Pastoral Framework for Hispanic Ministry*, n. 55.1.a.

40 Cfr. UNITED STATES CONFERENCE OF CATHOLIC BISHOPS, *Encuentro and Mission: A Renewed Pastoral Framework for Hispanic Ministry*, n. 55.2.c.

41 Cfr. UNITED STATES CONFERENCE OF CATHOLIC BISHOPS, *Encuentro and Mission: A Renewed Pastoral Framework for Hispanic Ministry*, n. 55.2.c.

42 Cfr. UNITED STATES CONFERENCE OF CATHOLIC BISHOPS, *Encuentro and Mission: A Renewed Pastoral Framework for Hispanic Ministry*, n. 56.3.c.

Among the various support structures available to ministers in the United States, the diocesan office of Hispanic ministry, when existent and adequately resourced, continues to be one of the most effective instruments to advance the Church's evangelizing mission with Latino/a Catholics. The diocesan office for Hispanic ministry should exist in the local church to

- «serve as a resource to parishes and other ministries»[43],
- «collaborate with schools, colleges, and universities, as well as with seminaries»[44],
- assist in the development of «catechetical, pastoral, and theological formation programs designed for Hispanics»[45],
- strengthen youth ministry initiatives[46],
- «promote legislation that supports educational opportunities for young people at risk and programs to reach new immigrants»[47],
- facilitate conversations related to ministry areas such as «youth, family, religious education, catechesis, liturgy, and advocacy»[48],
- «educate Hispanic Catholics about public policy issues and processes as well as basic community organizing skills… and promote political legislative action on issues affecting Hispanics and other Catholics, such as immigration, human rights, and education»[49], and
- actively participate in conversations about liturgical life in contexts where Latinos/as celebrate their faith[50].

A recent study on best practices in Hispanic ministry at the diocesan level concluded that a «well-established Office for Hispanic Ministry [OHM], has a competent director and/or staff in place, with direct access to the local ordinary who is bilingual to some degree. In arch/dioceses where Hispanic ministry is more

---

43 UNITED STATES CONFERENCE OF CATHOLIC BISHOPS, *Encuentro and Mission: A Renewed Pastoral Framework for Hispanic Ministry*, n. 57.2.a.

44 UNITED STATES CONFERENCE OF CATHOLIC BISHOPS, *Encuentro and Mission: A Renewed Pastoral Framework for Hispanic Ministry*, n. 55.2.a.

45 UNITED STATES CONFERENCE OF CATHOLIC BISHOPS, *Encuentro and Mission: A Renewed Pastoral Framework for Hispanic Ministry*, n. 55.3.a.

46 Cfr. UNITED STATES CONFERENCE OF CATHOLIC BISHOPS, *Encuentro and Mission: A Renewed Pastoral Framework for Hispanic Ministry*, 56.2.a.

47 UNITED STATES CONFERENCE OF CATHOLIC BISHOPS, *Encuentro and Mission: A Renewed Pastoral Framework for Hispanic Ministry*, n. 56.3.a.

48 UNITED STATES CONFERENCE OF CATHOLIC BISHOPS, *Encuentro and Mission: A Renewed Pastoral Framework for Hispanic Ministry*, n. 57.3.a.

49 UNITED STATES CONFERENCE OF CATHOLIC BISHOPS, *Encuentro and Mission: A Renewed Pastoral Framework for Hispanic Ministry*, n. 57.4.c.

50 Cfr. UNITED STATES CONFERENCE OF CATHOLIC BISHOPS, *Encuentro and Mission: A Renewed Pastoral Framework for Hispanic Ministry*, n. 58.3.a.

developed, the OHM is placed under direct supervision of the local ordinary or a member of the curia»[51]. Furthermore, «[b]est practice includes shared leadership, where Hispanics and other bilingual staff are members of the cabinet and other decision-making bodies in the arch/diocesan structure, and different ministerial offices have staff directly responsible for ministry development among Hispanics»[52]. This leadership model requires a sincere commitment on the part of bishops and diocesan leaders to make offices of Hispanic ministry integral components of their pastoral structures where collaboration with Latino/a leaders is valued and affirmed. The extent to which the Church can or cannot make these «best practices» standard practices will be the measure by which the institution will be effective in this regard.

.2. CHALLENGES

In past decades Latino/a leaders focused their attention on challenges such as marginalization, scarcity of resources, limited access to education, inadequate structures for leadership formation, and gathering space. Those challenges demanded specific responses and signaled that the time was ripe for the emergence of structures that made possible the growth of Hispanic ministry as currently we know it. While those situations still persist in many corners, today those involved in Hispanic ministry also see a new set of challenges that indicate that the time is ripe again to creatively renew present structures and give birth to new ones to further strengthen Hispanic ministry and leadership formation processes. Let us focus on three challenges.

First of all, as we mentioned above, in the early years of the 21st century U.S. Catholic witnessed the restructuring of several ecclesial organizations, the redefinition of the goals and identity of others, and the disappearance of quite a few. Restructuring has occurred nearly at every level: the USCCB, dioceses, parishes, and ministry networks. In this process, ecclesial structures supporting Hispanic ministry and programs of leadership formation have been significantly affected. Some dioceses and parishes have closed or reconfigured offices of Hispanic ministry, sometimes integrating them in multi-ministry offices with small budg-

---

51 UNITED STATES CONFERENCE OF CATHOLIC BISHOPS, COMMITTEE ON HISPANIC AFFAIRS, *Study On Best Practices for Diocesan Ministry among Hispanics/Latinos*, USCCB, Washington, D.C. 2006, 3, 5, 8. Resource available online at http://www.usccb.org/hispanicaffairs/BestPractices2. pdf (accessed March 26, 2010).

52 UNITED STATES CONFERENCE OF CATHOLIC BISHOPS, *Encuentro and Mission: A Renewed Pastoral Framework for Hispanic Ministry*, n. 9.

ets and an unclear sense of their actual mission. Economic bottom lines continue to burden Hispanic ministry and programs of leadership formation. A few structures have disappeared (e.g. National Organization for Catechesis with Hispanics, NOCH). Some regional offices for Hispanic ministry closed and others have lost vital sources of funding. A significant number of Hispanic pastoral leaders have lost their jobs and many lay women and men holding academic credentials do not see the prospects of job security in the Church and opt to work in the public sector or other private institutions. Despite these changes the Catholic Church continues to grow, due in large part to the millions of Catholic immigrants from predominantly Spanish-speaking countries now residing in the U.S. With several million more people to serve, the Church must continue its evangelizing mission yet with smaller budgets, less staff and limited resources to support the work of pastoral leaders. Support structures in every institution require change and adaptation. However, we must ask: what will be the operative method for restructuring, whose voices will be included, what languages will be considered and how will the goals hoped for be defined? Will the Church provide a prophetic example?

The second major challenge relates to the impact of the weakening of Hispanic ministry support structures of leadership and leadership formation established in the last decades. Based on the data gathered from a recent survey of twenty National and Regional Hispanic Catholic Ministry Organizational Initiatives commissioned by Fr. Allan Figueroa-Deck[53] in 2009, there is evidence that reducing resources for diocesan and parochial offices that work directly with U.S. Latinos/as is adversely affecting Hispanic ministry networks and consequently the institutions associated with them. The study revealed that the majority of these organizations have less than 5 staff members[54]; most address general issues related to Hispanic ministry and only a handful specialize in a particular ministry within Hispanic ministry[55]; the largest number of participants who benefit directly from the services offered by these organizations are lay women, followed by youth/young adults, priests, religious sisters and deacons[56]; 58 percent of the organizations have an annual organizational budget of

---

53 Fr. Allan Figueroa-Deck SJ is the first Executive Director of the newly created Secretariat for Cultural Diversity in the Church at the USCCB.

54 Cfr. DINGES W.D., *National and Regional Hispanic Catholic Ministry Organizational Initiatives: An Assessment*, Life Cycle Institute at The Catholic University of America, Washington, D.C. 2009, 5.

55 Cfr. UNITED STATES CONFERENCE OF CATHOLIC BISHOPS, *Encuentro and Mission: A Renewed Pastoral Framework for Hispanic Ministry*, n. 6.

56 Cfr. UNITED STATES CONFERENCE OF CATHOLIC BISHOPS, *Encuentro and Mission: A Renewed Pastoral Framework for Hispanic Ministry*, n. 9.

less than $50,000[57]; the heads of half of these organizations are salaried employees and the heads of the other half are volunteers[58]. Their major concerns focus on the lack of adequately trained leaders, the need to reinvent themselves each time there is change of leadership[59], and the fact that dioceses do not recognize their services as a priority[60]. The weakening of these organizational structures undoubtedly has a negative impact on initiatives for leadership formation among Catholic Hispanics. When diocesan and parochial offices of Hispanic ministry close their doors or become something else, Hispanic ministry support structures and networks lose membership, financial resources, and the potential beneficiaries of their services.

The third challenge relates to the redefinition of identities among major structures supporting Hispanic ministry. This challenge is in part the immediate result of the weakening of Hispanic ministry networks and some specialized offices serving Hispanic Catholics. The reduction of resources has led to three major situations: some of the Hispanic ministry support structures have disappeared (e.g. diocesan offices, national networks); others have shifted their *modus operandi* adopting a survival mode; others are exploring new partnerships with mainstream non-Hispanic ministry networks (a necessary process according to some, troublesome according to others). Hispanic leaders are very familiar with the first two. The third situation requires further commentary. Thanks to the increasing number of Hispanics throughout the country, mainstream ministry organizations have intensified their outreach to Latino/a leaders to join their ranks. At the same time, many Hispanic leaders have come to the conclusion that in a Church where Latinos/as constitute almost half of the Catholic population, uniting efforts with those ministry organizations that have a stronger voice and more resources is a wise strategy. Here we perceive a sense of intentional mutuality inspired by a common mission. Yet, at the practical level there are major questions that need to be addressed if such collaboration is to yield fruitful results. For the most part, mainstream ministry organizations have taken

---

57 Cfr. UNITED STATES CONFERENCE OF CATHOLIC BISHOPS, *Encuentro and Mission: A Renewed Pastoral Framework for Hispanic Ministry*, n. 12.

58 Cfr. UNITED STATES CONFERENCE OF CATHOLIC BISHOPS, *Encuentro and Mission: A Renewed Pastoral Framework for Hispanic Ministry*, n. 12.

59 Cfr. UNITED STATES CONFERENCE OF CATHOLIC BISHOPS, *Encuentro and Mission: A Renewed Pastoral Framework for Hispanic Ministry*, n. 16.

60 Cfr. UNITED STATES CONFERENCE OF CATHOLIC BISHOPS, *Encuentro and Mission: A Renewed Pastoral Framework for Hispanic Ministry*, n. 17.

too long to fully engage the complexity of the u.s. Hispanic experience and to adjust their agendas to reflect the concerns and questions of a culturally diverse Church. Often times the expectation is that Latinos/as —and others who are not considered mainstream— must accommodate to «business as usual» and «learn how things are done». Such attitude is reflected in ministry initiatives where Latino/a leaders are not present as creative minds at the very beginning of their reflections or are invited simply as consultants or asked to provide «a Hispanic perspective». New partnerships demand openness to new voices, new ways of seeing, and even new ways of proceeding. Failure to integrate Hispanic leadership *now*, considering the rapid growth of Hispanics in the Church, will undermine the good efforts of many of these ministry organizations. At the same time, Hispanic leaders have the obligation to continuously review strategies and commitments. Many of us need to widen the vision of Hispanic ministry as an effort that includes working with Spanish-speaking immigrants but cannot be limited to it because the u.s. Latino/a experience is much larger and more complex. Also, we need to overcome feelings of distrust towards others who do not share our most immediate concerns. It is imperative that more Latino/a leaders join the already existing ministry networks and become active participants in them. Hispanic ministry organizations can and must exist in this context to better articulate Hispanic perspectives. However, the affirmation of the work of these organizations does not exclude the necessary collaboration with mainstream, larger ministry networks. As the u.s. Catholic population in the 21ˢᵗ century becomes increasingly Hispanic, current ministry structures, networks, and organizations will have Latinos/as leading them and the topics of reflection will be determined according to the reality of our faith communities rather than according to predefined agendas. These partnerships must lead to renewed visions for leadership formation.

3
Conclusion

As Catholic theologians we offer the previous reflections about ministry and leadership formation within the context of the u.s. Hispanic experience as a starting point for further conversations. The 2009 National Symposium on the Present and Future of Catholic Hispanic Ministry in the United States at Boston

College was truly an opportunity to identify some of the most urgent questions in the minds of contemporary Hispanic Catholic leaders. The two areas we chose to explore in this essay (effective leadership and support structures for Hispanic ministry and leadership formation) bring together several of these questions. We must address them immediately, building on the wisdom of decades of *memoria histórica*, dialoguing with different voices in the Church, and looking at the future with renewed hope. We invite further conversation with Church leaders and theologians about leadership formation for ministry with a focus on the Latino/a Catholic experience in the United States. Such conversation requires authentic collaboration between lay and ordained leaders in the culturally diverse ecclesial communities where we share our faith and envision fresh models of leadership formation for the Church.

We invite Church leaders to remain attentive to how this conversation unfolds in the following forums: 1) the Federación of Institutos Pastorales (Federation of Pastoral Institutes); 2) national initiatives to articulate theologies and standards for lay ecclesial ministry; 3) the Academy of Catholic Hispanic Theologians of the United States (ACHTUS) and its sister networks of U.S. Catholic theologians; 4) the work of Catholic universities developing programs of Hispanic ministry and theology; 5) mainstream ministry networks; 6) national Hispanic ministry networks; and 7) the initiatives sponsored by the newly created Secretariat for Cultural Diversity in the Church at the USCCB. Our hope is that all these groups and voices will find ways to unite efforts, reflect *en conjunto*, and together propose a vision that makes the Church a stronger presence in our society in order to bring women and men closer to Jesus Christ.

EXCURSUS TO CHAPTER 7
On the Need for Inclusive Theological Reflection on Ministry and Leadership Formation

U.S. Catholics have been remarkably creative in the development of theological reflections on ministry and pastoral leadership, particularly in the decades following the Second Vatican Council. Without a doubt those reflections, articulated simultaneously in academic and pastoral contexts, have strongly influenced many of the Church's documents on lay and ordained ministry. U.S. Hispanic

Catholics have not been absent from these theological developments. Perhaps our most significant contribution as Latino/a theologians and pastoral leaders is the grounding of our reflections about ministry and leadership primarily on the lived experience of Latinos/as in the Church and in the larger society. By doing this, our theological reflections honor the particular experiences of Hispanic women and men in the immediacy of our ecclesial realities while remaining attentive to the culturally diverse nature of the ecclesial context in which we live.

1

Contexts, Themes, Sources

194

Among the many vibrant exchanges about ministry and leadership formation in our country today, Hispanic Catholics have a particular interest in conversations addressing lay ecclesial ministry[61], standards for ministry[62], and models of ministry in a diverse Church[63]. The participation of Latinos/as in these conversations is crucial in order to affirm the insights gained from processes such as the Encuentros, major documents on u.s. Hispanic Catholicism, and the contributions of the members of the Academy of Catholic Hispanic Theologians of the United States (ACHTUS).

---

61 Particularly the revision of documents such as *Co-Workers in the Vineyard of the Lord* and the development of theologies of lay ecclesial ministry in culturally diverse contexts.

62 The Federation of Pastoral Institutes / Federación de Institutos Pastorales (FIP) is an organization that brings together national, regional, diocesan and local institutes, committed to the formation and enrichment of Hispanic people at all levels and in their historic and cultural context. FIP is currently working on an updated version of its accreditation manual for pastoral leadership and the guidelines that member institutes will follow to excel in the formation for ministerial leadership of Catholic Hispanics enrolled in their programs. Various members of FIP actively participated in the conversation about Hispanic ministry and leadership formation during the 2009 National Symposium. More information about FIP is found at http://www.fipusa.com/.

63 See for instance Timothy Matovina's proposed approaches to Hispanic ministry in his essay in this book. Dr. Matovina will offer a slightly revised version of these approaches in a forthcoming book on Hispanic Catholicism. We are grateful to him for sharing a draft version of several chapters of this work. See also FIGUEROA-DECK A., «Models» in FIGUEROA-DECK A., TARANGO Y., and MATOVINA T. (eds.), *Perspectivas: Hispanic Ministry*, Sheed & Ward, Kansas City, MO 1995; JOHNSON-MONDRAGÓN K., «Ministry in Multicultural and National/Ethnic Parishes: Evaluating the Findings of the Emerging Models of Pastoral Leadership Project», Emerging Models of Pastoral Leadership Project, 2008, http://www.emergingmodels.org/doc/Multicultural%20 Report%20%282%29.pdf (accessed April 5, 2010).

There is no one perspective that fully captures the complexity of the Hispanic Catholic experience in the United States. Yet, it is possible to identify several elements in our shared experience that enrich conversations about ministry and leadership formation. U.S. Hispanic Catholics draw on powerful theological categories and a model of *teología de conjunto* that constitute a rich tradition that informs many of our conversations. From the Latin American ecclesial experience we have inherited theological categories such as the preferential option for the poor, the power of small ecclesial communities, and the missionary character of pastoral action in all its expressions. Rooted in our experience as Hispanic Catholics in the United States we continue to reflect about what it means to minister in *in-between* contexts such as mestizaje, exile, and social marginalization. A number of Hispanic Catholic thinkers are engaged in ecumenical explorations in light of the particularity of the Latino/a experience in the United States. Others are advancing reflections on intercultural perspectives about theology and ministry. From these conversations emerge key insights that Latino/a Catholics offer to further the conversations about ministry and leadership formation. In the pluralistic context in which U.S. Catholics share our faith, inclusive theologies of ministry need to incorporate these theological contributions.

The task of attending to Hispanic theological insights on ministry and leadership formation is a twofold process. On the one hand it requires revisiting the *memoria histórica* of the Latino/a Catholic community in the United States for the sake of understanding the origin and context of the categories that permeate our language and our reflections[64]. On the other hand, Latino/a theologians and ministry leaders must continuously create new categories and models to appropriately shape the formation of lay and ordained ministers in the culturally diverse context in which the Church in the United States is inserted. Many of those categories and models need to be developed in conversation with the different voices that constitute our ecclesial communities throughout the country. Latino/a contributions will then emerge from both an adequate understanding of the historical memory of the various Hispanic communities in the Church in the United States and the creative development of categories that respond to the most urgent questions emerging from our present, shared reality. This reflective process is certainly an invitation to go beyond the idea of simply

---

64 The essay by Jorge Presmaness and Alicia Marill in this book, for example, highlights some key ecclesiological categories that emerged from the various Encuentro processes which have shaped the understanding of ministerial leadership in many sectors of Hispanic ministry.

adding a «Hispanic perspective» to pre-established notions of ministry and leadership formation.

2

Important Considerations

As Catholics in the United States we are part of a new moment in our shared history and thus must work together to respond to the challenges that the 21ˢᵗ century has brought to our attention regarding formation for ministerial leadership. Because Hispanic Catholics are committed to share our contributions and concerns with the rest of the u.s. Catholic community in order to respond to these challenges, it is pertinent that we raise some important questions.

a) Mainstream definitions of ministry in the United States, both theologically and organizationally, often reflect perspectives that fail to take into consideration the voices of groups that are still deemed minorities —even when numerically those groups together constitute the majority of all u.s. Catholics. We must then ask some important questions: what do we mean when we speak of ministry? What kind of ministry are we forming our pastoral leaders for? How are theological reflections about ministerial formation addressing the questions emerging from all sectors of the Church, particularly from the marginalized? How do we include members of all communities to provide initial directions to answer such questions? This demands that we make preferential options in our reflections and the ways we form leaders in the Church.

b) Lay ecclesial ministers are the fastest growing body of women and men involved in pastoral service in the Church in the United States[65]. Their work and formation are at the center of conversations about professional standards that seek to guarantee quality and effectiveness. The collaborative effort of three national ministry organizations[66] led to the publication in 2003 of a common set of certification standards for lay ministry for their membership. In 2006 a new expanded edition of the standards was published adding the input of the Na-

---

65 Cfr. DᴇLAMBO D., *Lay Parish Ministers: A Study of Emerging Leadership*, National Pastoral Life Center, New York 2005, 44.

66 The three organizations are: the National Association for Lay Ministry (NALM), the National Conference for Catechetical Leadership (NCCL), and the National Federation for Catholic Youth Ministry (NFCYM).

tional Association of Pastoral Musicians (NPM). Both editions were approved by the United States Catholic Conference of Bishops' Commission on Certification and Accreditation. At the time of this writing, a new effort has been set in motion to review such standards and a new national alliance of ministry organizations has assumed the responsibility of leading the process[67]. Though large Hispanic ministry organizations are generally aware of the current standards and many use them in their formation programs, it is striking that among the members of the new alliance no Hispanic ministry network plays a leading role. How will Hispanic perspectives influence the core drafts of the new document? It is true that major organizations have Latino/a members, but in most cases these are very few in number. Are isolated consultations with some Hispanic leaders enough when such standards hope to regulate ministry for thousands of pastoral leaders in a Church where Latinos/as will soon constitute 50 percent of the Catholic population? What kind of ecclesiology is at play when major ministry organizations advance projects of this kind without affirming the leadership initiatives of Catholic Latinos/as and our organizations? The absence of a more meaningful participation of Hispanic leaders in these processes is a missed opportunity in the culturally diverse context in which we live.

c) The main locus of ministerial leadership in many sectors of the Church in the United States is widely assumed to be diocesan and parochial offices. Though such offices are important in many ways, U.S. Latino/a Catholics are also aware that many of our leaders are primarily formed and sustained in the context of ecclesial movements (e.g. Charismatic Renewal, Cursillo, small ecclesial communities) and many of our most effective leaders are evangelizing in their homes and neighborhoods. A contemporary theology of ministry must clearly affirm the meaning of *lo cotidiano* (the everyday) in the context of leadership and recognize the contributions of diverse spiritualities that sustain the lives of many lay leaders and their communities. How can we integrate these contributions and spiritualities into a wider theological reflection about ministry?

d) The largest sector of Hispanic Catholics in the United States is constituted by *jóvenes*. For decades Latino/a leaders have called for renewed attention to young Latinos/as since they are the present and the future of the Church in this

---

67 The Alliance member organizations are: Federation of Diocesan Liturgical Commissions, National Association for Lay Ministry, National Association of Pastoral Musicians, National Conference for Catechetical Leadership, and National Federation for Catholic Youth Ministry.

country[68]. What theological questions are young Latinos/as asking? How does the young Latino community challenge the way Catholics in the United States understand our relationship with the God of life through Jesus Christ in the Church? Thanks to the excellent work of organizations like Instituto Fe y Vida, the South East Pastoral Institute, and the network involved in the organization of the First National Encounter for Hispanic Youth and Young Adult Ministry, theological reflections about ministerial leadership have been significantly enriched with important and challenging questions that young Latinos/as have put forward to the entire Church in the United States[69]. Some of these questions are present in various ways in the conclusions of the First National Encounter for Hispanic Youth and Young Adult Ministry. For instance, young Latinos/as state:

- «[We need] personnel trained in *PJH* [*Pastoral Juvenil Hispana*] in diocesan offices and parishes; greater openness and attention from pastoral leaders and parishes, which translates into more participation of the *jóvenes* in the mission of the Church».

- There is need to foster «the creation of small communities of *PJH*, with an openness to people of other cultures and equal rights in the various activities of the Church»[70].

Do our programs of leadership formation train ministers who can effectively embrace and respond to the everyday reality of u.s. Hispanic youth? How are we empowering Hispanic youth to participate in the mission of the Church? Does our way of doing ministry affirm the contributions of small ecclesial communities to the u.s. Catholic experience? How do leaders in the Church sincerely affirm the gift of cultural diversity? What circumstances in the Church and in the larger society limit the full participation of Hispanic youth? We cannot afford to ignore such questions in our theological reflections and in our programs of ministerial leadership formation.

---

68 Cfr. *Prophetic Voices: Document on the Process of the III Encuentro Nacional Hispano de Pastoral*, USCC, Washington, D.C. 1986, n. 40-42, in UNITED STATES CONFERENCE OF CATHOLIC BISHOPS, *Hispanic Ministry: Three Major Documents*, USCCB, Washington, D.C. 1995; NATIONAL CONFERENCE OF CATHOLIC BISHOPS, *National Pastoral Plan for Hispanic Ministry*, USCC, Washington, D.C. 1987, n. 64-66, in USCCB, *Hispanic Ministry: Three Major Documents*, *Encuentro and Mission*, n. 55.2.a.b.; 70.

69 NATIONAL CATHOLIC NETWORK DE PASTORAL JUVENIL HISPANA —LA RED, *Conclusions: First National Encounter for Hispanic Youth and Young Adult Ministry*, USCCB, Washington, D.C. 2008.

70 NATIONAL CATHOLIC NETWORK DE PASTORAL JUVENIL HISPANA —LA RED, *Conclusiones: Primer Encuentro Nacional de Pastoral Juvenil Hispana*, Jo-16, p. 50.

e) For U.S. Latino/a Catholics the relationship between faith and culture has continuously been at the forefront of our reflections. How we live our faith is deeply shaped by how we live *lo cotidiano*, our customs, languages, traditions and practices. Likewise, how we interpret our *latinidad* is deeply informed by our Catholicism. Formation for ministerial leadership in Hispanic contexts cannot ignore the importance of Latino cultures. Because Latinos/as live our faith in a culturally diverse context, it is imperative that we develop intercultural theologies, methodologies of ministry and models of ministerial formation that honor the particularity of the Latino/a experiences. However, we must interpret these in dialogue with the experiences of women and men from other ethnic and cultural groups with whom we share and celebrate our Catholic identity. U.S. Latino/a Catholic theologians have done groundbreaking work setting the foundations of what is called an intercultural theology[71]. Such theology, according to U.S. Catholic theologian María Pilar Aquino, confronts all conditions of oppression and leads to integral liberation, builds on the platform of solidarity, engages the pluralistic dimension of reality, affirms difference, and seriously takes into consideration the historical and cultural experience of the people in their communities[72]. This is Catholic theology at its best. Thus, it becomes imperative that these insights be present in the processes of reflection about ministry and leadership formation in our communities.

f) Lastly, the day-to-day dynamic of pastoral work with Latinos/as normally unfolds in the particularity of parishes where frequently lay and ordained leaders from different generations and cultures hold a variety of ministerial perspectives that coexist in tension. The encounter of these perspectives in the life of the parish can be read as the encounter of diverse theologies of ministry that are shaped by particular socio-cultural experiences. We ask then, is it possible to speak of a theology of ministry within an ecclesiological framework that affirms the uniqueness of each of these perspectives, fosters a healthy tension among them, and leads to new forms of creative ministry? What needs to be

---

71 Cfr. AQUINO M.P., «Theological Method in U.S. Latino/a Theology: Toward an Intercultural Theology for the Third Millennium» in ESPÍN O. and DÍAZ M. (eds.), *From the Heart of Our People: Latino/a Explorations in Catholic Systematic Theology*, Orbis, Maryknoll, NY 1999, 6-48; ESPÍN O., «Toward the Construction of an Intercultural Theology of (Catholic) Tradition» in ESPÍN O., *Grace and Humanness: Theological Reflections Because of Culture*, Orbis Books, Maryknoll, NY 2007, 1-50; OSPINO H., «Foundations for an Intercultural Philosophy of Christian Education» in *Religious Education* 104, n.3 (2009) 303-314.

72 Cfr. AQUINO M.P., «Theological Method in U.S. Latino/a Theology: Toward an Intercultural Theology for the Third Millennium», 19-20.

done to integrate such theological perspectives in the processes of ministerial formation, from seminaries and universities to diocesan and parish leadership programs? How do we appropriately address cultural differences? These questions require the attention of theologians and pastoral ministers working *en conjunto.*

The above are not the only questions that occupy the minds and hearts of U.S. Latino/a Catholic leaders and theologians reflecting on Hispanic ministry and leadership formation. Nevertheless, these are among the most important concerns that require our most immediate attention at this historical juncture. It is urgent that pastoral leaders and theologians, Hispanic and non-Hispanic, make a concerted effort to address these questions in our works, our periodic meetings, conferences, and scholarly investigations in order to find the most appropriate language and directions to articulate our perspectives as a community of discourse rooted in a common faith. By doing so, we will then be in a better position to join broader conversations about ministry and leadership formation in the culturally diverse context in which we live our faith today[73].

---

[73] A good example of this reflection on what it means to be Catholic in a culturally diverse Church is the process and conclusions of the Encuentro 2000, http://www.usccb.org/hispanicaffairs/encuentro.shtml. See also the resources from the various conversations during the Catholic Cultural Diversity Network Convocation organized by the USCCB Secretariat for Cultural Diversity in the Church in May 2010, http://usccb.org/ccdnc/.

Address to the National Symposium on the Present and Future of Catholic Hispanic Ministry in the United States

The Most Rev. JOSÉ H. GÓMEZ, S.T.D. *Coadjutor Archbishop of Los Angeles,*

Chairman, U.S. Bishops' Committee on Cultural Diversity in 2009

June 8, 2009

Boston College

(At the time of the Symposium,
Archbishop Gómez served as the head of the
Archdiocese of San Antonio, TX.)

¡*Un saludo cordial muy queridos hermanos y hermanas!* It is great to be with you, my friends. I am honored to be invited to share my thoughts with such a distinguished group.

My friend, Hosffman Ospino, has asked me to talk about three issues: first, the major challenges facing Hispanic Catholics; secondly, the paths that we as leaders should take in addressing these challenges; and finally, some thoughts on how we might take initiative at this historic moment in which our people are about to become «numerical majority» in the United States.

I am happy to try to talk about all these things. But I want to start with some recent news items. As you all know, President Obama has recently nominated two Hispanics to high positions —a Cuban-American Catholic, Dr. Miguel Díaz, to be his Ambassador to the Vatican, and a Puerto Rican who was raised Catholic to serve on the Supreme Court, Judge Sonia Sotomayor.

I do not know either of these nominees, personally. But I find their biographies, as I have read them in the press, to be quite inspiring. And as I thought about what to say to you today, it occurred to me that their stories tell us a lot about our people and their experience over the last few generations in this country.

Dr. Díaz was born in Havana and is the son of a restaurant waiter. He is the first person in his family to attend college and he has gone on to become a respected theologian; he is very active in the Church, and is the father of four children.

Judge Sotomayor has an even more dramatic background. Her father died when she was 9 and she was raised in the Bronx. Her mother worked hard and sacrificed to send both her and her brother to Catholic schools all the way through high school. According to statements from the White House and from people who know her, Judge Sotomayor is no longer a practicing Catholic and indeed does not practice any religion.

Now, let me make myself clear. The reason I mention Professor Díaz and Judge Sotomayor has nothing to do with politics. I'm not interested in making any judgments on their religious faith, or their political views, or their qualifications for the posts for which they have been nominated. I mention them because I think their paths are instructive as we consider the future of our ministry to our Hispanic people.

Let me explain.

Here we have two leading Hispanics. Each has risen, within one generation —from homes where the parents had very limited educations and very little economic means— to achieve among the highest ranks in his or her respective fields. Each is now in line for a very prominent position in the government of this country. Each is a great «success story» of Hispanic immigration; the one continues to practice the Catholic faith he was brought up in, while the other does not.

In these two nominees we have a snapshot of larger patterns of religious practice and affiliation among our Hispanic population. The Pew Religious Landscape Survey from last year, and the Trinity College American Religious Identification Survey, which came out about a month ago, reach similar conclusions about the faith of our people. About 58 percent of Hispanics identify themselves as Catholic; about one quarter identify themselves as some brand of Protestant Christian; and between 10 and 12 percent describe themselves as having no religion.

These percentages represent a big change from 20 years ago, and even from 10 years ago. The number of Hispanics self-identifying as Catholics has declined from nearly 100 percent in just two decades, while the number who describe themselves as Protestant has nearly doubled, and the number saying they have «no religion» has also doubled.

I'm not a big believer in polls about religious beliefs and practice. But in this case the polls reflect pastoral experience on the ground and provide us with a graphic measure of what I believe to be the biggest challenge facing Hispanic Catholics in the years ahead.

Let me state the challenge bluntly and then explain what I mean. I'll put it in terms of the question that Jesus Christ once asked: *Pero, cuando el Hijo del hombre venga, ¿encontrará fe sobre la tierra?* «Nevertheless, when the Son of Man comes, will he find faith on earth?» (Luke 18:8)

That's the challenge, my friends. As Hispanics become more and more successful, more and more assimilated into the American mainstream, will they keep the faith? Which path are they going to follow? Will they stay Catholic or will they drift away —to Protestant denominations, to some variety of vague spirituality, or to no religion at all?

What will their relationship be to the Catholic Church? Will they live by the Church's teachings and promote and defend these teachings in the public square? Or will their Catholicism simply become a kind of «cultural» background, a personality trait, a part of their upbringing that shapes their perspective on the world but compels no allegiance or devotion to the Church?

These are all open questions as we move into the early 21st century. And the stakes are high, friends. Because historically speaking, Hispanics have always been more than an ethnic group. To be Hispanic has always been to be Catholic.

There are many factors involved in this drift. There is the simple reality of our relentless consumer culture. «Shopping around» is more than a metaphor for Americans, it is a way of life. People shop for churches and religions like they do everything else, and Hispanics in this country are no different. It's also true that Protestant proselytizers have been successful in playing on the poverty and insecurity of our people —by preaching a seductive «Gospel of wealth».

Another factor: we cannot underestimate the impact —let's be frank— of racism, both in American society and unfortunately in the Church. Our ugly, unproductive, and unfinished national debate over immigration has exposed that. If our people feel scapegoated in society and marginalized in Catholic life, it's only natural that they would look around for someplace that might welcome them and treat them with the dignity they deserve. And unfortunately, some people are going to reject Christianity altogether because they experience Christians treating them in ways that are not very Christian.

These are problems. But I think the most serious problem we face comes not so much from these factors as from the dominant culture in the United States, which is aggressively, even militantly secularized. This is a subject that unfortunately doesn't get much attention at all in discussions about the future of Hispanic ministry. But it's time that we change that.

In fact, I believe that unless we, as Hispanic leaders, develop a strategy for understanding and dealing with the secular culture, our pastoral plans and programs will never achieve the success we would hope for.

1

The Challenge of Secular Culture

Let me be clear about what I mean by secularized culture. There is a sociological theory that holds that secularization is the inevitable, almost natural outcome of modernization. In other words, religious faith is supposed to fade away and eventually disappear as a society becomes more technologically advanced, more educated and sophisticated. That theory might be a good explanation for how secularization happened in Europe. But here in the United States, secularization has involved a deliberate strategy of «de-Christianization», carried out by cultural elites over many years.

There is a good scholarly book on this called «The Secular Revolution», edited by Christian Smith of the University of North Carolina. Smith and his colleagues show how secularization was carried out by powerful interest groups in the areas of law and public policy, education, and the media.

The result is that what I call «practical atheism» has become the de facto state religion in America. The price of participation in our economic, political, and social life is that we essentially have to agree to conduct ourselves as if God does not exist. We can't talk about religion or faith in the workplace or in the public square. Sure, people still do, but those people are dismissed as zealots or «the Christian right».

This is all very strange for a country that was founded by Christians —in fact by Hispanic Catholics. Indeed, where I'm from, in San Antonio, the Gospel was being preached in Spanish and Holy Mass was being celebrated by Hispanics before George Washington was born. Before there was a Congress. Before there was a Wall Street.

But today, religion in the u.s. has been reduced to the area of private devotion and subjective emotion. Religion is something we do on Sundays or in our families, but is not allowed to have any influence on what we do the rest of the week —in our work, in our civic life. This separation of religion from public life has led to lots of other problems in our country. It has contributed to the rise of moral relativism, the presumption that there are no truths in the moral order, only different opinions, and points of view.

And more to my point —secularization has an «alarming effect» on everyone's practice of religion. We see this in the rise of the number of people who say they practice no religion at all. Never before in the history of our country have so many people lived without any day-to-day awareness of God. They don't hate God like atheists do. They've just forgotten who he is.

These secularizing forces put forth even more pressure on Hispanics and other immigrant groups. Why? Because immigrants already face severe demands to «fit in», to downplay what is culturally and religiously distinct about them; to prove that they are «real» Americans, too. A generation ago, we can hardly imagine a Hispanic saying he or she had «no religion», yet that number has doubled in just the past few years.

My friends, I believe we need to think hard about our culture. The first missionaries to this country studied the indigenous cultures in order to evangelize. We need to do the same thing. We need an approach to culture that is broader than concentrating simply on ministering to Hispanics. Definitely, we need to raise up Hispanic Catholics leaders, and we need a pastoral plan to educate Hispanics in the faith and to nourish them with the sacraments. But this must be part of a wider evangelical strategy. We need to commit ourselves again to the work of re-evangelization, to preaching the Gospel again to America.

I want to talk more about these things in a minute.

2
The Challenge of Poverty —Material and Spiritual

But before I do, I want to mention the second critical challenge that I think we face as Hispanic leaders. I'm going to label this second challenge —«poverty: material and spiritual».

In general terms, Hispanics in this country are following the classic immigrant model. The second and third generations of Hispanics are much better educated, much more fluent in the dominant language, and are living at a higher economic standard of living than the first generation.

But the troubling fact is that still about one-quarter of all Hispanics, no matter what generation, are living below the poverty line. And that number does not seem to be improving very much from generation to generation. Combine that with high school dropout rates of about 22 percent, and a dramatic rise in the number of Hispanic children being raised in single-parent homes —both strong indicators of future poverty— and I worry that we may be ministering to a permanent Hispanic underclass.

We have moral and social problems too. Our people have some of the highest rates of teen pregnancy, abortion, and out-of-wedlock births, of any ethnic group in the country. These are things we don't talk about enough. But we cannot write these issues off as just «conservative issues».

The hard truth is that many of our young people are making bad moral decisions that have enormous and permanent consequences —not only for them, but for our society and for the future of Hispanic culture in America. To my mind, these are serious «justice» issues. If we want justice for our young people, if we want what God wants for them —lives worthy of their great dignity as his sons and daughters— then we need to find ways to teach our young people virtue, self-discipline, and personal responsibility. Any realistic assessment of the future of our ministry must include consideration of these issues. Any meaningful pastoral plan must address this challenge.

3
The Only Path for Leadership: Jesus Christ

Ok. So far I have answered Hosffman's first question —the challenges I see facing our Hispanic people. Broadly speaking I've identified those challenges as the aggressive secular culture in the u.s., and the realities of material and spiritual poverty among our people.

Now for Hosffman's second question —what paths we should pursue in addressing these challenges.

My answer to this question is short —two words: Jesus Christ.

Jesus Christ has to be our way, our truth, and our life —for each of us personally and for our ministry as a whole. There can be no other path, no other paradigm or model for Hispanic ministry.

The only «reason» that Hispanic ministry exists in the first place is to fulfill the calling of Christ, the mission that he gave to his Church —to preach repentance and forgiveness of sins in his name to all nations, to baptize and make disciples, and to spread his teachings.

Hispanic ministry should mean only one thing —bringing Hispanic people to the encounter with Jesus Christ in his Church. Too often, I'm afraid, we lose sight of that. We get caught up in thinking about our plans, our programs; who has control; what's going on in the bureaucracy. Our intentions are always good. We want to find the best means to help our people. My worry is that we concentrate so much on the «means» that we end up mistaking the means for the end.

All our pastoral plans and programs presume that we are trying to serve Christ and his Gospel. But my brothers and sisters we can no longer simply *presume* Christ. We must make sure we are *proclaiming* him.

The proclamation of Jesus Christ must be the criterion against which we measure everything we do in Hispanic ministry. Are we making new disciples? Are we strengthening the faith of those who have already been made disciples? Is the knowledge and love of Christ spreading through our work?

The mission that Christ gave to his Church can be summed up in two words: preaching and teaching. *La predicación y la enseñanza.* Proclaiming the good news of salvation and teaching men and women to live according to all that Christ commanded. This is a good way for us to think about and organize our pastoral response to the challenges I have identified. Preaching and teaching. *La predicación y la enseñanza.*

4

La predicación y la enseñanza

First, we need to preach the Gospel. «The New Evangelization» has become a buzzword or catchphrase in the Church. This is good. It must now become a way of life, a way of discipleship, the basic mandate for our every ministry.

In our Hispanic ministries, we must understand that we are preaching the Good News to the poor. This is the reality, my friends. Many of our people are poor now and they are going to be poor for many years. They face discrimination and exploitation because of their poverty and their race. Millions of them are forced to live in the shadows because our lawmakers are not yet brave enough to fix our broken immigration system.

We need to preach the Good News of Christ to them. But we also need to show them that good news in action. I am more and more convinced that we must address the issues of Hispanic poverty with an intense practical emphasis on education —education in general and education in the faith.

Every expert on poverty tells us that education is the one key to getting out of it. That means, in the first place, we need to get those Hispanic drop-out rates down. It means we need to find new ways to keep our kids chaste and in school, and to instill in them the value of education. We need to push for real improvements in public education, and in public support for private education, especially in our poorest school districts. And we need to assemble all the resources of our own network of Catholic schools to meet this challenge.

Educating our people in the faith should also be an urgent priority. We need to find ways to teach the faith so that our people really «get it» —not just the intellectual content of the faith, but the true, life-changing power of the encounter with Jesus Christ.

We need to show them that our Catholic faith is a beautiful and complete way of life, one that brings joy and peace, and one that offers real answers to the problems of daily life. We need to teach the faith so that people not only want to live it, but are inspired to defend it and pass it on to others —in their homes, in their communities, in the places where they work.

My brothers and sisters, it is essential that our people know their own story, *our* story —the great story of Hispanic Catholicism in the Americas.

Do our people know that the Gospel was being preached in Spanish and the Holy Mass was being celebrated by Hispanics in our country in the 1560s —more than 200 years before the Declaration of Independence? Do they know the names and the lives of the great priests and lay missionaries, the saints and martyrs who brought the faith to this land?

Do they know about the more immediate *«memoria histórica»* of Hispanic ministry? The Encuentros, including «Encuentro 2000», the only official national celebration of the Jubilee Year? What about the Documents of the USCCB regarding Hispanic ministry?

How will our people come to know these things unless we are the ones who tell them? As leaders, we have to learn this great story ourselves, and promote creative ways of sharing that story with our people. We need to encourage devotion to our local saints —especially our Hispanic and Latin American saints and blesseds. Our people need to know that these holy men and women shared their faith, and their struggles against sin, injustice, and oppression.

They also need to know about the men and women who have dedicated their lives in recent years to the service of the Church in Hispanic ministry.

We also need to concentrate on raising up new leaders. We still do not have enough successful Hispanics taking on leadership roles in the Church or in our communities. There are a lot of reasons for this. Professional Hispanic men and women are still struggling hard to establish themselves in their fields. They still face a lot of racism and institutional barriers to success; it takes a lot of their energy and a lot of their time. There isn't a lot of either left-over to «give back» to the community, to the Church.

So we need to find ways to help them and encourage them to put their time, talents and treasure in the service of our people. We have to find a better way to market our organizations and to facilitate the participation of successful Hispanics in our ministries and activities.

But what we really must do is promoting the sense of discipleship among all our peoples. We need to remind them that all Catholics are called to be missionaries, to be leaders in proclaiming their faith, in preaching the Gospel with their lives.

That goes for us, too, my friends. Most of us here today are «professional Catholics». I say that with deep respect and gratitude for your service to Christ and his Church. But you have to remember that your work for the Church —in chanceries and parishes, in classrooms, in all your various ministries— does not exhaust your responsibilities as disciples. Your discipleship must extend into every area of your life.

We are all called to become better examples of the Gospel we're called to proclaim. If you lead, my friends, others will follow. I promise you that.

5

¡Somos Católicos!

My time is almost up. Let me turn to Hosffman's last question —how do we seize the initiative at this moment in history?

First, I think we need to consider what's really at stake. I hear a lot of talk these days about so-called «cultural Catholicism» as it relates to Hispanics. It's a category that's supposed to describe people who have been raised Catholic. They're supposed to have a unique dedication to working for social justice that stays with them even though they're no longer practicing their faith. «Cultural Catholicism» is supposed to be a good thing, a sign that Christian values have penetrated deep into a person's personality and outlook on life.

But I am reminded of some tough words that our Lord once spoke: *¿De qué le servirá al hombre ganar el mundo entero, si pierde su vida?* «For what does it profit a man, to gain the whole world and forfeit his life?» (Mark 8:36)

What good will it do our people to be a majority of Americans if we forfeit our Catholic faith in the process, if we lose our soul? Jesus Christ did not come to suffer and die so that he could make «cultural Catholics».

The Gospel is not an attitude or a philosophy of life. It is a relationship with the living God, a relationship that Christ himself intended to be profoundly *ecclesial;* that is, it is a relationship that we have through him, with him, and in him —*in his Church.*

We need to reject every short-cut, every attempt to reduce the Gospel to its lowest common denominator. Catholic principles can make society a better place to live, but only the fullness of the Gospel can bring men and women to eternal life.

To seize the moment, we need to embrace our identity as Catholics. ¡*Somos Católicos!* That means embracing the fullness of our heritage as Hispanic Catholics.

Carlos Fuentes, our great Mexican writer, has said, «You cannot have a living future if you have a dead past». He's right. The way forward in the future is to always be drawing from our past —not only from the words of Scripture, but from the great communion of saints.

In that spirit, I want to leave you this afternoon with reflections from two figures from our Hispanic Catholic heritage.

The first is Bartolomé de Las Casas, the great Dominican evangelist and champion of human rights. We all know his story. In fact, I was rereading his defense of the dignity of the Indians recently, and I was thinking that every word could be applied to our debates today about abortion.

What makes him so relevant for us is that he had some very simple yet powerful ideas about the evangelization of culture. From his classic, «The Only Way to Draw All People to a Living Faith», I offer you two points:

First, Fray Bartolomé says that Christ and the apostles evangelized by (a) winning people's minds with reasoned arguments; and (b) by attracting their hearts with gentle invitations and compelling motives.

That's a good way for us to think about our ministries, too. We need an approach to evangelizing our culture that is both intellectually rigorous and that is rooted in deep love for our brothers and sisters and a desire that they come to know Christ.

Second, Fray Bartolomé reminds us of something I just mentioned —that our mission is profoundly *ecclesial.* He says we have a «triple duty—The first, to preach the faith. The second, nourishing believers with the sacraments. The third, teaching believers nourished by the sacraments to keep the commandments of God and to live a good life».

Again —a very clear and simple path for us to follow. We evangelize, we educate, we bring men and women into the life of the Church, we feed them the Bread of Life, and we help them to live by all the teachings of Christ.

Finally, I want to propose that we reflect on the missionary work of Blessed Miguel Pro, the great Jesuit martyr of the Mexican persecution in the 1920s.

I think we all know his story, too. What we need is his conviction that Christ alone can save us. At a time when practicing the faith was a capitol crime, this conviction led him to risk his life every day to bring people to Christ in the Eucharist and in the sacrament of Penance.

We need his creativity, courage, and daring, to find new ways to bring our brothers and sisters to Christ.

My friends, in the future we must preach with the confidence of those who know the hope of the resurrection. If the God who raised Jesus from the dead is with us, what could we possibly have to fear?

Thank you for your attention this afternoon. I'm grateful for the chance to join you in this important discussion.

Let me leave you with Blessed Miguel's last words: ¡*Viva Cristo Rey!* («Long live Christ the King!»).

And I pray that Our Lady of Guadalupe, the mother of us all, watch over us and guide us in our service of her Son, especially these coming days as we discuss the present and future of Catholic Hispanic ministry in the United States.

Thank you.

Simposium Participant by Study Areas

1

Hispanic Ministry and U.S. Catholicism

1. Carmen Aguinaco

    President of The National Catholic Council for Hispanic Ministry (NCCHM)

2. Alejandro Aguilera-Titus

    Assistant Director, Secretariat of Cultural Diversity in the Church, USCCB

3. Rev. Richard Clifford, SJ

    Dean of Boston College's School of Theology and Ministry

4. Rev. Allan Deck, SJ

    Executive Director of the Secretariat of Cultural Diversity in the Church, USCCB

5. Bishop Ricardo García

    Bishop of Monterey, CA; Chair of the Subcommittee of Hispanic Affairs, USCCB

6. Archbishop José H. Gómez

    Coadjutor Archbishop of Los Angeles; Chairman, U.S. Bishops' Committee on Cultural Diversity in 2009

7. Dr. Timothy Matovina

    Professor of Theology, Director of the Cushwa Center for the Study of American Catholicism, University of Notre Dame

8. Mario Paredes

    President of the Catholic Association of Latino Leaders (CALL); Bible Society of America

9. Dr. Milagros Peña

    Professor of Sociology and Women's Studies, Associate Dean for Behavioral & Social Sciences, University of Miami

10. Enid Román

    President of the National Catholic Association of Diocesan Directors for Hispanic Ministry (NCADDHM)

2

Hispanic Ministry and Theology

. Dr. María Pilar Aquino

    Professor of Theology and Religious Studies, University of San Diego

2. Dr. Shawn Copeland
Associate Professor of Theology, Boston College

3. Dr. Roberto Goizueta
Professor of Theology, Boston College

4. Rev. Rafael Luévano
Associate Professor of Religious Studies, Chapman University

5. Dr. Alicia Marill
Associate Professor of Practical Theology, Director of Doctor of Ministry Program, Barry University

6. Dr. Carmen Nanko
Assistant Professor of Pastoral Ministry, Director of the Ecumenical Doctor of Ministry Program, Director of the Certificate in Pastoral Studies, Catholic Theological Union

7. Rev. Jorge Presmanes, O.P.

Assistant Professor of Practical Theology, Director of the Institute for Hispanic/Latino Theology and Ministry, Barry University

8. Dr. Nancy Pineda-Madrid
Assistant Professor of Theology and Latino/a Ministry, Boston College

9. Rev. Mark Wedig, O.P.
Professor of Liturgical Theology, Associate Dean for Graduate Studies in the College of Arts and Sciences, Chair of the Theology and Philosophy Department, Barry University

3

Hispanic Ministry, Evangelization, and Faith Formation

1. Carlos Aedo
Director of Religious Education for Hispanics, Archdiocese of Hartford

2. Santiago Cortés-Sjoberg
Loyola Press

3. William S. Dinger
President, William H. Sadlier, Inc.

4. Dr. Thomas Groome
Professor of Theology and Religious Education, Boston College

5. Dulce Jimenez
William H. Sadlier, Inc.

6. Dr. Hosffman Ospino

Assistant Professor of Hispanic Ministry and Religious Education, Director of Graduate Programs in Hispanic Ministry, Boston College

7. Jo Ann Paradise

Harcourt Religion Publishers

8. Jo Rotunno

RCL Benziger

9. Dr. Maruja Sedano

Director of the Office of Religious Education, Archdiocese of Chicago

10. Thomas McGrath

Loyola Press

11. Daniel Mulhall

RCL Benziger

4
Hispanic Ministry, Liturgy and Spirituality

Rev. Eduardo Fernández, SJ

Associate Professor of Pastoral Theology and Ministry, Jesuit School of Theology of Santa Clara

Rev. Raúl Gómez-Ruíz, S.D.S.

Professor and Vice President for Academic Affairs at the Sacred Heart School of Theology in Hales Corners, WI

Dr. Cecilia González-Andrieu

Assistant Professor of Theological Studies, Loyola Marymount University

Dr. Robert Hurteau

Director, Center for Religion and Spirituality, Loyola Marymount University

Rev. Alejandro López-Cardinale

Renew International

Pedro Rubalcava

Oregon Catholic Press

Rev. Juan Sosa

President, Instituto Nacional Hispano de Liturgia

Hispanic Ministry in the 21st Century

5
Hispanic Youth and Young Adult Ministry

1. Rev. José Burgués, Sch. P.
   Director, South East Pastoral Institute (SEPI)
2. Liliana Flores
   National Catholic Network de Pastoral Juvenil Hispana, La Red
3. Reinardo Malavé
   Chairperson First National Encounter for Hispanic Youth and Young Adult Ministry (2006)
4. Rev. Michael G. Lee, SJ
   Assistant Professor of Theological Studies, Loyola Marymount University
5. Walter Mena
   Director of Formation Programs, Instituto Fe y Vida
6. Ken Johnson-Mondragón
   Director of Research and Publications, Instituto Fe y Vida
7. Guadalupe Ospino
   Hispanic Ministry, St. Patrick Parish in Lawrence, MA
8. Sean Reynolds
   National Federation for Catholic Youth Ministry (NFCYM)
9. Víctor Valenzuela
   William H. Sadlier, Inc.

220

6
Hispanic Ministry and Social Justice

1. Sr. Sonia Avi, IHM
   Office of Hispanic Ministry, Diocese of Candem, NJ
2. Dr. Arturo Chávez
   President and CEO of the Mexican American Catholic College (MACC) in San Antonio, TX
3. Rev. Ken Davis, OFM, Conv
   Saint Joseph College Seminary, Saint Benedict, LA
4. Sr. Hilda Mateo, MGSpS
   Misioneras Guadalupanas del Espíritu Santo

Rev. Bill Rickle, sj
Director of the Institute on Migration, Culture, and Ministry
Bishop Jaime Soto
Bishop of Sacramento, CA; Chairman, U.S. Bishops' Committee on Cultural Diversity in 2010
Hope Villella
National Pastoral Life Center

7
Hispanic Ministry and Leadership Formation

Sr. Ruth Bolarte, IHM
President of the Federación de Institutos Pastorales
Rev. Wayne Cavalier, O.P.
Director, Congar Institute for Ministry Development
Paulina Espinosa
Director of the Hispanic Institute, Jesuit School of Theology of Santa Clara
Rev. Tom Florek, sj
Director, Instituto Cultural de Liderazgo en el Medio Oeste (ICLM)
Dr. Elsie M. Miranda
Assistant Professor of Practical Theology, Director of the Master of Arts in Practical Theology,
Director of Ministerial Formation, Barry University
Dr. Ana María Pineda
Associate Professor of Religious Studies, Santa Clara University
Luis Soto
Executive Director, Centro San Juan Diego, Denver, CO
Rudy Vargas
Executive Director, Northeast Hispanic Catholic Center
Rev. Richard Vega
President, National Federation of Priests Councils (NFPC)

Contributors

Arturo Chávez, Ph.D. is the President and CEO of the Mexican American Catholic College (MACC) in San Antonio, TX.

Raúl Gómez-Ruíz, S.D.S., Ph.D. is Professor and Vice President for Academic Affairs at the Sacred Heart School of Theology in Hales Corners, WI.

Ken Johnson-Mondragón, D.Min candidate is Director of Research and Publications at Instituto Fe y Vida in Stockton, CA.

Alicia Marill, D.Min. is Associate Professor and Director of the Doctor of Ministry Program at Barry University in Miami, FL.

Timothy Matovina, Ph.D. is Professor of Theology and the Director of the Cushwa Center for the Study of American Catholicism at the University of Notre Dame in South Bend, IN.

Elsie M. Miranda, D.Min. is Assistant Professor of Practical Theology, Director of the Master of Arts in Practical Theology, and Director of Ministerial Formation at Barry University in Miami, FL.

Hosffman Ospino, Ph.D. is Assistant Professor of Hispanic Ministry and Religious Education, Director of Graduate Programs in Hispanic Ministry at Boston College's School of Theology and Ministry in Boston, MA.

Jorge Presmanes, O.P., D.Min. is Assistant Professor of Theology and Director of the Institute for Hispanic/Latino Theology and Ministry at Barry University in Miami, FL.

2

El ministerio hispano en el siglo XXI: presente y futuro

Agradecimientos

Todo proyecto que hace la diferencia en nuestras organizaciones e instituciones es posible gracias a las personas creativas que nos rodean, las que apoyan y las que contribuyen con sus recursos, las que acompañan y las que trabajan incansablemente, las que inspiran y aquellas en quienes pensamos cuando nos proponemos una meta. El *Simposio Nacional sobre el Presente y Futuro del Ministerio Católico Hispano en los Estados Unidos* celebrado en Boston College en el año 2009 sin lugar a dudas reunió personas con todas estas cualidades. Muchas gracias a quienes hicieron posible el simposio y este libro.

Gracias a mis colegas en la Escuela de Teología y Ministerio (*School of Theology and Ministry*, STM, en inglés) de Boston College quienes creyeron y apoyaron la idea del simposio desde un principio. Agradezco sinceramente a Thomas H. Groome por su apoyo, acompañamiento y visión inspiradora; a Richard Clifford, SJ, primer decano de la Escuela de Teología y Ministerio, por afirmar la formación teológica y ministerial de líderes para el ministerio hispano como una prioridad en nuestra institución; a Nancy Pineda-Madrid y Roberto Goizueta por la bendición de su amistad. Agradezco especialmente a Rebecca Camacho, estudiante asistente para programas de ministerio hispano en Boston College durante el año 2009, quien junto con Maura Colleary hizo un trabajo espectacular en la parte logística del simposio. También extiendo mi agradecimiento a Katherine Klauser, estudiante asistente para programas de ministerio hispano en Boston College en el año 2010, y a todos los estudiantes de postgrado que trabajaron durante el simposio. Es un privilegio estar rodeado de los mejores.

Gracias a los académicos y administradores en las universidades que aceptaron la invitación a unirse a Boston College en la organización del simposio: Barry University, Loyola Marymount University y el Congar Institute for Ministry Development. Juntos hemos modelado aquello en lo que creemos: un esfuerzo de colaboración para el mayor bien de la Iglesia y la sociedad. Fue un privilegio trabajar con ustedes y espero que nuestra colaboración siga dando frutos.

Gracias a los teólogos y líderes eclesiales que sirvieron como lectores asignados para estos documentos en sus versiones originales: Alejandro Aguilera-Titus, Ruth Bolarte, IHM, Cecilia González-Andrieu, Michael G. Lee, SJ, Nancy Pineda-Madrid y Bill Rickle, SJ. Un agradecimiento especial a los líderes académicos que aceptaron la invitación a escribir los ensayos que hacen parte de esta colección. Sus ideas y observaciones sin duda alguna son contribuciones excepcionales a la reflexión contemporánea sobre la experiencia católica en los Estados Unidos.

Gracias a las siguientes casas editoriales, organizaciones e instituciones, incluyendo aquellas que prefieren no ser nombradas, cuyo patrocinio hizo posible que tuviéramos los recursos necesarios para celebrar el simposio y publicar este libro: Claretian Publications, Convivium Press, Harcourt Religion Publishers, Loyola Press, Northeast Pastoral Center, Oregon Catholic Press, Our Sunday Visitor, Inc., RCL Benziger, Renew International y William H. Sadlier, Inc. Gracias a las organizaciones nacionales que apoyaron el simposio y continúan avanzando la reflexión sobre el ministerio hispano en los Estados Unidos: Academia de Teólogos Católicos Hispanos de los Estados Unidos (ACHTUS), Asociación Nacional Católica de Directores Diocesanos para el Ministerio Hispano (NCADDHM), Consejo Nacional Católico para el Ministerio Hispano (NCCHM), y el Secretariado de Diversidad Cultural en la Iglesia, Oficina de Asuntos Hispanos de la Conferencia de Obispos Católicos de Estados Unidos.

Finalmente unas palabras profundas de agradecimiento a los pioneros y los grandes del ministerio hispano y la teología latina en este país a quienes admiración y elogio son debidos por sus contribuciones abundantes, las cuales son la base de gran parte de nuestro reflexionar; a las mujeres y los hombres que recientemente han hecho la opción preferencial de servir a los latinos como parte de la misión evangelizadora de la Iglesia en los Estados Unidos; y a los participantes en el Simposio Nacional sobre el Presente y Futuro del Ministerio Católico Hispano en los Estados Unidos del 2009. Qué gran honor caminar con ustedes en este momento de la historia.

Introducción

La experiencia católica estadounidense en el siglo XXI está siendo transformada profundamente por la presencia y contribuciones de los católicos hispanos[1]. Se estima que en el año 2010 los latinos constituimos cerca del 40 por ciento de la población total de los católicos en los Estados Unidos y dentro de unos años la mayoría de los católicos en el país será de origen hispano. A nivel nacional los latinos somos el 17 por ciento del total de la población estadounidense y según los demógrafos este número llegará al 25 por ciento a mediados de este siglo. ¿Qué significa esto para la Iglesia Católica y para los católicos latinos en particular?

Los católicos latinos recibimos el siglo XXI conscientes de los grandes logros que varias generaciones de católicos en los Estados Unidos, muchos de ellos hispanos, han conseguido durante varios siglos. Reconocemos que ser católicos estadounidenses significa mantenernos fieles a los principios de la fe cristiana que nos aviva y nos sostiene y al mismo tiempo nos llama a participar en la construcción de una sociedad justa y floreciente. Sabemos que nuestras culturas, tradiciones y convicciones son contribuciones importantes a la riqueza de la fe y de la vida católica en este país. Al mismo tiempo tenemos conciencia de que por un largo tiempo muchas de nuestras experiencias como pueblo han sido relegadas a las márgenes de la Iglesia y la sociedad; que muchas veces nuestros hermanos y hermanas en la fe católica no se han percatado de nuestras luchas y no han escuchado nuestras voces con verdadera atención. El siglo XXI es una oportunidad única para que los católicos en los Estados Unidos afirmemos la presencia y contribuciones de los católicos hispanos, fortalezcamos la herencia católica en este país y juntos forjemos una experiencia renovada de lo que significa ser católico estadounidense en el contexto culturalmente diverso dentro del cual damos testimonio de nuestra fe en Cristo resucitado. Para muchos de nosotros el contexto en el que esto ocurre es el ministerio hispano.

El ministerio hispano es la matriz desde la que entendemos la acción evangelizadora de la Iglesia con los latinos en los Estados Unidos. Muchas veces se habla del ministerio hispano como una forma especializada de trabajo pastoral liderada usualmente por latinos/as para el beneficio de otros latinos/as. Esto refleja sólo una parte de la realidad. Existen cientos de líderes que no son latinos y

---

[1] Nota importante sobre el uso del lenguaje. Los ensayos en este libro usan las palabras *latino* e *hispano* intercambiablemente. La presencia de ambas palabras con sus correspondientes variaciones femeninas *latina* e *hispana* indica que la conversación sobre cuál de ellos es preferible para referirse a los latinos/hispanos se mantiene abierta. El hecho de que un autor prefiera un término en un momento determinado no indica la exclusión de otras posibilidades.

están comprometidos de lleno con el ministerio hispano al igual que cientos de líderes hispanos sirviendo en círculos que no son exclusivamente latinos. A medida que el número de latinos/as crece en las parroquias y las diócesis alrededor del país, las líneas de diferenciación son cada vez menos claras. En muchos lugares hablar de ministerio hispano es hablar simplemente de ministerio a nivel general; y viceversa. Por consiguiente, el ministerio hispano en el siglo XXI ha de ser entendido como una responsabilidad de toda la Iglesia en los Estados Unidos. Todos los miembros de la Iglesia en este país estamos llamados a reconocer y a afirmar la experiencia católica latina en el contexto del ministerio pastoral. Por un lado, ese llamado exige acompañar a los latinos a medida que integramos nuestras vidas, visiones y esperanzas como parte de la amplia experiencia católica estadounidense. Por otro lado, todos los latinos necesitamos comprender plenamente la magnitud de la misión evangelizadora de la Iglesia en este país y asumir con espíritu renovado las posibilidades que dicha misión nos presenta. Esto ciertamente nos llevará a experimentar transformaciones profundas. Se trata de un proceso complejo que requiere que nos preguntemos: ¿qué traemos a la mesa de conversación? ¿Cómo evangelizamos y educamos en la fe? ¿De qué manera hacemos teología? ¿De qué manera presentamos a Cristo a nuestra juventud? ¿Cómo celebramos y vivimos nuestra fe? ¿Practicamos lo que creemos? ¿Cómo preparamos a nuestros líderes?

Para responder a estas preguntas vemos el presente como *experiencia vivida*. No se trata de un presente abstracto en el cual los eventos ocurren por accidente o sin consecuencias. El presente es donde vivimos, donde nos encontramos con Dios, donde entramos en relación unos con otros. Para los católicos hispanos en los Estados Unidos el presente es un momento histórico privilegiado en el que descubrimos la complejidad de nuestra diversidad. Es en nuestro presente que sabemos que la inmigración, el mestizaje y la globalización nos han hecho un nuevo pueblo y como pueblo nuevo entramos en diálogo con la Iglesia en los Estados Unidos, la sociedad en general y las comunidades latinoamericanas en donde muchos de nosotros todavía tenemos raíces profundas. En el presente reconocemos que los muchos retos que enfrentamos hacen que nuestra experiencia esté lejos de ser idílica. No obstante, aceptamos esos retos porque sabemos que ellos constituyen el crisol en el que se fortalece el carácter de nuestras comunidades al igual que el de las nuevas generaciones de católicos latinos. En el presente afirmamos nuestra identidad como discípulos misioneros de Jesucristo quienes tenemos en nuestras manos la responsabilidad de construir comunidades de fe y amor en las cuales todo el mundo pueda experimentar que Dios es real porque su presencia divina ha sido real en nuestras vidas. Vemos el presente como protagonistas de una nueva época y un futuro lleno de esperanza. Vemos el futuro con *esperanza fiel*. Como protagonistas de un nuevo momento en la historia del catolicismo estadounidense nos encontramos en una posición privilegiada, aunque intimidante en cierta manera, para proponer caminos que conduzcan a experimentar el Reino de Dios de maneras tanto tradicionales como nuevas. No podemos hacer esto solos ni mucho menos ignorando las muchas voces que nos acompañan en nuestras comunidades de fe. Ésta es una oportunidad para que los católicos hispanos en los Estados Unidos propongamos modelos renovados de acción pastoral, reflexión teológica y compromiso social que respondan a los tiempos cambiantes en los que vivimos. Como cristianos, permanecemos fieles a la llamada del Señor a ser sus discípulos; tenemos esperanza porque confiamos en el Dios de la vida cuya presencia nos acompaña en nuestro caminar histórico.

Sin embargo, hablar del presente e imaginar el futuro del ministerio hispano en la Iglesia Católica en los Estados Unidos no tendría mucho sentido si no honráramos nuestra *memoria histórica*. Dicha memoria nos recuerda las luchas y los sueños de muchos católicos latinos que celebraron su fe con convicción en esta tierra y levantaron sus voces para hablar en favor de sus hermanas y hermanos en los distintos momentos de una larga historia. Dicha historia antecede las grandes olas migratorias desde Europa que marcaron profundamente el carácter de nuestra sociedad; la guerra civil estadounidense, el nacimiento de los Estados Unidos como nación, el establecimiento de las primeras colonias inglesas e incluso la llegada de los peregrinos en Plymouth, MA. Antes de que todos estos acontecimientos históricos tan importantes ocurrieran, ¡los católicos hispanos ya estábamos presentes!

De manera particular en el siglo XX los católicos hispanos participaron en el movimiento de los derechos civiles y fortalecieron sus voces dentro de la Iglesia y la sociedad. La formación de grupos como PADRES y Las Hermanas y la fundación de instituciones como el Centro Cultural México Americano fueron verdaderos signos de esperanza. El Secretariado para Asuntos Hispanos dentro de la Conferencia de Obispos Católicos en sus distintas etapas fue una afirmación de la importancia de la presencia hispana en la Iglesia a nivel institucional. La consagración de Patricio Flores en 1970 como el primer obispo mexicoamericano en los Estados Unidos señaló un nuevo momento en el mundo del liderazgo eclesial, el cual se ha prolongado por medio de la consagración de un número creciente de obispos hispanos y la participación de más católicos latinos en posiciones claves de liderazgo eclesial. En el año 2010 José H. Gómez fue nombrado como arzobispo coadjutor de Los Angeles, la arquidiócesis más grande del país y sede cardenalicia, lo cual le abre la posibilidad de convertirse en el primer cardenal latino en la historia del catolicismo estadounidense. La creación de organizaciones nacionales, instituciones educativas y distintas oficinas enfocadas en el ministerio hispano alrededor del país canalizó los esfuerzos del liderazgo católico hispano y confirmó que trabajando en conjunto podemos hacer más. El número creciente de teólogos católicos hispanos estadounidenses ha expandido la influencia de nuestras contribuciones más allá del contexto de nuestras comunidades de fe e incursionado en el mundo de la academia. La mayoría de teólogos católicos hispanos participamos constantemente de la vida de nuestras comunidades de fe no sólo compartiendo las ideas que nacen en medio de nuestras reflexiones, sino también siendo sostenidos por la fe viva de nuestra gente. El número de obispos, sacerdotes, diáconos permanentes y religiosos hispanos sigue aumentando, aunque muy lentamente comparado con el resto de la población católica hispana. Los ministros eclesiales laicos latinos siguen siendo líderes claves en muchas de nuestras comunidades de fe. Pero ninguna serie de eventos en nuestra rica memoria histórica ha tenido tanto impacto en la formación de la identidad del liderazgo católico hispano como los procesos de Encuentro. Los Encuentros Nacionales Hispanos de Pastoral de 1972, 1977 y 1985, el Encuentro 2000, el cual abrió la espiritualidad y dinámica de Encuentro al resto de la Iglesia en los Estados Unidos bajo el liderazgo prominente de los católicos hispanos; y más recientemente el Primer Encuentro Nacional de Pastoral Juvenil Hispana del 2006 fueron espacios que en sus distintos momentos dieron voz a cientos de miles de personas, la mayoría de ellas latinos y latinas en todos los niveles de liderazgo en la Iglesia, para compartir de manera profética su visión y sus esperanzas. Estos procesos de Encuentro fueron oportunidades únicas para afirmar que nuestra presencia no es ni temporal ni insignificante y que aceptamos el reto de ser protagonistas de un futuro común con el resto de la población católica estadounidense caracterizada por su gran diversidad. En el espíritu de estos Encuentros, en 1987 los obispos católicos estadounidenses presentaron un *Plan Pastoral Nacional para el Ministerio Hispano* y también han escrito otros documentos reflexionando sobre la realidad hispana, dentro de los cuales se destaca *Encuentro y Misión: Un Marco Pastoral Renovado para el*

Ministerio Hispano, escrito en el año 2002. Es preciso que conozcamos y afirmemos nuestra memoria histórica, especialmente cuando miramos al presente y el futuro del ministerio hispano católico en el siglo XXI. Nuevas generaciones de líderes católicos están asumiendo responsabilidades ministeriales que requieren servir en comunidades en donde los católicos latinos están presentes. Estas personas se beneficiarán profundamente de la sabiduría, las voces y los movimientos que han guiado al ministerio hispano durante las últimas décadas.

Entre el 8 y el 10 de junio del 2009 nos dimos cita sesenta y dos líderes de distintas partes del país en Boston para afirmar nuestra memoria histórica, analizar nuestra experiencia presente con mirada crítica y juntos imaginar el futuro del ministerio hispano en la segunda década del siglo XXI. La razón de nuestra reunión fue el Simposio Nacional sobre el Presente y Futuro del Ministerio Católico Hispano en los Estados Unidos. Obispos, teólogos, académicos trabajando en distintos campos, líderes de oficinas nacionales, editores, líderes de grandes organizaciones nacionales abogando en favor del ministerio hispano y líderes parroquiales y diocesanos trabajando con católicos latinos en distintos niveles nos reunimos para reflexionar sobre los retos y las promesas del ministerio católico hispano en el país. El simposio fue organizado por Boston College en colaboración con Barry University de Miami, Loyola Marymount University de Los Angeles y el Congar Institute for Ministry Development de San Antonio. El trabajo en conjunto de estas instituciones académicas ha modelado un esfuerzo de colaboración que seguramente marcará la dinámica de la reflexión sobre el ministerio y la teología en la Iglesia Católica en los próximos años.

Los ensayos que hacen parte de este libro son la versión revisada de los documentos de estudio que inspiraron la conversación durante el simposio. Estos ensayos se presentan aquí como herramientas para que académicos, líderes y servidores trabajando con católicos latinos continúen la reflexión. De hecho, los ensayos son recursos valiosos para cualquier persona interesada en el presente y el futuro de la experiencia católica estadounidense en general, no sólo la de los hispanos.

En el capítulo primero Timothy Matovina ofrece un análisis del ministerio hispano dentro del contexto más amplio de la experiencia católica en los Estados Unidos. Su ensayo comienza con un recorrido histórico que señala el nacimiento de varias de las estructuras y los ministerios sirviendo a la comunidad católica hispana en este país, luego evalúa varias respuestas actuales a la presencia de los católicos latinos en la Iglesia a medida que nos integramos más de lleno a la experiencia católica estadounidense y concluye proponiendo una serie de pasos concretos para continuar la conversación en un momento en que latinas y latinos asumimos más papeles de liderazgo en la Iglesia.

En el capítulo segundo Hosffman Ospino reflexiona sobre lo que significa evangelizar y educar en la fe en el contexto particular del ministerio hispano. Su ensayo identifica algunos de los factores y situaciones más urgentes que definen la experiencia presente de los latinos en este país e indica cómo estas realidades deben ser cuidadosamente consideradas en la planeación de todo proceso evangelizador con los latinos. El autor invita a elaborar un marco analítico que guíe las distintas conversaciones sobre educación católica, la formación en la fe y la evangelización de los católicos hispanos en los Estados Unidos y propone siete bases claves para sostener dicho marco.

En el capítulo tercero Jorge Presmanes y Alicia Marill reflexionan sobre la relación entre el ministerio hispano y la reflexión teológica. Los autores parten de su experiencia personal trabajando con latinos en comunidades de fe católicas y de la de sus propios estudiantes en programas de postgrado en ministerio. El ensayo afirma que la experiencia vivida de los católicos latinos en la particularidad de nuestras comunidades de fe nos ofrece una eclesiología única que influye profundamente en nuestra reflexión teológica y nuestra práctica pastoral. La particularidad de la experiencia católica latina en los Estados Unidos ha sido una fuente abundante de categorías teológicas que informan tanto nuestras teologías como nuestra acción pastoral, lo sigue siendo en el presente y lo será en el futuro venidero.

En el capítulo cuarto Ken Johnson-Mondragón comparte la experiencia de varios años de investigación y análisis atento de la realidad de los jóvenes hispanos en los Estados Unidos. Su ensayo ofrece no sólo una lectura completa de la realidad actual de los jóvenes católicos latinos en el país, sino que también propone categorías valiosas para que agentes pastorales y educadores podamos usar en nuestro trabajo con este importante sector de la población católica. Este capítulo incorpora cuidadosamente las ideas y conclusiones de estudios recientes sobre juventud en los Estados Unidos e introduce a los líderes en el ministerio hispano a las conclusiones del Primer Encuentro Nacional de Pastoral Juvenil Hispana celebrado en el año 2006.

En el capítulo quinto Raúl Gómez-Ruíz reflexiona sobre la importante relación que existe entre la liturgia y la espiritualidad en el ministerio hispano. El ensayo nos invita a adentrarnos más profundamente en el mundo de la espiritualidad católica hispana, vivida consistentemente por medio de expresiones de catolicismo popular, y a descubrir sus conexiones íntimas con la vida litúrgica. El autor invita a apreciar más de lleno las categorías de mística y sacramentalidad en la experiencia católica latina en los Estados Unidos y demuestra convincentemente cómo estas realidades sostienen la vida de fe de nuestras comunidades y cómo conducen a los creyentes a asumir compromisos de acción pastoral.

En el capítulo sexto Arturo Chávez explora las conexiones entre el ministerio hispano y la justicia social. Su ensayo inserta esta reflexión en el contexto de conversaciones claves sobre temas como la economía, la educación, la inmigración y la dignidad humana, entre otros, los cuales exigen una participación activa por parte de los católicos hispanos. El autor nos recuerda que el discernimiento pastoral aplicado a asuntos de justicia social ha sido un elemento central en el ministerio hispano y ha de ser considerado una de nuestras contribuciones más significativas a la reflexión contemporánea sobre la experiencia católica estadounidense. Éste es un momento de oportunidades para los católicos hispanos y debemos dar lo mejor de nosotros en medio de las circunstancias actuales.

Finalmente, en el capítulo séptimo Hosffman Ospino y Elsie Miranda evalúan las posibilidades y esperanzas de los católicos latinos en un momento en el que estamos asumiendo más posiciones de liderazgo en la Iglesia. Los autores ofrecen un análisis general de acontecimientos, documentos y conversaciones recientes sobre la formación de líderes para el servicio eclesial en el contexto del ministerio hispano, consideran ciertas corrientes actuales que están influyendo la formación de líderes católicos hispanos y proponen varias direcciones para continuar la reflexión sobre esta área. El capítulo concluye afirmando la necesidad de una reflexión teológica más inclusiva sobre el ministerio y la formación para el liderazgo.

Ojalá que este libro contagie a sus lectores con la energía y la esperanza que experimentamos en el Simposio Nacional en Boston e inspire muchas más conversaciones en los próximos años.

El ministerio hispano y el catolicismo en los Estados Unidos

Timothy Matovina

El Padre José Antonio Díaz de León, el último fraile franciscano trabajando en Texas cuando ésta todavía era parte de México, murió misteriosamente en 1834 cerca de la ciudad de Nacogdoches al este de Texas. Un juez exoneró a un hombre angloamericano del asesinato de Díaz de León en medio de rumores que aseguraban que la muerte del sacerdote, causada por una herida de bala, había sido un suicidio. Los católicos mexicanos criticaron esta decisión como una falsedad. ¿Cómo podía ser que su párroco, quien había servido fielmente en la frontera de Texas por tantos años como sacerdote fuese a cometer tal acto de desesperación?

Siete años más tarde, los sacerdotes vicentinos John Timon y Jean Marie Odin hicieron una visita pastoral a Nacogdoches. Los clérigos lamentaron la situación de los católicos mexicanos notando que los angloamericanos con frecuencia los asesinaban y los expulsaban de sus tierras usurpándolas indiscriminadamente. El Padre Odin también informó que los angloamericanos habían reducido a cenizas el templo católico en el área. Aún así, éstos y otros visitantes observaron que los católicos laicos mexicanos continuaban reuniéndose en sus casas en días de fiesta en donde celebraban servicios litúrgicos semanales, ritos, e incluso funerales. En Nacogdoches el ministerio hispano se mantuvo vivo en gran medida gracias al esfuerzo de los laicos hasta que en 1847 el ahora obispo Odin asignó dos sacerdotes para reemplazar al Padre Díaz de León. El entusiasmo de los feligreses al recibir los sacramentos de parte de los nuevos pastores fue un testimonio de su fe inquebrantable en medio de aquel momento tumultuoso de cambio social[1].

Esfuerzos como los de los fieles de Nacogdoches nos permiten reconocer las bases del ministerio hispano tanto a nivel de comunidades como de iniciativas locales. Los católicos de habla hispana han estado activos en lo que hoy en día es los Estados Unidos casi el doble del tiempo de existencia de esta nación. La primera diócesis del nuevo mundo se estableció en 1511 en San Juan, Puerto Rico. Súbditos de la corona española establecieron la primera comunidad europea permanente dentro de las fronteras de los actuales cincuenta estados en San Agustín en la Florida en 1565, cuatro décadas antes del establecimiento de la primera colonia británica en Jamestown. En 1598 en lo que hoy en día es El Paso, Texas, súbditos españoles establecieron las bases permanentes del catolicismo en lo que hoy conocemos como el suroeste[2].

---

1 MATOVINA T., «Lay Initiatives in Worship on the Texas *Frontera*, 1830-1860» en *U.s. Catholic Historian* 12 (1994) 108-11.

2 Véanse algunas de las historias generales del catolicismo hispano en los Estados Unidos tales como los trabajos de SANDOVAL M., *On the Move: A History of the Hispanic Church in the United States*, segunda edición, Orbis, Maryknoll, NY 1990, 2006; MATOVINA T. Y POYO G.E. (eds.), *¡Presente!*

Aunque durante la mayor parte de la historia del catolicismo estadounidense los hispanos han permanecido como un grupo proporcionalmente pequeño y a menudo ignorado, a partir de la segunda guerra mundial sus números e influencia han aumentado dramáticamente. Olas de inmigrantes provenientes de diversas partes como Puerto Rico, Cuba, la República Dominicana, El Salvador, Guatemala, Nicaragua, Colombia, Perú, Ecuador y Argentina, junto con personas provenientes de México que han sido parte de un patrón migratorio constante, se han unido a la población hispana ya establecida, compuesta principalmente por católicos de origen mexicano. Más importante aún, aparte de las ya tradicionales comunidades católicas hispanas previamente concentradas en Nueva York, el suroeste y algunas ciudades del medio este estadounidense, hoy en día podemos encontrar comunidades latinas en toda la geografía del país, desde Seattle hasta Boston y desde Miami hasta Alaska.

Al acercarnos al quinto centenario de la fundación de la arquidiócesis de San Juan, un gran acontecimiento que da testimonio de la larga presencia católica hispana en territorios ahora asociados a los Estados Unidos, el ministerio hispano está atravesando por medio de importantes transiciones tanto a nivel de sus estructuras de apoyo como de los enfoques que empleamos en nuestras tareas pastorales. Incluso en lugares en donde los ministerios en español prosperan y florecen, los obispos y otros líderes están pidiendo una mayor integración de los hispanos en el resto de la vida de la Iglesia Católica en los Estados Unidos. Muchos tienen la esperanza puesta en la promesa brillante de un futuro de enriquecimiento mutuo entre los hispanos y el resto de la población católica. Pero si esa promesa se ha de cumplir, tenemos que confrontar los siguientes retos: renovar nuestra visión para el ministerio hispano, afirmar la igualdad en el liderazgo y promover una integración auténtica de los hispanos en la Iglesia y la sociedad.

1

Estructuras y ministerios

A pesar de su larga presencia en comunidades locales, el esfuerzo coordinado del ministerio hispano a nivel nacional no comenzó sino hasta 1945 cuando el arzobispo Robert Lucey de San Antonio propuso fundar el Comité Episcopal para

U.S. *Latino Catholics from Colonial Origins to the Present*, Orbis, Maryknoll, NY 2000; BADILLO D.A., *Latinos and the New Immigrant Church*, Johns Hopkins University Press, Baltimore, MD 2006.

Católicos de Habla Hispana (*Bishop's Committee for the Spanish Speaking*, en inglés). Los líderes del comité trabajaron para avanzar el ministerio hispano especialmente estableciendo consejos diocesanos católicos para los católicos de habla hispana. En 1970 Pablo Sedillo se convirtió en el nuevo director de esta iniciativa y sus operaciones se trasladaron a las oficinas nacionales de los obispos católicos en Washington D.C. Al observar que «no tenía fácil acceso a los núcleos administrativos más altos, es decir los secretariados» dentro de la Conferencia, Sedillo insistió durante cuatro años que la oficina hispana debería tener el estatus de un secretariado y finalmente los obispos aceptaron la sugerencia. Líderes de la arquidiócesis de Nueva York como el Padre Robert Stern y Encarnación Padilla de Armas, junto con Edgar Beltrán, quien anteriormente había trabajado para el Consejo Episcopal Latinoamericano (CELAM), fortalecieron los esfuerzos de Sedillo al igual que el progreso nacional del ministerio hispano con el proyecto de convocar el Primer Encuentro Nacional Hispano de Pastoral en 1972. Bajo la guía de Sedillo y la de su sucesor Ron Cruz, el Secretariado para Asuntos Hispanos de la Conferencia de Obispos jugó un papel central en la organización de éste y otros dos Encuentros nacionales en los que los católicos hispanos expresaron sus necesidades pastorales y su visión al igual que otros numerosos esfuerzos para promover el liderazgo latino y el ministerio hispano a nivel parroquial, diocesano, regional y nacional. El Secretariado también fue instrumental en el esfuerzo de organización del «Encuentro 2000», una iniciativa para unir líderes de los diversos grupos raciales y étnicos que hacen parte del catolicismo en los Estados Unidos, el cual culminó en una reunión nacional llamada *Muchos Rostros en la Casa de Dios: Una Visión Católica para el Tercer Milenio*[3]. Los obispos financiaron los Encuentros y los apoyaron con directivas como la carta pastoral de 1983 sobre el ministerio hispano, el *Plan Pastoral Nacional para el Ministerio Hispano* de 1987 y el documento *Encuentro y Misión: Un Marco Pastoral Renovado para el Ministerio Hispano* en el 2002[4].

---

3 SANDOVAL M., «The Organization of a Hispanic Church» en DOLAN J.P. y FIGUEROA DECK A. (eds.), *Hispanic Catholic Culture in the U.S.: Issues and Concerns*, University of Notre Dame Press, Notre Dame, IN 1994, 131-65, especialmente 139; STEVENS-ARROYO A.M., «The First Encounter» en *Prophets Denied Honor: An Anthology on the Hispano Church in the United States*, Orbis, Maryknoll, NY 1980, capítulo 8; UNITED STATES CONFERENCE OF CATHOLIC BISHOPS, FAQS *About Many Faces in God's House:* Encuentro 2000, http://www.nccbuscc.org/encuentro2000/questions.htm (página visitada en mayo del 2009).

4 NATIONAL CONFERENCE OF CATHOLIC BISHOPS (ahora conocida como UNITED STATES CONFERENCE OF CATHOLIC BISHOPS), *La Presencia Hispana: Esperanza y Compromiso*, USCC, Washington, D.C. 1984; idem, *Plan Pastoral Nacional para el Ministerio Hispano*, USCC, Washington, D.C. 1988. Ambos documentos se encuentran en UNITED STATES CONFERENCE OF CATHOLIC BISHOPS,

Aparte de los esfuerzos de los obispos, diversas iniciativas regionales y nacionales para el ministerio hispano surgieron rápidamente tales como la fundación de PADRES (*Padres Asociados por los Derechos Religiosos, Educativos, y Sociales*) en 1969 y el establecimiento de Las Hermanas en 1972. A lo largo de las siguientes décadas los católicos latinos establecieron diferentes organizaciones nacionales para apoyar y promover el trabajo de los latinos sirviendo como ministros en la liturgia, diáconos, seminaristas, catequistas, teólogos, historiadores de la Iglesia, jóvenes y directores diocesanos del ministerio hispano. También establecieron institutos pastorales como el Centro Cultural México Americano (MACC, sigla en inglés, el cual ahora se llama Colegio Católico México Americano) en San Antonio, el Centro Pastoral Hispano del Nordeste en Nueva York y el Instituto Pastoral del Sureste (SEPI) en Miami, los cuales sirven como centros para estudiar español y formación pastoral al igual que como promotores del ministerio hispano y la justicia en la Iglesia y la sociedad. En 1991 el sacerdote jesuita Allan Figueroa Deck guió la iniciativa de fundar el Consejo Nacional Católico para el Ministerio Hispano (NCCHM, sigla en inglés), un grupo que acoge cerca de sesenta organizaciones católicas hispanas[5].

La reestructuración de la Conferencia de Obispos Católicos de Estados Unidos (USCCB, sigla en inglés) estableció en el año 2007 un nuevo Secretariado de Diversidad Cultural en la Iglesia cuyo propósito es fomentar la unidad eclesial y a responder a las necesidades espirituales de los católicos latinos, afroamericanos, asiáticos y las personas provenientes de las islas del Pacífico, indígenas estadounidenses, migrantes y refugiados. En medio de este proceso se disolvió el Comité Episcopal para Asuntos Hispanos y se cerró el Secretariado para Asuntos Hispanos. Uno de los objetivos de esta reestructuración es integrar a los hispanos y a otros grupos históricamente menos representados para que participen más plenamente en la vida y la misión de la Iglesia en los Estados Unidos,

---

Ministerio Hispano: Tres Documentos Importantes, USCCB, Washington, D.C. 1995. UNITED STATES CONFERENCE OF CATHOLIC BISHOPS, *Encuentro y Misión: Un Marco Pastoral Renovado para el Ministerio Hispano*, USCCB, Washington, D.C. 2002, http://www.usccb.org/hispanicaffairs/encuentromissionsp.shtml. Citas tomadas de estos documentos importantes aparecen en contexto más adelante en este ensayo.

5 RODRÍGUEZ E., «The Hispanic Community and Church Movements: Schools of Leadership» en DOLAN J.P. y FIGUEROA DECK A. (eds.), *Hispanic Catholic Culture in the U.S.*, 206-39; MEDINA L., *Las Hermanas: Chicana/Latina Religious-Political Activism in the U.S. Catholic Church*, Temple University Press, Philadelphia 2004; MARTÍNEZ R.E., PADRES: *The National Chicano Priest Movement*, University of Texas Press, Austin 2005; BURGUÉS J.P., *SEPI 1978-2008: 30 Años de Evangelización en el Sureste y en la Nación*, Centro de Artes Gráficas, Miami 2008.

asegurando su participación en las cinco metas prioritarias que los obispos se propusieron recientemente: fortalecer el matrimonio; promover vocaciones al sacerdocio y a la vida religiosa; fomentar la formación en la fe y la práctica sacramental; afirmar la vida y la dignidad de la persona humana; y apreciar la diversidad cultural, con un énfasis especial en el ministerio hispano en el espíritu del Encuentro 2000[6].

Un buen número de líderes en el ministerio hispano expresaron su preocupación al reconocer que por medio de la reestructuración de la Conferencia de Obispos Católicos se perdió un gran instrumento de apoyo a sus esfuerzos a nivel nacional y el símbolo más prominente de la visibilidad hispana dentro del catolicismo estadounidense: el secretariado. En agosto del 2007 el Consejo Nacional Católico para el Ministerio Hispano convocó un simposio de líderes católicos hispanos reconocidos quienes enviaron una declaración de preocupación y compromiso al Comité Episcopal para Asuntos Hispanos (que aún estaba activo hasta su última reunión en noviembre del 2007). La declaración agradeció a los obispos «que se expresaron en contra de la decisión de la Conferencia de Obispos Católicos de integrar estructuralmente el Secretariado para Asuntos Hispanos dentro de la nueva Oficina [*sic*] para la Diversidad Cultural en la Iglesia». El documento también advirtió que esta decisión «puede causar un impacto negativo en el cuidado pastoral y en la formación de líderes hispanos» cuyos números crecientes, «desafíos y oportunidades excepcionales… requieren unos medios y un apoyo institucional que pueden quedar diluidos si se agrupa la pastoral hispana junto a otras pastorales étnicas y raciales». La declaración lamentó que el plan para el nuevo Secretariado de Diversidad Cultural en la Iglesia «divide estructuralmente a la Iglesia en dos grupos: el de los católicos blancos y el de los católicos no blancos, según la Oficina Estatal del Censo». Los líderes hispanos concluyeron con una serie de recomendaciones para responder a estas preocupaciones en la implementación de las cinco prioridades pastorales y el plan de reestructuración de la USCCB, los cuales prometieron apoyar firmemente a pesar de sus desacuerdos[7].

6 Para una visión general de las cinco prioridades y los objetivos que los obispos establecieron para cada una de ellas, véase http://www.usccb.org/priorities/ (página visitada en mayo del 2009).
7 Consejo Nacional Católico para el Ministerio Hispano (NCCHM), «Response to the USCCB Reorganization» in *Origins* 37 (10 de enero del 2008) 486-7.

Los cambios recientes en la Conferencia de Obispos Católicos son el reflejo de realidades más amplias que están transformando significativamente las estructuras de apoyo al ministerio hispano. Los recursos económicos para la financiación de proyectos se han reducido alarmantemente. Ya se han disuelto grupos como la Organización Nacional de Catequesis Hispana (NOCH) y varios más están en peligro inminente de desaparecer. Algunas oficinas regionales para el ministerio hispano creadas a partir del Segundo Encuentro Nacional Hispano en 1977 están prácticamente extintas y muchas de las organizaciones nacionales hispanas se han debilitado o están asumiendo modelos operacionales más autosuficientes. Algunas organizaciones católicas «dominantes» que operan a nivel nacional han demostrado un deseo alentador de incorporar más líderes hispanos como es el caso del foro de catequesis con hispanos dentro de la Conferencia Nacional para el Liderazgo Catequético (NCCL, sigla en inglés), el cual Alex Sandoval, un joven educador religioso de Texas, ayudó a establecer. Aún así, una tarea crucial para quienes estamos comprometidos con el futuro del ministerio hispano es promover las organizaciones nacionales e institutos que son más eficaces en la coordinación y orientación de nuestros esfuerzos. Afortunadamente el Padre Allan Figueroa Deck, cuyo nombramiento como director ejecutivo del nuevo Secretariado de Diversidad Cultural en la Iglesia fue recibido y apoyado cálidamente por los líderes hispanos, ha lanzado una iniciativa para crear un foro nacional con líderes experimentados en el ministerio hispano dirigido precisamente a fortalecer nuestras estructuras nacionales y regionales.

Sea cual fuere el éxito que alcancemos en la revitalización de estas estructuras, el gran desafío reside en que la mayoría de las iniciativas dentro del ministerio hispano giran alrededor de las comunidades locales mucho más de lo que se experimentó desde la segunda guerra mundial, ahora cuando las vocaciones sacerdotales y los recursos en las diócesis y parroquias son cada vez menos. El punto es que, ya sea por necesidad o según un plan, los ministerios hispanos y otros ministerios florecen mucho más cuando están arraigados en iniciativas locales como en el caso de Nacogdoches durante esos años difíciles después del asesinato del padre José Antonio Díaz de León.

Hay muchas cosas ocurriendo a nivel local. Hace veinte años el P. Allan Figueroa Deck identificó tres modelos comunes en el ministerio hispano: el tradicionalista, el reformista y el transformador[8]. Las condiciones cambiantes den-

8 FIGUEROA DECK A., «Hispanic Ministry Comes of Age» en *America*154 (1986) 400-02.

tro de la Iglesia y la sociedad, incluyendo cierres de parroquias y controversias sobre inmigración, junto con la expansión geográfica de la creciente población latina a través del territorio estadounidense, han transformado el contexto del ministerio hispano. Los siguientes cuatro enfoques dibujan un mapa colectivo de las visiones operantes entre muchos líderes actualmente involucrados en el ministerio. Dichas opciones no son mutuamente excluyentes; más bien reflejan distintos énfasis y prioridades. En cada enfoque ofrezco una breve evaluación de sus fortalezas y debilidades.

Un primer enfoque se pudiera llamar movimiento. Los veteranos y veteranas que enfatizan este enfoque ayudaron a crear y fortalecer el ministerio hispano durante varias décadas. Algunos sirvieron como líderes desde el mismo Primer Encuentro Nacional Hispano en 1972 e incluso antes. La preocupación central de estos líderes ha sido crear condiciones de visibilidad para los hispanos dentro del catolicismo en los Estados Unidos y hacer que tanto el liderazgo como el ministerio hispano sean una prioridad. Muchos han aplicado las lecciones aprendidas a raíz de su participación en movimientos sociales y de organización comunitaria para resaltar las preocupaciones de los hispanos en la Iglesia Católica en este país. Según *Encuentro y Misión*, estos líderes ayudaron a forjar una «memoria histórica» que ilumina la «identidad singular» y la «rica historia de los católicos hispanos en Estados Unidos» (n. 11). Los miembros de este grupo son quienes usualmente se muestran más frustrados con las transiciones estructurales recientes y con el estado general del ministerio hispano. Para ellos estos cambios pueden parecer como un rechazo o un retroceso en cuanto a los logros obtenidos con su propia sangre, sudor y lágrimas. Estos líderes nos recuerdan que cualquier conversación sobre el futuro tiene que sostenerse en una comprensión crítica del pasado. Su fidelidad, compromiso por la justicia, experiencia y sabiduría son de mucho valor.

Un segundo grupo es constituido por los nuevos inmigrantes. Las iniciativas relacionadas con el ministerio hispano en los Estados Unidos tienden a concentrarse más en la experiencia de los inmigrantes. Sus ritos y devociones tradicionales, el reconocimiento de sus necesidades espirituales y materiales, el uso preferencial del español y el compromiso de los pastores que les acompañan en solidaridad hacen que este grupo se pueda organizar más fácilmente a través de comunidades de fe vibrantes. La preponderancia del clero latino nacido fuera de los Estados Unidos —un análisis estadístico reciente indica que cinco de cada seis de los 2.900 sacerdotes latinos ejerciendo el ministerio en los

Estados Unidos nacieron fuera del país[9]— hace posible la prevalencia de un ministerio hispano enfocado en los inmigrantes y realizado primordialmente en español. Algunos programas diseñados para orientar a los sacerdotes inmigrantes se encuentran establecidos en Oblate School of Theology en San Antonio, Loyola Marymount University en Los Angeles y St. Patrick's Seminary en Menlo Park, California, pero desafortunadamente estos programas no llegan a todos estos sacerdotes que vienen a servir en los Estados Unidos[10]. Como consecuencia, los nuevos líderes inmigrantes con frecuencia conocen poco o nada de los acontecimientos históricos esquematizados anteriormente, los cuales han definido el desarrollo del ministerio hispano. Estos líderes tienden a equiparar el ministerio hispano con el apostolado en español; muchas veces juzgan negativamente a los latinos que no hablan español muy bien y poco conocen o no se identifican de lleno con su tradición cultural hispana. Sin embargo, estos líderes también traen mucha energía y un gran espíritu a las parroquias, los movimientos apostólicos, los grupos de oración y las luchas diarias de los inmigrantes para sobrevivir y afirmar su dignidad. Sus vínculos con Latinoamérica son vitales para nutrir el sentido de comunión y misión hemisféricas al cual nos llamaron el Papa Juan Pablo II en la su exhortación apostólica *Ecclesia in America* en 1999 y el Papa Benedicto XVI en su discurso inaugural en la V Conferencia General del Episcopado Latinoamericano y del Caribe en Aparecida, Brasil en el 2007. Aún más, la dedicación de los nuevos líderes inmigrantes es esencial para el resto de hermanos y hermanas inmigrantes quienes se encuentran entre los más olvidados y vulnerables dentro de la sociedad estadounidense.

Un tercer grupo de líderes es el de los integracionistas, quienes acentúan el deseo de incorporar a los latinos en todos los niveles de la Iglesia y la sociedad. Muchos defensores de este enfoque son servidores eclesiales en parroquias y diócesis donde una presencia hispana significativa ha florecido en las dos últimas décadas. Éste es un escenario en el que los latinos son relativamente recién llegados en muchas comunidades euroamericanas ya establecidas. Cada vez son más los casos en que una misma parroquia católica sirve a más de dos grupos lingüísticos, agravando el desafío práctico de servir a una congregación tan diversa cuyo párroco con frecuencia está agobiado por todo el trabajo que esto

---

9   UNITED STATES CONFERENCE OF CATHOLIC BISHOPS, SECRETARIADO DE DIVERSIDAD CULTURAL EN LA IGLESIA, ASUNTOS HISPANOS, «Recordando el pasado con gratitud», http://www.usccb.org/hispanicaffairs/recordandopasado.shtml (página visitada el 9 de enero del 2010).

10 HOGE D. R. Y OKURE A., *International Priests in America: Challenges and Opportunities*, Liturgical Press, Collegeville, MN 2006.

implica. Con o sin intención, algunos esfuerzos de integración marchan a un ritmo y modo particular que los hispanos perciben como un intento de asimilación forzada. Frecuentemente, los feligreses establecidos resisten los esfuerzos de los latinos para transformar la vida parroquial con el argumento de que «nuestros antepasados construyeron esta iglesia» o «nosotros estábamos aquí primero». Aún así, las preocupaciones teológicas de los integracionistas sobre la unidad eclesial y la necesidad de trabajar juntos para promover la vida y la misión de la Iglesia son cruciales cuando se implementan con respeto mutuo. Es más, incluso desde la perspectiva más particular del catolicismo hispano, los integracionistas ofrecen una luz para entender la realidad pastoral de la transición generacional masiva en la población latina en los Estados Unidos: las proyecciones actuales indican que en las próximas tres décadas el número de latinos de tercera generación se triplicará, el de segunda generación se duplicará y el porcentaje total de inmigrantes de primera generación descenderá[11]. Los integracionistas nos recuerdan que los esfuerzos de los padres de familia y los líderes pastorales para formar a los jóvenes latinos en la fe católica, así como la manera en que estos jóvenes latinos practiquen su fe según se van integrando en la Iglesia y en la sociedad, serán decisivos para las próximas décadas del catolicismo en los Estados Unidos.

Un cuarto grupo de liderazgo, el de jóvenes, incorpora de hecho muchas de las perspectivas de los demás enfoques, especialmente el de los nuevos inmigrantes y el de los integracionistas. Sin embargo, dada su visión, su vitalidad, y sus números —los latinos constituyen casi la mitad de los católicos estadounidenses menores de 25 años y más de tres cuartas partes de los católicos menores 18 años en Texas, Nuevo México, Arizona y California— los líderes latinos jóvenes merecen una categoría por separado. Ken Johnson-Mondragón señala que los adolescentes latinos pueden identificarse según cuatro categorías pastorales distintas: trabajadores inmigrantes, buscadores de identidad, integrantes a la cultura dominante, pandilleros y jóvenes de alto riesgo. Un tratamiento más extenso de estas categorías y de los líderes que los sirven se encuentra en el ensayo sobre ministerio hispano y Pastoral Juvenil Hispana en este volumen. Es suficiente afirmar que, como lo implican las cuatro categorías de Johnson-Mondragón, los jóvenes latinos se enfrentan a muchos desafíos. Sin embargo, como in-

---

11 RODRÍGUEZ G., *Mongrels, Bastards, Orphans, and Vagabonds: Mexican Immigration and the Future of Race in America*, Pantheon, New York, NY 2007, 254.

dican las conclusiones del Primer Encuentro Nacional de Pastoral Juvenil Hispana en el año 2006, «[l]a nueva vida que están dando a nuestra Iglesia proviene del celo apostólico de jóvenes que, habiendo puesto a Jesús en el centro de su vida, dedican horas y más horas a compartir y fomentar la fe de sus compañeros»[12]. Aunque este «celo apostólico» y el énfasis en una evangelización vigorosa que lo acompaña de ninguna manera están limitados a los jóvenes latinos, a menudo se consideran como los elementos que son más sobresalientes en el enfoque ministerial actual en el ministerio con los jóvenes hispanos.

2
Incorporación

252   Los anteriores enfoques ministeriales reflejan una preocupación central y permanente propia del catolicismo en los Estados Unidos: el afán de incorporar diversos grupos y a los recién llegados en una comunidad de fe unificada. Un aspecto controversial que sobresale con frecuencia es el cómo alcanzar esa meta de incorporación. Muchos católicos interesados en este asunto lo abordan en medio del debate sobre si los latinos deben mantener el idioma español y su propia herencia cultural a medida que adoptan el lenguaje dominante y la cultura de los Estados Unidos. Algunas entrevistas con líderes diocesanos y parroquiales realizadas como parte de un informe del Comité Episcopal para Asuntos Hispanos en 1999 revelan desacuerdos entre los católicos estadounidenses sobre el tema de «incorporación vs. asimilación». El reporte del estudio indicó que «existe una tensión constante entre quienes proponen que la mejor manera de incorporar a los hispanos en la Iglesia es asimilándolos rápidamente a la experiencia católica y la cultura dominante en los Estados Unidos y quienes defienden que una verdadera incorporación exige que primero se acoja a los hispanos en sus propios términos». Un grupo mantuvo que «forzar a los hispanos a asimilarse inmediatamente sólo reiteraría su estatus subalterno dentro de la Iglesia» y propuso que se ofrecieran sacramentos y otras actividades en español, llamando y

---

12 JOHNSON-MONDRAGÓN K., «Socioreligious Demographics of Hispanic Teenagers» en JOHNSON-MONDRAGÓN K. (ed.), *Pathways of Hope and Faith Among Hispanic Teens: Pastoral Reflections and Strategies Inspired by the National Study of Youth and Religion*, Instituto Fe y Vida, Stockton, CA 2007, 19-20, 33-9; NATIONAL CATHOLIC NETWORK DE PASTORAL JUVENIL HISPANA —LA RED, *Conclusiones: Primer Encuentro Nacional de Pastoral Juvenil Hispana*, PENPJH, USCCB, Washington, D.C. 2008, 12.

formando a líderes hispanos, y, «sólo cuando la comunidad católica hispana se haya fortalecido lo suficientemente», incorporarlos más ampliamente a la vida parroquial. Otro grupo insistió que dicha «visión gradual» corre el «riesgo de cometer los mismos errores del pasado, de producir pequeñas parroquias nacionales con actitudes excluyentes que dividen a la Iglesia»[13].

El papel integrador de la parroquia nacional o étnica en la experiencia de los inmigrantes católicos de origen europeo es bien conocido. En un principio estas parroquias fueron refugios donde los inmigrantes nutrían su fe y abrigaban un sentido de pertenencia que les llevaba a sentir la comunidad como suya en una tierra extranjera. A lo largo del tiempo estas parroquias nacionales permitieron que los descendientes de los inmigrantes se integraran en la sociedad estadounidense y en la vida eclesial desde una posición bastante firme[14]. Hoy la norma en la mayoría de las diócesis es que existan parroquias integradas o multiculturales aunque en realidad muchas de estas congregaciones podrían ser descritas más exactamente como estructuras «americanizadoras» que buscan la asimilación de los recién llegados o, por el contrario, parroquias «segmentadas» en las que dos o más grupos comparten el mismo templo pero en la práctica permanecen aislados unos de otros[15]. Entre las razones históricas que exigieron un cambio de estrategia pastoral y llevaron a considerar opciones distintas a las parroquias nacionales tenemos: el rápido descenso en el número de inmigrantes europeos y sus descendientes participando activamente en estas comunidades étnicas y el eventual abandono de dichas comunidades, el deterioro de los edificios que usaron comunidades inmigrantes en el pasado, la pérdida de fe de algunos descendientes de inmigrantes que identifican el catolicismo con aquellas prácticas «arcaicas» de las comunidades reunidas en la antigua parroquia nacional, la cada vez más pronunciada escasez de sacerdotes y de recursos

13 COMITÉ EPISCOPAL PARA ASUNTOS HISPANOS, *Hispanic Ministry at the Turn of the New Millennium*, NCCB, Washington, D.C. 1999, sección de entrevistas de campo, n. 2, http://www.nccbuscc.org/hispanicaffairs/study.shtml (página visitada en mayo del 2009).

14 El importante estudio de Silvano Tomasi sobre los inmigrantes italianos en Nueva York se cita a menudo para demostrar esta tesis de gran influencia. TOMASI S.M., *Piety and Power: The Role of Italian Parishes in the New York Metropolitan Area, 1880-1930*, Center for Migration Studies, Staten Island, NY 1975.

15 JOHNSON-MONDRAGÓN K., «Ministry in Multicultural and National/Ethnic Parishes: Evaluating the Findings of the Emerging Models of Pastoral Leadership Project», 9-10, reporte y presentación durante la conferencia de National Ministry Summit: Emerging Models of Pastoral Leadership conference, abril del 2008, http://www.emergingmodels.org/doc/Multicultural%20Report%20(2).pdf (página visitada en junio del 2009).

económicos, y la opinión de que las parroquias nacionales conducen a la fragmentación del cuerpo de Cristo.

Encuentro y Misión expresó sus reservas sobre un «modelo "multicultural"» que con frecuencia diluye la «identidad y la visión del ministerio hispano» y que excluye «al personal del ministerio hispano en el proceso de toma de decisiones» (n. 69). Los obispos señalaron que «[e]l compromiso de los hispanos a ser participantes activos y ofrecer sus singulares contribuciones, de *incorporarse* a la vida de la Iglesia y la sociedad en vez de simplemente *asimilarse*, ha sido un valor y principio primordial para los hispanos en el ministerio». (n. 14, énfasis en el original). Un líder hispano laico se lamentó de la siguiente manera: «Me desanima el hecho de que nosotros los hispanos no contamos en esta parroquia. Somos muchos los que venimos a misa y nuestras misas están verdaderamente llenas del espíritu. Pero todo el poder está en manos de un pequeño grupo de feligreses establecidos (quienes no son hispanos) que contribuyen mucho dinero a la Iglesia»[16].

Los hispanos a menudo responden a la idea de parroquias integradas con lo que se pudiera llamar una «dinámica de parroquia nacional», la cual diríamos es la lección más clara que debemos tener en cuenta en la historia del ministerio hispano durante el último medio siglo. Conscientemente o no, al igual que los inmigrantes de origen europeo que establecieron las parroquias nacionales, los latinos intentan establecer y mantener las celebraciones de fiestas religiosas, movimientos de renovación, organizaciones piadosas y otras estructuras de vida católica que les permitan pasar por lo menos del sentimiento de ser objeto de hospitalidad en una comunidad eclesial que pertenece a otras personas a uno de llegar a casa en su propia comunidad eclesial. Teológicamente, el considerable activismo eclesial de los latinos a lo largo de este último medio siglo hace eco a las mismas convicciones de los muchos millones de recién llegados a lo largo de la larga saga del catolicismo en los Estados Unidos: la casa de Dios no es santa sólo porque todos somos bienvenidos; la casa de Dios es santa porque todos pertenecemos como miembros sinceramente valorados en este hogar.

Sin embargo, los líderes pastorales están profundamente preocupados sobre la dinámica de la incorporación de los latinos en la Iglesia Católica en los Estados Unidos y en el resto de las estructuras de la sociedad. Como señalaron nuestros obispos en *Encuentro y Misión*: «[El ministerio hispano] debe ser visto

16 COMITÉ EPISCOPAL PARA ASUNTOS HISPANOS, *Hispanic Ministry at the Turn of the New Millennium*, sección de entrevistas de campo, n. 8.

como parte integral de la vida y misión de la Iglesia en este país. Debemos ser incansables en nuestros esfuerzos de promover y facilitar la participación plena de los católicos hispanos en la vida de la Iglesia y en su misión» (n. 60). Tales declaraciones afirman que el ministerio hispano no se trata sólo o principalmente de la realidad hispana sino que es algo que afecta la catolicidad de toda la Iglesia en los Estados Unidos.

Muchos líderes eclesiales se mantienen particularmente atentos a lo que la dinámica de integración significa en cuanto a la vitalidad de la permanencia de los latinos en la Iglesia y el tema de la unidad de las parroquias cada vez más diversas culturalmente en los Estados Unidos. La mayoría de los latinos —un 60 por ciento según la Oficina del Censo de los Estados Unidos— no son inmigrantes. El impacto de la tasa de nacimiento y de residencia en los Estados Unidos en cuanto al uso del idioma es importante: mientras que más de la mitad de los adultos latinos hablan exclusiva o primordialmente español en sus hogares, dos tercios de los adolescentes latinos hablan exclusiva o primordialmente inglés entre sus amigos[17]. Los líderes latinos insisten en la necesidad de más iniciativas para el ministerio entre los jóvenes latinos nacidos en los Estados Unidos, una necesidad claramente articulada en el Primer Encuentro Nacional de Pastoral Juvenil Hispana. Obispos, párrocos y directores diocesanos expresan cada vez más su deseo de que los líderes pastorales hispanos no sólo proporcionen un servicio pastoral excelente en las comunidades hispanas, sino que también sirvan como «gente puente»: mujeres y hombres que sean fuentes de unidad construyendo puentes entre los latinos y los demás miembros de la Iglesia con quienes comparten su fe[18].

Los latinos católicos en los Estados Unidos exhiben tanto una dinámica de parroquia nacional como la tendencia a integrarse como lo hicieron los católicos de origen europeo. Lo que más los distingue como grupo es que en su caso *ambas* dinámicas han estado ocurriendo simultáneamente por un periodo más extendido. Ningún grupo en la historia de los Estados Unidos se ha visto confrontado con una expansión poblacional similar a la de los hispanos en cuanto a la presencia de inmigrantes y sus descendientes, de habla inglesa u otra lengua, recién llegados y residentes establecidos. Una encuesta nacional en el año 2000 confirmó que los latinos valoran tanto su herencia étnica como la vida en los

17 JOHNSON-MONDRAGÓN K., «Socioreligious Demographics of Hispanic Teenagers», 24.
18 GURZA A., «*Ni Aquí* Nor There» en *u.s. Catholic* 73 (2008) 12-17.

Estados Unidos: mientras que el 89 por ciento de los hispanos encuestados reconocieron que para ellos es importante «mantener sus culturas», el 84 por ciento de entrevistados en el mismo grupo afirmaron también que es importante «que los latinos cambien para poder integrarse al resto de la sociedad tal como en la idea de un crisol de culturas [*melting pot*, en inglés]». Las conclusiones del Primer Encuentro Nacional de Pastoral Juvenil Hispana incluyeron la declaración de la misión de los delegados representando a los jóvenes en la cual se afirma: «Aspiramos a ser parte de la sociedad en EUA, sin perder nuestra identidad y raíces culturales»[19].

La *simultaneidad* de la solidaridad étnica y la continua ola migratoria *junto con* la transición generacional en la Iglesia y la sociedad estadounidense —lo cual ha sido evidente entre los hijos de inmigrantes católicos latinos al menos desde cerca de 1920— a menudo es ignorada tanto por los católicos hispanos como por el resto de la comunidad católica. Por una parte se escuchan con frecuencia pronunciamientos tales como: «De cualquier manera se asimilarán más o menos dentro de una generación o quizás un poco más. Al ofrecerles servicios en español lo único que hacemos es retrasar el proceso. Otros grupos de inmigrantes también se sintieron "presionados" cuando llegaron. Éste es tan solo un grupo más que está experimentando el ajuste a la vida en los Estados Unidos. Ya pasará». Dichas afirmaciones ignoran realidades tales como la llegada continua de nuevos inmigrantes, la influencia que tiene la cercanía de la frontera en cuanto a la retención del idioma y la cultura, el poder de los medios de comunicación en español, la adaptabilidad de muchos latinos nacidos en los Estados Unidos para mantener sus costumbres y su habilidad de hablar español, y las enseñanzas de la Iglesia sobre el respeto a las tradiciones de fe y la herencia cultural de un grupo. Por otro lado, algunos líderes en el ministerio hispano se centran sólo en estas realidades y desestiman o pasan por alto el número considerable de latinos que sólo hablan inglés, cuyas conexiones con la herencia hispana son débiles, practican su fe primordialmente en parroquias que no son hispanas o incluso han dejado el catolicismo para ser parte de otra denominación o simplemente no practican ninguna forma de religión. La fe vibrante de los inmigrantes católicos en muchas parroquias hispanas alimenta el concepto erróneo de que la gran mayoría de los hispanos mantendrán indefinidamente

---

19 GOLDSTEIN A. y SURO R., «A Journey in Stages: Assimilation's Pull Is Still Strong, But Its Pace Varies» en *Washington Post*, January 16, 2000, A1; NATIONAL CATHOLIC NETWORK DE PASTORAL JUVENIL HISPANA —LA RED, *Conclusiones: Primer Encuentro*, 51.

sus lazos culturales y la habilidad de hablar español. La implementación de enfoques pastorales unilaterales son inadecuados en este contexto, tanto aquellos que enfatizan una asimilación acelerada y el uso exclusivo del inglés como aquellos que promueven un separatismo étnico prolongado y el establecimiento de ministerios sólo en español.

Cuando se integra la vitalidad de los ministerios hispanos al resto de la vida de la Iglesia, los latinos tienen la oportunidad tanto de recibir como de contribuir a la vida católica en los Estados Unidos. El celo y el genio organizacional de los católicos en este país permitieron establecer los sistemas privados de educación, salud y servicios sociales más grandes del mundo. A pesar de los profundos desafíos económicos y de personal a los que deben enfrentarse las escuelas católicas para aumentar el acceso de los latinos cuando sea posible, estas instituciones son particularmente uno de los recursos más eficaces para que los padres latinos ofrezcan a sus hijos una formación en la fe y un mejor futuro. Lamentablemente sólo un 3 por ciento de los niños latinos están matriculados en escuelas católicas elementales y secundarias[20]. El énfasis en la parroquia como el corazón de la experiencia católica, muy característico en los Estados Unidos, anima a los latinos a fortalecer sus tradiciones culturales y familiares sostenidas por la fe católica. La parroquia invita a un compromiso más profundo con la Iglesia como comunidad sacramental en la que todos están unidos en una fe y una misión común. Varios programas de formación de fe y liderazgo urgen a los latinos a ampliar su conocimiento de la fe católica y a vivirla como catequistas, directores de pastoral juvenil, diáconos y por medio de otros compromisos. Por ejemplo, los programas de formación para el diaconado permanente son relativamente raros en Latinoamérica pero en muchas diócesis en los Estados Unidos son bastante vibrantes. A nivel nacional el número de diáconos permanentes hispanos es casi similar al número de sacerdotes hispanos. La amplia gama de grupos étnicos y raciales en la Iglesia Católica en los Estados Unidos, que es al mismo tiempo la institución más diversa del mundo dentro de una misma nación, invita a los latinos y los demás católicos en esta comunidad de fe a aceptar aquella unidad enraizada en la fe y el bautismo que sobrepasa toda división humana.

---

20 Véase EL EQUIPO DE TRABAJO DE LA UNIVERSIDAD DE NOTRE DAME RESPECTO A LA PARTICIPACIÓN DE LOS NIÑOS Y FAMILIAS LATINAS EN ESCUELA CATÓLICAS, *Para alentar el espíritu de una nación: familias latinas, escuelas católicas y oportunidades educativas*, University of Notre Dame, 12 de diciembre del 2009, http://catholicschooladvantage.nd.edu/assets/19177/nd_ltf_report_final_spanish_12.2.pdf (página visitada el 8 de enero del 2010).

Por su parte, los latinos tienen mucho que ofrecer al catolicismo en los Estados Unidos y a la sociedad en general, especialmente sus tradiciones y su fe católica y la disposición para entrar en diálogo con su fe cuando se trata de luchar por la justicia. Como señalaron nuestros obispos en su carta pastoral sobre el ministerio hispano de 1983, los latinos poseen valores vitales tales como el respeto por la dignidad de cada persona, un amor profundo por la vida familiar, un hondo sentido de comunidad, un aprecio de la vida como don precioso de Dios y una fuerte y auténtica devoción a María, la Madre de Dios (n. 3). Haciendo eco a su carta pastoral, en *Encuentro y Misión* los obispos declararon que «[l]os católicos hispanos son una bendición de Dios y una presencia profética que ha convertido a muchas diócesis y parroquias en unas comunidades de fe más acogedoras, vibrantes, y evangelizadoras» (n. 6).

Citemos tan sólo un ejemplo. Los hispanos contribuyen una experiencia renovada a la presencia pública del catolicismo en los Estados Unidos junto con un estilo de participación que trasciende enfoques particulares en el momento del diálogo sobre políticas que afectan la vida del pueblo. El fallecido Cardenal Avery Dulles afirmó que «los flujos migratorios desde áreas culturalmente católicas como Latinoamérica… tienen el potencial de aumentar la influencia de la Iglesia en la cultura estadounidense»[21]. Esta influencia incluye expresiones públicas de religiosidad tales como la devoción a Jesús crucificado y su madre sufriente el día de Viernes Santo. Patricia, una líder del Vía Crucis en el vecindario de Pilsen en Chicago, resume el poder de estos acontecimientos de la siguiente manera: «Cristo sufrió hace dos mil años pero continúa sufriendo hoy. Su pueblo sufre. Nos lamentamos y sollozamos. Pero al mismo tiempo somos un pueblo alegre… Así que esto no es una historia, no es un cuento de hadas. Ocurrió y sigue ocurriendo ahora». Para estos participantes la fuerza del ritual reside en su capacidad de mediar un encuentro con Dios que transciende las distinciones limitantes como las que existen entre Pilsen y el Monte Calvario, Chicago y Jerusalén, nuestra era «secular» y el tiempo «sagrado» de Jesús. Estos creyentes participan de tradiciones religiosas no simplemente como representaciones piadosas sino como acontecimientos sagrados que son integrados en la vida dia-

---

21 DULLES A., «The Impact of the Catholic Church on American Culture» conferencia ofrecida en el John Paul II Cultural Center, Washington, D.C., el 13 de noviembre del 2001, reportada en *America* 185 (2001) 5. Véase también DULLES A., «The Impact of the Catholic Church on American Culture» en RAUSCH T.P. (ed.), *Evangelizing America*, Paulist Press, Mahwah, NJ 2004, 11-27, especialmente 23-4.

ria y que animan a los devotos a luchar por la transformación de sus vidas personales y colectivas. El sociólogo de la religión Stephen Warner, quien es luterano, comentó después de su primera experiencia en las procesiones de Viernes Santo organizadas por la comunidad de la catedral de San Fernando por las calles del centro de San Antonio: «Muchos de estos rituales me resultaban extraños… Frente a nosotros vimos una representación realista del sufrimiento y muerte de Jesús, la crueldad de sus verdugos y el dolor de su madre. No había nada metafórico, nada simplemente figurativo, nada genérico sobre estos ritos. Y sin embargo, como anglo, no me sentí excluido». Haciendo eco a esas observaciones, el antiguo párroco de San Fernando, el Padre Virgilio Elizondo, asegura que «el amor de los latinos por los ritos públicos es una contribución que hacemos a la sociedad estadounidense. Pienso que hay un hambre de esto en la vida de quienes viven en los Estados Unidos. Te permite entrar en la fuerza de una experiencia colectiva»[22].

3
Futuro

Nos enfrentamos por lo menos a tres desafíos formidables si aceptamos afirmar el potencial de mutuo enriquecimiento entre los latinos católicos y el resto de la comunidad eclesial. El primero de ellos exige sabiamente renovar nuestra visión para el ministerio hispano. A nivel nacional y regional debemos ser lo suficientemente astutos como para reconocer que en el ambiente actual, a excepción de que ocurra algo completamente inesperado o un acto de la providencia divina, el debilitamiento de algunas de las estructuras por las que muchos hemos trabajado infatigablemente es irreversible. El desafío más urgente es reorganizar nuestros esfuerzos para que sean más eficaces que nunca en la promoción de los ministerios a nivel local en las diócesis y las parroquias. Para hacer esto hemos de tener una discusión franca sobre cuáles de nuestras actuales estructuras nacionales y regionales son más esenciales para sostener los ministerios

22 DAVALOS K.M., «"The Real Way of Praying": The Via Crucis, *Mexicano* Sacred Space, and the Architecture of Domination» en MATOVINA T. y RIEBE-ESTRELLA G. (eds.), *Horizons of the Sacred: Mexican Traditions in U.S. Catholicism*, Cornell, Ithaca, NY 2002, 60; WARNER R.S., «Elizondo's Pastoral Theology in Action: An Inductive Appreciation» en MATOVINA T. (ed.), *Beyond Borders: Writings of Virgilio Elizondo and Friends*, Orbis, Maryknoll, NY 2000, 50; ROURKE M., «A Return to Ritual» en *Los Angeles Times*, 18 de marzo de 1997, E8.

locales. ¿Debemos enfocarnos en organizaciones con un reconocido historial de logros como catalizadores en una región tal como lo ha hecho SEPI en el sureste? ¿Deberíamos considerar los vínculos vitales que ciertas organizaciones tienen con las comunidades eclesiales locales tales como la Asociación Nacional Católica de Directores Diocesanos para el Ministerio Hispano (NCADDHM, sigla en inglés), cuyos miembros tienen una influencia directa en las diócesis en las que sirven? ¿Debemos trabajar estratégicamente con las actuales organizaciones de la «cultura dominante» como es el caso del foro de catequesis con hispanos en NCCL, el cual se estableció después de la desaparición de NOCH? Estos criterios pueden ser vistos como prioridades sólidas desde las cuales podemos iniciar una conversación honesta. La mayor tragedia será entrar en este discernimiento con un provincialismo poco visionario desde el cual queramos simplemente defender nuestros propios intereses y permitiéramos que nuestras organizaciones nacionales y regionales tuvieran que reestructurarse siguiendo algo parecido a una ley de sobrevivencia del más fuerte.

Siendo las parroquias y las diócesis los lugares en donde principalmente se avanza el ministerio hispano, necesitamos que en ellas se haga más análisis de los cuatro enfoques descritos anteriormente al igual que la propuesta de otras posibilidades a considerar. El propósito de esas conversaciones no es defender cuál enfoque es mejor que los otros. Ciertamente, el discernimiento sobre cuál enfoque debe ser usado no debe depender principalmente de las preferencias del líder pastoral sino de las necesidades de la comunidad de fe a la que se sirve. Muchos de nuestros líderes pastorales combinan sabiamente elementos de uno y otro enfoque. Todo líder pastoral debe identificar su propia visión fundamental para el ministerio hispano, es decir el conjunto de percepciones y prioridades al que muchas veces nos adherimos inconscientemente. Éste es un primer paso clave para hacer un examen crítico sobre nuestros diversos enfoques en la pastoral y determinar cómo podemos ponernos más eficazmente al servicio de Cristo y de la Iglesia.

Al discernir la renovación del ministerio hispano de manera que responda a jóvenes y ancianos, inmigrantes y residentes establecidos, y a la enorme diversidad de católicos hispanos, un segundo desafío clave al que nos enfrentamos es la igualdad en el liderazgo en todos los niveles eclesiales. Para llegar a ello tenemos que reconocer quiénes somos. La Iglesia Católica en los Estados Unidos no es una comunidad abrumadoramente inmigrante como lo fue hace un siglo, ni tampoco es simplemente una comunidad «americanizada» como a menudo se asume. Más bien es una iglesia con líderes católicos mayormente de origen euroamericano en todos los niveles con grandes comunidades de inmigrantes latinos, asiáticos y africanos que están creciendo numéricamente, y grandes grupos de católicos latinos nacidos en los Estados Unidos, afroamericanos y algunos indígenas estadounidenses. Nuestros antepasados en la fe nos enseñaron que la estrategia más eficaz para construir una Iglesia diversa pero unida es llamar y preparar líderes de todos los grupos que constituyen nuestra comunidad eclesial, haciendo esfuerzos deliberados para asegurarnos que los líderes de cada grupo participen activamente en aquellas decisiones que nos afectan a todos. Tenemos que aprender de la sabiduría de los doce apóstoles quienes llamaron a siete hombres griegos a servir como diáconos en respuesta a las quejas de que las viudas griegas recibían un trato desigual al de las viudas judías (He 6,1-6). Así resolvieron una dificultad pastoral entre los grupos étnicos y simultáneamente enriquecieron la Iglesia con nuevos líderes.

La formación de líderes pastorales en sus propias comunidades es con frecuencia el eje de atención de los católicos hispanos. Este tema se resaltó como una «gran prioridad» en el Estudio sobre Mejores Prácticas en el Ministerio Hispano/Latino Diocesano en el 2006[23] y fue una de las cuatro dimensiones específicas del *Plan Pastoral Nacional para el Ministerio Hispano*. El promover la formación para el liderazgo y la igualdad tendrá un efecto significativo que se reflejará en otras áreas del ministerio hispano tales como una mejor planificación pastoral, una mejor evangelización y un esfuerzo misionero más vibrante al cual también invitó el *Plan Pastoral Nacional*. ¿Cómo podríamos trabajar para que aumente el número de agentes pastorales hispanos eficaces? Una manera de hacerlo es evaluando la actividad pastoral diocesana y parroquial con una pregunta como la siguiente: «¿cómo fomentará esta actividad el surgimiento de un liderazgo más eficaz?» Por ejemplo, un programa de preparación bautismal se considerará eficaz no sólo si ofrece una catequesis inspiradora sino también cuando identifica, llama y prepara nuevos líderes para participar en la tarea catequética. Sabiendo que muchas parejas de padres y padrinos que asisten a las clases de preparación bautismal tienen una relación poco cercana con su parroquia, una estrategia eficaz es seleccionar tácticamente a las parejas cuya fe

23 UNITED STATES CONFERENCE OF CATHOLIC BISHOPS, COMITÉ EPISCOPAL PARA ASUNTOS HISPANOS, *Study on Best Practices for Diocesan Ministry among Hispanics/Latinos*, Washington, D.C. 2006, 4, http://www.usccb.org/hispanicaffairs/BestPractices2.pdf (página visitada en junio del 2009).

católica es reanimada cuando bautizan a su hijo/a, invitarlas y prepararlas para que compartan su testimonio con otros padres de familia. Este testimonio «de padres a padres» puede ser un medio eficaz para que el Espíritu Santo obre en las vidas de quienes buscan el bautismo para sus hijos y necesitan una reanimación similar de su propia vida de fe.

Sin embargo, la formación de líderes no se puede limitar a los ministerios litúrgicos ni se puede reducir a «los mismos de siempre» o cualquier otro grupo privilegiado. A menudo los nuevos líderes no se comprometen hasta que el personal diocesano, los párrocos u otros servidores eclesiales los invitan. Con frecuencia el número creciente de latinos educados formalmente y de clase media, muchos de los cuales se relacionan con la Iglesia sólo marginalmente o muchas veces no tienen relación alguna con la institución, son una fuente con mucho potencial para el liderazgo. Uno de los temas centrales en las agendas de las organizaciones parroquiales al igual que en las reuniones pastorales y de planificación debe ser la discusión constante sobre quiénes han de ser invitados para ser parte de programas de formación y participar en ministerios específicos.

Una de las necesidades más urgentes es la de fomentar vocaciones hispanas al sacerdocio y a la vida religiosa. Los inmigrantes europeos regularmente contaban con servicios pastorales de religiosos, mujeres y hombres, y sacerdotes provenientes de sus países de origen, quienes a su vez facilitaron el acceso a las autoridades eclesiales y les ayudaron a participar en procesos de toma de decisión. Ningún grupo ha tenido una escasez de vocaciones religiosas tan notable cuando se compara con el tamaño de su población como los latinos católicos. La proporción de sacerdotes hispanos con relación al laicado católico hispano en los Estados Unidos es aproximadamente de 1 a 10.000, más o menos diez veces más laicos por sacerdote que la proporción general para el resto de la población católica estadounidense[24]. Los diáconos permanentes, las religiosas y líderes pastorales que no son latinos, pero que hablan español y conocen la cultura, han ayudado a llenar el vacío, aunque sólo de manera parcial. Las razones para explicar la escasez de vocaciones hispanas son variadas pero muchos líderes latinos resaltan una historia de pocas oportunidades educativas, prejuicio racial en los seminarios, fuertes lazos familiares entre los hispanos que impiden a los posibles candidatos dejar sus círculos familiares, y patrones culturales que en-

---

24 UNITED STATES CONFERENCE OF CATHOLIC BISHOPS, SECRETARIADO DE DIVERSIDAD CULTURAL EN LA IGLESIA, ASUNTOS HISPANOS, «Recordando el pasado con gratitud».

tran en conflicto con el requisito del celibato obligatorio. Hoy en día algunos seminarios, obispos y otros líderes han iniciado esfuerzos para aumentar las vocaciones hispanas al sacerdocio tales como la arquidiócesis de San Antonio que en el año 2009 ordenó el grupo más grande de sacerdotes desde 1930; más de la mitad de los ordenados fueron hispanos. A nivel nacional, sin embargo, los hispanos constituyeron sólo un 12 por ciento de los sacerdotes ordenados en el 2009[25]. Como consecuencia, el bajo número de sacerdotes hispanos y religiosos nacidos en los Estados Unidos reduce las posibilidades de ofrecer modelos para motivar nuevas vocaciones al igual que el desarrollo de ministerios que involucren las generaciones más jóvenes y a otros latinos a medida que se adaptan a la vida en los Estados Unidos. Oración, motivación y apoyo a las vocaciones sacerdotales son prioridades que se han resaltado por mucho tiempo y no podemos dejar de promover estas acciones en ningún momento.

Un tercer gran desafío es aquel de experimentar una visión eclesial de integración arraigada en el Evangelio y en dos mil años de reflexión como parte de la tradición de la Iglesia. Algo que debemos evitar con seguridad es equiparar la unidad con la uniformidad. La expectativa de que los hispanos, incluyendo los inmigrantes recién llegados, participen en misas y eventos parroquiales en inglés para facilitar la «unidad» con frecuencia conducen a una armonía superficial. En el peor de los casos esta expectativa causa frustración, resentimiento y la decisión trágica de que los hispanos no regresen y abandonen la participación en la vida parroquial en la Iglesia. Es bueno recordar que los inmigrantes católicos europeos lograron integrarse completamente en el trascurso de tres generaciones, tiempo durante el cual, gracias a su deseo de pertenecer a sus comunidades y a las circunstancias que dieron lugar a éstas, muchos de ellos se congregaban en parroquias nacionales. Mirando retrospectivamente, su incorporación gradual fue prudente ya que permitió armonizar tanto la práctica de su fe católica como la unidad étnica europea en parroquias estadounidenses. Una estrategia prudente como ésta junto con detallada atención al progreso gradual aliviarían las tensiones que a menudo encontramos en las parroquias y las diócesis que están experimentando un aumento notable en el número de hispanos que llegan a ellas.

25 UNITED STATES CONFERENCE OF CATHOLIC BISHOPS, nota de prensa, «Ordination Class 2009 Has Many Asian-Born, Despite Low Percentage of Asian Catholics in the United States», abril 20 del 2009, http://www.usccb.org/comm/archives/2009/09-083.shtml (página visitada en mayo del 2009).

Una incorporación auténtica requiere respeto mutuo, escuchar a otros y permitir que sus perspectivas influyan sobre las nuestras. Esto exige no sólo la participación de los hispanos en las parroquias y las diócesis, sino también la integración de sus perspectivas en conversaciones en niveles más altos y su participación en los procesos de toma de decisiones que tienen que ver con la dirección de la experiencia católica en los Estados Unidos. Estas perspectivas revelan una brecha fundamental entre muchos católicos hispanos y el resto de católicos de origen europeo. En las últimas cuatro décadas los católicos euroamericanos han enfocado más su atención en las dinámicas internas de la Iglesia: reformas litúrgicas, la voz y el papel del laicado, disensión u obediencia a la ética sexual y otras doctrinas de la Iglesia, el ejercicio adecuado de la autoridad, y la cuestión de quiénes son llamados a la ordenación sacerdotal. El enfoque en estos temas tiende a producir debates marcados por la polarización entre facciones «liberales» y «conservadoras». Dicho enfoque es tan familiar y común entre los católicos estadounidenses que su aplicación al debate público en caso de acontecimientos tales como la crisis generada por el escándalo después de conocerse el problema de abuso sexual de niños por parte de sacerdotes o la selección de un nuevo pontífice es más un reflejo impulsivo que una opción consciente. Los medios de comunicación refuerzan este enfoque dialéctico con su tendencia a cubrir casi todas las historias que se refieren a la Iglesia Católica con comentarios de católicos posicionados a la «derecha» o la «izquierda» de un asunto determinado, pero rara vez consultan a los hispanos, de quienes se asume pueden ser parte de cualquiera de las dos facciones, o pronto lo serán.

En las últimas décadas los hispanos han optado más por acentuar la misión de la Iglesia pidiendo frecuentemente más fondos para las oficinas de ministerio hispano, iniciativas con los jóvenes, esfuerzos para servir necesidades sociales y programas de formación y capacitación de líderes. También han dedicado sus esfuerzos a aumentar el número de misas en español, de obispos hispanos, de celebraciones de fiestas que son parte de sus tradiciones hispanas y de programas de formación dirigidos a seminaristas y otros líderes hispanos con el propósito de integrar la realidad cultural de la comunidad. Aunque estos esfuerzos incluyen y reflejan intentos de reforma interna en áreas como la liturgia y la participación en el liderazgo eclesial, en general apuntan más al deseo de equipar a la Iglesia adecuadamente para servir y acompañar a sus miembros hispanos en la fe y en sus luchas diarias.

En otras palabras, por un lado los líderes católicos hispanos con frecuencia perciben a la Iglesia Católica como una institución muy importante que puede hacer mucho para apoyar a sus hermanos y hermanas que sufren. Por otro lado, los líderes católicos estadounidenses de origen o descendencia europea tienden a preocuparse más de asuntos de democratización y de adaptación de la Iglesia al ambiente de los Estados Unidos o, en el caso contrario, a debatir la idea alarmante de que el catolicismo estadounidense de hecho ha progresado tanto en esta línea que ahora es más estadounidense («americano») que católico. Una de las posibilidades más esperanzadoras para facilitar la incorporación de los hispanos en la Iglesia Católica en los Estados Unidos es su potencial para transcender este impase. Tanto en parroquias como en organizaciones nacionales, la tendencia hispana de enfocarse en la misión de la Iglesia nos recuerda que no se trata tanto de que la Iglesia tenga una misión sino de que la misión evangelizadora de Jesucristo llama a la Iglesia a existir. Involucrar a los hispanos en los procesos de toma de decisiones requiere dejar atrás los viejos hábitos de asumir que sus posiciones se ajustan a las perspectivas y paradigmas existentes. Sabremos que la incorporación de los hispanos ha echado raíces profundas cuando la visión e intuiciones de los líderes hispanos sean parte central de nuestras deliberaciones colectivas como comunidad de fe, sin importar qué tan débiles o fuertes sean articuladas a través de los canales que buscan manejar la opinión católica. Esto no es simplemente un reto pragmático para asegurar la retención de los feligreses hispanos ni una estrategia sociológica para lograr la cohesión de un grupo. Ante todo se trata de un gran desafío eclesial: ser la Iglesia que el Evangelio nos llama a ser para todo el pueblo de Dios.

El ministerio hispano, la evangelización y la formación en la fe

Hosffman Ospino

lido para indagar sobre cómo los católicos hispanos en los Estados unidos están respondiendo a los anteriores interrogantes en sus comunidades. Como académico me propuse comenzar con cuatro hipótesis de trabajo:

1) Los católicos latinos en el suroeste estadounidense, una región en donde la presencia hispana data de siglos, ya han dado pasos importantes para resolver varios de los retos que ahora enfrentan los latinos en otras partes del país cuya presencia es comparativamente más reciente. Sus modelos de formación en la fe y evangelización pueden ser usados por otros católicos latinos en otras partes adaptándolos a las necesidades locales.

2) Los educadores religiosos y agentes pastorales católicos latinos están bien familiarizados con los procesos de los Encuentros y sus conclusiones, los varios documentos de los obispos estadounidenses sobre el ministerio hispano y otros recursos eclesiales sobre formación en la fe que guían la conversación en distintos foros alrededor del país.

3) Teniendo en cuenta que los católicos hispanos constituyen casi la mitad de la población de la Iglesia en los Estados Unidos, en algunos lugares más de la mitad, los procesos de reflexión sobre formación en la fe, evangelización, capacitación de líderes pastorales, educación católica y el elaboración de materiales para la catequesis en todos los niveles de la Iglesia involucran y afirman el liderazgo de un número amplio de voces hispanas.

4) Los líderes católicos que no son latinos no adelantan procesos cruciales de reflexión dentro de las áreas enumeradas en la anterior hipótesis sin primero entrar en conversación con líderes y expertos hispanos y así asegurarse que la complejidad de la experiencia hispana es tenida en cuenta.

¿Fueron estas hipótesis el resultado de la ingenuidad, el idealismo o una simple esperanza? No estoy seguro pero ésa fue la manera como mi sentido pastoral percibía un orden ideal para la acción pastoral. De hecho, esto es lo que he oído que muchos líderes católicos hispanos quisieran lograr. Después de varios años de investigación, práctica ministerial y múltiples conversaciones, la situación se revela más compleja de lo que inicialmente pensaba. El diálogo sobre el ministerio hispano normalmente se mueve en distintas direcciones gracias a la dinámica cambiante de factores como los siguientes: olas constantes de inmigración desde Latinoamérica, el número relativamente pequeño de líderes hispanos en posiciones de liderazgo en todos los niveles de la Iglesia, la inconveniencia de que el ministerio hispano no sea entendido como una preocupación de todos los miembros de la Iglesia, la falta de voluntad para cambiar el status quo en algunos sectores, prejuicios raciales y culturales, la expectativa de que los católicos hispanos eventualmente se «ajustarán» (léase asimilarán) a los modelos pastorales que se consideran como normativos, los recursos limitados para llevar a cabo iniciativas creativas, la débil implementación de políticas y planes, y la inhabilidad de líderes tanto latinos como de otros grupos étnicos de entender con claridad la complejidad de la experiencia hispana, entre otros. Estos factores hacen que sea difícil mantener una conversación sostenida sobre esta realidad tan importante.

El reto no es necesariamente la falta de visión o de deseo de hacer que las cosas trabajen para el bien de todos. De hecho, hay muchas visiones, muy buenas intenciones y gran energía alrededor de los asuntos relacionados con la evangelización y la formación en la fe entre los católicos hispanos. Sin embargo, en este momento histórico es urgente que estos esfuerzos sean interpretados a la luz de un marco analítico que ayude a todos los católicos, tanto latinos como de otros grupos étnicos, a leer apropiadamente nuestra experiencia actual y proponer estrategias prácticas que ayuden a responder mejor a las necesidades de formación en la fe de los católicos hispanos. En el año 2002 los obispos católicos de los Estados Unidos promulgaron una declaración pastoral muy importante llamada *Encuentro y Misión: Un Marco Pastoral Renovado para el Ministerio Hispano*[2]. En este documento, fruto de la conversación con líderes hispanos de todo el país, los obispos propusieron una visión actualizada para el ministerio hispano al comienzo del nuevo milenio. Los obispos y los líderes hispanos afirmaron las intuiciones y experiencias recogidas durante varias décadas de reflexión sobre la realidad hispana católica estadounidense. *Encuentro y Misión* sigue siendo un marco de referencia válido dentro del cual otros marcos deben diseñarse, tal como el que propongo en estas páginas.

El presente ensayo es un ejercicio de reflexión práctica que busca proveer ciertas direcciones que conduzcan a la formulación de un marco analítico para la evangelización y la formación en la fe de los católicos hispanos en los Estados Unidos. Dicho marco analítico exige una revisión de la manera en que hacemos pastoral, evangelizamos, educamos cristianos en nuestras comunidades, creamos materiales para la formación en la fe y preparamos la siguiente generación de líderes para servir a la comunidad católica en este país. Para lograr esto tene-

---

2 UNITED STATES CONFERENCE OF CATHOLIC BISHOPS, *Encuentro y Misión: Un Marco Pastoral Renovado para el Ministerio Hispano*, USCCB, Washington, D.C. 2002, http://www.usccb.org/hispanicaffairs/encuentromissionsp.shtml.

mos que *observar el contexto* en donde estas actividades tienen lugar, *evaluar* lo que funciona y lo que no funciona bien e *imaginar* direcciones, quizás nuevas y más creativas, que nos guíen para llevar a cabo efectivamente la misión de educar en la fe a los católicos hispanos[3].

1

Una mirada rápida a nuestra realidad

La misión evangelizadora de la Iglesia en los Estados Unidos está actualmente siendo transformada por una serie de circunstancias únicas que exigen análisis organizados y la propuesta de estrategias efectivas. Al comienzo del siglo XXI nos encontramos ante retos urgentes tales como el bajo número de católicos que van a la iglesia con regularidad, la escasez de sacerdotes, corrientes secularizadoras, una transición compleja en el liderazgo eclesial, indiferencia en cuanto a la religión institucionalizada, falta de conocimiento de los elementos básicos de la fe, un pluralismo creciente, divisiones generacionales que causan dolor y, todavía, poca claridad sobre cómo responder estratégicamente a la presencia de millones de inmigrantes católicos que vienen de todas partes del mundo. El rápido crecimiento de la población hispana católica, actualmente el 40 por ciento de la población católica en el país, ocurre en medio de este contexto. Sin embargo, no sólo los católicos hispanos tenemos que preocuparnos de estos retos sino que al mismo tiempo tenemos que atender a otros retos que son particulares a nuestra realidad socio-cultural tales como los niveles altos de pobreza, una presencia débil en posiciones de liderazgo en la sociedad y en la Iglesia, los bajos niveles educativos, la inadecuada atención pastoral que se ha dado a los jóvenes latinos, las tasas altas de deserción de la Iglesia y la falta de recursos adecuados para llevar a cabo una evangelización organizada[4].

---

3 El método básico de reflexión pastoral *ver-juzgar-actuar* está integrado de varias maneras en este ensayo. El método en sus distintas variaciones ha sido particularmente de gran valor en los muchos procesos de estudio pastoral y consulta entre los católicos hispanos en los Estados Unidos tales como los Encuentros nacionales, la planeación pastoral, las pequeñas comunidades eclesiales y la reflexión teológica católica latina estadounidense. Cfr. *Encuentro y Misión*, n. 21.

4 Cfr. *Encuentro y Misión*, n. 63-75.

Todos estos retos afectan profundamente el *qué* y el *cómo* de la formación en la fe en las comunidades sirviendo a los católicos hispanos. En cuanto al *qué*, no hay duda que los educadores católicos conocemos los elementos básicos de la fe que estamos llamados a compartir. Para ello contamos con recursos excelentes como las Sagradas Escrituras, el Catecismo de la Iglesia Católica, los Directorios General y Nacional para la Catequesis, las guías catequéticas y muchos otros recursos preparados por casas editoriales, educadores y teólogos. Estos recursos nos recuerdan que hay convicciones centrales que todos los cristianos católicos debemos conocer. Al mismo tiempo nos dejan saber que hay distintas maneras de llegar a conocer dichas convicciones. Los educadores religiosos y catequistas trabajando en contextos hispanos tenemos que saber discernir qué elementos de la tradición cristiana se relacionan más directamente con la experiencia de las latinas y los latinos que vienen a nuestras comunidades a aprender sobre Dios y a profundizar sus convicciones de fe. Tales elementos servirán como puertas de entrada que llevarán a los latinos a un encuentro más dinámico con el conjunto de la tradición de fe y así les ayudarán a apreciar la armonía de las verdades que constituyen nuestra fe cristiana. La experiencia común que determina el punto de partida para la formación en la fe en las distintas comunidades latinas no siempre será el mismo. En algunos casos la experiencia común es la inmigración; en otros, el exilio; en otros, la experiencia de las mujeres hispanas luchando por sus familias en este país; en otros, alguna forma de marginación; en otros, la búsqueda de identidad en una sociedad e iglesia culturalmente diversas. Por consiguiente, los líderes catequéticos deben formularse dos preguntas en el momento de definir el currículo, el *qué* en los proceso de formación en la fe entre los católicos latinos: 1) ¿de qué manera se relaciona el contenido que compartimos con la experiencia actual de los latinos y latinas que vienen a conocer sobre Dios y a profundizar sus convicciones de fe? 2) ¿Qué elementos de la tradición cristiana podemos introducir primero a partir de dicha experiencia para llevar a los latinos a una mejor apreciación de los elementos centrales de nuestra fe?

Cuando hablamos del *cómo*, incursionamos en el campo de las pedagogías y las estrategias para la formación en la fe. En las últimas décadas los católicos en los Estados Unidos han sido bendecidos con la propuesta de varios modelos de formación en la fe que buscan responder al análisis maduro de lo qué significa ser cristianos en esta sociedad. Algunos de estos modelos han nacido en medio del diálogo con las ciencias sociales y otros con las ciencias humanas; algunos incluso han explorado la dimensión política de la formación en la fe[5]. Algunos enfoques han restablecido modelos de formación en la fe que sirvieron en el pasado y son percibidos como de gran ayuda en el contexto actual (ej. el movimiento kerigmático[6] y el catecumenado[7]). Otros se han enfocado en dinámicas comunitarias[8]. Algunos afirman el uso de catecismos, otros el de las Sagradas Escrituras. Los católicos latinos en general hemos participado, y lo seguimos haciendo, en procesos de formación en la fe que usan estos modelos. Sin embargo, tenemos que hacernos la siguiente pregunta: *¿responden verdaderamente estos modelos a la experiencia compleja de ser católico hispano en los Estados Unidos?*

Para responder a esta pregunta tenemos que considerar al menos tres factores:

Primero, muchos de estos modelos pedagógicos son implementados principalmente en contextos institucionales: escuelas, universidades, programas parroquiales de formación en la fe. Sin embargo, la presencia de los hispanos en estos contextos es considerablemente limitada[9]. No todas las parroquias sirviendo latinos tienen programas para los jóvenes hispanos. No todos los jóvenes hispanos encuentran las dinámicas tradicionales de pastoral juvenil (*youth and young adult ministry*) atractivas o incluso abiertas a invitarles a participar en la

5 Cfr. O'HARE P. (ed.), *Foundations of Religious Education*, Paulist Press, New York, NY 1978; GROOME T.H., *Christian Religious Education: Sharing Our Story and Vision*, Jossey-Bass Publishers, San Francisco, CA 1980.

6 Véase JUNGMANN J.A., *The Good News Yesterday and Today*, traducido (resumido) y editado por William A. Huesman, William H. Sadlier, New York, NY 1962.

7 *Rito de la Iniciación Cristiana de Adultos*, Liturgical Press, Collegeville, MN 1991, aprobado por la conferencia nacional de obispos católicos y confirmado por la sede apostólica para uso en las diócesis de los Estados Unidos de América; UNITED STATES CONFERENCE OF CATHOLIC BISHOPS, *Sentíamos arder nuestro corazón: Plan pastoral de Estados Unidos para la formación en la fe del adulto*, USCCB, Washington, D.C. 1999.

8 Véase HUEBSCH B., *Whole Community Catechesis in Plain English*, Twenty-Third Publications, Mystic, CT 2002; Generations of Faith Project, http://www.generationsoffaith.org/

9 En el año 2000 sólo el 10.7 por ciento de todos los estudiantes en las escuelas católicas a nivel primario y secundario eran hispanos. El mismo año sólo el 8.2 por ciento de todos los estudiantes matriculados en 260 universidades católicas en el país era hispano. Sólo la mitad de todos los niños católicos en edad escolar participan en programas parroquiales de educación religiosa. Cfr. FROEHLE B.T. y GAUTIER M.L., *Catholicism USA: A Portrait of the Catholic Church in the United States*, Center for Applied Research in the Apostolate [CARA], Washington, D.C. 2000, 63-86, citado en UNITED STATES CONFERENCE OF CATHOLIC BISHOPS, *Directorio Nacional para la Catequesis*, USCCB, Washington, D.C. 2005, C, 4A, nota 25; MCGRATH R.J., «Students in Catholic Schools» en HUNT T.C., JOSEPH E.A., y NUZZI R.J. (eds.), *Catholic Schools Still Make a Difference: Ten Years of Research, 1991-2000*, segunda edición, National Catholic Educational Association, Washington, D.C. 2004, 84; PETTIT J., *Enrollment in Catholic Higher Education in the United States: 1980 to 2000*, Catholic Higher Education Research Cooperative, Rockville Centre, NY 2004, 5, http://www3.villanova.edu/cherc/research/pdf_j_pettit_enrollment.pdf (página visitada el 15 de enero del 2010).

vida de la Iglesia[10]. No todos los hispanos se adaptan al sistema escolarizado convencional según distintos niveles que caracteriza la mayoría de los programas parroquiales de catequesis; muchos no lo entienden. Cientos de miles de familias católicas hispanas no participan en programa de formación en la fe alguno.

Segundo, un gran número de estos enfoques pedagógicos reflejan modelos culturales de reflexión e interacción con los que con frecuencia muchos católicos hispanos no están familiarizados, especialmente los inmigrantes recién llegados. A menudo dichos modelos requieren que los participantes dediquen grandes cantidades de tiempo y de recursos. Aunque dicha expectativa se ajusta a la experiencia de los católicos que están más establecidos a nivel social y cultural, quienes tienen el privilegio de dedicar tiempo y recursos, ésta poco toma en cuenta las muchas limitaciones de la mayoría de las familias hispanas. Los hispanos en los Estados Unidos en general confrontan problemas urgentes tales como la pobreza generalizada: «mientras que la tasa de pobreza para los blancos no hispanos es del 8 por ciento, la de los afroamericanos es del 24.1 por ciento, la de los hispanos del 21.8 por ciento y la de los indígenas estadounidenses del 23.2 por ciento»[11]. Los bajos niveles de educación entre los hispanos son preocupantes: cerca del 30 por ciento de la población latina en programas de educación secundaria abandona la escuela (siendo los inmigrantes el grupo más afectado), sin contar con que el 15 por ciento de los estudiantes latinos no llega a la secundaria[12]; sólo el 54 por ciento de los latinos que se gradúan de la secundaria van a programas universitarios y de este grupo la mitad va a instituciones de dos años, entre los cuales la mayoría nunca procede a obtener un título profesional (*bachelor's degree*, en inglés)[13]. Algunos estudios indican que en general los cristianos católicos hispanos son más pobres y menos educados que los cristianos

10 Cfr. CERVANTES C.M. y JOHNSON-MONDRAGÓN K., «Pastoral Juvenil Hispana, Youth Ministry, and Young Adult Ministry: An Updated Perspective on Three Different Pastoral Realities» en *Perspectives on Hispanic Youth and Young Adult Ministry*, Publicación 3, Instituto Fe y Vida, Stockton, CA 2007; *Encuentro y Misión*, n. 70.

11 CATHOLIC CHARITIES USA, «Poverty and Racism: Overlapping Threats to the Common Good» en *Origins* 37, n. 34 (2008) 539. En enero del 2010, debido a la crisis económica actual que afecta a los Estados Unidos, el nivel de pobreza promedio entre los hispanos estadounidenses aumentó al 23.2 por ciento.

12 Cfr. GÁNDARA P. y CONTRERAS F., *The Latino Education Crisis: The Consequences of Failed Social Policies*, Harvard University Press, Cambridge, MA 2009, 22-23; CARGER C.L., «Dropout Rates» en DIAZ L. (ed.), *Latino Education in the U.S.*, Rowman & Littlefield Education, Lanham, MD 2008, 106-108; Véase también VÉLEZ W., «The Educational Experience of Latinos in the United States» en RODRÍGUEZ H., SÁENZ R., y MENJÍVAR C. (eds.), *Latinas/os in the United States: Changing the Face of America*, Springer, New York, NY 2008, 129-148.

13 Cfr. GÁNDARA P. y CONTRERAS F., *The Latino Education Crisis*, 24.

protestantes hispanos[14]. Aunque está comprobado que las escuelas católicas son un gran recurso para asegurar altos niveles de educación y éxito académico entre las minorías étnicas, sólo el 3 por ciento de los latinos estudia en escuelas católicas en este país[15]. Tanto la pobreza como los bajos niveles de educación ponen a los católicos hispanos en posiciones de desventaja que comprometen seriamente su formación en la fe[16]. Bajo estas circunstancias, millones carecen del tiempo, los recursos y la experiencia cultural para provocar trasformaciones necesarias en sus comunidades de fe y en el resto de la sociedad.

Tercero, los procesos de formación en la fe en los Estados Unidos se valen notablemente de materiales producidos por casas editoriales, teólogos y otros profesionales. La industria de producción de libros, recursos pedagógicos, guías, trabajos académicos y recursos electrónicos, entre otros, para el apoyo de la formación de los católicos en los Estados Unidos es quizás una de las fortalezas más evidentes del catolicismo en este país, aunque se puede convertir en su propio talón de Aquiles si no logra entender a tiempo los cambios demográficos que están transformando nuestras comunidades eclesiales. En general la industria editorial sirve prioritariamente las necesidades de los católicos de habla inglesa, especialmente aquellos que pudiéramos decir que se identifican con experiencias católicas más establecidas. Aún así, hay que resaltar la labor de aquellas compañías que han respondido al desafío de publicar materiales bilingües (inglés y español), sólo en español, y sólo en inglés aunque incorporando perspectivas latinas. El camino ya está hecho y tenemos que seguir adelante. Para responder a las necesidades más inmediatas de la formación en la fe de la población latina que crece rápidamente en términos de sus números, algunos líderes hispanos han optado por importar libros desde Latinoamérica y España. Aunque estos materiales son de bastante ayuda, muchos de ellos no reflejan la experiencia católica latina en los Estados Unidos y, francamente, no ayudan a los latinos a formar una identidad como miembros de la Iglesia en este país. Algunos

---

14 Cfr. DAVIS K.G., HERNÁNDEZ A., y LAMPE P.E., «Hispanic Catholic Leadership: Key to the Future» en HERNÁNDEZ E.I., PEÑA M., DAVIS K.G., y STATION E. (eds.), *Emerging Voices, Urgent Choices: Essays on Latino/a Religious Leadership*, Brill, Boston, MA 2006, 40-45.

15 Véase EL EQUIPO DE TRABAJO DE LA UNIVERSIDAD DE NOTRE DAME RESPECTO A LA PARTICIPACIÓN DE LOS NIÑOS Y FAMILIAS LATINAS EN ESCUELA CATÓLICAS, *Para alentar el espíritu de una nación: familias latinas, escuelas católicas y oportunidades educativas*, University of Notre Dame, 12 de diciembre del 2009, http://catholicschooladvantage.nd.edu/assets/19177/nd_ltf_report_final_spanish_12.2.pdf (página visitada el 8 de enero del 2010).

16 Cfr. UNITED STATES CONFERENCE OF CATHOLIC BISHOPS, *Directorio Nacional para la Catequesis*, Introducción, 4c.

líderes y editoriales recurren a la práctica de traducir libros y otros recursos del inglés al español. Una vez más, muchas de estas traducciones son de gran ayuda pero no utilizan el potencial de latinas y latinos que son teólogos, educadores religiosos y profesionales en otras áreas, quienes pudieran crear materiales originales en inglés y en español reflejando la profundidad y la riqueza de la experiencia católica hispana estadounidense.

Muchos modelos contemporáneos de formación en la fe en los Estados Unidos tienen un gran impacto en la definición de la experiencia católica hispana, sin embargo estos mismos exhiben serias limitaciones en el momento de responder a algunas dimensiones críticas de dicha experiencia. Con frecuencia dichos modelos sirven a los latinos que son considerados más «americanizados», gracias a su nacimiento o al proceso de aculturación que han experimentado, y a aquellos que pueden acomodarse con más facilidad a los estándares de la cultura dominante. Algunos educadores religiosos y líderes pastorales hacen un trabajo admirable adaptando estos modelos a las necesidades de las comunidades hispanas. Aún así, un gran número de hispanos no es servido apropiadamente a nivel pastoral en nuestras comunidades de fe y su formación catequética está en riesgo por falta de modelos renovados y recursos creativos que respondan a sus necesidades particulares. Es urgente que los líderes eclesiales, los académicos, los educadores religiosos, las casas editoriales y todos quienes estamos involucrados en procesos de evangelización y formación en la fe entendamos los múltiples contextos en los que viven los católicos que hacen parte de la diversidad cultural de nuestras comunidades eclesiales. Por un lado, es necesario entender la complejidad de la experiencia de ser católico hispano en los Estados Unidos. Por otro, hay que aprovechar los espacios para la formación en la fe y los dones que los católicos hispanos contribuyen a partir de sus experiencias culturales y religiosas.

Al comenzar la segunda década del siglo XXI, necesitamos evaluar a la luz de nuestra experiencia católica actual los modelos tradicionales de formación en la fe que han sido propuestos desde contextos históricos y culturales particulares. Necesitamos marcos renovados para la formación en la fe entre los católicos hispanos y, en última instancia, para todos los católicos en los Estados Unidos.

2

Realidad compartida, preocupación de todos

ᘓᔕᕘ

El éxito de nuestras conversaciones sobre la evangelización y la formación en la fe de los católicos hispanos depende de qué tan profundamente entendamos la experiencia general del catolicismo estadounidense. Al mismo tiempo, para elaborar modelos de evangelización y formación en la fe para los católicos estadounidenses tenemos que tener en cuenta la experiencia de los latinos y aquellas de los otros grupos que constituyen la diversidad cultural de nuestra Iglesia[17].

Propongo que consideremos cinco situaciones claves que afectan nuestra realidad actual. Primero, comenzamos el siglo XXI reivindicando el sentido religioso y espiritual de la realidad. Contrario a las muchas predicciones de que el nuevo siglo estaría marcado por un secularismo totalizante y del fin de las instituciones religiosas, somos testigos de una renovada búsqueda de Dios y del deseo de pertenecer a comunidades de fe[18]. Lo que sí es distinto en este momento es que las iglesias «históricas» o tradicionales no son percibidas como las fuentes exclusivas de las respuestas a esa búsqueda de Dios y de sentido, ni siquiera entre los mismos católicos. Es más común que mujeres y hombres tomen sus propias decisiones sobre el tipo de asociación religiosa que prefieren tener; muchos escogen las convicciones de fe que quieren aceptar y rechazan otras; los creyentes de hoy desean expresar su voz en el proceso de establecer criterios y estándares de realización religiosa. Esto es un fenómeno conocido ampliamente entre las generaciones más jóvenes[19]. Un número altísimo de católicos no van a sus iglesias pero aún se sienten identificados con el catolicismo como tradición religiosa y quieren que sus hijos sean bautizados; muchos integran prácticas

---

17 Al tener en cuenta los cambios demográficos en miles de comunidades católicas alrededor del país, hablar de ministerio hispano literalmente significa hablar de ministerio católico en general, y viceversa. En otras palabras, los investigadores, agentes pastorales y organizaciones preocupadas por los asuntos relacionados con la evangelización y la formación en la fe en los Estados Unidos no pueden darse el lujo de tratar la experiencia hispana como un fenómeno aislado ni mucho menos como algo secundario o simplemente una realidad que preocupa sólo a los hispanos.

18 Cfr. UNITED STATES CONFERENCE OF CATHOLIC BISHOPS, *Directorio Nacional para la Catequesis,* 11B; CELAM, *Aparecida: V Conferencia General del Episcopado Latinoamericano y del Caribe: Documento Conclusivo,* CELAM, Bogotá, Colombia 2007, n. 52.

19 HORELL H.D., «Cultural Postmodernity and Christian Faith Formation» en GROOME T.H. y HORELL H.D. (eds.), *Horizons and Hopes: The Future of Religious Education,* ed., Paulist Press, New York, NY 2003, 83-89.

que no son cristianas como parte de su vida espiritual; muchos están afiliados con varias organizaciones religiosas. Algunas de las personas que estudian esta realidad la identifican como postmodernismo y otras la refutan como puro relativismo. Lo que es interesante es el hecho que vivimos en un momento histórico en el que la gente tiene sed de Dios en medio de un contexto pluralista. Si la Iglesia no encuentra caminos creativos y apropiados para responder a la búsqueda de Dios de las mujeres y los hombres contemporáneos y no habla un lenguaje que estas personas puedan entender, lo más seguro es que irán a otro lado donde sí encuentren esto[20].

Segundo, el catolicismo estadounidense está atravesando por un proceso de transiciones múltiples: de un modelo cultural euroamericano de ser católico a uno que es más diverso a nivel cultural, con una influencia más notable de tradiciones culturales y religiosas hispanas. De un catolicismo en gran parte establecido socialmente en la clase media a uno que está echando rápidamente raíces en barrios y grandes centros urbanos. De un catolicismo dominante a uno considerablemente definido por experiencias inmigrantes y marginales. De modelos de liderazgo que dependen primordialmente de personal capacitado profesionalmente a modelos de liderazgo carismático que florecen en las bases pero necesitan formación apropiada para tener un impacto en las distintas estructuras eclesiales y sociales. De perspectivas de liderazgo que se concentran en «lo local» a perspectivas que prestan seria atención a «lo global» gracias a las nuevas dimensiones transnacionales del catolicismo en un mundo globalizado. Todas estas transiciones exigen un nuevo marco analítico que preserve las mejores contribuciones a los procesos de formación en la fe y del liderazgo que los católicos estadounidenses han avanzado hasta hoy, pero que al mismo tiempo incorpore de manera creativa las nuevas perspectivas y voces que están surgiendo en cada esquina de la Iglesia en los Estados Unidos. No hacer esto nos dejaría a merced de modelos anacrónicos e indiferentes a la realidad actual que eventualmente debilitarían el proceso de formación en la fe de los católicos en el país.

---

20 El número de cristianos estadounidenses abandonando sus iglesias tradicionales y cambiando de afiliación religiosa ha incrementado rápidamente en las últimas dos décadas. Gracias a las continuas olas migratorias desde Latinoamérica, en su mayoría católicos, el crecimiento de la Iglesia en los Estados Unidos se ha mantenido estable. Sin embargo, si separáramos el fenómeno hispano por un momento podríamos observar un descenso poblacional dramático. Cfr. KOSMIN B.A., y KEYSAR A., *ARIS 2008: Summary Report*, Institute for the Study of Secularism in Society and Culture, Trinity College, Harford, CT 2008, http://livinginliminality.files.wordpress.com/2009/03/aris_report_2008.pdf (página visitada el 15 de abril del 2009).

Tercero, ser católico en los Estados Unidos significa experimentar lo mejor de la «catolicidad», especialmente expresada en la riqueza de la diversidad cultural de la Iglesia[21]. El catolicismo en los Estados Unidos es una rica mezcla de tradiciones culturales, lingüísticas y religiosas. Ciertamente éste no es un fenómeno nuevo en una comunidad eclesial que desde el principio ha sido formada por inmigrantes de todas partes del mundo. Sin embargo, en distintos momentos de la historia los católicos estadounidenses se han inclinado hacia la idea de una experiencia estándar y dominante que con frecuencia ignora voces, prácticas y perspectivas que no se conforman con aquello que se asume como normativo. Lo interesante es que estas distintas voces, prácticas y perspectivas, usualmente vivas en las márgenes de la Iglesia y de la sociedad, nunca han dejado de influenciar la experiencia católica estadounidense. Hoy en día estamos más atentos a su presencia y sus contribuciones porque están convirtiéndose, irónicamente y sin perder la vitalidad de su diversidad, en la nueva norma de la experiencia católica.

Aunque los católicos hispanos constituimos el grupo étnico más grande dentro de la Iglesia en este país, tenemos que tener cuidado de no asumir que la experiencia hispana es un fenómeno homogéneo. Existen en medio de nosotros muchas experiencias hispanas, cada una marcada por particularidades de carácter cultural, lingüístico, histórico y religioso. Entre estas muchas experiencias, quizás el desafío más importante que tenemos los educadores religiosos y los agentes pastorales trabajando con católicos latinos es la realidad multigeneracional de nuestro pueblo. Las necesidades pastorales de la primera y segunda generación de hispanos son muy distintas, aunque no completamente aisladas, de las de los latinos de tercera, cuarta y otras generaciones. Factores tales como el idioma, la socialización, las perspectivas históricas, la comunicación intergeneracional y la identidad cultural, entre otros, juegan un papel importante que exigen el desarrollo de enfoques evangelizadores distintos al igual que de la habilidad de entrar en diálogo con una variedad de interrogantes, dependiendo del grupo con el que estemos trabajando. Un marco analítico para la formación en la fe de los católicos hispanos tienen que tener en cuenta la diversidad que caracteriza las varias experiencias coexistentes en nuestras comunidades latinas y facilitar el desarrollo de pedagogías basadas en esas experiencias.

---

21 Con relación al concepto de «catolicidad» véase SCHREITER R., *The New Catholicity: Theology between the Global and the Local*, Orbis Books, Maryknoll, NY 1997.

Cuarto, el bajo nivel de conocimiento básico sobre la fe entre quienes viven en los Estados Unidos debe ser una preocupación constante para los educadores religiosos y agentes pastorales de todas las tradiciones religiosas[22]. Desafortunadamente no hay suficientes datos de investigación científica sobre los niveles de dicho conocimiento entre los católicos estadounidenses, pero podemos asumir que éste también es un gran problema en nuestras comunidades. El *Directorio Nacional para la Catequesis* observa que casi la mitad, quizás más, de todos los niños católicos y la mayoría de los jóvenes católicos no reciben catequesis formal:

> Actualmente, en los Estados Unidos están inscritos [*sic*] en los programas de catequesis parroquial el 52 por ciento de los niños católicos en edad escolar, mientras que el 16 por ciento de los niños de escuela primaria están matriculados en escuelas católicas. Tal vez el 2 por ciento recibe enseñanza en su hogar y el porcentaje de jóvenes católicos que cursan la escuela secundaria y que no reciben catequesis sistemática es generalmente un número más elevado[23].

Aún más, muchos católicos no practican su fe activamente y no tienen claridad sobre cómo integrar los valores cristianos básicos en sus propias vidas. Los católicos hispanos no son necesariamente la excepción. No obstante, los católicos hispanos en general bautizan a sus hijos en grandes números, tienen un sentido profundo de lo sagrado y su espiritualidad es continuamente sostenida por prácticas de religiosidad popular. Por consiguiente, las limitaciones y consecuencias del bajo conocimiento de los elementos centrales de la fe deben ser analizadas junto con la fe del pueblo vivida y expresada en lo cotidiano. Ambas perspectivas tienen que estar presentes al momento de proponer las bases de un marco analítico para la formación de la fe nacido dentro del contexto de la Nueva Evangelización[24].

Quinto, el éxito de la misión evangelizadora de la Iglesia y el de sus procesos de formación en la fe depende en gran parte de los líderes que los llevan a cabo. La Iglesia Católica en los Estados Unidos ha sido bendecida con vocaciones

---

22 Véase PROTHERO S., *Religious Literacy: What Every American Needs to Know —and Doesn't*, Harper San Francisco, San Francisco, CA 2007.

23 FROEHLE B.T. Y GAUTIER M.L., *Catholicism USA*, en UNITED STATES CONFERENCE OF CATHOLIC BISHOPS, *Directorio Nacional para la Catequesis*, 4A, nota 25.

24 Ésta es la propuesta de *Encuentro y Misión*. Cfr. *Encuentro y Misión*, n. 25-28.

abundantes al sacerdocio ministerial, la vida consagrada y el ministerio eclesial laico. A pesar del descenso en el número de sacerdotes y religiosos, nuevas formas de liderazgo pastoral siguen germinando[25]. Sin embargo, el número de líderes hispanos preparados adecuadamente para evangelizar y educar en la fe no incrementó paralelamente al número de católicos latinos en las comunidades durante la segunda parte del siglo xx y la primera década del siglo xxi. Es urgente promover más vocaciones al liderazgo eclesial entre los latinos y ampliar su acceso a la formación académica al nivel de universidades y seminarios para poder servir mejor sus comunidades. Además, en una comunidad eclesial culturalmente diversa como la nuestra en los Estados Unidos, todos los ministros de todas las tradiciones culturales y étnicas tienen que ser equipados con las competencias y sensibilidades culturales apropiadas para servir la abundante diversidad que encontramos en nuestras comunidades. Esto ciertamente requiere una comprensión adecuada de la realidad en la que evangelizamos y educamos en la fe, y un compromiso firme de dialogar con todas las voces que constituyen la Iglesia en los Estados Unidos.

Las cinco situaciones anteriores nos permiten ver qué tan compleja es la realidad en la que estamos llamados a evangelizar y a educar en la fe a los católicos hispanos. Con seguridad la lista pudiera ser más larga. Compartimos esta realidad común con todos los católicos en el país y, en cierta manera, con todos los católicos del continente[26]. El avance de reflexiones y la creación de recursos para la evangelización y la formación en la fe entre los católicos hispanos tienen que responder continuamente a los desafíos de nuestro contexto. Para ello es imperativo que afirmemos las fortalezas de nuestras comunidades.

3

Bases claves para la evangelización y la formación en la fe entre los católicos hispanos

Las observaciones anteriores nos ubican ante un panorama que nos permite entender mejor la situación en la cual nos encontramos actualmente con relación a la experiencia católica en los Estados Unidos. Dichas observaciones nos ayudan a identificar las preocupaciones más urgentes que requieren de nuestra aten-

25 Cfr. DeLAMBO D., *Lay Parish Ministers: A Study of Emerging Leadership*, National Pastoral Life Center, New York, NY 2005.
26 Cfr. *Aparecida*, n. 33-59; 98-100.

ción a medida que proponemos pedagogías, programas y materiales para la evangelización y la formación en la fe entre los católicos hispanos.

Ahora es momento de contemplar siete *bases claves* o dimensiones que son parte íntima de la experiencia de la mayoría de los católicos hispanos en este país y deben tenerse en cuenta en la formulación de cualquier marco analítico para la formación en la fe y la evangelización. Varios documentos y conversaciones sobre el ministerio hispano ya han identificado la centralidad de estas bases claves[27]. Es urgente que volvamos a ellas y las evaluemos regularmente con el objeto de ver si están realmente presentes en nuestras metodologías y en los recursos que usamos para la evangelización y la formación en la fe entre los hispanos.

3.1. CATOLICISMO CULTURAL

284

La mayoría de los latinos y latinas en los Estados Unidos se identifica como miembros de la tradición cristiana católica[28]. Sin embargo, no todos los católicos latinos practican su fe activamente[29]. La mayoría de los católicos latinos

---

27 De interés particular es el *Plan Pastoral Nacional para el Ministerio Hispano*, publicado en 1988. Véase UNITED STATES CONFERENCE OF CATHOLIC BISHOPS, *Ministerio Hispano: Tres Documentos Importantes*, USCCB, Washington, D.C. 1995, 59-98. Véase también *Encuentro y Misión*. Para los educadores religiosos el *Directorio Nacional para la Catequesis* es un recurso de mucho valor. En el desarrollo de estas reflexiones incorporo ideas e intuiciones recogidas en las conclusiones y reportes de tres importantes reuniones recientes en las cuales tuve la oportunidad de participar: 1) Simposio sobre Formación en la Fe entre Latinos/Hispanos, organizado por el Secretariado de Diversidad Cultural en La Iglesia, Baltimore, diciembre 5 del 2008; 2) Simposio sobre cambios paradigmáticos en el ministerio católico hispano nacional, convocado por el Consejo Nacional Católico para el Ministerio Hispano, en San Antonio, TX, agosto 28-29 del 2007; y 3) consulta nacional *Soy catequista: dignidad, vocación, y misión del catequista* en University of Notre Dame, South Bend, IN, noviembre 7-9 del 2006.

28 Es difícil establecer un número exacto. En el año 2009 el Pew Forum on Religion and Public Life publicó los resultados de un estudio sobre los latinos estadounidenses y el tema de la religión. El estudio estimó que el 68 por ciento de todos los latinos en el país son católicos, aunque la afiliación a la Iglesia puede variar según distintos factores tales como la edad, la educación y el estatus socioeconómico. Véase THE PEW FORUM ON RELIGION AND PUBLIC LIFE, *Changing Faiths: Latinos and the Transformation of American Religion*, Pew Hispanic Center, Washington, D.C. 2007, 6, http://pewforum.org/newassets/surveys/hispanic/hispanics-religion-07-final-mar08.pdf (página visitada el 30 de marzo del 2009). Los resultados de la encuesta sobre afiliación religiosa entre los estadounidenses (*American Religious Identification Survey*, ARIS 2008, en inglés) publicada en el 2009 indica que el 59 por ciento de los hispanos se identifican como católicos. Es interesante observar que dicho número indica un descenso en términos de auto-identificación en comparación con los resultados de una encuesta similar en 1990 cuando el 66 por ciento de los hispanos dijeron ser católicos. Véase KOSMIN B.A. Y KEYSAR A., *ARIS 2008*, 14.

29 Se estima que el 42 por ciento de los católicos hispanos van a misa al menos una vez a la semana. Cfr. THE PEW FORUM ON RELIGION AND PUBLIC LIFE, *Changing Faiths*, 16. Personalmente creo que este número es más pequeño que lo que el estudio indica. Hace varios años la Oficina de

compartimos lo que pudiera llamarse un catolicismo cultural (el cual no debe ser confundido con lo que se conoce como catolicismo nominal[30], aunque algunas veces ambas categorías coinciden) que permea nuestra visión de la realidad y la manera como entendemos a Dios, la humanidad, la naturaleza y la vida. Este catolicismo cultural tiene sus raíces en la influencia enorme que las instituciones católicas han ejercido sobre las estructuras sociales, políticas y culturales de las sociedades latinoamericanas desde la época colonial. El catolicismo, tanto en un sentido estricto como en un sentido más amplio, se comunica por medio de la cultura. Aún cuando la mayoría de los católicos latinos nacieron y han crecido en los Estados Unidos, el catolicismo cultural continúa siendo un gran elemento que marca la identidad latina, incluso entre los cristianos protestantes latinos[31]. Líderes eclesiales, académicos, organizaciones, educadores religiosos y agentes pastorales no podemos asumir los costos de ignorar la importancia de esta realidad.

También es importante observar que el catolicismo cultural en la experiencia hispana estadounidense no es necesariamente un indicador de homogeneidad religiosa. La experiencia hispana en general se puede describir como la coexistencia de distintas maneras de ser católico, las cuales, aunque tienen sus raíces en convicciones comunes de fe, son determinadas por una multiplicidad de experiencias históricas, culturales y eclesiales[32]. Los enfoques y recursos que han de usarse para la evangelización y la formación en la fe entre los católicos hispanos deben incorporar tantas de estas experiencias como sea posible y así mantener abierta la posibilidad de ser adaptadas a la realidad particular de cada grupo. La idea de que «los mismos recursos son válidos para todos los contextos» puede quizás producir resultados inmediatos pero después de cierto período la experiencia práctica indica que dicha idea es metodológicamente ineficaz.

Apostolado Hispano de la arquidiócesis de Boston reportó que cerca del 13 por ciento de los católicos hispanos en esta iglesia local iban regularmente a una misa dominical. Este último número parece reflejar más la realidad que los líderes pastorales observan en sus comunidades cada semana.

30 Uso las categorías de catolicismo «nominal» y «cultural» siguiendo el trabajo del sociólogo Allen Spitzer en su ensayo «The Culture Organization of Catholicism» en *The American Catholic Sociological Review* 19, n. 1 (1958) 2-3.

31 Cfr. GONZÁLEZ J.L., *Mañana: Christian Theology from a Theological Perspective*, Abingdon Press, Nashville, TN 1990, 66.

32 Aunque las experiencias de cruzar la frontera en búsqueda de mejores oportunidades, vivir en el exilio y escapar de circunstancias violentas pueden tener elementos comunes, cada una conduce a una lectura diferente de la historia y de la presencia de Dios en las comunidades latinas constituidas por las personas que experimentan dichas experiencias.

3.2. FAMILIA Y COMUNIDAD

El catolicismo hispano con frecuencia se describe como una realidad socio-religiosa fundamentada sólidamente en los valores tradicionales de familia y comunidad[33]. Una vez más, podemos afirmar que esta dimensión es otra manifestación de la influencia de la evangelización católica en la experiencia cultural latina ordinaria. Es en la familia y la comunidad que los católicos latinos formamos primordialmente nuestra identidad cultural y religiosa[34], lo cual emerge como una convicción contracultural en una sociedad en la que actitudes individualistas tienden a prevalecer[35]. La familia juega un papel importante en el desarrollo de las relaciones humanas y la estabilidad de la comunidad. Mientras que el concepto de familia tradicional —papá, mamá e hijos— es central en la experiencia de comunidad entre los hispanos, hablar de familia con frecuencia incluye otras relaciones de sangre, políticas, religiosas, de compadrazgo y amistad. Por consiguiente, los esfuerzos evangelizadores y los procesos de formación en la fe entre los hispanos serán fortalecidos cuando se afirmen modelos que integren de lleno esa experiencia de familia y comunidad. Por ejemplo, el modelo de pequeñas comunidades eclesiales es bien conocido entre los católicos hispanos[36]. Estas comunidades son flexibles, invitan a la participación y abren espacios para ejercer el liderazgo. Junto a estas pequeñas comunidades eclesiales hay que resaltar el impacto evangelizador y el dinamismo de los movimientos apostólicos y su habilidad de afirmar la dimensión comunitaria de la experiencia religiosa. Entre ellos podemos destacar la Renovación Carismática Católica con la cual se identifica aproximadamente el 54 por ciento de los católicos hispanos activos en la vida eclesial[37]. Tanto educadores religiosos como agentes pastorales necesitamos trabajar de cerca con los movimientos apostólicos para facilitar procesos de formación en la fe que fortalezcan la unidad de las comunidades eclesiales en las cuales están presentes.

---

[33] Véase por ejemplo la carta pastoral publicada por los obispos de los Estados Unidos en enero de 1984, «*La Presencia Hispana: Esperanza y Compromiso*, USCC, Washington, D.C. 1984» en UNITED STATES CONFERENCE OF CATHOLIC BISHOPS, *Ministerio Hispano: Tres Documentos Importantes*, 3; *Encuentro y Misión*, n. 15; 56.2.

[34] Véase GOIZUETA R., *Caminemos con Jesús. Hacia una teología del acompañamiento*, Convivium Press, Miami, FL 2009, 77-85.

[35] Cfr. GOIZUETA R., *Caminemos con Jesús. Hacia una teología del acompañamiento*, Convivium Press, Miami, FL 2009, 85-100.

[36] Cfr. UNITED STATES CONFERENCE OF CATHOLIC BISHOPS, *Plan Pastoral Nacional para el Ministerio Hispano*, 37-38; *Encuentro y Misión*, n. 40-42.

[37] Cfr. THE PEW FORUM ON RELIGION AND PUBLIC LIFE, *Changing Faiths*, 29-38.

Al mismo tiempo, «asumir» que todos los latinos compartimos un mismo sentido de familia y comunidad requiere de un poco de análisis crítico. Los líderes eclesiales, académicos y educadores religiosos no podemos caer en la tentación de idealizar estas dimensiones de la experiencia católica hispana. Es verdad que los católicos latinos en principio valoramos el ideal de familia, pero las familias latinas en los Estados Unidos son parte de una crisis seria en la que no se encuentran solas[38]. En el año 2006 el 42 por ciento de los niños hispanos nacieron en medio de relaciones familiares donde el matrimonio no existía; en el mismo año, la mitad de las mujeres latinas nacidas en los Estados Unidos y el 35 por ciento de mujeres latinas inmigrantes que tuvieron hijos lo hicieron como madres solteras[39]. Las parejas hispanas inmigrantes tienen una tasa más baja de divorcio que las parejas nacidas en el país, pero sus hijos nacidos y educados en los Estados Unidos tienden a replicar exactamente las tendencias del resto de la población: cerca del 50 por ciento de los matrimonios en los Estados Unidos terminan en divorcio[40]. Miles de familias hispanas viven divididas por causa de separaciones transnacionales, largas horas de trabajo y la lucha continua para adaptarse a la nueva cultura. En este contexto los esfuerzos evangelizadores y las iniciativas de formación en la fe necesitan adoptar un doble enfoque: por un lado, afirmar las imágenes positivas de familia y comunidad que son parte íntima de la visión de la vida del pueblo latino; por otro, responder directamente a los desafíos a los que se enfrentan las familias hispanas y proponer procesos de sanación.

3.3. LA FE DEL PUEBLO: CATOLICISMO POPULAR

Las tradiciones espirituales y teológicas más profundas del catolicismo se hacen vida plenamente por medio de la liturgia, la máxima expresión del culto cristiano que conduce hacia una experiencia profunda del Misterio Pascual[41]. Mientras que la liturgia mantiene su primacía entre todas las formas de expresión cultural en la vida de la Iglesia, dicha primacía no limita o niega el valor de expre-

---

38 Cfr. *Encuentro y Misión*, n. 56.2.

39 GONZÁLEZ F., *Hispanic Women in the United States*, Pew Hispanic Center, Washington, D.C. 2007, revisado el 14 del mayo del 2008, 9, http://pewhispanic.org/files/factsheets/42.pdf (página visitada el 15 de abril del 2009).

40 Cfr. CHERLIN A.J., *The Marriage-Go-Round: The State of Marriage and the Family in America Today*, Alfred A. Knopf, New York, NY 2009, 4; 180.

41 Cfr. *Sacrosanctum Concilium*, n. 10, 61. Véase también el ensayo de Raúl Gómez-Ruíz en esta colección.

siones de espiritualidad como las que son parte del catolicismo popular: «Así pues, Liturgia y piedad popular son dos expresiones cultuales que se deben poner en relación mutua y fecunda»[42].

Las prácticas de catolicismo popular juegan un papel importante en la mediación de la relación entre Dios y la humanidad en la vida diaria[43]. Un gran número de teólogos católicos latinos estadounidenses y líderes eclesiales hemos visto en el catolicismo popular una fuente de inmenso valor que constantemente ayuda a los hispanos a entender lo que significa estar en relación con el Dios de la Revelación en la particularidad de nuestra historia. El catolicismo popular ofrece a mujeres y hombres los medios necesarios para profundizar en los misterios de la fe que se celebran en la liturgia. Algunas veces, éste es el único lenguaje que los desposeídos tienen disponible para articular su experiencia de Dios[44]. El catolicismo popular sostiene la vida de fe fuera del contexto de las celebraciones litúrgicas y revela el amor de Dios quien se hace presente a mujeres y hombres en sus experiencias cotidianas[45].

El potencial pedagógico del catolicismo popular es evidente cuando vemos la amplia práctica de estas expresiones en la vida de muchas comunidades a través del país: procesiones, devociones, celebraciones marianas, veneración de los santos, novenas, etc. La experiencia católica hispana es rica en prácticas que están particularmente relacionadas con la cultura de nuestro pueblo tales como las posadas, las quinceañeras y los altarcitos, entre otras. Así, el poder del catolicismo popular para facilitar procesos de evangelización y formación en la fe es único. Los programas y recursos diseñados para la formación en la fe entre los hispanos deben poner atención a estas expresiones e integrarlas estratégicamente como contenido y método de la mejor manera posible. Aún en situaciones cuando estas expresiones son la única forma de celebración ritual que los creyentes practican con regularidad, los catequistas y agentes pastorales tenemos la responsabilidad de afirmar la relación apropiada entre el catolicismo popu-

---

42 Cfr. CONGREGACIÓN PARA EL CULTO DIVINO Y LA DISCIPLINA DE LOS SACRAMENTOS, *Directorio sobre la piedad popular y la liturgia: principio y orientaciones,* Ciudad del Vaticano 2001, n. 58, http://www.vatican.va/roman_curia/congregations/ccdds/documents/rc_con_ccdds_doc_20020513_vers-direttorio_sp.html (página visitada el 16 de marzo del 2009).

43 Cfr. GOIZUETA R., *Caminemos con Jesús,* 49-53.

44 Cfr. GONZÁLEZ J.L., *Mañana,* 61.

45 Véase OSPINO H., «Unveiling the Human and the Divine: The Revelatory Power of Popular Religiosity Narratives in Christian Education» en *Religious Education* 102, n. 3 (2007) 328-339.

lar y la vida litúrgica[46]. Los excesos y las interpretaciones limitadas no deben convertirse en una excusa para ignorar el potencial de estas prácticas para mediar pedagogías de fe[47].

3.4. UNA IGLESIA EN SOLIDARIDAD

Los principios de la Doctrina Social de la Iglesia no son un secreto cuando las comunidades de fe tienen que confrontar constantemente situaciones que requieren de reflexión y acción inmediata a la luz de las convicciones centrales de la tradición cristiana. Los católicos hispanos en los Estados Unidos enfrentamos desafíos importantes que exigen reflexión continua sobre lo que significa ser cristianos en medio de condiciones adversas tales como la pobreza, el racismo, la explotación, la marginación, etc. En muchas diócesis y parroquias alrededor del país el ministerio hispano opera en colaboración directa con oficinas y departamentos de servicio social. Trabajar en el ministerio hispano exige que nos involucremos constantemente en asuntos que requieren mediación, resolución de conflictos y justicia social.

Las iniciativas relacionadas con la evangelización y la formación en la fe entre los hispanos serán completas y efectivas cuando en verdad nos lleven a entender con claridad que somos una iglesia que debe estar en solidaridad con quienes más lo necesitan. Las palabras del Papa Pablo VI nos ofrecen una luz en este sentido:

> La evangelización no sería completa si no tuviera en cuenta la interpelación recíproca que en el curso de los tiempos se establece entre el Evangelio y la vida concreta, personal y social, del hombre [sic]. Precisamente por esto la evangelización lleva consigo un mensaje explícito, adaptado a las diversas situaciones y constantemente actualizado, sobre los derechos y deberes de toda persona humana, sobre la vida familiar sin la cual apenas es posible el progreso personal, sobre la vida comunitaria de la sociedad, sobre la vida internacional, la paz, la justicia, el desarrollo; un mensaje, especialmente vigoroso en nuestros días, sobre la liberación[48].

289

---

46 Cfr. CONGREGACIÓN PARA EL CULTO DIVINO Y LA DISCIPLINA DE LOS SACRAMENTOS, *Directorio sobre la piedad popular y la liturgia*, n. 59.
47 Cfr. CONGREGACIÓN PARA EL CULTO DIVINO Y LA DISCIPLINA DE LOS SACRAMENTOS, n. 57.
48 PABLO VI, *Evangelii Nuntiandi*, n. 29.

Educar en la fe a los católicos latinos tiene que ser una llamada permanente a hacer una opción preferencial por los pobres y por aquellas personas, hispanas y de otros grupos étnicos, quienes viven bajo circunstancias en las cuales su dignidad humana se afirma completamente. Los recursos y pedagogías de formación en la fe dentro de este contexto deben servir para identificar las causas primarias de la injusticia social que afecta la vida de millones de latinos/as y de muchas otras personas en nuestra sociedad. Hablar de Doctrina Social de la Iglesia y de solidaridad cristiana y afirmar que vivir nuestra fe en la vida diaria tiene implicaciones sociales no harán diferencia alguna en los procesos de educación religiosa y ministerio hispano si dichos compromisos no llevan a responder directamente a las circunstancias específicas que definen la vida cotidiana de millones de latinas y latinos en los Estados Unidos.

290   3.5.   INMIGRACIÓN

Muy relacionado con la base clave anterior, la inmigración surge como uno de los asuntos más urgentes que necesitamos tener en cuenta hoy en día en cualquier proceso de evangelización y formación en la fe entre los católicos hispanos. La mayoría de latinos en los Estados Unidos somos inmigrantes o hijos de inmigrantes que han llegando al país en las últimas cinco décadas. Como consecuencia, la inmigración es un asunto central en toda reflexión sobre identidad latina. La inmigración es un problema complejo que afecta varias áreas de la experiencia hispana estadounidense tales como la cultura, las relaciones personales, las leyes internacionales, la política, la religión, la economía y el acceso a educación[49].

Un marco analítico para la formación en la fe entre los hispanos debe poner la inmigración al centro de toda conversación. Una de sus metas más importantes tiene que ser ayudar a todos los católicos estadounidenses a entender mejor no sólo la complejidad de los asuntos relacionados con este fenómeno, sino también las consecuencias negativas que la indiferencia y el activismo anti-inmigrante pueden tener. Los recursos que usamos en iniciativas catequéticas necesitan facilitar un mejor diálogo sobre cómo la inmigración toca directamente las vidas de casi la mitad de los católicos en el país (e indirectamente las

---

49   Un buen recurso que describe la complejidad del asunto migratorio en la vida de los católicos, hispanos y no hispanos, en los Estados Unidos es el proyecto Justicia para los Inmigrantes (*Justice for Immigrants*, en inglés) patrocinado por los obispos católicos estadounidenses: http://www.justiceforimmigrants.org/

vidas de la otra mitad), cuáles son las mejores herramientas que nos ofrece nuestra tradición cristiana para reflexionar sobre esta realidad, cómo la experiencia católica en los Estados Unidos ha sido transformada gracias a la inmigración en distintos momentos de su corta historia y por qué es importante que todos los católicos, no solo los hispanos, estemos familiarizados con las enseñanzas de la Iglesia sobre migración.

Encuentro y Misión propuso la Nueva Evangelización como la dimensión eclesial desde la cual se entienden todos los compromisos relacionados con el trabajo pastoral con los católicos latinos[50]. Dicha preocupación por la evangelización también se halla claramente presente en otros documentos como el *Plan Pastoral Nacional para el Ministerio Hispano* y las conclusiones de los Encuentros[51]. Al corazón de la evangelización se encuentra la convicción de que la Iglesia está en un estado permanente de misión cuya meta última es guiar a mujeres y hombres a un encuentro transformador con Jesucristo. Así, *Encuentro y Misión* nos recuerda que los católicos en los Estados Unidos hemos optado repetidamente por un estilo de evangelización marcado por un fuerte carácter misionero[52]. Tal opción misionera garantiza la dinamicidad de un ministerio que busca permear todas las estructuras de la vida de la Iglesia y la sociedad.

En el contexto de la Nueva Evangelización, el discipulado y la opción misionera surgen como dos nociones esenciales. Esto fue confirmado por el espíritu de la v Conferencia General del Episcopado Latinoamericano y el Caribe en Aparecida, Brasil en el año 2007. Allí los obispos latinoamericanos propusieron que la evangelización actual tiene que ser entendida en términos de formar discípulos misioneros de Jesucristo[53] en una Iglesia que está en un estado permanente de misión[54]. Estas dos imágenes sintetizan la larga tradición de reflexión sobre el discipulado y la opción misionera que ha permeado las conversaciones entre

---

50   Véase *Encuentro y Misión*, n. 25-34.
51   Cfr. *Plan Pastoral Nacional para el Ministerio Hispano*, n. 37-50; Voces Proféticas: El Documento del Proceso del iii Encuentro Nacional Hispano de Pastoral, sección iv, publicado por los obispos de los Estados Unidos en agosto de 1986, en UNITED STATES CONFERENCE OF CATHOLIC BISHOPS, *Ministerio Hispano: Tres Documentos Importantes*, 34-35.
52   Cfr. *Encuentro y Misión*, n. 56-57.
53   Cfr. *Aparecida*, n. 129-153.
54   Cfr. *Aparecida*, n. 151.

los católicos latinoamericanos y los católicos hispanos en los Estados Unidos durante varias décadas. A la luz de las conclusiones de Aparecida, los obispos latinoamericanos lanzaron una misión continental cuya meta es animar la vocación misionera de los cristianos, fortaleciendo las raíces de su fe y despertando su responsabilidad para que todas las comunidades cristianas se pongan en estado de misión permanente.

Se trata de despertar en los cristianos la alegría y la fecundidad de ser discípulos de Jesucristo, celebrando con verdadero gozo el «estar-con-Él» y el «amar-como-Él» para ser enviados a la misión. «No podemos desaprovechar esta hora de gracia. ¡Necesitamos un nuevo Pentecostés! ¡Necesitamos salir al encuentro de las personas, las familias, las comunidades y los pueblos para comunicarles y compartir el don del encuentro con Cristo, que ha llenado nuestras vidas de "sentido", de verdad y amor, de alegría y de esperanza!»

Así, la misión nos lleva a vivir el encuentro con Jesús como un dinamismo de conversión personal, pastoral y eclesial capaz de impulsar hacia la santidad y el apostolado a los bautizados, y de atraer a quienes han abandonado la Iglesia, a quienes están alejados del influjo del evangelio y a quienes aún no han experimentado el don de la fe[55].

Un marco analítico para la formación en la fe sólo tiene sentido total cuando se entiende como parte del contexto más amplio de la evangelización. Así, los procesos, pedagogías y recursos para la formación en la fe entre los católicos hispanos en los Estados Unidos deben diseñarse con el espíritu de la Nueva Evangelización y conducir a la formación de discípulos misioneros. El catolicismo en el continente está en un estado permanente de misión. Esto requiere que las iniciativas de formación en la fe expliquen claramente de qué se trata esta misión, su contenido y sus metas. Es urgente que las generaciones presentes y futuras de educadores religiosos se preparen para trabajar en conjunto en esta misión común. En el contexto de una Iglesia culturalmente diversa, ser discípulos misioneros de Jesucristo significa permanecer atentos a las experiencias que marcan profundamente la identidad de nuestras comunidades, valorar la riqueza de nuestra tradición cristiana mediada a través de siglos de reflexión en distintas culturas y vivir en solidaridad con la humanidad más allá de nuestro mundo más inmediato y nuestras fronteras.

---

55 CELAM, *La Misión Continental para una Iglesia Misionera: Orientaciones*, CELAM, Bogotá, Colombia, 2008, n. 2, http://www.celam.org/principal/index.php?module=PostWrap&page= Mision_Home (página visitada el 25 de marzo del 2009).

Los católicos estadounidenses, tanto hispanos como de otros grupos étnicos, tenemos la responsabilidad de unirnos a la misión continental con nuestros mejores recursos, contribuciones e ideas.

3.7. DIMENSIÓN PÚBLICA DE LA FE CATÓLICA

La presencia católica hispana en los Estados Unidos es esencial al momento de hablar de la identidad de la Iglesia y la sociedad en esta esquina del mundo. Cada día más y más católicos hispanos somos parte de conversaciones en distintos niveles que afectan la vida de toda nuestra sociedad en las cuales se requiere contribuir con la sabiduría del cristianismo católico. Entramos a ser parte de estas conversaciones como católicos y como latinos estadounidenses. Al mismo tiempo, el crecimiento de la presencia de los católicos hispanos en la Iglesia y la sociedad ha servido como una oportunidad para girar la atención hacia preocupaciones que están íntimamente relacionadas con la realidad hispana (ej. la experiencia bicultural, nuestra relación con Latinoamérica, las tradiciones intelectuales y religiosas latinas).

Las iniciativas de formación en la fe y de evangelización entre los católicos hispanos tienen que preparar a los latinos para responder adecuadamente a los desafíos de entrar en las distintas conversaciones públicas que ocurren en la Iglesia y en el resto de la sociedad. Sería un grave error considerar que los católicos hispanos somos espectadores pasivos en estas importantes conversaciones o ignorar nuestras contribuciones. Los programas y recursos para la formación en la fe usados en nuestras comunidades deben ofrecer introducciones sólidas a las grandes preocupaciones que afectan *nuestras* vidas en *nuestro* contexto. Estos programas y recursos tienen que preparar a los católicos latinos para familiarizarse con la riqueza de la tradición cristiana, el origen de los interrogantes que ocupan a mujeres y hombres en nuestra sociedad, y los caminos más indicados para participar con nuestra propia voz en las arenas públicas de la Iglesia y la sociedad.

Esto requiere que asumamos, y diseñemos cuando sea necesario, pedagogías de formación en la fe que afirmen el potencial de los latinos y nos ayuden a apropiar nuestra fe de manera crítica para así participar más de lleno en la vida pública. Aunque ésta debe ser la meta de la catequesis en todos los niveles, es urgente que nos enfoquemos en programas de formación en la fe para adultos que lleven a entender mejor las dimensiones públicas del catolicismo.

4
Una mirada al futuro

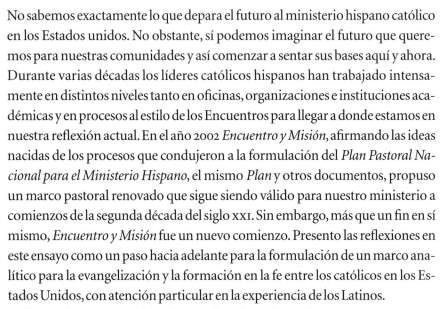

No sabemos exactamente lo que depara el futuro al ministerio hispano católico en los Estados unidos. No obstante, sí podemos imaginar el futuro que queremos para nuestras comunidades y así comenzar a sentar sus bases aquí y ahora. Durante varias décadas los líderes católicos hispanos han trabajado intensamente en distintos niveles tanto en oficinas, organizaciones e instituciones académicas y en procesos al estilo de los Encuentros para llegar a donde estamos en nuestra reflexión actual. En el año 2002 *Encuentro y Misión,* afirmando las ideas nacidas de los procesos que condujeron a la formulación del *Plan Pastoral Nacional para el Ministerio Hispano,* el mismo *Plan* y otros documentos, propuso un marco pastoral renovado que sigue siendo válido para nuestro ministerio a comienzos de la segunda década del siglo XXI. Sin embargo, más que un fin en sí mismo, *Encuentro y Misión* fue un nuevo comienzo. Presento las reflexiones en este ensayo como un paso hacia adelante para la formulación de un marco analítico para la evangelización y la formación en la fe entre los católicos en los Estados Unidos, con atención particular en la experiencia de los Latinos.

Por ende, las cuatro hipótesis descritas al comienzo de este ensayo permanecen como esperanza para el ministerio hispano en general y los procesos de formación en la fe y la evangelización entre los católicos hispanos en particular:

1) Necesitamos articular creativamente modelos y recursos para la formación en la fe y la evangelización que puedan ser compartidos en las distintas comunidades sirviendo a los católicos hispanos. Dichas iniciativas tienen que reflejar la particularidad de nuestra experiencia como latinos en este país. Aunque estos modelos y recursos necesariamente tendrán que se adaptados a la particularidad de las circunstancias socioculturales y religiosas de cada comunidad, deberán servir como puntos de partida para las nuevas comunidades trabajando con católicos hispanos.

2) Los educadores religiosos y agentes pastorales católicos hispanos tenemos que familiarizarnos profundamente con los procesos y conclusiones de los Encuentros, los distintos documentos sobre el ministerio hispanos respaldados o escritos por los obispos católicos estadounidenses, los trabajos de los teólogos católicos latinos y otros recursos eclesiales sobre formación en la fe que guían la conversación sobre este asunto en distintos foros alrededor del país.

3) Los católicos hispanos tenemos que seguir haciendo el esfuerzo de participar en todos los procesos de reflexión sobre la formación en la fe, la evangelización, la formación para el liderazgo, la educación católica y la creación de materiales para la catequesis en todos los niveles de la vida de la Iglesia, e incrementar dicha participación cuando sea necesario.

4) Los católicos que no son hispanos y están trabajando en organizaciones e instituciones que desarrollan recursos y proponen iniciativas para la formación en la fe y la evangelización en la Iglesia en los Estados Unidos deben trabajar con los líderes y los expertos hispanos en los distintos campos como parte de sus equipos. Estos líderes y expertos latinos traerán su experiencia profesional y sus perspectivas llamando la atención hacia la complejidad, los desafíos y las contribuciones de la experiencia católica hispana al resto de la Iglesia y de la sociedad.

El ministerio hispano y la reflexión teológica

Jorge Presmanes y Alicia Marill

1

Introducción

Que «toda política es local» es un axioma acuñado por Thomas «Tip» O'Neill, quien fuera presidente de la Cámara de Representantes en el Congreso de los Estados Unidos por muchos años. Este adagio sigue recordando a los servidores públicos elegidos popularmente que siempre deben permanecer atentos a las necesidades diarias de sus constituyentes en la base o sus carreras políticas serán muy cortas. En línea con «Tip» O'Neill, la hermenéutica ministerial que sostiene esta reflexión es que «toda teología es local». En otras palabras, «toda teología tiene que ser local» a no ser que esté desconectada del contexto eclesial y social de los fieles y así se torne irrelevante para quienes viven más allá del contexto de nuestras instituciones académicas. Éste es el reto que nos presentan nuestros estudiantes en programas de formación para el ministerio cuyo punto de entrada al discurso teológico es su experiencia ministerial particular.

La relación entre los ministerios hispanos y la reflexión teológica que exploraremos en las siguientes páginas tiene su fuente en la praxis pastoral concreta de nuestros estudiantes latinos en programas de formación para el ministerio, tanto en nuestra maestría en teología práctica y el doctorado en ministerio en nuestra universidad, ofrecidos en inglés, y nuestro programa de maestría en ministerio pastoral para hispanos a en el Instituto Pastoral del Sureste (SEPI), el cual se enseña en español. Aunque la mayoría de nuestros estudiantes son ministros eclesiales laicos en la Iglesia Católica, nuestro estudiantado también está constituido por sacerdotes y religiosos católicos al igual que ministros protestantes ordenados. Cada uno de estos ministros adelanta un trabajo de reflexión teológica desde la particularidad de su contexto eclesial y ministerial con la esperanza de responder mejor a las necesidades pastorales de las personas a quienes sirven. Teniendo en cuenta la diversidad de los contextos ministeriales y las funciones que nuestros estudiantes ejercen, pensamos que hablar de «ministerio hispano» es una abstracción inadecuada. No hay un «ministerio hispano» sino varios ministerios hispanos que son definidos por la especificidad pastoral, religiosa, cultural, social, económica, política, geográfica e histórica de cada contexto eclesial y ministerial.

En este ensayo sugerimos que el área de estudio conocida hoy en día como *teología práctica* nos provee la base teórica para este proyecto. La teología práctica es una subdisciplina que está emergiendo rápidamente en el mundo de los estudios teológicos, la cual opera desde una modalidad *praxis-teoría-praxis*. Sin substituir la necesidad que tiene la teología de hacer investigación histórica y sistemática, los teólogos prácticos reorientan la tarea teológica para que esta reflexión comience y culmine en el contexto ministerial de la teología. El examen profundo del lugar en donde los teólogos comienzan su reflexión es necesario para que la tarea teológica emerja de la práctica de la fe de las comunidades. Por consiguiente, toda teología comienza con una «descripción densa» de la «práctica orientada hacia la teoría»[1]. La descripción de los prejuicios y presuposiciones propios de la reflexión teológica y el ministerio libera a la teología de ser un instrumento para enmascarar dichas presuposiciones.

Finalmente, afirmamos que lo que ha sostenido a la reflexión teológica hispana/latina en los Estados Unidos por cerca de 30 años han sido sus metodologías basadas en la praxis. La exigencia de las comunidades hispanas que están creciendo rápidamente en los Estados Unidos ha sido el núcleo del trabajo de la Academia de Teólogos Católicos Hispanos de los Estados Unidos (ACHTUS, sigla en inglés). Es más, las reflexiones de organizaciones como el Consejo Nacional Católico Para el Ministerio Hispano Católico (NCCHM, sigla en inglés) se han valido abiertamente de enfoques prácticos para su trabajo. Así podemos decir que la teología práctica y la teología hispana/latina estadounidense son compañeras naturales de diálogo. En este ensayo usamos contribuciones provenientes de ambos campos.

Desde el prisma de la posición social de nuestros estudiantes, nuestra propia práctica ministerial y las contribuciones de la teología práctica, esta reflexión responderá a las dos preguntas que se nos han encomendado. En primer lugar, *¿qué preguntas para la teología surgen de la experiencia actual del ministerio hispano en los Estados Unidos?* En segundo lugar, *¿de qué manera se beneficia el ministerio hispano de la investigación teológica actual en este país, con atención especial a la teología católica latina estadounidense?* Ambas preguntas son bastante amplias y pudieran ser respondidas de muchas maneras. Limitaremos nuestra respuesta a la exploración de tres áreas de práctica pastoral: inculturación e interculturalidad, praxis ministerial y eclesiología. Reconocemos que una reflexión adecuada sobre cada una de estas realidades teológicas y su correspondiente praxis pastoral requeriría una plataforma mucho más amplia que el presente

1 BROWNING D., *Fundamental Practical Theology: Descriptive and Strategic Proposals,* University of Chicago Press, Chicago 1996, 1-12; 75-93.

análisis. Sin embargo, consideramos que la siguiente reflexión puede ser el comienzo de un estudio más exhaustivo de la relación entre teología y el ministerio en el presente contexto de la experiencia católica hispana en los Estados Unidos.

2

Inculturación e interculturalidad

Por décadas los líderes de nuestra comunidad han retado a quienes ejercen posiciones de liderazgo en la Iglesia en los Estados Unidos a asumir un enfoque inculturado del ministerio. Este método en el ministerio tiene sus raíces en la certeza de que la cultura no sólo es la clave epistemológica que abre las puertas al entendimiento de un grupo particular de personas o de una sociedad[2], sino que también es el camino por medio del cual la Buena Nueva del Evangelio puede ser comunicada efectivamente en el contexto de la misión evangelizadora de la Iglesia[3].

Con frecuencia el enfoque prevalente de acción pastoral que busca responder de manera específica a la dimensión cultural es la adaptación en lugar de la inculturación. Dicho enfoque impacta negativamente la efectividad de la praxis ministerial. Adaptación es un término que ha sido empleado en documentos eclesiales para referirse al tema de la evangelización transcultural. Robert Schreiter demuestra que adaptación es una clasificación que se usó ampliamente en círculos misiológicos en el período entre las dos guerras mundiales y continuó siendo usado con frecuencia hasta el sínodo sobre la evangelización en Roma en 1974[4]. Este método misiológico se entendió como un proceso por medio del cual «la fe» era adaptada o acomodada en cierto grado limitado para comunicar el mensaje del Evangelio en un contexto cultural específico. Schreiter afirma que la adaptación como práctica ministerial es «inadecuada por su idea simplista y extremamente estática de la cultura —como si la cultura pudiera leer con facilidad que una adaptación se puede prescribir con ligereza y que este proceso ocurre de una vez para siempre en una cultura que no cambia»[5].

2 ESPÍN O., «Grace and Humanness: A Hispanic Perspective» en *Journal of Hispanic/Latino Studies* 2, n. 2 (1994) 134-135.

3 FIGUEROA DECK A., «A Latino Practical Theology: Mapping the Road Ahead» en *Theological Studies* 65 (2004) 292-293.

4 SCHREITER R., «Faith and Cultures: Challenges to a World Church» en *Theological Studies* 50 (1989) 746.

5 SCHREITER R., «Faith and Cultures: Challenges to a World Church» en *Theological Studies* 50 (1989) 746.

Inculturación es el término utilizado con más frecuencia en círculos católicos para describir la relación propia entre fe y cultura[6]. En la tradición protestante el término que regularmente se usa es contextualización y por ello ambos términos se usan intercambiablemente en los estudios investigativos sobre este tema. La palabra «contextualización» fue usada en primer lugar por un grupo de estudio comisionado por el Fondo para la Educación Teológica en 1972, mientras que el término «inculturación» se comenzó a usar en la tradición católica desde comienzos de los años sesentas para referirse al diálogo entre la fe cristiana y las culturas del mundo como parte de la praxis evangelizadora de la Iglesia[7].

En un artículo titulado «Christianity as Faith and Culture» (Cristianismo como fe y cultura), Yves Congar demuestra que la inculturación, cuando es vista como el principio de correlación entre fe y cultura, está al centro de la misión cristiana. Congar define la fe como la respuesta del ser humano a la llamada de Dios a una relación propia con Dios y con el pueblo de Dios. Esta llamada sólo puede llegar a la persona en su particularidad cultural pero al mismo tiempo «trasciende esa particularidad»[8]. «Cada vez que el hombre [*sic*], por medio de la fe», escribe Congar, «entra a compartir la vida de Jesucristo, él [*sic*] vive dentro de los límites y las formas particulares de su propia situación, un misterio único y concreto de valor universal absoluto»[9]. Para Congar la fe es el «principio interno» de la unidad católica. Es el lugar de la unidad porque la fe está necesariamente entrelazada con la historia y la cultura. Congar continúa:

> Las iniciativas reveladoras de Dios por un lado y la fe que responde a ellas por otro no existen sino en lo concreto, y en los puntos de encuentro del tiempo y el espacio, del contexto social, de la expresión. La respuesta de la fe no es la respuesta de alguien, de un sujeto humano concreto, a no ser que sea dada, vivida, expresada en la carne de una humanidad concreta. Por eso la revelación y la Iglesia son católicas sólo en lo particular. «Particular» se opone a lo «general» pero no a lo «católico». Las realizaciones o expresiones particulares de la fe católica son *«pars pro toto»*, *«totum in parte»*[10].

6 SCHREITER R., «Faith and Cultures: Challenges to a World Church» en *Theological Studies* 50 (1989) 747.

7 SCHREITER R., «Faith and Cultures: Challenges to a World Church» en *Theological Studies* 50 (1989) 747.

8 CONGAR Y., «Christianity as Faith and Culture» en *East Asian Pastoral Review* 18, n. 4 (1981) 304.

9 CONGAR Y., «Christianity as Faith and Culture» en *East Asian Pastoral Review* 18, n. 4 (1981) 305.

10 CONGAR Y., «Christianity as Faith and Culture» en *East Asian Pastoral Review* 18, n. 4 (1981) 305 (Traducción al español por parte del editor).

El ministerio como inculturación es entonces el proceso por medio del cual la universalidad del mensaje del Evangelio es predicado por la Iglesia y al cual los fieles responden en lo concreto del tiempo y en la particularidad de la cultura. Como resultado, la clave de la inculturación está en la capacidad de la Iglesia de descubrir una unidad de fe diversamente expresada a través de las estructuras simbólicas y las prácticas sociales de una cultura específica.

Distinta a la adaptación, una perspectiva inculturada del ministerio no hace absolutos aquellos elementos de la tradición que fueron modelados en una cultura y luego son traducidos a otra. Al contrario, en el proceso de inculturación la fe y la cultura son puestas en una relación de diálogo intercultural abierto cuya meta es el enriquecimiento tanto de la comunidad cultural y la tradición de fe. Desafortunadamente, en la práctica lo que más se define como «inculturación» es «adaptación». Porque la inculturación como método ministerial con frecuencia es despojado de su esencia intercultural, sugerimos que un término alternativo para referirse a la praxis misionera de la Iglesia puede ser «interculturación».

La teología intercultural es un movimiento teológico emergente que «conscientemente opta por la interculturalidad como [su] eje metodológico central»[11]. Siguiendo el trabajo filosófico de Raúl Fornet-Betancourt, María Pilar Aquino afirma que la teología intercultural ofrece un reto a la identidad cristiana policéntrica manifestada en el «excesivo carácter monocultural del cristianismo occidental»[12]. «Interculturación» como método para el ministerio puede ser un término más apropiado que «inculturación» porque la interculturalidad apunta más claramente a la interacción entre fe y cultura al centro del proyecto ministerial de la comunidad latina. Como podemos ver, el agente pastoral en la comunidad latina está llamado a algo más que simplemente «adaptar» el mensaje cristiano a las culturas hispanas o a traducir una perspectiva «anglosajona» de la tradición al español como método pastoral. En lugar de ello, el punto de partida de la evangelización como interculturación comienza con un entendimiento crítico del «contexto histórico de cada pueblo y cada cultura» presentes en la comunidad de fe en la cual la praxis pastoral está inserta[13]. Este enfoque

---

11 AQUINO M.P., «Theological Method in u.s. Latino/a Theology: Toward an Intercultural Theology for the Third Millennium» en ESPÍN O. y DÍAZ M. (eds.), *From the Heart of Our People: Latino/a Explorations in Catholic Systematic Theology*, Orbis, Maryknoll, NY 1999, 35.

12 AQUINO M.P., «Theological Method in u.s. Latino/a Theology: Toward an Intercultual Theology for the Third Millennium» 35.

13 AQUINO M.P., «Feminist Intercultural Theology: Toward a Shared Future of Justice» en AQUINO M.P. y ROSADO-NUÑEZ M.J. (eds.), *Feminist Intercultural Theology: Latina Explorations for a Just World*, Orbis, Maryknoll, NY 2007, 14.

intercultural es esencial para el ministerio en el contexto latino debido al carácter multicultural de la comunidad hispana católica.

Por más de veinte años la misión evangelizadora de la Iglesia en la comunidad hispana se ha beneficiado significativamente de la reflexión sistemática de los teólogos latinos trabajando en la academia enfocados en la experiencia de fe de la comunidad mexicoamericana, la cual representa cerca del 64 por ciento de nuestro pueblo[14]. Por ejemplo, las obras de Virgilio Elizondo, Allan Figueroa Deck, Roberto Goizueta, Arturo Bañuelas, Timothy Matovina, Orlando Espín, y Nancy Pineda-Madrid, entre otros, son importantes contribuciones a la teología desde el contexto de la experiencia mexicoamericana. En menor escala lo mismo se puede decir de la reflexión teológica de la experiencia religiosa cubanoamericana. Las investigaciones de Miguel Díaz, Michelle González, Fernando Segovia, Ada María Isasi-Díaz y otros han hecho posible grandes avances dentro del discurso teológico desde la ubicación social de los cubanoamericanos. Creemos que es crucial continuar teologizando no sólo desde el contexto social de estas comunidades, sino también desde el contexto cultural de otras culturas hispanas presente entre nosotros. Tal proyecto investigativo facilitará el avance del ministerio como interculturación dentro de la comunidad hispana católica.

A través de la historia de la praxis misionera cristiana se han propuesto varios paradigmas de evangelización para responder a contextos culturales e históricos específicos[15]. El desarrollo de métodos de interculturación es crucial para asegurar la efectividad de un ministerio que atiende a la especificidad de la cultura porque la cultura es una realidad dinámica y cambiante[16]. Por consiguiente, es urgente que los agentes pastorales y los teólogos permanezcan atentos al dinamismo cultural y continúen buscando nuevos métodos de interculturación. En su libro *La Cosecha: Harvesting Contemporary United States Hispanic Theology (1972-1998)*, Eduardo Fernández correlaciona los esfuerzos de reflexión teológica hispana estadounidense con los modelos de teología contextual de Stephen Bevans. Con este ejercicio Fernández ha avanzado el estudio de la relación entre fe y cultura desde el prisma del contexto hispano estadounidense y ha dado a quienes trabajan en el ministerio en la comunidad latina un instru-

14 U.S. CENSUS BUREAU, «Facts for Features: Hispanic Heritage Month 2009, Sept 15 - Oct 15», http://www.census.gov/Press-Release/www/releases/archives/facts_for_features_special_editions/013984.html (página visitada en enero 12 del 2009).

15 BOSCH D., *Transforming Mission: Paradigm Shifts in Theology of Mission*, Orbis Books, Maryknoll, NY 1991, 181-182.

16 SCHREITER R., «Faith and Cultures: Challenges to a World Church», 746.

mento para ampliar los métodos de interculturación que emplean en su trabajo pastoral[17]. Creemos que el ministerio hispano se puede beneficiar considerablemente del un mayor desarrollo de modelos y métodos de interculturación en el contexto de las muchas culturas presentes entre los católicos hispanos en los Estados Unidos. Tal reflexión teológica optimizará notablemente muchas de las competencias cros-culturales que necesitan nuestros agentes pastorales.

3
Praxis ministerial

La mayoría de quienes hemos trabajado en el ministerio hispano por décadas, tanto a nivel diocesano, regional y nacional hemos participado y nos hemos beneficiado de los procesos de Encuentro. Aún así, muchos de los que están trabajando en el ministerio hispano hoy en día conocen poco sobre los Encuentros y otros procesos históricos de los ministerios pastorales en la comunidad latina. Con frecuencia nuestros agentes pastorales ignoran iniciativas claves al igual que la importancia de los logros históricos obtenidos por sus predecesores al establecer ministerios entre los hispanos, afirmando la especificidad de nuestra cultura. Para remediar este vacío, quienes estamos involucrados en la formación de agentes pastorales en la comunidad hispana tenemos que enseñar esta tradición como parte de la historia de las comunidades eclesiales latinas en los Estados Unidos. Para este propósito el libro clásico editado por Moisés Sandoval *Fronteras: A History of the Latin American Church in the USA Since 1513* es un recurso invaluable para la formación histórica de nuestros estudiantes[18]. Una historia más contemporánea de las comunidades eclesiales latinas en los Estados Unidos escrita a partir del contexto de cuatro centros urbanos (San Antonio, Nueva York, Miami y Chicago) es el libro escrito por David Badillo, *Latinos and the New Immigrant Church*[19]. Aunque estas obras históricas son de gran valor para la reflexión teológica y el ministerio, se necesita más investigación histórica sobre la fe y la experiencia eclesial de los hispanos.

---

17 FERNÁNDEZ E., *La Cosecha: Harvesting Contemporary United States Hispanic Theology 1972-1998*, Liturgical Press, Collegeville, MN 2000. Véase también BEVANS S., *Models of Contextual Theology*, Orbis Books, Maryknoll, NY 1992.

18 SANDOVAL M. (ed.), *Fronteras: A History of the Latin American Church in the USA Since 1513*, MACC, San Antonio, TX 1983.

19 BADILLO D.A., *Latinos and the New Immigrant Church*, Johns Hopkins University Press, Baltimore, MD 2006.

La historia de los hispanos en los Estados Unidos indica que muchos aspectos del contexto ministerial de la comunidad latina han cambiado desde que la organización del ministerio hispano a nivel nacional fue establecida oficialmente. Sin embargo, el método de planeación pastoral que se forjó con las bases a través de los procesos de Encuentro puede ser considerado tan relevante hoy en día como lo fue profético cuando se propuso[20]. Desde sus primeros momentos, la preocupación más urgente de los procesos de Encuentro y de la metodología de planeación pastoral hispana fue que los ministerios respondieran directamente a la realidad concreta de los latinos y que la participación de *la base* en el proceso de planeación fuera una prioridad.

La clave metodológica de los procesos de Encuentro afirmó la necesidad de reflexión sobre la praxis tanto al comienzo como al final. Así se estableció una teología práctica hecha desde el reverso de la historia y desde la experiencia humana. Esta metodología continúa siendo un «discernimiento pastoral que se enfoca en las necesidades y aspiraciones de los fieles, juzga esa realidad a la luz de las Sagradas Escrituras y la Tradición, y se concretiza en acción transformadora»[21]. Popularmente conocido como *ver-juzgar-actuar-evaluar*, este proceso continúa siendo el método de planeación pastoral preferido por muchos en las comunidades eclesiales latinas en los Estados Unidos.

Nuestro compromiso con estudiantes en procesos de formación para el ministerio exige una reflexión teológico-práctica determinada por la praxis de la comunidad hispana. Así, pensamos que es necesario adelantar más investigación teológica basada en la praxis como parte del trabajo académico de los teólogos hispanos. Mientras que apoyamos el trabajo de los teólogos latinos contemporáneos, resaltamos que el punto de partida de las teologías latinas no se debe dejar de lado. Un esfuerzo renovado de reflexión teológica basado en la praxis será instrumental para mediar la brecha que con frecuencia existe entre la teoría y la experiencia de fe diaria al nivel de la base.

Sugerimos que el área en la que hay mayor desconexión entre el trabajo académico de los teólogos latinos estadounidenses y el trabajo pastoral es en el ministerio de formación en la fe. Consistentemente el ministerio de formación en

---

20 INSTITUTO PASTORAL DEL SURESTE, *Memoria Histórica Común: Proceso Pastoral Hispano en los EE.UU.*, SEPI, Miami, FL 2004.

21 UNITED STATES CONFERENCE OF CATHOLIC BISHOPS, *Encuentro y Misión: Un Marco Pastoral Renovado para el Ministerio Hispano*, USCCB, Washington, D.C. 2002, 21, http://www.usccb.org/hispanicaffairs/encuentromissionsp.shtml.

la fe desde la base emerge como la preocupación primaria de los agentes pastorales en nuestros programas de teología y ministerio. Mientras que se hacen esfuerzos a nivel local y diocesano para responder al ministerio de formación en la fe, estos programas siguen atrayendo pocas personas cuando los comparamos con los altos números de latinos en nuestras comunidades eclesiales. Aún más, esa formación con frecuencia carece en gran medida de un diálogo con la reflexión que adelantan los teólogos latinos/hispanos estadounidenses en la academia.

Para la gran mayoría de latinos, el ministerio de formación en la fe se actualiza en el contexto de la parroquia, su liturgia y en los distintos movimientos eclesiales que sostienen a nuestras comunidades. Muchas veces las reflexiones teológicas y los análisis profundos no llegan a estos ambientes. Por ejemplo, existe una brecha entre el discurso teológico académico y las cristologías que operan al nivel de la base. Afirmadas por la predicación en la liturgia y otras prácticas que están presentes en movimientos eclesiales populares, muchas cristologías de la base siguen enfatizando a un Cristo imperial que está alejado y distante de la experiencia humana y tienden a centrarse excesivamente en la divinidad de Jesús, casi al punto de ignorar su humanidad. Mientras que el trabajo de Virgilio Elizondo en *El caminar del Galileo* y Roberto Goizueta en *Caminemos con Jesús: hacia una teología del acompañamiento* acentúan al Jesús histórico que sufre gracias a su solidaridad liberadora con los pobres, las cristologías que regularmente predominan en la base son aquellas que se enfocan más en la legitimación del sufrimiento impuesto sobre la humanidad como voluntad de Dios en lugar de una cristología que infunda en los fieles la convicción de ser autores de su propia historia y destino[22]. Es más, si estas cristologías prevalentes en nuestras comunidades se llevan al extremo pueden promover un docetismo contemporáneo en el cual la humanidad de Cristo se minimiza a tal punto que eventualmente se pudiera llegar a su negación total. Por ello creemos que los ministerios hispanos se pueden beneficiar de más investigación sobre las cristologías neotestamentarias teniendo en cuenta las culturas latinas en los Estados Unidos que hablan de interpretaciones liberadoras de Jesús. También creemos que hay que elaborar soteriologías que correspondan a dicha investigación cristológica. Finalmente, deducimos que esta reflexión cristológica y soteriológica influenciará las teologías operativas sobre Dios en el contexto ministerial hispano en los Estados Unidos.

---

22 ELIZONDO V., *El Caminar del Galileo: Promesa México-Americana*, MACC, San Antonio, TX 2002; GOIZUETA R., *Caminemos con Jesús. Hacia una teología del acompañamiento*, Convivium Press, Miami, FL 2009.

Otro ejemplo que ilustra la brecha que existe entre el trabajo académico de los teólogos latinos y el ministerio de formación en la fe es el área de la teología moral. Nuestra experiencia, al igual que la de nuestros estudiantes, revela el hecho lamentable de que la predicación y la catequesis sacramental en nuestras comunidades están cimentadas en una visión de la vida moral considerablemente individualista. Tal mentalidad moral promueve espiritualidades que se enfocan sólo en la vida interior y limitan y oscurecen las demandas de justicia social del Evangelio[23]. Creemos que esta ética primordialmente individualista que con frecuencia existe en muchas de nuestras comunidades suplanta la responsabilidad de transformar las estructuras sociales que perpetúan la opresión de los latinos[24]. A pesar de que los teólogos latinos han escrito bastante sobre asuntos de justicia, los ministerios hispanos necesitan beneficiarse del avance de teologías morales que reflejen la situación social de los hispanos en los Estados Unidos. Esta preocupación ética promueve un enfoque de la vida moral que subraya la reflexión ética social que educa para confrontar las fuerzas que marginan y oprimen a los hispanos en nuestro país.

4
Eclesiología

Con gran influencia de los movimientos de comunidades eclesiales de base en Latinoamérica, los procesos de Encuentro nacieron de metodologías de reflexión eclesiológica basadas en la comunidad. Al centro de la eclesiología de los Encuentros, y posteriormente en el *Plan Pastoral Nacional para el Ministerio Hispano*, se halla una teología bautismal que exige a los bautizados comprometerse de manera total e integral en la misión de la Iglesia. Para ello el modelo de Iglesia de los Encuentros se cimentó sobre los conceptos de comunión y participación: *comunión* en la misma fe en Jesucristo y en su misión; *participación* en la construcción del Reino de Dios[25]. En su libro, *Comunidades eclesiales de base: alcance y desafío de un modo nuevo de ser Iglesia*, Marcello Azevedo señala la interrelación entre comunión y participación como un aspecto crucial para la eclesiología y

---

23 GONZÁLEZ J. Y GONZÁLEZ C., *Liberation Preaching: The Pulpit and the Oppressed*, Avingdon Press, Nashville 1980, 23.
24 DE LA TORRE M., *Doing Christian Ethics from the Margins*, Orbis Books, Maryknoll, NY 2004, 56.
25 *Encuentro y Misión*, n. 37-39.

la teología, el cual se constituyó en un elemento integral del modelo de Iglesia que adoptó el *Plan Pastoral Nacional*:

> Comunión —*koinonia*— como dimensión esencial para la efectividad y credibilidad de la comunidad de fe, vivida como aquello que se profesa y se testimonia, que anuncia y denuncia, que establece entre los seres humanos amor y justicia, en la verdad y la libertad. Participación entendida como un compromiso de todos, en la variedad de personas y de vocaciones, ya sea como la edificación y el servicio de la misma comunidad —*diakonia*— o como la construcción de una sociedad de acuerdo con todo el alcance de los postulados de la fe[26].

La eclesiología de comunión y participación detrás del *Plan Pastoral Nacional* fue bienvenida por las comunidades eclesiales latinas en los Estados Unidos teniendo en cuenta el número cada vez más reducido de sacerdotes y religiosos sirviéndoles y el hecho de que los latinos habían sido continuamente excluidos del proceso de toma de decisiones dentro de las estructuras de la Iglesia[27]. Como resultado, el modelo de Iglesia que la comunidad latina adoptó en los procesos de Encuentro confrontó una praxis eclesial de privilegio que limita o absolutiza el poder de una élite conformada ya sea por sacerdotes, religiosos o líderes laicos. En el marco referencial de esta eclesiología latina, todos los miembros de la comunidad son reconocidos como iguales y todos comparten la misión de Jesucristo. Decir que todos los miembros son igualmente responsables de llevar a cabo la misión de la Iglesia no significa que no hay diferencias entre los miembros de la comunidad. Existen diferencias, pero éstas son para servir mejor a la comunidad. En otras palabras, los distintos papeles permiten que una diversidad de funciones se realicen. Todos los bautizados, los religiosos y los ordenados participan de la misma función carismática fundamental que es la construcción de la comunidad eclesial[28].

26 AZEVEDO M., *Comunidades eclesiais de base e inculturação da fé: a realidade das CEBs e sua tematização teórica, na perspectiva de uma evangelização inculturada*, Edições Loyola, São Paulo, Brasil, 1986, 207 (traducción al español por parte del editor). Para una breve historia del desarrollo de la eclesiología de comunión véase GAILLARDETZ R., *Ecclesiology for a Global Church: A People Called and Sent*, Orbis Books, Maryknoll, NY 2008, 85-131.

27 NATIONAL CONFERENCE OF CATHOLIC BISHOPS, *Plan Pastoral Nacional para el Ministerio Hispano*, USCC, Washington, D.C. 1987, n. 67, en UNITED STATES CONFERENCE OF CATHOLIC BISHOPS, *Ministerio Hispano: Tres Documentos Importantes*, USCCB, Washington, D.C. 1995.

28 AZEVEDO M., *Comunidades eclesiais de base e inculturação da fé*, 217.

Este modelo eclesial de corresponsabilidad entre iguales continúa reconociendo las diferencias entre quienes son ordenados para servir y aquellos que no lo son. La eclesiología nacida de los procesos de Encuentro no asumió una agenda de deconstrucción de las estructuras eclesiales. Por el contrario, el ministerio del Orden continúa siendo integral en la perspectiva latina de la Iglesia viéndolo como necesario para el gobierno y la dirección pastoral de la comunidad[29]. El modelo latino de Iglesia invitó a los ordenados y al resto de líderes eclesiales a subsistir en la asamblea y a asumir su lugar dentro de la comunidad.

Nuestra experiencia indica que hay numerosas eclesiologías que operan en nuestras comunidades hispanas hoy en día. Muchas, lamentablemente, no reflejan el modelo profético de Iglesia detrás de los procesos de Encuentro. Mientras que la teología de los Encuentros fluye de la dignidad del Bautismo manifestada por medio de la comunión y la participación, la eclesiología de muchas de nuestras comunidades continúa siendo caracterizada por estructuras patriarcales que absolutizan el poder del clero. Esta dinámica eclesial se atribuye a factores históricos, sociales y culturales que van más allá de esta reflexión. De todos modos, el número de latinos en los Estados Unidos ha incrementado substancialmente desde que se escribió el *Plan Pastoral Nacional*. A pesar de ello, muchos latinos todavía se encuentran en las márgenes de las estructuras de liderazgo eclesial en todos los niveles. Por estas razones la eclesiología de comunión y participación sigue siendo más vital que nunca para transformar y promover la misión evangelizadora de la Iglesia en la comunidad hispana.

Un ejemplo similar de reflexión sobre eclesiología de comunión y participación es el reciente documento de los obispos de los Estados Unidos *Colaboradores en la viña del Señor: un recurso para guiar el desarrollo del ministerio eclesial laico*. *Colaboradores* presenta una reflexión válida sobre el ministerio eclesial laico, la formación de los ministros eclesiales laicos y las implicaciones pastorales del ministerio de los bautizados. La observación del teólogo católico Richard Gaillardetz quien sugiere que el papel, función y responsabilidades de los ministros eclesiales laicos requieren una reflexión eclesial, litúrgica y sacramental más profunda se puede entender como una extensión de la eclesiología de comunión y participación[30]. El reto teológico de Gaillardetz es importante para los

29 FIGUEROA DECK A., «A Pox on Both Your Houses: A View of Catholic Conservative-Liberal Polarities from the Hispanic Margin» en WEAVER M.J. y APPLEBY R.S. (eds.), *Being Right: Conservative Catholics in America*, Indiana University Press, Bloomington, IN 1995, 101.
30 GAILLARDETZ R., *Ecclesiology for a Global Church*, 147.

teólogos latinos teniendo en cuenta la necesidad de reflexionar sobre conceptos claves que sostienen el documento *Colaboradores en la Viña del Señor* desde una perspectiva hispana.

Nuestros estudiantes hispanos en programas de ministerio eclesial laico afirman que un punto importante que necesita desarrollarse dentro de una teología del ministerio es la relación entre los ministros laicos y el clero en los Estados Unidos. Una vez más, Gaillardetz ofrece una luz con la propuesta de expandir el papel de los ministros laicos en la Iglesia en los Estados Unidos:

> La Iglesia norteamericana ha luchado por la búsqueda de una teología del ministerio capaz de hacer justicia a su nueva situación ministerial. Muchos miembros del clero estadounidense se han sentido amenazados por el número ascendente de ministerios que ahora ejercen los laicos. Algunos críticos ven el ministerio eclesial laico como una distracción de la enseñanza del Concilio, el cual indica que la esfera propia de la actividad de los laicos es en el mundo. Un número significativo de ministros laicos se han quejado de ser tratados como auxiliares ministeriales por parte del clero[31].

La dinámica de conflicto entre los ministros laicos y el clero impide una mejor apreciación del modelo de Iglesia como comunión y participación de los procesos de Encuentro. Aún más, lo que Gaillardetz indica que necesita ser explorado por las teologías contemporáneas sobre el ministerio se hace más difícil en la comunidad hispana por la presencia de clero nacido y formado en Latinoamérica quienes con frecuencia ven con desconfianza el papel cada vez más notorio del laicado en el contexto norteamericano. Esta dinámica, exacerbada por la falta de vocaciones al sacerdocio entre los hispanos nacidos en los Estados Unidos, se puede atribuir en parte al hecho de que «sólo en Norteamérica la renovación de la vida parroquial propuesta por el Concilio Vaticano II en verdad tuvo lugar»[32]. Por ello el clero nacido y formado fuera de este país con frecuencia tiene limitaciones para entender el papel del ministro laico en el contexto postconciliar de la Iglesia en los Estados Unidos y cómo el crecimiento del número de los ministros laicos ha sido instrumental en la revitalización de la vida parroquial[33]. Otra razón que contribuye a la relación conflictiva entre los ministros eclesiales laicos latinos en los Estados Unidos y el clero nacido y for-

---

31 GAILLARDETZ R., *Ecclesiology for a Global Church*, 148.
32 GAILLARDETZ R., *Ecclesiology for a Global Church*, 148.
33 GAILLARDETZ R., *Ecclesiology for a Global Church*, 148.

mado en Latinoamérica es el hecho que estos miembros del clero no participaron de los procesos de Encuentro y por consiguiente no han sido expuestos al modelo de Iglesia que nació de estos procesos.

A la luz de estos desafíos eclesiales y ministeriales que enfrenta la comunidad latina en los Estados Unidos, sugerimos que los ministerios hispanos se beneficiarán de más investigación sobre cinco elementos eclesiológicos importantes. Primero, se necesita proponer teologías latinas del Bautismo que afirmen el sacerdocio de los fieles[34]. Segundo, los ministerios hispanos se fortalecerán con la articulación de teologías del ministerio que exploren los conflictos en la dinámica eclesial entre el clero y los ministros laicos en nuestras comunidades. Tercero, el avance de teologías latinas católicas y sus espiritualidades correspondientes avanzarán el crecimiento ministerial y espiritual de los laicos en la comunidad hispana. Cuarto, se necesita más investigación eclesiológica sobre el papel, función y responsabilidades de los laicos que conduzcan a una eclesiología de comunión y participación renovada. Quinto, considerando la realidad multicultural de la Iglesia en los Estados Unidos, esperamos que los teólogos latinos en la academia desarrollen las tan necesitadas eclesiologías interculturales que permitirán una experiencia de Iglesia donde «hay un lugar para todos los pueblos y donde la dignidad humana y los derechos humanos sean posibles»[35].

5

Conclusión

Durante los últimos 30 años la teología latina y el ministerio hispano han necesitado de su propia reflexión para generar categorías fundamentales y sistemáticas que correlacionen nuestra experiencia con la tradición teológica. En este proceso, el trabajo académico producido por los teólogos católicos hispanos ha extendido el horizonte del discurso teológico para beneficiar no solo a los ministerios hispanos, sino también para enriquecer a la comunidad teológica en general. Sus trabajos de reflexión teológica desde una perspectiva académica se han enfocado en la especificidad de la cultura y sus contribuciones han ofre-

---

34 Véase WOODS S. (ed.), *Ordering the Baptismal Priesthood*, Liturgical Press, Collegeville, MN 2003; también PHILLIBERT P., *The Priesthood of the Faithful: Key to a Living Church*, Liturgical Press, Collegeville, MN 2005.

35 AQUINO M.P., «Feminist Intercultural Theology», 16.

cido a nuestros estudiantes herramientas muy valiosas para analizar su propia experiencia de fe al igual que la de las distintas culturas que constituyen nuestra comunidad hispana estadounidense. Esta investigación ha ofrecido a los agentes pastorales en procesos de formación teológica los métodos necesarios para la reflexión que les permiten ver sus ministerios como un *locus theologicus* de teología práctica.

Una contribución muy importante a los contextos de ministerio latino ha sido la amplia reflexión teológica de ACHTUS sobre las prácticas religiosas de los hispanos en los Estados Unidos. Dichos análisis no solo ofrecen una mejor apreciación de la práctica de las devociones populares como fuente de revelación y como texto teológico[36], sino que también proveen modelos metodológicos para la investigación teológica particularmente desde una ubicación cultural y social[37]. Desde el prisma del ministerio al nivel de la base, pensamos que es importante proponer teologías prácticas que se valgan de la religiosidad popular como instrumento de evangelización y al mismo tiempo como medios para cuestionar devociones que son inconsistentes con la tradición tanto en términos de ortodoxia como de ortopraxis[38].

La Academia de Teólogos Católicos Hispanos de los Estados Unidos ha sido un instrumento clave de concientización para la comunidad latina en este país en cuanto a la relación entre la justicia y los temas de pobreza y opción preferencial por los pobres, la dignidad humana, la experiencia muchas veces trastornarte del mestizaje y el exilio de los latinos, y la marginalización de las mujeres latinas. Sin embargo, lo que con frecuencia no se resalta es que el conjunto de trabajos producidos por los miembros de ACHTUS de hecho ha modelado una praxis liberadora que da voz a un pueblo que en muchas ocasiones ha sido silenciado sistemáticamente por la cultura dominante en los Estados Unidos, en ciertos sectores de la Iglesia en Norteamérica y del discurso teológico académico.

Nuestros estudiantes se refieren a la teología hispana/latina como un tesoro escondido que necesita ser compartido con más entusiasmo con la comunidad hispana en general. Para ello creemos que hay que ofrecer estrategias para que

---

36 Para una análisis general sobre el *sensus fidelium* como fuente de revelación dentro de la religiosidad popular hispana estadounidense véase ESPÍN O., *The Faith of the People: Theological Reflections on Popular Catholicism*, Orbis Books, Maryknoll, NY 1997.

37 GOIZUETA R., *Caminemos con Jesús*, 43.

38 ESPÍN O., «Tradition and Popular Religion: An Understanding of the Sensus Fidelium» en FIGUEROA DECK A. (ed.), *Frontiers of Hispanic Theology in the United States*, Orbis Books, Maryknoll, NY 1992, 65-66.

dicho compartir sea posible. Afirmamos los esfuerzos que se están haciendo para traducir las obras de los teólogos latinos al español para su estudio tanto en el contexto estadounidense como latinoamericano. También recomendamos más diálogo entre los teólogos y los agentes pastorales y vemos necesaria la elaboración de materiales teológicos que sean accesibles al nivel de la base. Al contemplar el futuro del ministerio hispano en los Estados Unidos, creemos que las ideas y desafíos de nuestros estudiantes, resaltados en este ensayo, ayudarán a avanzar una reflexión más amplia sobre la relación entre los ministerios hispanos y el discurso teológico latino contemporáneo en este país.

El ministerio hispano y la pastoral juvenil hispana

KEN JOHNSON-MONDRAGÓN

Nosotros, jóvenes católicos,
miembros de la Pastoral Juvenil Hispana en Estados Unidos,
nos sentimos llamados y comprometidos con la misión de la Iglesia,
a formarnos y capacitarnos integralmente en la acción,
y a evangelizar con amor a los jóvenes hispanos desde su realidad.

Queremos ofrecer a inmigrantes y ciudadanos,
la verdad siempre nueva y alegre del Evangelio,
resaltando los verdaderos valores evangélicos,
y haciendo un esfuerzo por llegar a
quienes más necesitan la Buena Nueva,
no conocen a Dios
o se han desviado del camino de Jesús.

Nos proponemos cumplir esta misión,
a través del testimonio de nuestra vida
y nuestro liderazgo profético entre la juventud,
invirtiendo nuestros dones y talentos
en una acción evangelizadora y misionera
donde viven, trabajan, estudian y se divierten nuestros compañeros,
siguiendo siempre el ejemplo de Jesús
y fortaleciéndonos en la Eucaristía[1].

La *Declaración de la misión de la Pastoral Juvenil Hispana*, presentada anteriormente, fue preparada y aprobada por los 1.680 jóvenes hispanos delegados al Primer Encuentro Nacional de Pastoral Juvenil Hispana (Encuentro o PENPJH) en el año 2006. Estos delegados representaron más de 40.000 jóvenes latinos que participaron en los encuentros parroquiales, diocesanos y regionales en todo el país. Esta declaración es un hecho clave en la historia del ministerio hispano en los Estados Unidos porque, por medio de ella, los delegados presentes en el encuentro indicaron que:

- están concientes de su identidad como una comunidad joven, latina y católica, presente en todo el país
- aceptan con todo el corazón la misión de la Iglesia como suya

1 NATIONAL CATHOLIC NETWORK DE PASTORAL JUVENIL HISPANA —LA RED, *Conclusiones: Primer Encuentro Nacional de Pastoral Juvenil Hispana*, USCCB, Washington, D.C. 2008, 54.

- son protagonistas de su misión como discípulos de Jesús, sin depender de la iniciativa de líderes adultos para comenzar a realizarla
- necesitan ayuda de la Iglesia para recibir formación apropiada, guía al seguir el ejemplo de Jesús y participación plena en la Eucaristía.

La madurez de la Pastoral Juvenil Hispana (PJH) —como un ministerio con sus propios principios, visión y estructuras de liderazgo a nivel nacional, regional y local— constituye el contexto para cualquier conversación sobre el trabajo pastoral con adolescentes y jóvenes adultos en el siglo XXI. Sin embargo, este ministerio depende de los jóvenes que ejercen su liderazgo en él; es un ministerio arraigado en los lenguajes y culturas de los jóvenes hispanos; está animado gracias a su celo profético por la evangelización y la santidad, como respuesta al Bautismo; responde a la realidad de la gente joven involucrada, especialmente a los obstáculos y retos que encuentran en la vida diaria; y ofrece formación en la fe católica para construir el Reino de Dios.

Esta descripción de la Pastoral Juvenil Hispana parece ser bastante clara, pero genera varias preguntas importantes. ¿Cuáles son los obstáculos y retos que los jóvenes hispanos enfrentan en su vida diaria? ¿De qué manera la cultura y el lenguaje impactan la experiencia y el entendimiento de la fe cristiana, según la tradición católica? ¿Qué formación tienen nuestros líderes en el ministerio y qué recursos pastorales y catequéticos están disponibles para asistirles en su tarea? ¿De qué manera la Iglesia, en general, responde a sus jóvenes latinos? ¿Cuál es el estado actual de la formación religiosa entre los jóvenes hispanos?

Este ensayo responde a varias de las preguntas anteriores, en tres partes. La primera parte presenta el contexto contemporáneo de la PJH en los Estados Unidos; la segunda ofrece una visión general de la PJH en EEUU hoy; y la tercera ofrece algunas reflexiones sobre esfuerzos que se han dado en la historia y tareas para crecer en este campo.

1

El contexto contemporáneo de la Pastoral Juvenil Hispana en los Estados Unidos

Las *Conclusiones del PENPJH* ofrecen una breve historia de la PJH en los Estados Unidos. Describen sus raíces en Latinoamérica; su desarrollo a través del proceso de los tres Encuentros Nacionales Hispanos de Pastoral; su relación con modelos tradicionales de *youth and young adult ministry* (ministerios con adolescentes y con adultos jóvenes en inglés) en el país, y su crecimiento más recien-te[2]. Este contexto histórico constituye el marco referencial de la primera parte de este ensayo.

En el año 2002 el Instituto Fe y Vida publicó una evaluación de la Pastoral Juvenil Hispana mostrando evidencia clara de los retos materiales y espirituales más importantes que enfrentan los jóvenes hispanos. A pesar de que los obispos católicos en los Estados Unidos se comprometieron a una opción misionera preferencial a favor de los pobres y los jóvenes en el ministerio hispano[3], el reporte reveló que «la mayoría de los programas parroquiales de *youth ministry* en los EEUU llegan sólo a un segmento pequeño de adolescentes latinos católicos, mien-tras que los programas dirigidos directamente a los jóvenes hispanos son pocos y limitados en cuanto a su capacidad y profundidad»[4].

En los años posteriores a esa evaluación preliminar, el proceso que condujo al PENPJH (2005-2006) ha estimulado esfuerzos en parroquias y diócesis para mejorar y aumentar el cuidado y el acompañamiento pastoral de los jóvenes hispanos. Además, los hallazgos del Estudio Nacional sobre Adolescentes y Re-ligión (NSYR, sigla en inglés, 2003-2008) han dado una luz sobre el estado actual de la formación religiosa y los retos pastorales que nacen de las diferencias de idioma, cultura y estatus socioeconómico, entre los adolescentes hispanos. Te-niendo en cuenta la abundancia de información disponible gracias a éstas y otras fuentes, éste es un momento oportuno para evaluar una vez más dónde estamos en nuestro ministerio «con, hacia y desde la juventud hispana»[5].

2 NATIONAL CATHOLIC NETWORK DE PASTORAL JUVENIL HISPANA —LA RED, *Conclusiones: Primer Encuentro Nacional de Pastoral Juvenil Hispana*, USCCB, Washington, D.C. 2008, 19-22.

3 NATIONAL CONFERENCE OF CATHOLIC BISHOPS, *Plan Pastoral Nacional para el Ministerio Hispano*, USCC, Washington, D.C. 1987, n. 51-56; 64-66, in UNITED STATES CONFERENCE OF CATHOLIC BISHOPS, *Ministerio Hispano: Tres Documentos Importantes*, USCCB, Washington, D.C. 1995.

4 JOHNSON-MONDRAGÓN K., *The Status of Hispanic Youth and Young Adult Ministry in the United States: A Preliminary Study*, Instituto Fe y Vida, Stockton, CA 2002, 30.

5 Esta frase es tomada del objetivo específico #3 del PENPJH, *Conclusiones*, 27. La frase captura la esencia de la acción evangelizadora en PJH tal como ha sido articulada en Latinoamérica: un ministerio que es realizado «desde la juventud» es un ministerio que está informado y responde al contexto inmediato y global de las vidas de los jóvenes. Al mismo tiempo es un ministerio que depende de los dones de los jóvenes para desarrollar e implementar una respuesta pastoral. Una descripción completa de la articulación latinoamericana de este ministerio se puede en-contrar en CONSEJO EPISCOPAL LATINOAMERICANO, *Civilización del amor: Tarea y esperanza*, CELAM, Sección de Juventud, Santa Fé de Bogotá, Colombia 1995, 2ª Parte, Sección III, n. 2.1-2.2.

1.1. CAMBIOS DEMOGRÁFICOS

Tal como indica la gráfica 1, los jóvenes latinos ya constituyen la mitad de los católicos menores de 18 años en los Estados unidos, y el pueblo latino constituirá la mayoría de la población católica en menos de 40 años. Por consiguiente, el trabajo pastoral de nuestra Iglesia en este siglo será marcado por un cambio demográfico enorme hacia una población latina mayoritaria. En este contexto tenemos que preguntarnos: ¿está nuestra Iglesia preparada para responder a este cambio constructivamente, preparando líderes y ofreciendo servicios pastorales que satisfagan las necesidades de toda la comunidad católica?

GRÁFICA 1

Proyección poblacional católica estadounidense por edad, raza/etnicidad y año

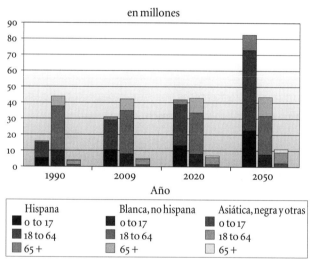

Basado en: RSL 2007, ICR Omnibus 2008, NSRI 1990, LNPS 1990, Censo 1990, los estimados de la población nacional en 2009 del u.s. Census Bureau y proyecciones del Pew Hispanic Center.

Debido al crecimiento elevado en el número de inmigrantes latinos entre las edades de 20 y 25 años, como muestra la gráfica 2, casi la mitad de los jóvenes católicos hispanos nacieron fuera del país. Además, los latinos más jóvenes en los Estados Unidos hoy en día son en su mayoría hijos de inmigrantes. Como resultado, su experiencia al crecer entre dos culturas tendrá gran impacto en la vida de nuestra Iglesia, a medida que maduran como jóvenes y eventualmente toman su lugar entre nuestros líderes —o no lo hacen— según sea la calidad de formación en la fe y capacitación para el liderazgo que reciban.

Hispanos en los Estados Unidos por edad y generación en 2009

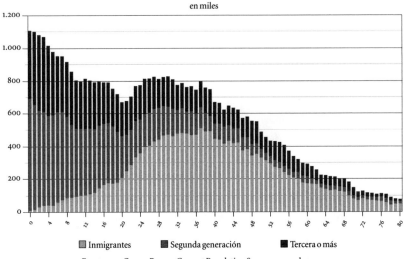

en miles

Inmigrantes   Segunda generación   Tercera o más

Fuente: u.s. Census Bureau Current Population Survey, marzo de 2009

La gráfica 3 ofrece una última mirada a la realidad demográfica de la pastoral juvenil en la Iglesia Católica, según la etnicidad, raza y generación de la población total de adolescentes y jóvenes católicos. Esta comparación muestra claramente que los inmigrantes constituyen el grupo más grande de jóvenes adultos católicos hispanos, mientras que los hijos de los inmigrantes predominan entre los adolescentes. Es importante indicar también que, de acuerdo con estimados del Instituto Fe y Vida, los hispanos ya sobrepasan a los blancos como el segmento poblacional católico más grande entre adolescentes en edad de escuela preparatoria.

Estimado poblacional de jóvenes católicos en los Estados Unidos por edad, raza/etnicidad y generación en 2009

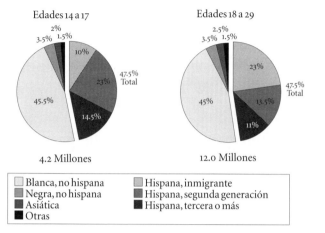

Basado en: RSL 2007, ICR Omnibus 2008 y los estimados de la población de Estados Unidos del U.S. Census Bureau, julio 1 de 2009

1.2. ASPECTOS CLAVES DEL CONTEXTO SOCIOCULTURAL

Para ayudar a situar la experiencia diaria de los jóvenes latinos en los Estados Unidos es necesario resaltar algunas diferencias entre jóvenes hispanos y blancos, en general, y contrastar la realidad de los jóvenes católicos hispanos y blancos cuando hay información disponible. Los resultados investigativos presentados aquí vienen de varias fuentes reunidas y publicadas por el Instituto Fe y Vida[6].

1.2.1. *IDIOMA*

- El 58 por ciento de los adolescentes hispanos habla español en casa, al igual o en mayor proporción que el inglés, incluyendo el 47 por ciento de los adolescentes hispanos nacidos en EEUU.
- El 62 por ciento de los jóvenes latinos (entre 18 y 29 años) dice que no habla inglés «bien».

6 INSTITUTO FE Y VIDA, «Pastoral Juvenil Hispana: Datos recientes» en *Perspectives on Hispanic Youth and Young Adult Ministry* 4, Instituto Fe y Vida Stockton, CA 2007, recurso electrónico, http://www.feyvida.org/research/researchpubs.html

Estas estadísticas reflejan la proporción de inmigrantes e hijos de inmigrantes que aparecen en la gráfica 2. Para la mayoría de personas, el lenguaje que se habla en casa tiende a ser el lenguaje preferido para la oración y la fe.

1.2.2. *ESTATUS MIGRATORIO*

- Aunque la Oficina del Censo no mantiene información sobre estatus migratorio, se estima que al menos la mitad de los jóvenes latinos *inmigrantes* son indocumentados.
- Junto con los datos del censo presentados en la gráfica 3, esto indica que en general cerca del 80 por ciento de los jóvenes hispanos en los Estados Unidos, tiene ciudadanía o residencia legal[7].

1.2.3. *EDUCACIÓN*

- Más del 30 por ciento de los hispanos entre los 20 y 29 años en el año 2007 no había terminado la preparatoria, comparado con sólo 7 por ciento de los blancos de la misma edad.
- Sólo el 15 por ciento de los hispanos entre las edades de 25 y 29 años había terminado estudios universitarios en programas de cuatro años u otros programas más avanzados, comparado con el 34 por ciento de los blancos de la misma edad.
- La diferencia para los católicos es aún mayor: entre los padres de adolescentes católicos en el Estudio Nacional sobre Adolescentes y Religión, el 38 por ciento de padres blancos y el 39 por ciento de madres blancas tenían al menos un título universitario, en comparación con el 12 por ciento de las madres y el 8 por ciento de los padres hispanos[8].

Capítulo 4

323

---

7 INSTITUTO FE Y VIDA, «Pastoral Juvenil Hispana: Datos recientes» en *Perspectives on Hispanic Youth and Young Adult Ministry*, 3, 5.

8 INSTITUTO FE Y VIDA, «Pastoral Juvenil Hispana: Datos recientes» en *Perspectives on Hispanic Youth and Young Adult Ministry*, 3, 5. En esta sección solo se mencionan los resultados correspondientes a blancos e hispanos del Estudio Nacional sobre Adolescentes y Religión debido a que las muestras de las encuestas no incluyeron suficientes participantes católicos de grupos negros, asiáticos, indígenas y otros grupos que permitieran una comparación apropiada.

1.2.4. ECONOMÍA FAMILIAR

No es sorpresa que estas diferencias también se reflejan en los ingresos familiares y posesiones materiales:

- El 26 por ciento de los hogares católicos hispanos en el Estudio Nacional sobre Adolescentes y Religión tenía un ingreso anual de menos de $20.000 dólares y sólo 14 por ciento de más de $60.000 dólares; esto ofrece una comparación de 4 por ciento y 52 por ciento, respectivamente, con relación a hogares de familias blancas católicas.

- Similarmente, el 75 por ciento de los padres católicos hispanos dijo que tenía deudas o sólo lo justo y necesario, mientras que sólo el 1 por ciento dijo que tenía «muchos» ahorros y bienes. Entre los padres católicos blancos, sólo el 41 por ciento dijo que tenía deudas o sólo lo justo y necesario, y el 13 por ciento dijo que tenía «muchos» ahorros y bienes.

- También los padres católicos blancos tenían casi el doble de probabilidades de ser dueños de su propia casa, comparados con los padres católicos hispanos (82 por ciento vs. 46 por ciento)[9].

1.2.5. MATRIMONIO E HIJOS

- El 49 por ciento de las latinas entre los 16 y 30 años estaba criando un hijo o varios, y el 19 por ciento de las latinas en estas edades eran madres solteras; esto se compara con el 27 por ciento y el 10 por ciento respectivamente, entre las mujeres no latinas[10].

- Los hispanos también tienden a casarse más temprano que otros grupos. El 31 por ciento de los hispanos entre las edades de 16 a 30 años está casado o lo ha estado, comparado con el 25 por ciento del resto de la población de la misma edad[11].

- El 62 por ciento de los adolescentes católicos hispanos tiene padres casados, comparado con el 76 por ciento de los adolescentes católicos blancos[12].

9 INSTITUTO FE Y VIDA, «Pastoral Juvenil Hispana: Datos recientes» en *Perspectives on Hispanic Youth and Young Adult Ministry*, 4.
10 U.S. CENSUS BUREAU, *Current Population Survey for March*, 2009.
11 U.S. CENSUS BUREAU, *Current Population Survey for March*, 2009.
12 JOHNSON-MONDRAGÓN K., «Youth Ministry and the Socioreligious Lives of Hispanic and White Catholic Teens in the U.S.» en INSTITUTO FE Y VIDA, *Perspectives on Hispanic Youth and Young Adult Ministry* 2, Instituto Fe y Vida, Stockton, CA 2005, 3, recurso electrónico, http://www.feyvida.org/research/researchpubs.html.

1.2.6. *CONDUCTA DE ALTO RIESGO Y CRIMINAL*

Las tasas de conductas de alto riesgo y de conductas criminales en los jóvenes hispanos, son significativamente más altas que en los jóvenes blancos:

- Los jóvenes hispanos tienen 50 por ciento más de probabilidades de intentar suicidarse; casi tres veces más, de ser encarcelados; más de tres veces, de que las chicas queden embarazadas o que los chicos dejen a una joven adolescente embarazada, y aproximadamente 30 veces más, de ser miembros activos de una pandilla[13].

- La excepción a este patrón es el abuso de drogas y alcohol: los adolescentes católicos hispanos y blancos reportaron niveles similares en el uso de marihuana y, entre los adolescentes que indicaron haberse embriagado en el último año, los católicos blancos lo hicieron 33 por ciento más que los católicos hispanos[14].

Estos factores de riesgo están relacionados al incremento de las probabilidades que tienen los jóvenes hispanos de estar expuestos a situaciones de violencia y abuso en el hogar, la escuela y los vecindarios, así como contar con menos supervisión y guía por parte de los padres, y estar sujetos a experiencias de discriminación y estereotipos negativos.

2

Visión general de la Pastoral Juvenil Hispana en los Estados Unidos hoy

La primera parte de este ensayo demostró que el segmento hispano de la población juvenil católica está creciendo mucho más rápido que el resto de la población de la misma edad y está marcado por diferencias socioculturales con relación a otros jóvenes católicos. Sin duda, muchas de esas diferencias impactan el bienestar espiritual, emocional, intelectual y físico de los jóvenes católicos hispanos. Ciertamente la información disponible demuestra que muchos jóvenes latinos están tomando decisiones nefastas con consecuencias terribles para ellos, sus hijos, nuestra Iglesia y el resto de la sociedad. Con esto en mente, esta segunda parte examina el estado de la formación en la fe y el cuidado pastoral de los jóvenes hispanos.

13 INSTITUTO FE Y VIDA, «Pastoral Juvenil Hispana: Datos recientes», 5.
14 JOHNSON-MONDRAGÓN K., «Youth Ministry and the Socioreligious Lives of Hispanic and White Catholic Teens in the U.S.», 22.

2.1. IDENTIDAD RELIGIOSA, FORMACIÓN EN LA FE
Y PRÁCTICAS RELIGIOSAS

El fenómeno de los hispanos abandonando la Iglesia Católica para ir a comunidades evangélicas y pentecostales continúa siendo discutido y analizado ampliamente[15], pero existe una pregunta más fundamental sobre la formación en la fe que están recibiendo los jóvenes católicos latinos. Muchos de los jóvenes católicos hispanos entrevistados en el Estudio Nacional sobre Adolescentes y Religión hablaron con convicción sobre su identidad católica pero su compromiso de fe se reflejó débilmente en sus prácticas religiosas y su habilidad de articular lo que creen. En general, los adolescentes católicos hispanos practican más devociones religiosas a nivel personal y familiar, mientras que los adolescentes católicos blancos tienden a estar más involucrados en actividades parroquiales[16]. Aún así, ambos grupos tienden a describir su fe como una expresión de «deísmo terapéutico moralista» (*moralistic therapeutic deism*, MTD, en inglés)[17], más que una vivencia correcta de las enseñanzas de la Iglesia.

Lo que es motivo de preocupación pastoral es que aún los padres de familia católicos latinos, que están comprometidos con su fe e involucrados en la parroquia, tienen dificultad para comunicar la fe a sus hijos adolescentes, lo que contrasta con la experiencia de los padres de familia católicos blancos comprometidos con su fe. El análisis del Estudio Nacional sobre Adolescentes y Religión describió esta realidad en el siguiente pasaje:

«Los hijos de padres católicos latinos "comprometidos" con su fe, en la muestra del Estudio Nacional sobre Adolescentes y Religión, comparados con los hijos blancos de un grupo similar de padres, tienen menos de la mitad de probabilidades de participar en la misa semanal; menos de un tercio, de participar en un grupo juvenil en la Iglesia;

15 Véase un análisis reciente de este fenómeno en THE PEW FORUM ON RELIGION AND PUBLIC LIFE, *Changing Faiths: Latinos and the Transformation of American Religion*, Pew Hispanic Center, Washington, D.C. 2007, 41-48, http://pewforum.org/newassets/surveys/hispanic/hispanics-religion-07-final-mar08.pdf (página visitada en enero 11 del 2010).

16 JOHNSON-MONDRAGÓN K., (ed.), *Pathways of Hope and Faith Among Hispanic Teens: Pastoral Reflections and Strategies Inspired by the National Study of Youth and Religion*, Instituto Fe y Vida, Stockton, CA 2007, 97-100; 324.

17 Deísmo terapéutico moralista (Moralistic Therapeutic Deism) es un término propuesto por Christian Smith, el investigador principal del Estudio Nacional sobre Adolescentes y Religión, para describir una actitud generalizada de «me vale» que caracteriza la fe religiosa de la mayoría de los adolescentes en los Estados Unidos hoy en día. Para una descripción de este término en relación con los adolescentes hispanos vea JOHNSON-MONDRAGÓN K., (ed.), *Pathways of Hope and Faith Among Hispanic Teens*, 72-74; 324.

menos de una cuarta parte, de ir a una escuela católica; menos de una quinta parte, de ser líderes de un grupo juvenil, y menos de una sexta parte, quizás menos, de asistir a un retiro religioso o a una experiencia de campamentos de verano»[18].

Las razones que llevan a esta desconexión entre los padres latinos y sus hijos adolescentes son complejas y varían de familia en familia y de parroquia en parroquia, pero dos factores sobresalen: 1) muchos de los adolescentes latinos nacidos en los Estados Unidos no se identifican fácilmente con las expresiones y tradiciones de sus padres inmigrantes, debido a la gran brecha cultural que experimentan con ellos[19], y 2) las diferencias de idioma, cultura y clase social que muchos adolescentes latinos experimentan con relación a otros adolescentes y líderes adultos en sus parroquias, con frecuencia los lleva a no participar en programas de *youth ministry,* especialmente cuando la parroquia sólo ofrece un modelo de trabajo pastoral con adolescentes[20].

2.2. VOCACIONES AL MINISTERIO ECLESIAL

La falta de compromiso de los adolescentes católicos latinos refleja de muchas maneras la poca atención y, en algunos casos, el racismo tangible con el que la Iglesia Católica —como institución— ha respondido a las necesidades pastorales de sus miembros hispanos de todas las edades, a través de los años[21]. Las consecuencias de esta falta de atención no pueden ser más evidentes que en las estadísticas relacionadas con vocaciones religiosas y ministeriales:

- El 11 por ciento de los diáconos católicos estadounidenses es hispano
- El 9 por ciento de los obispos católicos estadounidenses es hispano
- El 6 por ciento de los sacerdotes católicos estadounidenses es hispano, y el 83 por ciento de ellos, nacieron fuera de los Estados Unidos
- El 4 por ciento de los ministros eclesiales laicos estadounidenses es hispano
- El 2 por ciento de los religiosos consagrados (hombres y mujeres) estadounidenses es hispano

18 JOHNSON-MONDRAGÓN K., (ed.), *Pathways of Hope and Faith Among Hispanic Teens,* 100; 324. INSTITUTO FE Y VIDA, «Pastoral Juvenil Hispana: Datos recientes», 6-7.
19 Vea CERVANTES C. y JOHNSON-MONDRAGÓN K., «Las dinámicas de cultura, fe y familia en la vida de los adolescentes hispanos, y sus implicaciones para la pastoral con adolescentes» en INSTITUTO FE Y VIDA, *Perspectives on Hispanic Youth and Young Adult Ministry* 5, Instituto Fe y Vida, Stockton, CA 2008, recurso electrónico, http://www.feyvida.org/research/researchpubs.html.
20 NATIONAL CATHOLIC NETWORK DE PASTORAL JUVENIL HISPANA —LA RED, *Conclusiones,* 33.
21 JOHNSON-MONDRAGÓN K., (ed.), *Pathways of Hope and Faith Among Hispanic Teens,* 326-329.

- El 1 por ciento de los sacerdotes nacidos en los Estados Unidos es hispano[22].

Desde otra perspectiva, la proporción entre laicos y sacerdotes puede verse como una medida del grado de identificación y compromiso institucional en la comunidad católica. Actualmente hay cerca de 1.900 laicos católicos por cada sacerdote católico en los Estados Unidos. Por el contrario, hay cerca de 10.000 laicos católicos latinos por cada sacerdote latino, y la diferencia se dispara a 30.000 laicos católicos hispanos nacidos en los Estados Unidos por cada sacerdote latino nacido en el país[23]. Quizás esto no es una sorpresa, pues es difícil pedir un compromiso de por vida a los jóvenes latinos en una institución con un récord mediocre e irregular de dedicación a las comunidades hispanas, a pesar de los grandes ideales articulados por los obispos estadounidenses en el *Plan Pastoral Nacional para el Ministerio Hispano* y otros documentos sobre el ministerio hispano.

2.3. CATEGORÍAS PASTORALES DE JÓVENES LATINOS

Avanzar un compromiso eclesial en favor de los jóvenes latinos requerirá un esfuerzo organizado para crear programas acogedores que respondan a sus preocupaciones y necesidades pastorales. En este sentido, los efectos alienadores de las diferencias lingüísticas, culturales y sociales entre quienes participan en *youth ministry*, con frecuencia pasan desapercibidos. La variedad de circunstancias pastorales que existen entre los jóvenes hispanos (sin mencionar a los jóvenes católicos de otras razas/etnicidades) es un llamado a crear espacios y programas pastorales que respondan a segmentos particulares de la población juvenil. El Estudio Nacional sobre Adolescentes y Religión describe cuatro categorías pastorales distintas de jóvenes hispanos para ayudar a que los líderes pastorales reconozcan esta diversidad[24]. Esa información no será repetida aquí en detalle, pero se presenta articulada en las siguientes tablas:

---

22 INSTITUTO FE Y VIDA, «Pastoral Juvenil Hispana: Datos recientes», 8.
23 INSTITUTO FE Y VIDA, «Pastoral Juvenil Hispana: Datos recientes», 8.
24 JOHNSON-MONDRAGÓN K., (ed.), *Pathways of Hope and Faith Among Hispanic Teens*, 33-39.

TABLA 1

Categorías pastorales de los jóvenes hispanos

Trabajadores Inmigrantes	
· La mayoría habla español	· Poca educación escolar
· La mayoría de origen mexicano	· Tienen familias grandes
· Muchos son indocumentados	· Motivados y esperanzados
· Más del 74% es católico	· Dispuestos a trabajar duro
· Buscan el apoyo moral y espiritual de la iglesia	
· La mayoría tiene pocos recursos económicos	
· Les interesa formar grupos y comunidades juveniles	

Buscadores de Identidad	
· La mayoría es bilingüe	· Pocos van a la universidad
· La mayoría nació en EUA	· Poco autoestima
· Son hijos de inmigrantes	· No tienen motivación
· Terminan la preparatoria con dificultad	
· Algunos buscan refugio en el alcohol, la droga o el sexo	
· Encuentran esperanza en el trabajo, la familia o los amigos	
· Se encuentran en la clase media baja	

Integrantes a la Cultura Dominante	
· La mayoría habla inglés	· Motivados y esperanzados
· La mayoría nació en EUA	· Dispuestos a trabajar duro
· Van a la universidad y algunos asisten a escuelas privadas	
· No les interesa insertarse en la comunidad hispana pobre	
· A menudo abandonan la Iglesia Católica	
· Tienden a despreciar a otros jóvenes hispanos	
· La mayoría pertenece a la clase media alta	

Pandilleros y Jóvenes de Alto Riesgo	
· Inglés y español limitados	· Poca educación escolar
· La mayoría nació en EUA	· Ira contra la sociedad
· Viven en los barrios latinos	· Experimentan desesperanza
· La mayoría está desempleada	· Muchos son encarcelados
· Muchos consumen y/o venden la droga	
· La mayoría tiene pocos recursos económicos	
· Se acercan a la iglesia solamente en programas especializadas	

TABLA 2

Necesidades pastorales de los jóvenes hispanos por categoría

	Trabajadores Inmigrantes	Buscadores de Identidad	Integrantes a la Cultura Dominante	Pandilleros y Jóvenes de Alto Riesgo
Vida espiritual	Necesitan formar comunidades de fe con base en su cultura de origen	Necesitan asesoría y acompañamiento para integrar su fe y su vida en la transición cultural	Necesitan guía para superar el individualismo y consumismo, y valorar la espiritualidad hispana	Necesitan la fe para sanar las heridas y pasar del enojo y el odio al perdón
Desarrollo intelectual	Necesitan un sistema alternativo de educación	Necesitan motivación para terminar la preparatoria y proponerse estudios universitarios	Necesitan ayuda financiera y orientación para entender el sistema educativo de EUA	Necesitan un sistema alternativo de educación
Madurez afectiva y socialización	Necesitan un ambiente sano para desarrollar relaciones sociales	Necesitan ayuda para crecer su autoestima y seguridad en si mismos	Necesitan personas que sean modelo de integración social y cultural	Necesitan un lugar y un grupo a los que pertenecer y personas que sean buenos modelos
Adquisición de virtudes humanas	Necesitan apoyo para no caer en el vicio / adicciones	Necesitan guía y orientación en la vida	Necesitan valorar el servicio a la comunidad y la justicia social	Necesitan consejería para superar los hábitos y actitudes malos
Porcentaje de jóvenes / adolescentes hispanos	25% a 45% / 10% a 20%	25% a 45% / 40% a 50%	15% a 25% / 20% a 30%	10% a 15% / 10% a 15%

Por supuesto, la proporción relativa de jóvenes latinos en cada categoría dependerá de cada lugar. Sin embargo, las necesidades pastorales de cada categoría son tan distintas, que es difícil imaginar un solo programa o un grupo que pudiera responder efectivamente a las necesidades de todos. Así, la Pastoral Juvenil Hispana es más efectiva cuando ofrece una respuesta pastoral diferenciada por medio de una variedad de estructuras, programas, eventos y actividades diseñados a servir segmentos específicos de la población juvenil en la parroquia o la diócesis, según sus necesidades particulares. Mientras más programas y actividades ofrezca una parroquia, más oportunidades de que los jóvenes católicos en la comunidad encuentren un hogar espiritual y una comunidad para crecer en la fe.

Es importante reconocer que no todos los jóvenes católicos están listos para integrarse en un programa intensivo de catequesis y formación en la fe. El hogar y los ambientes sociales de muchos jóvenes latinos con frecuencia están dominados por valores contrarios al Evangelio tales como:

- Consumismo que valora a las personas por lo que compran
- Presión social para buscar satisfacción inmediata en el sexo, las drogas y otras conductas de alto riesgo
- Individualismo extremo que ve a otras personas como objetos a ser utilizados para beneficio o placer personal
- Secularismo que margina las convicciones y valores religiosos
- Experiencias de dominación, violencia, racismo, sexismo, abuso y discriminación vistas como aspectos «normales» de la vida, ante las cuales nada podemos hacer
- Juicio moral disminuido causado por adicciones

En estos ambientes, un ministerio efectivo puede requerir un período de pre-evangelización que incluya actividades diseñadas para ganar la confianza de los jóvenes sin que se sientan juzgados, al tiempo que participan de actividades seguras y constructivas para orientar su vida. El compromiso amoroso, el testimonio personal de fe y las preguntas profundas de los líderes —adultos y jóvenes— gradualmente estimularán en estos jóvenes un deseo mayor por entender la fe, una conversión y una espiritualidad más profunda, cuando estén listos. También puede ser necesario catequizar a la comunidad sobre cómo acoger y aceptar a los jóvenes como son, para minimizar la experiencia común de ser juzgados o rechazados por los adultos en la comunidad parroquial por no «parecer» jóvenes católicos buenos.

2.4. DESARROLLO Y ORGANIZACIÓN DE TRES RESPUESTAS PASTORALES COMPLEMENTARIAS

Aunque todavía no podemos decir que la Iglesia ofrece una respuesta integral a las necesidades pastorales de las cuatro categorías de jóvenes latinos en todas las parroquias, existen tres ministerios que proveen respuestas parciales: *youth ministry* (pastoral con adolescentes), *young adult ministry* (pastoral con adultos jóvenes entre 18 y 39 años, sean solteros o casados o con hijos, generalmente con estudios universitarios), and Pastoral Juvenil Hispana. Tal como se mencionó anteriormente, los elementos claves del desarrollo de la Pastoral Juvenil Hispana, incluyendo sus raíces en Latinoamérica y un recorrido breve por su proceso histórico de inculturación en la Iglesia Católica en este país, se pueden encontrar en las *Conclusiones del PENPJH*[25]. Los esfuerzos tradicionales de *youth ministry* y *young adult ministry* también tienen su historia y su desarrollo particular como esfuerzos diferenciados en los Estados Unidos.

Un elemento común entre estas respuestas es que cada ministerio ha desarrollado su propio conjunto de principios operativos y organizaciones nacionales para apoyar a los líderes a nivel diocesano y parroquial:

- *Youth ministry* usa el documento *Renovemos la Visión: Fundamentos para el Ministerio con Jóvenes Católicos* (publicación de USCCB) y se apoya en las siguientes dos organizaciones: la National Federation for Catholic Youth Ministry (NFCYM) y National Association of Catholic Youth Ministry Leaders (NACYML).
- *Young adult ministry* usa el documento *Hijos e Hijas de la Luz: Plan Pastoral para el Ministerio con Jóvenes Adultos* (publicación de USCCB) y se apoya en las siguientes tres organizaciones: la National Catholic Young Adult Ministry Association (NCYAMA), la Catholic Campus Ministry Association (CCMA), y la National Association of Diocesan Directors of Campus Ministry (NADDCM).
- Pastoral Juvenil Hispana usa los siguientes dos documentos *Civilización del amor: Tarea y esperanza* (publicado por el Consejo Episcopal Latinoamericano, Sección de Juventud) y las *Conclusiones del PENPJH* (publicación de USCCB); y se apoya en la siguiente organización: la National Catholic Network de Pastoral Juvenil Hispana —La Red.

A pesar de los mejores esfuerzos por parte de las organizaciones nacionales y de los ministerios que representan, muchos jóvenes hispanos no son atendidos pastoralmente. Los jóvenes latinos que viven en situaciones de alto riesgo pocas veces se benefician de esfuerzos pastorales organizados que les sirvan y la mayoría de jóvenes «buscadores de identidad» no se sienten a gusto ni en los grupos tradicionales de *youth and young adult ministry* ni en la PJH (asumiendo que su parroquia es una de las pocas que ofrece opciones), por lo cual simplemente no participan. Estos jóvenes «estrujados culturalmente» son los que tienen más probabilidad de perder su fe e identidad católica en su vida adulta, con

---

25 NATIONAL CATHOLIC NETWORK DE PASTORAL JUVENIL HISPANA —LA RED, *Conclusiones*, 19-22.

frecuencia debido a un proceso que empieza con el rechazo de la cultura de sus padres y lleva eventualmente al rechazo de la fe[26].

2.5. DISTINTOS ENFOQUES PASTORALES Y LA PROTECCIÓN DE LOS ADOLESCENTES

Es importante reconocer algunas de las diferencias centrales entre el enfoque tradicional de *youth ministry* y el de Pastoral Juvenil Hispana. En primer lugar, aunque *youth ministry* se describe como un ministerio hacia, con, por y para adolescentes[27], en el contexto estadounidense se asume que los adolescentes sólo ejercerán liderazgo bajo la dirección de adultos —asalariados o voluntarios— responsables por todo lo que ocurre en el ministerio. Hay límites en lo que los líderes pueden y no pueden hacer, debido a su edad, incluso en el caso de líderes entre los 18 y 25 años de edad. Además, a partir de los escándalos sobre abuso sexual a comienzos de este siglo, los obispos han implementado un *Estatuto para la Protección de Niños y Jóvenes* cuyas normas se aplican en casi todos los programas de *youth ministry*.

Por el contrario, la pastoral juvenil en Latinoamérica es un ministerio de los jóvenes a sus compañeros, generalmente sin un líder asalariado e incluso sin un adulto voluntario asignado para guiar las reuniones[28]. En los Estados Unidos *La Red* ha definido la PJH como un ministerio de jóvenes hispanos solteros entre las edades de 16 y 30 años, con sus compañeros[29], aunque existen grupos que sirven a una población más amplia en muchos lugares. Con la publicación del *Estatuto* de los obispos, el liderazgo pastoral a nivel diocesano y parroquial se ha encontrado ante el desafío de asegurarse que la PJH ofrezca un ambiente seguro para sus participantes menores de 18 años. Esto es especialmente problemático si se considera que muchos de los jóvenes adultos —líderes y participantes— están indocumentados, lo cual les hace temerosos de cualquier tipo de verificación de récord criminal. Como resultado, algunas parroquias y diócesis han op-

---

26 Para una descripción de los patrones más comunes de adaptación entre padres inmigrantes y sus hijos naciones en los Estados Unidos, véase CERVANTES C. Y JOHNSON-MONDRAGÓN K., «Las dinámicas de cultura, fe y familia en la vida de los adolescentes hispanos, y sus implicaciones para la pastoral con adolescentes», 3-5.

27 UNITED STATES CATHOLIC CONFERENCE, DEPARTMENT OF EDUCATION, *A Vision of Youth Ministry: Edición Bilingüe*, Washington, D.C., USCC 1986, 6-7.

28 CERVANTES C. Y JOHNSON-MONDRAGÓN K., «Pastoral Juvenil Hispana, Youth Ministry, and Young Adult Ministry: An Updated Perspective on Three Different Pastoral Realities» en INSTITUTO FE Y VIDA, *Perspectives on Hispanic Youth and Young Adult Ministry* 3, Instituto Fe y Vida, Stockton, CA 2007, 3.

29 NATIONAL CATHOLIC NETWORK DE PASTORAL JUVENIL HISPANA —LA RED, *Conclusiones*, 23.

tado por separar las edades, mientras que otras han designado los grupos como «ministerio intergeneracional» asignando líderes que han sido capacitados y obtenido las debidas verificaciones para supervisar adolescentes durante actividades en grupos pequeños[30].

Aunque cada diócesis ha encargado a alguien para asegurarse de que las parroquias cumplan con las normas del *Estatuto*, es importante reconocer que hay muchos movimientos apostólicos en la Iglesia que sirven a los jóvenes hispanos, con frecuencia sin mucha supervisión de la parroquia o de la diócesis. Los encuentros diocesanos llevados a cabo como preparación para el PENPJH incluyeron representantes de más de 60 movimientos distintos, 67 por ciento de los cuales reportaron trabajar con jóvenes y adolescentes juntos[31], y en la mayoría de las diócesis no hay estructuras claras de responsabilidad para asegurarse que sus líderes están preparados para proveer la protección requerida por los obispos en el *Estatuto*. De hecho, varias anécdotas pastorales sugieren que un número significativo de grupos de jóvenes de distintas edades, ni siquiera saben que es un asunto que necesita abordarse —en algunos casos debido a una decisión práctica por parte del personal diocesano de dejar que los ministerios sigan funcionando como tal, en lugar de imponer normas que serían difíciles de seguir pastoralmente.

2.6. OTRAS DIFERENCIAS IMPORTANTES CON RELACIÓN A YOUTH MINISTRY

Además de las diferencias en cuanto a la manera de agrupar a los jóvenes según sus edades, la PJH y *youth ministry* dependen de distintas formas de liderazgo, enfrentan diversos retos y usan modelos diferentes en áreas claves del cuidado y acompañamiento pastoral de los jóvenes en la Iglesia. Cuando los párrocos y los líderes diocesanos no entienden estas diferencias, usualmente el resultado es que un ministerio se suspende en favor del otro. Por consiguiente, es importante reconocer la complementariedad de los enfoques para poder extender el ministerio hacia y con los jóvenes latinos en parroquias y diócesis. Veamos algunas diferencias clave entre estos dos ministerios:

---

30 Para una presentación sobre los puntos a favor y en contra de tener grupos integrados con jóvenes de distintas edades versus grupos separados según la edad, véase JOHNSON-MONDRAGÓN K., (ed.), *Pathways of Hope and Faith Among Hispanic Teens*, 342-344.

31 JOHNSON-MONDRAGÓN K., (ed.), *Pathways of Hope and Faith Among Hispanic Teens*, 99.

- Estructuras de liderazgo. Siendo un ministerio entre compañeros, la PJH está organizada por medio de estructuras de liderazgo compartido, en las que el papel del líder se rota periódicamente, basándose en los dones y la disponibilidad de cada persona para que todos los participantes tengan oportunidades de desarrollar sus habilidades para liderar sin importar su edad[32]. También, el equipo de liderazgo en la PJH rara vez incluye un coordinador profesional asalariado —una posición que es cada vez más común en programas de *youth ministry*, especialmente en parroquias mejor posicionadas económicamente[33]. En contraste, los equipos de la PJH buscan orientación y supervisión de un adulto que pueda asesorarlos (ej. un sacerdote, un director espiritual, un miembro del equipo pastoral de la parroquia o el coordinador diocesano de *pastoral juvenil*), sin que usualmente esté presente en las reuniones periódicas del grupo, la comunidad o movimiento.

- Personal parroquial y formación para el liderazgo. Idealmente cada parroquia que sirve un número significativo de latinos debería tener un asesor adulto para la PJH en su equipo pastoral. Esto proveería estabilidad y continuidad al ministerio en tiempos de transición y crisis al igual que asesoría permanente y desarrollo continuo de liderazgo. Sin embargo, pocas parroquias con inmigrantes latinos tienen los recursos económicos para contratar un profesional de tiempo completo para este ministerio. Además, existe un vacío crítico de líderes adultos con capacitación para asesorar y avanzar la PJH, credenciales académicas para ejercer un ministerio profesional y habilidades lingüísticas y culturales que se requieren para este rol —aún entre los sacerdotes y directores parroquiales de educación religiosa. Como resultado, frecuentemente ministerios enteros son desmantelados cuando hay un cambio de liderazgo en la parroquia, mientras que otros ministerios son vulnerables debido a la inexperiencia del equipo de liderazgo o ante los cambios que ocurren cuando las circunstancias de la vida requieren que líderes establecidos pasen el liderazgo a otras personas.

- Coordinación y apoyo diocesano. En este contexto, se ha comprobado que una de las estructuras más efectivas para apoyar la PJH en las parroquias y los movimientos, es el coordinador diocesano de pastoral juvenil capaci-

---

32 NATIONAL CATHOLIC NETWORK DE PASTORAL JUVENIL HISPANA —LA RED, *Conclusiones*, 57.

33 El Estudio Nacional sobre Adolescentes y Religión reveló que los adolescentes blancos tienen un 50 por ciento más de posibilidades de tener un director de pastoral juvenil de tiempo completo en sus parroquias que los adolescentes hispanos. Véase JOHNSON-MONDRAGÓN K., (ed.), *Pathways of Hope and Faith Among Hispanic Teens*, 90-92.

tado profesionalmente. En contraste con el trabajo de la mayoría de directores diocesanos de *youth ministry* —cuyo ministerio consiste más que todo en apoyar, ofrecer recursos y capacitar líderes parroquiales para trabajar con jóvenes— los coordinadores diocesanos de la PJH tienen que estar más involucrados en los ministerios que apoyan.

En parroquias en donde la PJH no existe todavía, a ellos se les puede pedir que ayuden a identificar, invitar, motivar y capacitar a un equipo de líderes voluntarios para establecer el ministerio. Otra de las tareas importantes del coordinador diocesano es mediar el diálogo entre los jóvenes y los agentes de pastoral parroquiales que no entienden el modelo de PJH completamente o quienes están empeñados en tener un solo programa de pastoral «para todos» los jóvenes. Aún más, es prácticamente imposible que las parroquias ofrezcan niveles avanzados de formación pastoral, teológica y de liderazgo para este ministerio por su propia cuenta, por lo que la formación y el apoyo a los líderes voluntarios en las parroquias y los movimientos es un factor crítico en la misión del coordinador diocesano.

· *Pastoral de conjunto.* La Pastoral Juvenil Hispana también se diferencia de programas tradicionales de *youth ministry* y *young adult ministry* en cuanto a su énfasis en una pastoral de conjunto —un concepto ministerial que no tiene un equivalente exacto en inglés, pero que con frecuencia se traduce como «*communion in mission*» (comunión en misión). Una dimensión de este enfoque ministerial ocurre cuando varios grupos y movimientos colaboran en la organización de eventos y celebraciones que atraen grandes grupos. Debido a la fuerte dimensión comunitaria de las culturas latinas, la PJH florece cuando las reuniones regulares de un grupo se complementan con la experiencia periódica de reuniones más grandes. Ésta es la manera más efectiva de acoger a los jóvenes que llegan recientemente al ministerio, mantener la energía y el compromiso de los que ya están involucrados, y ayudar a formar nuevos líderes a través de un proceso de formación-en-la-acción. La carta pastoral de los obispos latinoamericanos sobre pastoral juvenil enfatiza que el establecimiento de redes, reuniones y colaboración entre grupos debe ocurrir en distintos niveles: en la parroquia, entre parroquias, en la diócesis, así como a los niveles regional, nacional e internacional[34].

---

34 CONSEJO EPISCOPAL LATINOAMERICANO, *Civilización del Amor*, 3ª Parte, n. 4.1 - 4.2.

- Un ministerio diferenciado. Otro aspecto de pastoral de conjunto que resaltan los obispos latinoamericanos es la importancia de coordinar esfuerzos pastorales entre varios ministerios, tales como los modelos tradicionales de pastoral con adolescentes (*youth ministry*) y con jóvenes adultos (*young adult ministry*), pastoral carcelaria, ministerio hispano, trabajo con pandillas, la PJH, apostolado familiar, apostolado con los enfermos y discapacitados, pastoral migrante, pastoral universitaria, y otras[35]. Sólo por medio de la coordinación de estos esfuerzos será que jóvenes procedentes de distintos ámbitos y con diversas necesidades tengan garantizado el acceso a la formación en la fe, el cuidado pastoral, acompañamiento y oportunidades para participar en la vida y la misión de la Iglesia.

- Perspectivas sobre evangelización y vocación. Al ser articulado como un ministerio de jóvenes hacia jóvenes, la PJH concede gran importancia al protagonismo de los jóvenes en la tarea de la evangelización[36]. Fiel a la misión de la Iglesia[37], la PJH entiende que la proclamación y la inculturación[38] del Evangelio son la responsabilidad de todos los jóvenes católicos como respuesta a su Bautismo[39]. De hecho, la evangelización no está completa hasta que los evangelizados asuman su misión como evangelizadores[40]. De manera similar, el discernimiento de una vocación enraizada en el llamado bautismal común —un «proyecto de vida»— está al fondo de la PJH porque define quienes somos como seguidores de Cristo[41].

En contraste, la teoría y la práctica del modelo tradicional de *youth ministry* en los Estados Unidos ofrecen a los adolescentes poca preparación para participar en la evangelización de la Iglesia llevando a los otros jóvenes la palabra de la Buena Nueva. El trabajo de evangelización es visto por los adoles-

---

35 CONSEJO EPISCOPAL LATINOAMERICANO, *Civilización del Amor*, 3ª Parte, n. 3.2 - 3.4.

36 NATIONAL CATHOLIC NETWORK DE PASTORAL JUVENIL HISPANA —LA RED, *Conclusiones*, 54-55, 57, especialmente PJ-22, #3. Véase también CONSEJO EPISCOPAL LATINOAMERICANO, *Civilización del Amor*, 2ª Parte, Sección I, n. 1.2 y Sección III, n. 2.2.

37 Véase PAUL VI, *Evangelii Nuntiandi*, n. 14, 17-18, 22 y 29.

38 Una explicación más profunda del concepto de inculturación y su aplicación a la pastoral juvenil se puede encontrar en CERVANTES C. y JOHNSON-MONDRAGÓN K., «Las dinámicas de cultura, fe y familia en la vida de los adolescentes hispanos, y sus implicaciones para la pastoral con adolescentes», 5-10.

39 NATIONAL CATHOLIC NETWORK DE PASTORAL JUVENIL HISPANA —LA RED, *Conclusiones*, 13-15, 54, 60-61.

40 *Evangelii Nuntiandi*, n. 24.

41 Cfr. CONSEJO EPISCOPAL LATINOAMERICANO, *Civilización del Amor*, 2ª Parte, Sección I, n. 2.3.1. La frase «*proyecto de vida*» aparece 35 veces en el documento.

centes primordialmente como la tarea de los adultos en la comunidad, especialmente aquellos adultos que son líderes en el trabajo pastoral con adolescentes[42]. Al mismo tiempo, mientras que es cierto que existen recursos vocacionales para el *youth ministry* en inglés, éstos usualmente se destinan a jóvenes en el último año de secundaria, mientras que la orientación vocacional durante otras etapas en el ministerio, es casi inexistente.

3
Evaluemos el camino

Teniendo en cuenta los retos sociales y pastorales descritos anteriormente, la declaración de la misión de la Pastoral Juvenil Hispana, llena de fe y visionaria, articulada por los delegados al Encuentro de jóvenes (ver inicio de este ensayo) es aún más extraordinaria. Sin embargo, la realidad pastoral exige que nos preguntemos si esta declaración refleja la intención y el entendimiento colectivo de *todos* los jóvenes católicos hispanos en los Estados Unidos. La respuesta breve a la pregunta es: no —no en cuanto a la gran mayoría de ellos.

3.1. LOGROS RECIENTES

Con todo lo anterior, la descripción general del contexto pastoral oculta —en cierta manera— otra verdad: la pastoral con, hacia y desde la juventud hispana ha progresado notablemente en los años posteriores al estudio preliminar del Instituto Fe y Vida en 2002, a pesar de que han habido retrocesos en algunos lugares y que todavía queda mucho trabajo por hacer. La siguiente lista describe algunos de los avances notables en este ministerio durante los últimos siete años.

a) Desarrollo de un liderazgo diocesano y nacional para la Pastoral Juvenil Hispana. Gracias en gran parte a *La Red* por liderar el proceso del Encuentro, más diócesis ahora tienen personal dedicado al ministerio con los jóvenes hispanos. Un signo de esperanza es que algunas diócesis comenzaron a contratar directores bilingües de *youth and young adult ministry* quienes tienen la responsabilidad de dirigir estos ministerios en inglés y español. Sin embargo, los líderes bilingües y biculturales que son calificados y tienen la experiencia necesaria para ocupar estas posiciones son todavía muy pocos.

---

42 UNITED STATES CONFERENCE OF CATHOLIC BISHOPS, *Renovemos la Visión: Fundamentos para el Ministerio con Jóvenes Católicos*, USCCB, Washington, D.C. 1997, 37-39.

b) El crecimiento del papel de *La Red* como una importante organización trabajando en colaboración con otras organizaciones ministeriales a nivel nacional. El papel destacado de *La Red* es particularmente evidente en su colaboración continua con la NFCYM y el Secretariado para los Laicos, el Matrimonio, la Vida Familiar y la Juventud de la Conferencia de Obispos Católicos de Estados Unidos. Esta colaboración está ayudando a que el trabajo de la NFCYM sea más inclusivo, y su fruto está siendo manifiesto en el desarrollo de un *Plan estratégico de cinco años para la Pastoral Juvenil Hispana* como resultado del Encuentro[43].

c) Celebración del Primer Encuentro Nacional de Pastoral Juvenil Hispana y la publicación de sus *Conclusiones.* Los logros y limitaciones del Encuentro son una radiografía de la posición en la que se encuentra la Iglesia en su compromiso con los jóvenes latinos. Aún más, en el mismo documento de las *Conclusiones del* PENPJH tenemos un relato bilingüe de la historia, contexto teológico y pastoral, visión, principios, necesidades pastorales y mejores prácticas y modelos articulados por los mismos jóvenes con el consentimiento y apoyo de los obispos estadounidenses.

d) Investigación sociológica sólida sobre la realidad religiosa de los jóvenes latinos. La muestra nacional, representando adolescentes y jóvenes encuestados y entrevistados en el Estudio Nacional sobre Adolescentes y Religión, provee información confiable de las creencias y prácticas religiosas de los adolescentes en los Estados Unidos hoy en día. En el libro *Pathways of Hope and Faith Among Hispanic Teens,* un grupo interdisciplinario de nueve escritores contribuyeron desde distintas perspectivas con un análisis de los jóvenes que participaron en dicho estudio. Este trabajo es un recurso de mucho valor para cualquier persona preparándose para trabajar pastoralmente con la juventud católica latina.

e) Amplia disponibilidad de programas de formación para Pastoral Juvenil Hispana. El Instituto Pastoral del Sureste (SEPI) y varias diócesis del país han desarrollado programas de formación para líderes y asesores en la PJH. Además, el Instituto Fe y Vida tiene un equipo pastoral móvil que tiene la capacidad de proveer formación a distintos niveles en cualquier diócesis del país que lo solicite y ofrece un programa intensivo anual de una semana (*Progra-*

---

43 El texto completo del *Plan estratégico de cinco años para la* PJH está disponible en línea en http://www.laredpjh.org.

ma Nacional de Verano) para la formación de líderes cuyas diócesis no ofrecen una oportunidad similar. Finalmente, varios movimientos apostólicos han desarrollado sus propios programas y recursos para la formación de líderes.

f) Incremento de recursos humanos en la comunidad católica, tanto entre hispanos como otros grupos. Durante el proceso del Encuentro y después de éste, muchos directores, coordinadores y líderes de *youth ministry* se han percatado de la necesidad de incrementar su capacidad de servir a los adolescentes hispanos. Además, el mismo proceso del Encuentro fue diseñado como un proceso de formación-en-la-acción que ha forjado una nueva generación de líderes latinos para la PJH y *youth ministry* en comunidades latinas.

3.2. ÁREAS QUE NECESITAN MÁS ATENCIÓN

Los logros alcanzados sólo han sido posibles gracias a los esfuerzos coordinados de miles de líderes en programas católicos de *youth ministry, young adult ministry* y Pastoral Juvenil Hispana. Sin embargo, la realidad pastoral descrita en la primera parte de este ensayo revela que hay mucho más por hacer. Dicha información no será resumida aquí. En lugar de ello, esta sección se enfocará en los avances estructurales que deben ocurrir para facilitar una respuesta integral a las necesidades pastorales de los jóvenes latinos a nivel local, diocesano, regional y nacional.

a) Elaborar un plan pastoral integral a nivel nacional que agrupe los distintos ministerios y organizaciones ministeriales para el cuidado pastoral y el acompañamiento de *toda* la juventud católica (adolescentes y jóvenes de toda raza, cultura e idioma). Este plan pastoral necesita ser presentado como una respuesta a la realidad social, cultural, lingüística, educativa y espiritual de la juventud de hoy, entre los cuales los latinos constituyen casi la mitad. Al evaluar esta realidad, se debe poner atención especial a la situación actual de las familias al igual que a la habilidad de los padres para servir como modelos y guías confiables en la formación en la fe de sus hijos. Además, debe haber herramientas para ayudar a que los agentes de pastoral diocesanos y parroquiales realicen un análisis de la realidad local, para que elaboren planes pastorales que respondan a las necesidades locales.

Será crucial preparar líderes para que vean el conjunto completo de necesidades que los jóvenes bajo su cuidado pueden tener —especialmente los que son parte de la gran mayoría que actualmente no participa en programas pastorales— y que propongan un enfoque diferenciado para responder a las diversas necesidades pastorales en la parroquia a través de programas, grupos, movimientos, eventos, actividades y servicios. El plan debe proveer una guía para el desarrollo de esfuerzos de evangelización y servicio en los que los jóvenes mismos sean los protagonistas. Al mismo tiempo, el plan debe ofrecer criterios para discernir en qué circunstancias se deben implementar esfuerzos de pre-evangelización como la respuesta más inmediata. Finalmente, deben presentarse criterios pastorales y teológicos para ayudar a los líderes a identificar las necesidades urgentes y fundamentales que deben ser consideradas como prioridad en su ministerio.

b) Estructurar los ministerios juveniles basados en una eclesiología que entienda la parroquia como comunidad de comunidades. Con frecuencia los programas de *youth ministry* son limitados debido a una convicción teológica errónea que asume que la multiplicación de programas a favor de los jóvenes puede dividir la parroquia[44]. En este sentido las *Conclusiones del PENPJH* son bien claras:

> «El liderazgo de la pastoral juvenil, el ministerio hispano y el *youth and young adult ministry* está cada vez más consciente de que los programas y actividades propios para la cultura dominante, no favorecen la participación de adolescentes y jóvenes hispanos, aunque hablen inglés. Esto sucede debido a las diferencias económicas, culturales, educacionales, geográficas y lingüísticas, especialmente cuando la pastoral en la parroquia se limita a un solo grupo juvenil» (énfasis añadido)[45].

Como respuesta, las parroquias de los Estados Unidos harán bien en seguir un consejo de la v Conferencia General del Episcopado Latinoamericano y del Caribe en Aparecida, Brasil:

> «La renovación de las parroquias al inicio del tercer milenio exige reformular sus estructuras, para que sea una red de comunidades y grupos, capaces de articularse logrando que sus miembros se sientan y sean realmente discípulos y misioneros de Jesucristo en comunión»[46].

---

44 Para una presentación sobre las circunstancias culturales y pastorales que pueden contribuir a esta visión errónea, y para una articulación del modelo «comunidad de comunidades» véase JOHNSON-MONDRAGÓN K., (ed.), *Pathways of Hope and Faith Among Hispanic Teens*, 332-339; 345-352.

45 NATIONAL CATHOLIC NETWORK DE PASTORAL JUVENIL HISPANA —LA RED, *Conclusiones*, 32-33.

46 CELAM, *Aparecida: v Conferencia General del Episcopado Latinoamericano y del Caribe: Documento Conclusivo*, CELAM, Bogotá, Colombia 2007, n. 172.

c) Incrementar la colaboración y el diálogo con los líderes y organizaciones pastorales en Latinoamérica. La cita anterior es una respuesta clara a la llamada del Papa Juan Pablo II a las parroquias a convertirse en una «comunidad de comunidades y movimientos», en *Ecclesia in America*[47]. También resalta la esperanza de que la Iglesia en el Continente Americano comience a verse como una sola Iglesia continental en colaboración sincera entre los países del norte y del sur. Tal como este ensayo ha demostrado, la práctica de *youth and young adult ministry* en los Estados Unidos se beneficiaría al ofrecer mayor consideración a las orientaciones de *Civilización del Amor: Tarea y Esperanza* al igual que a las prioridades pastorales del *Documento de Aparecida*. Tal intercambio de ideas y prácticas sería el primer paso en el desarrollo de una pastoral de conjunto genuina entre el norte y el sur.

d) Incrementar la colaboración y el diálogo con los líderes y organizaciones de los demás ministerios católicos en los Estados Unidos. Dado el tamaño de la población católica hispana, ya no se puede aceptar (si es que en algún momento se consideró aceptable) que documentos clave dirigidos a toda la Iglesia estadounidense o sobre iniciativas pastorales con implicaciones para todos los católicos en los Estados Unidos —especialmente la juventud— se escriban sin representación apropiada de los latinos, en los momentos de tomar decisiones fundamentales y hacer ediciones finales. Ya existen iniciativas de este estilo en las que se está trabajando para desarrollar orientaciones y criterios para el futuro de la catequesis, la evangelización, la educación católica, la formación de líderes eclesiales laicos y la promoción de vocaciones al servicio eclesial. La PJH tiene mucho que contribuir a estas áreas y *La Red* tiene que ser parte de la conversación al igual que un ente motivador de estos esfuerzos.

e) Diseñar estrategias y respuestas para vencer los obstáculos estructurales para la PJH. Algunos de los mayores retos que encontramos actualmente en este ministerio son:

• *Formación pastoral y reflexión teológica.* Muy pocos líderes diocesanos, sacerdotes y directores de *youth ministry* tienen un conocimiento adecuado de las necesidades, visión, misión, principios e historia de la PJH. Como consecuencia, sus convicciones pastorales, equívocas con frecuencia, no les permiten ofrecer un apoyo efectivo a este ministerio y en muchos casos les llevan a cerrarlo o a bloquear su establecimiento en la parroquia o la

47 JUAN PABLO II, *Ecclesia in America*, n. 41.

diócesis[48]. Aún más, la formación pastoral y teológica limitada de muchos jóvenes adultos trabajando en la PJH continúa siendo un obstáculo para formar y sostener los ministerios que se les han encargado. Desafortunadamente, la falta de atención al cuidado pastoral de la juventud latina también es evidente en los programas de formación para el ministerio hispano y entre los teólogos latinos/hispanos. Como resultado, aún nuestros líderes mejor preparados en el ministerio hispano con frecuencia carecen de la formación para apoyar y abogar en favor de la PJH.

- *Educación académica.* El bajo nivel educacional de los «trabajadores inmigrantes» latinos y las altas tasas de deserción escolar entre los adolescentes hispanos nacidos en los Estados Unidos conspiran para limitar el grupo de líderes latinos calificados que puedan cursar estudios académicos para servir en la pastoral o para obtener una posición ministerial pagada en la Iglesia. Al mismo tiempo, cientos de escuelas católicas de primaria y secundaria están a punto de ser cerradas, mientras que millones de familias católicas de bajos recursos no logran cubrir sus necesidades educacionales debido al pobre desempeño de las escuelas públicas donde asisten sus hijos. Esto requiere una iniciativa nacional para mejorar la educación académica de los inmigrantes católicos, sus hijos y otros grupos raciales/étnicos, tanto en las escuelas católicas como las públicas.

- *Asuntos de inmigración.* La condición de indocumentados que viven muchos de los inmigrantes jóvenes, lo cual les limita acceso a becas, posiciones de liderazgo en el ministerio con adolescentes y en general trae inestabilidad a sus vidas, hace que sea difícil realizar un beneficio de la inversión en su formación para trabajar en la PJH o *youth ministry*. Los obispos estadounidenses han declarado como prioridad abogar por los inmigrantes, pero esto no se ha extendido lo suficiente para que muchas parroquias o grupos católicos de acción política se unan a esfuerzos locales y nacionales para una reforma migratoria integral fundamentada en los principios de la Doctrina Social de la Iglesia.

- *Pastoral de conjunto.* La falta de coordinación entre los modelos tradicionales de *youth and young adult ministry* y la PJH han contribuido a una tasa baja de participación por parte de jóvenes hispanos nacidos en los Estados Unidos, quienes hablan principalmente inglés y no están en la universidad ni planean ir. Un trabajo pastoral efectivo con estos jóvenes requerirá colabora-

---

48 El capítulo 10 de JOHNSON-MONDRAGÓN K., (ed.), *Pathways of Hope and Faith Among Hispanic Teens* describe diez factores que nuestra Iglesia necesita tener en cuenta para que el ministerio con jóvenes hispanos se haga parte vital de las comunidades. Véase páginas 321-359.

ción y supervisión compartida entre el ministerio hispano, *youth and young adult ministry*, Pastoral Juvenil Hispana y los movimientos apostólicos.

f) Incrementar los recursos humanos, económicos y programáticos para la PJH. Esto requerirá una inversión significativa en la formación de líderes en todos los niveles, tanto en inglés como en español, para que los líderes de *youth ministry* puedan mejorar y expandir su ministerio mientras los líderes jóvenes inmigrantes trabajando en la PJH hacen lo mismo. Quizás el primer paso práctico y sin mucho costo sería la contratación de un director diocesano de la PJH. Esta persona sería responsable de coordinar la formación de líderes en parroquias y movimientos apostólicos, ofreciendo apoyo continuo a sus esfuerzos ministeriales y motivándoles a ser parte de un proceso de formación-en-la-acción y una pastoral de conjunto.

Por otro lado, hay pocos materiales para guiar programas y pocos recursos audiovisuales disponibles para apoyar la PJH. Igualmente, es difícil encontrar recursos bilingües para ayudar a los padres hispanos a superar los conflictos lingüísticos y culturales que frecuentemente experimentan con sus hijos, al querer cumplir su papel como primeros educadores en la fe. Desafortunadamente, la mayoría de los recursos elaborados para los programas tradicionales de *youth and young adult ministry* o la pastoral juvenil latinoamericana no se acomodan muy bien al contexto latino estadounidense. Se requerirá una inversión substancial por parte de la Iglesia en general y por parte de las editoriales católicas en particular para desarrollar la capacidad de los líderes en la PJH y de parte de los artistas latinos para crear recursos que apoyen estos ministerios.

Finalmente, modelos creativos y efectivos para financiar estos esfuerzos necesitan ser desarrollados a nivel local y diocesano y ser compartidos nacionalmente. El papel de *La Red* en el apoyo y avance continuo de la PJH a nivel nacional se ha hecho indispensable, pero todavía sigue operando sólo con líderes voluntarios, sin una oficina central para archivos y comunicaciones. Considerando que *La Red* ha aceptado la responsabilidad de abogar por la mitad de todos los jóvenes católicos en los Estados Unidos, tiene que haber más apoyo institucional y filantrópico para este ministerio.

g) Crear estándares de certificación para coordinadores de *youth ministry* y la PJH diseñados para equipar a ministros tanto en programas tradicionales como latinos para llevar a cabo una pastoral efectiva con, hacia y desde la juventud hispana. Hay cinco organizaciones que actualmente están revisando las *Normas Nacionales para Certificación de Ministros Eclesiales Laicos*. Teniendo en cuenta el tamaño y la amplia presencia geográfica de la población católica hispana, los normas nacionales deben reflejar las competencias y metodologías requeridas para el ministerio en comunidades hispanas. Aún más, los estándares específicos para líderes de *youth ministry* deben incluir competencias basadas en la visión, necesidades y principios para el ministerio con adolescentes hispanos descritos en las *Conclusiones del* PENPJH. *La Red* también debe participar en este proceso de revisión proponiendo estándares de certificación de líderes, coordinadores y consejeros de la PJH.

4

Conclusión

344

Los desafíos pastorales que enfrentan los jóvenes hispanos en los Estados Unidos son inmensos y, sin duda alguna, contribuyen a la siguiente conclusión del Estudio Nacional sobre Adolescentes y Religión: «Los adolescentes latinos como grupo son religiosamente más inarticulados y descomprometidos que otros adolescentes católicos a pesar de que sus padres demuestran un mayor compromiso con su fe que los padres católicos blancos»[49]. Ciertamente sus necesidades son diversas y su presencia numerosa en las comunidades católicas alrededor del país. Requiere un esfuerzo coordinado de toda la Iglesia para ofrecerles un cuidado pastoral adecuado, formación en la fe y una invitación a participar en la vida y misión de la Iglesia.

La buena noticia es que nuestra comunidad católica ha sido bendecida con miles de jóvenes inmigrantes que son líderes en la PJH y miles más de directores y coordinadores de *youth ministry* en parroquias y movimientos apostólicos alrededor del país. Además, tenemos el mapa que nos ayudará a servir y motivar a los jóvenes hispanos en las *Conclusiones del* PENPJH y el *Plan estratégico de cinco años para la Pastoral Juvenil Hispana*. Todo lo que se necesita en este momento es que nuestra Iglesia asuma la voluntad institucional para implementar este plan por medio de una pastoral de conjunto genuina en parroquias y diócesis a lo largo de todo el país. Al llevar a cabo este proceso, los esfuerzos de *youth ministry*, *young adult ministry*, y la PJH serán un modelo de cómo unir el ministerio hispano con el resto de los ministerios católicos para forjar una Iglesia renovada en los Estados Unidos en el siglo XXI.

49 JOHNSON-MONDRAGÓN K., (ed.), *Pathways of Hope and Faith Among Hispanic Teens*, 324.

El ministerio hispano, la liturgia y la espiritualidad

RAÚL GÓMEZ-RUÍZ

1

Introducción

Al caer la tarde, los participantes en la primera conferencia Raíces y Alas (1992) nos reunimos en la capilla de la Universidad Loyola Marymount para hacer la oración de apertura[1]. Los organizadores del evento pidieron de antemano a los miembros del Instituto Nacional Hispano de Liturgia[2] que prepararan las oraciones y celebraciones eucarísticas de la conferencia y yo, uno de sus miembros, tuve que coordinar esta oración. El *ordo* para el 14 de agosto de 1992 indicaba que, según la tradición, las vísperas en esta fecha deberían hacerse en honor de la Dormición de la Virgen. Éste fue nuestro punto de partida: usamos la estructura general de la liturgia pero añadimos elementos devocionales hispanos para darle vida. Pedimos a los participantes, tanto mujeres como hombres, que se ofrecieran como voluntarios para presidir, leer, predicar, etc. Para comenzar, una mujer silenciosamente entró por el pasillo desde la parte de atrás portando una urna con incienso. La siguieron cuatro hombres que cargaban un anda con una imagen yacente de la Virgen, cubierta con una tela transparente. Quienes llevaban las velas acompañaban el anda seguidos de los líderes de la oración. Los hombres reposaron la imagen al lado del altar y la mujer la incensó. Los participantes estaban sorprendidos al ver esto y era palpable que estaban profundamente concentrados en el silencio de la procesión. Las vísperas continuaron como de costumbre: himnos, salmos y cántico, lectura, reflexión, Magnificat y oraciones de los fieles; luego se incluyó algo más: se invitó a todos a acercarse a colocar flores sobre la imagen y a ofrecer una oración en silencio por los difuntos. Una música suave acompañaba este acto contribuyendo a su solemnidad y belleza. Al volver a sus bancas, muchos lloraron emocionados. Todos los que quisieron pusieron una flor sobre la imagen de la Virgen y la oración terminó de manera usual con una bendición y la despedida. Se dejó la imagen al lado del altar para que quienes quisieran volver a orar más tarde pudieran hacerlo. Muchos de los presentes me dijeron que nunca habían sido movidos por una liturgia así y estaban

---

1 Esta primera reunión de líderes de organizaciones comprometidas con el ministerio hispano en los Estados Unidos fue convocada por el Consejo Nacional Católico para el Ministerio Hispano (NCCHM, sigla en inglés) y tuvo lugar en la sede de Loyola Marymount University en Los Ángeles del 14 al 17 de agosto de 1992.

2 El Instituto Nacional Hispano de Liturgia o *National Hispanic Institute of Liturgy* tiene sus oficinas en The Catholic University of America en Washington, D.C.

impresionados de cómo unos cuantos toques de piedad devocional hispana[3] pudieran añadir tanto significado sin alterar la integridad de las vísperas. Aprovechar la devoción hispana a la Virgen, reconocer el dolor de la muerte, ser acompañados por los ministros en una oración bilingüe, usar flores, velas, incienso y música, todo esto junto sirvió para inculturar la liturgia y ayudar a los participantes a que vieran las conexiones entre ésta y sus expresiones de espiritualidad o mística[4].

La liturgia como fundamento de la mística hispana y, por tanto, el punto de partida del ministerio entre los hispanos en los Estados Unidos todavía debe ser examinada y apreciada más plenamente. La religiosidad popular, por el contrario, ha sido el centro primordial de nuestros esfuerzos pastorales y de la reflexión teológica entre los latinos y otras personas involucradas en el ministerio hispano[5]. En círculos católicos, estas expresiones de espiritualidad están a menudo marcadas por actitudes y prácticas que reflejan la adopción y adaptación de elementos teológicos, litúrgicos y espirituales que se podrían denominar como catolicismo popular.

Reconociendo el papel del catolicismo popular en la espiritualidad hispana, los obispos de los Estados Unidos en su carta pastoral de 1984 *La Presencia Hispana: Esperanza y Compromiso* señalaron que la «espiritualidad hispana es un ejemplo de la profundidad con que el cristianismo puede penetrar las raíces de

3 Con frecuencia se privilegia el uso del término «hispano» para nombrar los esfuerzos pastorales con personas que hablan español en los Estados Unidos. Aunque es bastante amplio, dada la falta de homogeneidad de quienes se identifican con él, creo que el término describe a los pueblos del mundo que comparten conexiones históricas y familiares con España, un elemento común que es clave para quienes se identifican como hispanos. A este respecto véase el trabajo de GRACIA J., *Hispanic/Latino Identity: A Philosophical Perspective*, Blackwell, Malden, MA 2000.

4 El *Plan Pastoral Nacional para el Ministerio Hispano* (publicado en 1988; de aquí en adelante PPNMH) define *mística* como «las motivaciones y valores profundos que dan vida al proceso del pueblo, crean experiencias de fe y producen una espiritualidad que da incentivo a la vida y a la pastoral». Véase PPNMH, «D. Terminología» en NATIONAL CONFERENCE OF CATHOLIC BISHOPS, *Plan Pastoral Nacional para el Ministerio Hispano*, USCC, Washington, D.C. 1988, 98, en UNITED STATES CONFERENCE OF CATHOLIC BISHOPS, *Ministerio Hispano: Tres Documentos Importantes*, USCCB, Washington, D.C. 1995. Es importante señalar que esta definición aparece en el PPNMH después del Tercer Encuentro y los eventos de reflexión teológica que le siguieron. En estos eventos se usó el término antes de cualquier definición clara de su significado. Como consecuencia cuando uso el concepto «expresiones de espiritualidad» lo hago siguiendo los documentos, incluyendo el PPNMH.

5 Uso el término «religiosidad popular» intencionalmente para incluir las expresiones de espiritualidad que algunos llaman religión popular, piedad o prácticas devocionales. Todos son intentos de describir una realidad compleja: la experiencia de una realidad transcendente o la fe en ésta y su incorporación a la vida diaria, especialmente entre aquellos que no son parte de las élites religiosas. Para una discusión amplia sobre este tema véase GÓMEZ-RUÍZ R., *Mozarabs, Hispanics, & the Cross*, Orbis Books, Maryknoll, NY 2007, 166-169.

una cultura»[6]. Conociendo la centralidad de la liturgia, los obispos invitaron a establecer un puente entre la religiosidad popular y la liturgia. En este ensayo exploro algunas de las razones por las que la religiosidad popular hispana se ha mantenido al centro de la reflexión teológica y pastoral y luego doy algunas razones por las que el papel de la liturgia como fundamento de la espiritualidad y del ministerio hispano tiene que ser examinado y valorado con más atención. Termino con algunas sugerencias para seguir la reflexión y el diálogo sobre este tema.

2
Razones para enfocarse primordialmente en la religiosidad popular hispana
৩৯০

El Tercer Encuentro Nacional Hispano de Pastoral (1985) fue un momento decisivo en la historia reciente de la pastoral hispana[7]. Un aspecto central de este Tercer Encuentro fue su mística o «expresión de espiritualidad». Dos reuniones posteriores de reflexión teológica después del Tercer Encuentro ayudaron a identificar lo que esto significa y sus ideas fueron expresadas principalmente por medio un *Credo* que aparece en el *Plan Pastoral Nacional para el Ministerio Hispano* (*ppnmh*)[8].

La espiritualidad identificada a través del proceso del Tercer Encuentro se encuentra expresada en la octava y última sección del Credo que se desarrolló ahí. La primera parte dice: «Creemos en María, nuestra Madre, quien tomó nuestra cultura hispana bajo su protección, quien nos ha acompañado y nos acompañará siempre en nuestro caminar, trabajando para llevar el mensaje de Jesús al mundo entero»[9]. La segunda parte continúa: «Creemos en la intercesión de nuestra Madre querida y en su ejemplo de humildad, simplicidad y disponibilidad, que son base de nuestra cultura hispana». Por tanto, la espiritualidad que emerge del *Credo* es principalmente de naturaleza mariana, devocional y popu-

---

6 NATIONAL CONFERENCE OF CATHOLIC BISHOPS, *La Presencia Hispana: Esperanza y Compromiso*, USCC, Washington, D.C. 1984, n. 12, 0, en UNITED STATES CONFERENCE OF CATHOLIC BISHOPS, *Ministerio Hispano*, 16.

7 La metodología y los compromisos adquiridos fueron publicados en *Voces Proféticas: Documento del Proceso del III Encuentro Nacional Hispano de Pastoral*, USCC, Washington, D.C., 1986, en UNITED STATES CONFERENCE OF CATHOLIC BISHOPS, *Ministerio Hispano*.

8 Estos tuvieron lugar en Seattle con la participación de 35 líderes pastorales hispanos en octubre de 1985 y en Tucson en enero de 1986 con la participación de 17 obispos del antiguo comité especializado para asuntos hispanos. Véase también la nota 4 en este ensayo.

9 Ésta y la siguiente cita se encuentran en *Voces Proféticas*, 48.

lar. Lo que falta aquí es la influencia que ha tenido el Movimiento Carismático entre los hispanos, con su énfasis en las experiencias afectivas del Espíritu y su atención a las Sagradas Escrituras.

Incluso en la segunda sección principal del *Credo* en la que se expresa la fe en Cristo, el énfasis es puesto en la identificación con el Cristo sufriente. Dividida en cinco declaraciones, esta sección comienza diciendo: «Creemos en nuestra identificación con Cristo, como pueblo sufrido que somos, reconocemos al igual que Él, la dignidad de todos los seres humanos y su liberación por medio del amor»[10]. Aunque ambos ejemplos del Credo indican una tendencia liberacionista de la espiritualidad identificada a través de la reflexión teológica pastoral, los dos se apoyan en lo que identifico como las raíces culturales de la espiritualidad hispana.

Es interesante notar que ni el *Credo* ni las reflexiones teológicas pastorales posteriores identifican la liturgia como un factor importante en la mística hispana[11]. Esto se puede observar a pesar del hecho de que la liturgia fue instrumental para proporcionar una mística para el Tercer Encuentro y de que los obispos en *La Presencia Hispana* invitaron a prestar atención a la liturgia, aunque tomando «medidas para celebrar el culto en español o en forma bilingüe, según las tradiciones y costumbres del pueblo al que se sirve». Aún más, los obispos afirmaron que esto «nos debe llevar a estudiar mejor las formas de oración de los hispanos», especialmente aquellas que nacen en el hogar hispano teniendo en cuenta que éste «se ha convertido tradicionalmente para ellos en el centro de la fe y del culto». Así pues, «se debe valorar y alentar la celebración de las fiestas tradicionales y las ocasiones especiales en el hogar»[12]. Esto sugiere que la mística hispana en sus raíces es más devocional y popular que litúrgica. También revela cierta tendencia a un romanticismo que exige más reflexión.

El énfasis en las prácticas devocionales populares se reitera en el *Plan Pastoral Nacional para el Ministerio Hispano*. El PPNMH declara que la «espiritualidad o mística del pueblo hispano nace de su fe y de su relación con Dios… La espiri-

---

10 *Voces Proféticas*, 47.

11 Juan Sosa, miembro del grupo de estudio que discutió la relación entre el ministerio hispano, la liturgia y la espiritualidad en el Simposio Nacional del 2009 en Boston College y participante en el Tercer Encuentro, señaló que el *Credo* no comparte la mística generada por el aspecto litúrgico del Encuentro sino que de hecho la ignora. Por consiguiente, los autores del *Credo* no reflejaron la plenitud de lo que experimentaron. En su opinión, esto se debe a que el liderazgo hispano no siempre ha considerado la liturgia como un elemento esencial de la espiritualidad hispana.

12 NATIONAL CONFERENCE OF CATHOLIC BISHOPS, *La Presencia Hispana*, n. 12a.

tualidad penetra todos los aspectos de la vida y por tanto se manifiesta con gran variedad»[13]. Esta afirmación de religiosidad popular es una afirmación de la cultura hispana que sin lugar a dudas ha estado marcada por una rica vida devocional tanto en el hogar, como lo demuestran los altarcitos, y en las calles, como se ve en las procesiones y peregrinaciones frecuentes que atraen grandes multitudes.

Probablemente éste era el énfasis que se necesitaba en ese momento, ya que las voces dominantes en la Iglesia en los Estados Unidos transmitían antipatía hacia las prácticas religiosas populares. Este «sentimiento encontrado» con relación a la religiosidad popular ha continuado presente a pesar de las afirmaciones de los obispos de los Estados Unidos e incluso de la Santa Sede[14]. Encontré esta situación en un estudio sobre el ministerio hispano realizado en 1998-1999. El antiguo Comité Episcopal para Asuntos Hispanos nos encargó a Manuel Vásquez y a mí que proporcionáramos información cualitativa sobre el ministerio hispano. Uno de los once temas y desafíos claves que identificamos en nuestro informe de 1999 señalaba la tensión entre la religiosidad popular y la evangelización. En el informe reportamos que «a los ojos de algunos pastores, las devociones populares no son más que un "catolicismo del día" que se centra en rituales y símbolos, enfatizando momentos de fervor que son importantes aunque aislados, que no se traducen en una transformación profunda y duradera ni en una participación permanente en la vida de la iglesia»[15]. Descubrimos que algunos pastores pretendían eliminar las prácticas devocionales populares mientras que otros las veían meramente como peldaños para llegar a una «mayor madurez en la fe» que deberán abandonarse una vez se logre dicha madurez. El estudio muestra que donde la celebración de los sacramentos ha sido el principal enfoque pastoral en el ministerio hispano, se ha tendido más a una celebración con poca catequesis y poca atención a la dimensión ética de la vida sacramental[16]. Por consiguiente muchas veces las parroquias se convierten en «fábricas de sacramentos».

13 UNITED STATES CONFERENCE OF CATHOLIC BISHOPS, *Plan Pastoral Nacional para el Ministerio Hispano,* n. 16.

14 UNITED STATES CONFERENCE OF CATHOLIC BISHOPS, *Ejercicios devocionales populares: preguntas y respuestas básicas,* USCCB, Washington, D.C. 2003; CONGREGACIÓN PARA EL CULTO DIVINO Y LA DISCIPLINA DE LOS SACRAMENTOS, *Directorio sobre la piedad popular y la liturgia. Principios y orientaciones,* BAC, Madrid, 2004.

15 UNITED STATES CONFERENCE OF CATHOLIC BISHOPS, SECRETARIADO PARA ASUNTOS HISPANOS, *Hispanic Ministry Study,* USCCB, Washington, D.C. 1999, sección III, 6, www.usccb.org/hispanic affairs/studygomez.shtml (disponible sólo en inglés).

16 UNITED STATES CONFERENCE OF CATHOLIC BISHOPS, SECRETARIADO PARA ASUNTOS HISPANOS, *Hispanic Ministry Study,* USCCB, Washington, D.C. 1999, sección III, 7.

Ciertamente la religiosidad popular es un rasgo notable de la espiritualidad hispana. Los teólogos hispanos la han estudiado bien, los pastoralistas hispanos la han promovido, y la jerarquía de la Iglesia la ha afirmado. Muchos han escrito sobre cómo las prácticas devocionales hispanas han sostenido la fe católica incluso cuando la Iglesia parecía no valorar apropiadamente a los hispanos. Yo, sin embargo, mantengo que una de las razones por las cuales la religiosidad popular ha sido tal fuerza de sustento es porque ha emergido y ha sido nutrida en un contexto cultural primordialmente católico en el cual todas las dimensiones sacramentales de su drama y belleza pueden florecer. Específicamente, América Latina ha estado impregnada de un catolicismo cultural que se refuerza periódicamente por medio de expresiones públicas de fe con un carácter altamente devocional[17]. Las procesiones de Semana Santa, las fiestas patronales y las peregrinaciones regulares han servido para inspirar en el pueblo un sentido de lo sagrado y del conjunto de las creencias católicas. Marcada por ritos, color, música y la participación de grandes multitudes (aún cuando muchos son tan sólo espectadores), la religiosidad popular hispana ha sido capaz de cautivar los sentidos y la imaginación de quienes la practican, no sólo como expresión de fe sino también como un medio para diferenciar la identidad y expresar un orgullo nacional[18]. Por consiguiente, es razonable pensar que debe ser valorada y debemos intentar recrearla en el contexto cultural de los Estados Unidos. Esto ocurrió también entre otros grupos de inmigrantes profundamente marcados por la experiencia católica tales como los italianos, los polacos y los irlandeses en sus primeras generaciones en los Estados Unidos, quienes contaron con el apoyo de los líderes de la Iglesia[19].

17   Esto no pretende menospreciar las manifestaciones de este fenómeno en el suroeste de los Estados Unidos, las cuales son muy antiguas aunque ciertamente no muy comunes.

18   Esta intuición se apoya en la respuesta personal de Cecilia González-Andrieu a este ensayo como parte de su participación en el Simposio Nacional del 2009 en Boston College. En sus comentarios González-Andrieu señala acertadamente que: «Esta falta de homogeneidad, mientras que simultáneamente retiene la característica de "diferencia", hace que lo que tradicionalmente se conocen como prácticas religiosas aparezcan como maneras de resistir asimilación, de subrayar la identidad nacional y de fortalecer la comunidad. Creo que la necesidad cultural y política de ser reconocido es posiblemente la motivación principal que lleva a preservar muchas prácticas religiosas. Esto no quiere decir que éstas hayan perdido su significado religioso, sin embargo nos invitan a considerar más cuidadosamente el papel del ritual religioso, la sacramentalidad y la espiritualidad en la preservación de la identidad y la estrategia de resistencia». Véase también, GÓMEZ-RUÍZ R., *Mozarabs, Hispanics, & the Cross*, introduction and Chapter 1, 8-9.

19   Véase entre otros, TAVES A., *The Household of Faith: Roman Catholic Devotions in Mid-Nineteenth-Century America*, University of Notre Dame Press, Notre Dame, IN 1986. Lamentablemente muchos abandonaron sus prácticas de fe nutridas por su cultura una vez que se asimilaron o ascendieron en la escala social, algo que parece estar ocurriendo también entre muchos hispanos.

El énfasis en el catolicismo popular se ve reforzado por los esfuerzos pastorales característicos del ministerio hispano en los Estados Unidos. Desde el comienzo de los años setentas, su enfoque, y por tanto sus beneficiarios, han sido inmigrantes latinoamericanos recién salidos de ese contexto cultural católico. Allí la liturgia ha sido con frecuencia un área reservada casi exclusivamente al fuero del clero y la religión popular se ha mantenido en la vida diaria del pueblo[20]. Como consecuencia, la liturgia se ha considerado menos importante para los que trabajan en el ministerio con los hispanos en los Estados Unidos debido a la idea de que es un área de preocupación de los especialistas, es decir aquellas personas formadas, educadas y seleccionadas para esta tarea. Aunque esencial, la liturgia a menudo ha sido juzgada como anticuada, formal y restrictiva y, por lo tanto, como algo que poco tiene que ver con las necesidades pastorales «reales» del pueblo. Así, la supuesta separación de la mística hispana como religiosidad popular por encima o contraria a la liturgia ha sido inadvertidamente reafirmada en el curso de los procesos de Encuentro. Es laudable que la noción de una mística hispana que abarca las dos realidades haya comenzado a emerger. Éste es un paso importante ya que la religiosidad popular y la liturgia son encuentros con Dios que atraen, inspiran y dan vida a los fieles ofreciéndoles caminos para expresar su respuesta a ese encuentro, formal e informalmente, oficial y extraoficialmente, como resistencia y adhesión a lo que significa ser católico. Así, el papel de la religiosidad popular como encuentro con Dios debe ser examinado más profundamente por *todos* los católicos y el papel de la liturgia en dicho encuentro necesita más atención por parte de todos los católicos hispanos.

---

20 Hay muchas razones históricas, culturales y pastorales por las cuales la liturgia se limitó a ser un área de interés casi exclusivo del clero y las prácticas religiosas populares un área de interés primordialmente entre los laicos, mucho de lo cual fue fomentado por el propio clero. Especialmente durante la conquista y la evangelización subsecuente de las Américas, los francisc-- dominicos y agustinos, entre otros, usaron las prácticas religiosas populares como u- interpretar la liturgia y catequizar y así atraer a la gente al catolicismo. Véase, ᵗ Preaching: The Witness of Our Latin Eyes» en DAVIS K.G. Y PRESMANES J. (-- *Culture in Latino Congregations*, Liturgy Training Publications, Cʰⁱ «The Liturgical Roots of Hispanic Popular Religiosity» en DAVⁱ- *Mesa y Musa*, second edition, World Library Publications, S-ᵗ

3

Razones por las que la liturgia debe ser examinada y valorada más profundamente

⊘

Cuando empecé mis estudios doctorales en liturgia en 1994 sabía que un eje central de la reflexión teológica hispana en ese momento era la religiosidad popular. Aunque éste sigue siendo un punto de gran interés para los teólogos hispanos, en aquel momento parecía ser el único. Estaba preocupado porque cuando se mencionaba la liturgia, mis héroes en la academia solían pasarla por alto diciendo que «la liturgia es demasiado importante como para dejársela a los liturgistas». No estoy seguro de lo que eso significa exactamente, aunque creo que estoy de acuerdo en cuanto que es preciso que escuchemos otras voces aparte de los liturgistas cuando se trata de reflexionar teológicamente sobre la liturgia. Sin embargo, la expresión indica que hay que buscar una manera de hablar sobre la relación entre la religiosidad popular y la liturgia, especialmente en el contexto hispano en los Estados Unidos. Ésta es la preocupación de los obispos también expresada en *Encuentro y Misión: Un Marco Pastoral Renovado para el Ministerio Hispano*[21]. Es más, contrario a la experiencia en otros países de habla hispana en el resto del mundo, el principal contacto que tiene nuestro pueblo con su fe católica en los Estados Unidos es a través de la misa en sus parroquias y no en las calles llenas de personas participando constantemente de eventos y expresiones devocionales.

Algunos factores identificados en el estudio sobre el ministerio hispano indican que está ocurriendo un gran cambio entre los católicos hispanos. El estudio confirmó que la mayoría de los esfuerzos en el ministerio hispano estaban dirigidos a inmigrantes recién llegados. En cierto sentido esto se entendía en los años setentas hasta mediados de los noventas cuando todavía grandes números de inmigrantes, principalmente de México, estaban llegando al igual que un número ascendente de centro y suramericanos. En particular los mexicanos traían un fuerte sentido de identidad católica y acudían a sus parroquias más cercanas buscando ayuda. Las diócesis respondieron estableciendo oficinas de ministerio hispano y muchas comenzaron a tomar el PPNMH como modelo para sus planes diocesanos. Junto con mecanismos de asistencia para conseguir vi-

---

21 UNITED STATES CONFERENCE OF CATHOLIC BISHOPS, *Encuentro y Misión: Un Marco Pastoral Renovado para el Ministerio Hispano*, USCCB, Washington, D.C. 2002, n. 34, 58.1, 58.2 y 58.4, http://www.usccb.org/hispanicaffairs/encuentromissionsp.shtml.

vienda, trabajos, y responder a asuntos migratorios, los pastoralistas identificaron la necesidad de una catequesis básica e instrucción doctrinal.

Lo que se perdió de vista en este esfuerzo fueron las necesidades pastorales de los hispanos ya establecidos, muchos de los cuales eran de segunda, tercera e incluso cuarta generación. Mientras que los inmigrantes recién llegados hablaban principalmente español y a menudo buscaban las formas tradicionales de práctica religiosa que habían experimentado en sus países de origen, los hispanos más establecidos se estaban acomodando a la liturgia en inglés y al enfoque más privado de la vida devocional que generalmente caracteriza la experiencia católica dominante en los Estados Unidos. Junto con este factor, un rasgo preocupante que identificamos fue el que llamamos «síndrome de la segunda generación»[22]. Con relación a éste, los pastoralistas que entrevistamos expresaron incertidumbre sobre cómo servir al número creciente de hispanos que no hablan español, los que suelen abandonar la escuela, tienen una baja autoestima y/o se sienten inseguros sobre su identidad. Además, estos pastoralistas expresaron preocupación por el conflicto entre las distintas generaciones de hispanos, incluyendo grupos pertenecientes a distintas olas migratorias y distintas nacionalidades. Estas preocupaciones persisten. Desafortunadamente desde 1999 muchas oficinas diocesanas de ministerio hispano se han cerrado o se han consolidado en «oficinas de ministerios multiculturales». Esto también ocurrió a nivel nacional con la reorganización de la Conferencia de Obispos Católicos de Estados Unidos en el 2008 y el establecimiento del nuevo Secretariado de Diversidad Cultural en la Iglesia[23]. Todo esto afecta significativamente las condiciones del trabajo pastoral en el ministerio hispano tanto con latinos de primera generación como con aquellos que ya están más establecidos.

Otro factor a tener en cuenta es que, en medio de los esfuerzos por tratar de recrear las prácticas devocionales tradicionales y la celebración de los sacramentos al estilo latinoamericano, son comunes los conflictos entre distintos grupos nacionales e incluso entre miembros de un mismo grupo debido a las grandes diferencias sobre cómo se deben celebrar ciertos sacramentos y ritos[24]. En par-

22 UNITED STATES CONFERENCE OF CATHOLIC BISHOPS, SECRETARIADO PARA ASUNTOS HISPANOS, *Hispanic Ministry Study*, sección II, parágrafo 4. Con relación a los hispanos y la liturgia véase http://cara.georgetown.edu/Symposium.html.

23 Véase http://www.usccb.org/hispanicaffairs/indexsp.shtml. Para una crítica de esta tendencia ver CASARELLA P., «Recognizing Diversity after Multiculturalism» in *New Theology Review* 21, n. 4 (2008) 17.

24 Es importante observar también que no todos los grupos de latinoamericanos participan en prácticas religiosas populares puesto que éstas parecen asociarse principalmente con los po-

ticular, esta realidad se puede ilustrar con lo que ocurre con las advocaciones marianas que los latinos quieren honrar y cómo celebrarlas en sus comunidades. La competencia entre los distintos grupos y la escasez de recursos tienden a crear facciones y resentimientos a este respecto.

Más importante aún, pienso, es un factor que tiene que ver con la manera de fomentar y mantener la identidad católica. En América Latina se puede absorber el espíritu católico del ambiente sin tener que ir a la iglesia, gracias a las expresiones públicas de fe y los ritos de paso que de vez en cuando llevan a la gente a los templos tales como bautismos, primeras comuniones, quinceañeras, bodas y funerales. Estos acontecimientos, impregnados de un gran simbolismo, marcan la vida ordinaria sin exigir mucha participación en la liturgia y por ello pareciera que no fuese muy importante involucrarse en la parroquia. ¡No es de extrañar que la liturgia se perciba como algo que le compete sólo al clero! A pesar de esto, en la mayor parte del contexto estadounidense, la parroquia y sus actividades son básicamente los únicos recursos que muchos católicos latinos tienen a su alcance[25].

Si uno quiere entrar en contacto con su propia identidad como católico hispano o profundizar en su propia fe en el contexto estadounidense, generalmente uno debe ir a misa. Creo que una razón para ello tiene que ver con el concepto de separación de Iglesia y Estado que limita las demostraciones públicas de la fe. Esto ha fomentado la privatización de la fe y ha sido reforzado gracias a la necesidad de solicitar permisos y pagar cuotas para organizar procesiones o peregrinaciones. De hecho, los sistemas establecidos restringen y muchas veces desaniman la celebración de estas expresiones tradicionales de fervor religioso en público a no ser que prometan algún beneficio económico a la ciudad y se puedan justificar como oportunidades para incrementar el turismo. Un buen ejem-

---

bres o menos educados, los cuales desafortunadamente son la gran mayoría de la población. Por lo tanto, se esperaría que los inmigrantes de las clases altas participaran en actividades a las que nunca habían estado vinculados y esto puede ser una fuente de conflicto. La identificación de la religiosidad popular con los pobres en algunas de las culturas latinoamericanas también puede llevar a pensar que el «ascenso social» y la «asimilación» a la cultura dominante estadounidense exigiría el rechazo de las prácticas devocionales y, en algunos casos, del propio catolicismo.

25 Pedro Rubalcava, miembro del grupo de estudio que discutió la relación entre el ministerio hispano, la liturgia y la espiritualidad en el Simposio Nacional del 2009 en Boston College, señaló que existen excepciones notables en cuanto a esta actitud dependiendo del área del país. Al mismo tiempo Rubalcava indicó que el catolicismo popular continúa ejerciendo poder sobre la imaginación religiosa de los hispanos de distintas generaciones.

plo de esto es la Semana Santa en San Antonio, TX[26]. Aún si se pudieran conseguir los permisos fácilmente, el clima en la mayoría de las ciudades de los Estados Unidos no permite realizar celebraciones muy elaboradas como procesiones de Semana Santa que duren todo un día. En Milwaukee, donde trabajo, la Semana Santa se celebra a menudo en medio de bajas temperaturas, lluvia y a veces nieve. Parece que el mismo ambiente conspirara para restringir y limitar las demostraciones públicas de la fe que pudieran fomentar la identidad católica y su renovación espiritual periódica más allá de la liturgia. Es más, la mayoría de las parroquias se centran en programas de formación religiosa más que en la animación de una rica vida devocional centrada en la parroquia.

A pesar de estos factores, en el estudio de 1999 descubrimos que los hispanos están siendo fuerza de renovación en muchas parroquias abandonadas por inmigrantes de otras etnicidades que estuvieron antes allí. Encontramos evidencia de parroquias vibrantes animadas por prácticas devocionales adaptadas a las condiciones presentes al igual que con una vida litúrgica abundante. Los programas de formación y ministerio en español que promueven las oficinas de ministerio hispano han atraído a los hispanos y han aprovechado la gran sed de conocimiento de la Biblia y de lo que significa ser católico. Parece que esta sed ha aumentado porque la gente sigue asistiendo a las liturgias para poder sostener o robustecer su fe, su espiritualidad y su identidad[27]. A medida que la gente llega a escuchar las lecturas y las homilías que explican las Escrituras y lo que creen los católicos, y al ser animados a asumir roles en la liturgia, muchos han respondido deseando aprender más no sólo sobre la Biblia sino también sobre la liturgia.

Un gran ejemplo de ello es el testimonio de Juan y Martha Andrade[28]. He tenido la oportunidad de conocer a esta pareja muy bien en los últimos veinte años en los que he celebrado la Eucaristía y otros sacramentos en la parroquia de San Jacinto en el sur de Milwaukee. Juan y Martha son inmigrantes de primera generación. Llegaron a los Estados Unidos cuando eran jóvenes y se conocieron en Chicago. Juan, el mayor de varios hermanos que le han seguido a Milwaukee,

---

26 En 1998 participé como experto en un grupo de estudio que observó, analizó y reflexionó sobre los eventos organizados por el personal pastoral de la catedral de San Fernando en San Antonio, TX. El estudio estuvo financiado por la Fundación Lilly y el Centro Cultural México-Americano; más tarde nuestras aportaciones fueron publicadas en diversas fuentes.

27 Éste, por supuesto, es el mejor de los casos. Desafortunadamente, a menudo los hispanos se han encontrado con poca acogida y han dejado el catolicismo para ir a otras denominaciones o simplemente han dejado de identificarse con cualquier iglesia.

28 Uso sus nombres e historia con permiso.

soñaba con ahorrar dinero para establecer un negocio en su país de origen. Martha fue a Chicago con el sueño de superarse por medio de la educación. Se conocieron en un baile, se enamoraron, se casaron y se trasladaron a Milwaukee donde sus tres hijos, ahora adultos, nacieron, se criaron y se educaron.

Con el deseo de mantener su identidad católica, la familia Andrade fue a San Jacinto, la cual estaba cerca de su vivienda en ese momento. Ésta era una parroquia sirviendo originalmente inmigrantes polacos. A medida que su situación económica mejoró, Martha terminó una carrera en el campo de los negocios en una universidad católica para mujeres y se convirtió en consejera financiera con una amplia clientela entre hispanos del sur de Milwaukee. Pero Martha deseaba más que simplemente ir a misa. Comenzó a servir como lectora y luego ministro de la Eucaristía, llevando a Juan con ella. Al mismo tiempo se involucró en el comité del festival parroquial y le preguntó al párroco si podría iniciar un «consejo parroquial hispano» para ayudar a organizar celebraciones hispanas como las fiestas de Nuestra Señora de Guadalupe o la Purísima y también para responder a otras necesidades pastorales de la comunidad de habla hispana. Pasado un tiempo también involucró a sus cuñadas y a las familias de éstas en diversas actividades. Martha eventualmente logró que el consejo parroquial fuera bilingüe y se convirtió en uno de sus líderes laicos. Hoy en día es uno de los tres síndicos de la parroquia.

Martha atribuye su compromiso con la parroquia a la liturgia. Ha trabajado para mejorar las celebraciones y participa en programas diocesanos de formación litúrgica. Ha invitado a familiares y a amigos a involucrarse en los programas de educación religiosa de la parroquia y ha ayudado a introducir ciertas prácticas devocionales que los hispanos siguen celebrando en sus hogares hasta el día de hoy. Esto incluye la oración del novenario de las Posadas en la iglesia en lugar de hacerlo por las calles, seguido del rezo del rosario y una convivencia. Ella ha animado a otros a desarrollar sus talentos y a usarlos en la liturgia y otras celebraciones, por ejemplo enseñando a los niños a bailar danzas tradicionales en honor a la Virgen. Martha también ve su servicio de aconsejar a otros sobre asuntos financieros como un ministerio inspirado en los valores que ha recibido de la liturgia. En nuestro estudio, Manuel Vásquez y yo encontramos que en muchos lugares «la comunidad hispana ha liderado una renovación de las prácticas devocionales y ha aumento las actividades parroquiales centradas en el crecimiento espiritual»[29]. Esto es cierto en el caso de San Jacinto. No son sólo los

---

29 UNITED STATES CONFERENCE OF CATHOLIC BISHOPS, SECRETARIADO PARA ASUNTOS HISPANOS, *Hispanic Ministry Study,* sección II, parágrafo 5.

esfuerzos de Martha sino también los de aquellos que como ella han descubierto en la liturgia una fuente de motivación para realizar su potencial. La liturgia les ha inspirado a unir esfuerzos y a buscar maneras de renovar y reinterpretar sus prácticas devocionales en el contexto en el que viven y celebran el culto.

Tal como vemos en el ejemplo de Juan y Martha, los mismos hispanos están estableciendo puentes entre la religiosidad popular y la liturgia y también han atraído a latinos de distintas generaciones a participar en la vida de la Iglesia. Esta sencilla razón es más que suficiente para que quienes trabajamos y reflexionamos sobre el ministerio hispano tomemos la liturgia más seriamente que hasta ahora. No se trata de restar importancia a la religiosidad popular sino de afirmar que la liturgia no es el campo exclusivo del clero y de unos pocos expertos. Una manera de establecer los puentes necesarios es reconocer los elementos comunes entre las prácticas de religiosidad popular y la liturgia, su mediación de la presencia de Dios que revitaliza, sana, acompaña y santifica a quienes las practican a través de un encuentro con Cristo. Esto es a lo que llamamos sacramentalidad.

4
La sacramentalidad como clave para comprender la mística hispana

∽

La sacramentalidad tiene que ver en gran parte con la experiencia religiosa y su actualización a través de los ritos y las celebraciones específicas que fomentan y expanden esta experiencia. Es decir, en este acontecimiento, mediado por signos y símbolos, participamos en un encuentro transformador y vivificante con Cristo. Somos divinizados en este intercambio sagrado cuando Dios entra en nuestra realidad para que participemos en la realidad divina. O como dice la oración que usamos cuando se mezclan el vino y el agua durante la celebración eucarística: «El agua unida al vino sea signo de nuestra participación en la vida divina de quien ha querido compartir nuestra condición humana»[30]. En cierto modo todas las experiencias que tenemos de encuentro con Cristo tienen un hilo conductor y se ritualizan a diario para que podamos continuar encontrándonos con Él en nuestras vidas y encontremos nuestras vidas en Él.

---

30 Cfr. *Misal Romano*.

Porque el encuentro con Cristo es central en nuestra identidad como católicos, los teólogos que estudian los sacramentos se enfocan en lo que estos son, cómo funcionan y lo que significan[31]. En cierta manera, los sacramentos se entienden desde el misterio de la encarnación: hacen presente la actividad salvadora de Cristo en nuestra carne, en nuestra humanidad. San Isidoro de Sevilla (murió en 636) propuso la idea del *aspecto memorial* de los ritos sacramentales como un aspecto importante para considerar[32]. Así pues, la sacramentalidad tiene que ver con la anamnesis y la encarnación. Y estas ideas incorporan los conceptos de signo y símbolo. Tal como lo han señalado los miembros de la Academia de Teólogos Católicos Hispanos de los Estados Unidos (ACHTUS, sigla en inglés), la religiosidad popular está llena de signos y símbolos al igual que de ritos y acciones a través de los cuales nos encontramos con lo sagrado.

Por esta razón, la sacramentalidad es un área que merece ser estudiada con más profundidad. Es una conversación compleja y extensa en la que los teólogos hispanos y los pastoralistas tienen que participar más de lleno[33]. En mi opinión, la conversación se empobrece si falta nuestra voz. Debemos hablar más sobre la sacramentalidad desde la perspectiva hispana. Aunque para nosotros la sacramentalidad se arraiga en los sacramentos, no se limita a ellos. Profundamente insertada en la visión del mundo hispano está el sentido de que la acción y la gracia de Dios abundan a nuestro alrededor, arriba, abajo y a través de nosotros[34].

---

[31] Véase la historia de los sacramentos de MARTOS J., *Doors to the Sacred: A Historical Introduction to Sacraments in the Catholic Church*, edición revisada y actualizada, Liguori/Triumph, Liguori, MO 2001.

[32] Véase OSBORNE K.B., OFM, *Sacramental Theology: A General Introduction*, Paulist Press, New York/Mahwah 1988, 23-24. Osborne hace referencia al texto de Isidoro de Sevilla: *Etimologías*.

[33] Otros miembros de ACHTUS y del Instituto Nacional Hispano de Liturgia han explorado el concepto de sacramentalidad como parte de sus trabajos. Por ejemplo, DÍAZ M.H., *On Being Human: U.S. Hispanic and Rahnerian Perspectives*, Orbis Books, Maryknoll, NY 2001, particularmente el capítulo 3; MATOVINA T. y RIEBE-ESTRELLA G. (eds.), *Horizons of the Sacred: Mexican Traditions in U.S. Catholicism*, Cornell, Ithaca, NY 2002; GARCÍA-RIVERA A. «Community and Communion: The Language of the Sacraments» en GÓMEZ-RUÍZ R., SDS (ed.), *Languages of Worship/El Lenguaje de la Liturgia*, Liturgy Training Publications, Chicago 2004; DAVIS K.G., OFM,Conv. (ed.), *Misa, Mesa y Musa*, segunda edición, World Library Publications, Schiller Park, IL 1997; DAVIS K.G., OFM,Conv. (ed.), *Misa, Mesa, y Musa, Vol 2: Liturgy in the U.S. Hispanic Church*, World Library Publications, Franklin Park, IL 2008. Los siguientes dos trabajos examinan el tema de la sacramentalidad desde una perspectiva postmoderna y una de teología estética respectivamente: EMPEREUR J. y FERNÁNDEZ E., *La Vida Sacra: Contemporary Hispanic Sacramental Theology*, Rowman & Littlefield, Lanham, MD 2006; GARCÍA-RIVERA A. y SCIRGHI T., *Living Beauty: The Art of Liturgy*, Rowman & Littlefield, Lanham, MD 2007.

[34] Reflexiono sobre este tema en detalle en el siguiente artículo: GÓMEZ R., SDS, «Preaching the Ritual Masses among Latinos» en DAVIS K.G. y PRESMANES J. (eds.), *Preaching and Culture in Latino Congregations*, 103-119. El mismo artículo aparece en *Chicago Studies* 39, n. 3 (2000) 295-311.

La sacramentalidad es la experiencia del encuentro con algo santo, significativo y transformador; es el deseo de repetir esa experiencia a través de acciones y retenerla por medio de objetos que participan en la experiencia y la extienden en la propia vida. Esto es lo que hacen los sacramentos y los sacramentales. Es más, la sacramentalidad es un término relacional que implica encuentro, respuesta y transformación. Es un dinamismo que genera y destella, que permea los sacramentos y los sacramentales, al cual llamamos gracia. La sacramentalidad también se encuentra en diversos eventos y situaciones en lo cotidiano, los cuales transforman nuestra propia vida y nos atraen hacia un encuentro con Cristo con tal de que tengamos ojos para ver y oídos para oír. Las prácticas devocionales asociadas por los hispanos con los sacramentos y con el uso de sacramentales, tales como bendiciones y objetos bendecidos, llevan a este encuentro y a una respuesta a la acción de Dios, a la gracia de Dios en la propia vida y el deseo de prolongar esa experiencia en una relación marcada por ritos, prácticas y objetos que ayudan a revivir esa experiencia. En algunos casos la transformación que ocurre gracias al acontecimiento exige que sea simbolizada con una variedad de objetos y acciones que reafirman el cambio con relación a lo sagrado y generan una nueva identidad. En el caso del bautismo, algunos hispanos simbolizan por medio del bolo o monedas arrojadas al aire por el padrino el nacimiento de un nuevo cristiano lleno de la abundancia de la gracia. En el caso de la quinceañera, la joven es ahora una mujer de fe que da gracias públicamente por ello. En el caso del matrimonio, un lazo atado alrededor de la pareja en el día de su boda simboliza que los esposos están indisolublemente unidos para toda la vida sin importar lo que ocurra. ¿Cómo podemos cerrar la brecha entre la religiosidad popular y la liturgia para que se pueda comprender más profundamente la mística hispana y se reflexione sobre ella como una fuerza para el futuro del ministerio hispano en los Estados Unidos?

5
Sugerencias para la reflexión y el diálogo

Ofrezco cuatro sugerencias que podrían ayudar a cerrar la brecha entre la religiosidad popular y la liturgia con el deseo de dar un paso hacia adelante en el ministerio hispano. Estas sugerencias tienen que ver con 1) una reflexión más intencional sobre la sacramentalidad como base de la mística hispana, 2) el uso del poder de la liturgia y de la religiosidad popular como instrumentos para la inculturación de esa mística, 3) la identificación y capacitación de líderes en la comunidad para llevar a cabo estos esfuerzos, y 4) la explicitación de las conexiones entre la mística hispana y la experiencia litúrgica y espiritual dominante en la Iglesia Católica en los Estados Unidos.

1) *Reflexionar más intencionalmente sobre la sacramentalidad.* La reflexión sobre cómo la sacramentalidad se expresa entre los hispanos nos ayudará a promover la construcción de puentes y atender a las necesidades pastorales de los hispanos de distintas generaciones en los Estados Unidos. La revisión de los ritos sacramentales de la Iglesia Católica ha generado una teología sacramental vibrante. Como resultado de esta reflexión hoy en día consideramos la sacramentalidad como parte integral de la vida litúrgica, el culto, y tenemos una mejor apreciación de la liturgia como expresión de participación en la sacramentalidad por medio de los sacramentos[35].

Podemos contribuir especialmente a la conversación sobre la sacramentalidad usando la categoría de relación. Roberto Goizueta ha señalado que nuestra identidad como hispanos está claramente unida a nuestra interconexión dentro de lo que llamamos «familia» o «comunidad»[36]. Existimos en relación; es decir, nuestra identidad como individuos depende del grupo al que pertenecemos. Para los hispanos esto es fruto de nuestra historia como mezcla de razas, lenguas y culturas —nuestro mestizaje y mulatez— que nos han ayudado a abrirnos a otros, a recibir al extranjero y a incorporar diversas costumbres y perspectivas. Dora Tobar afirma que este rasgo proporciona un principio de comunión y un profundo encuentro que la liturgia debe y puede celebrar[37]. Este principio de comunión es operante en nuestro esfuerzo de hacer teología en conjunto. Reflexionar juntos teológicamente también implica un principio de reconciliación al exponer nuestros pensamientos más íntimos y tratar de reconciliar o unir muchos puntos de vista. Hacemos esto para descubrir quién es Dios y quiénes somos nosotros con relación a Dios y a los demás.

---

35 Esto aparece en el *Catecismo de la Iglesia Católica*, segunda edición (1997); toda la discusión sobre los sacramentos se encuentra en la sección sobre la liturgia, segunda parte: La celebración del misterio cristiano.

36 Véase GOIZUETA R.S., «The Symbolic World of Mexican American Religion» en MATOVINA T. y RIEBE-ESTRELLA G. (eds.), *Horizons of the Sacred*, 121; idem, «The Symbolic Realism of U.S. Latino/a Popular Catholicism» en *Theological Studies* 65, n. 2 (2004) 258.

37 TOBAR D.E., «El Lenguaje de la cultura hispana y la liturgia» en GÓMEZ R., SDS (ed.), *Languages of Worship/El Lenguaje de la Liturgia*, 71, citando Puebla, n. 409.

Los términos relacionales hispanos tienen una riqueza única que puede revelar modos para entender y hablar de sacramentalidad como un encuentro transformador y significativo con Cristo en lo cotidiano y en el culto. Me refiero a términos que no se traducen exactamente en inglés o simplemente no se nombran para señalar una gama de relaciones existentes en la comunidad latina. Hay términos de compadrazgo tales como padrino o madrina y sus correspondientes ahijado y ahijada. Los padrinos no son solamente testigos sino que son otros padres; los ahijados son «afiliados» o miembros de la propia prole, no como vínculo de sangre sino de espíritu[38]. Tocayos y tocayas, primo hermano, prima hermana, tío abuelo, tía abuela, comadre y compadre son sólo una muestra de las maneras de crear, nombrar y fomentar una red de relaciones con y dentro de nuestras comunidades. Es principalmente en las relaciones donde encontramos el sentido de la vida, la vida como bendición, la vida como algo sagrado. Estar fuera o no ser parte de una red de relaciones es prácticamente como estar muerto en vida.

Existimos en medio de nuestras relaciones. Al entrar en relación nos situamos al centro de una fuerza que nos lleva más allá de nosotros mismos a un lugar donde se aprende a negociar y a tomar posturas frente a distintos asuntos, a entrar en mutualidad y compromiso, a formar lazos de amistad y amor, y a repararlos cuando sea necesario. En ese lugar somos llamados a vivir en medio de las exigencias que se hacen sobre nuestro tiempo, nuestras emociones y nuestra independencia para así aprender a confiar y renunciar, dar y recibir. En otras palabras, en la compleja dinámica de nuestras relaciones nos hacemos plenamente humanos. La sacramentalidad de nuestras relaciones tiene que ver con el reconocimiento de que somos incompletos sin los demás. Al buscar la plenitud *con* y *en* la otra persona, tanto en el caso de Dios como el de los demás seres humanos, encontramos la plenitud de la vida desde la cual Dios nos ha amado y a la que nos atrae más profundamente. En esta dinámica nos convertimos en aquello para lo que Dios nos ha creado y compartimos la cruz de Cristo al morir a nosotros mismos y convertirnos en fuente de vida nueva para los demás. Es decir, estar en relación nos lleva a experimentar lo sagrado y divino. Estar en relación es una realidad sacramental.

---

38 La raíz de la palabra para afiliados es el latín *affilii*, es decir, hijos adoptados.

En las relaciones que experimentan los hispanos a menudo veo la centralidad de Cristo, aunque con frecuencia es un Cristo débil y pequeño ya sea al comienzo de su vida o al final, pero dependiente de nosotros y reflejado en las actitudes que tenemos frente a los inocentes y los ancianos[39]. Veo la importancia de la encarnación, el acontecimiento sacramental de la integración humana y divina en el cual Dios y la humanidad habitan juntos. La encarnación proporciona el sentido de que Dios se puede encontrar en los asuntos de la vida diaria, en lo cotidiano. Nuestras actitudes y prácticas religiosas nos conectan con la vida de la Trinidad reforzando nuestro énfasis en la familia, el compromiso de acompañar a los que sufren y la necesidad de celebrar la fiesta que da sentido unificador a la vida. El español, parte integral de nuestra identidad, con el carácter religioso de nuestros dichos, expresiones y música, media lo que es significativo para nosotros y lo que nos proporciona el sentido de ser pueblo de Dios. Objetos aparentemente ordinarios como los milagritos moldeados en forma de partes del cuerpo humano y acontecimientos ordinarios como los sacrificios personales y los juramentos son mediadores de un encuentro con Dios que puede conducir a una acción ética. ¿No es eso de lo que se tratan en realidad las mandas y las promesas? Considero que nuestras ritualizaciones tales como nuestro modo particular de hacer la señal de la cruz, el papel del sufrimiento y el papel de lo femenino, especialmente el de María, en nuestra espiritualidad también median un encuentro con Cristo que nos da vida, nos transforma y nos completa. Nuestra mística es verdaderamente poderosa.

2) *Usar el poder de la liturgia y de la religiosidad popular como instrumentos para la inculturación de la mística hispana.* En la liturgia definimos nuestras relaciones a través de bautizos, primeras comuniones, quinceañeras, bodas e incluso sepelios. También las definimos con los santos y lo divino a través de fiestas patronales y una amplia gama de prácticas religiosas que han tomado sus símbolos de la liturgia, tales como los altarcitos y las veladoras, los despojos y los ensalmes, las procesiones y las cofradías. De este modo los principales aconteci-

---

[39] «Débil» en este caso se refiere al juicio que algunos hicieron de la condición física de Jesús en estas situaciones. Como bien señala Cecilia González-Andrieu, «Cristo no es débil en el camino al Calvario, ni es débil en la cruz al morir una muerte terrible por nosotros —creo que la religiosidad hispana reconoce en Cristo una fuerza indomable, una fuerza profunda para resistir y continuar, para perseverar en la fe ante toda dificultad. Veo esto especialmente cuando comparo algunas piezas de arte de América latina con otras parecidas que fueron creadas en un contexto europeo —Cristo es poderoso en su sufrimiento y en su muerte en el contexto latinoamericano. También creo que esto se traduce al Cristo de otras comunidades sufrientes, tal como las africanas» (comunicación personal con el autor por medio de correo electrónico, 16 de julio del 2009).

mientos sacramentales identificados por la Iglesia se prolongan en celebraciones adyacentes que hemos creado a lo largo del tiempo. Aquí es donde lo cotidiano se encuentra con el culto y viceversa. Aquí es donde los hispanos podemos hacer una gran contribución a la liturgia basados en esta relación.

A través de la liturgia las personas son convocadas a ser parte de una asamblea, a una relación de individuos llamados para ser constituidos como Pueblo de Dios. Allí se convierten en Cuerpo de Cristo y en Templo del Espíritu Santo, es decir la Iglesia, por acción del Espíritu. El edificio del templo es un símbolo de esto y tiene un papel evangelizador. Por tanto, el edificio mismo debe ser digno y hermoso para que quienes se reúnen ahí sientan que están en la casa de Dios. Las imágenes sagradas que se encuentran en las iglesias en donde los hispanos están presentes atraen a la gente por su diseño: han de ser revestidas, articuladas, móviles, sacadas en procesión para que la gente se sienta atraída a ellas. Estas imágenes evocan a las personas que representan y funcionan como íconos tridimensionales. Al salir en procesión llaman la atención, atraen a las personas y las invitan a regresar a la iglesia poniendo así en práctica la convicción de que la liturgia es fuente y culmen de la actividad y la vida de la Iglesia. En cierto sentido se convierten en instrumentos del Espíritu Santo para convocar a la Iglesia[40]. Así como el catolicismo popular ha usado ritos, símbolos, el ambiente y actividades que incorporan todos los sentidos, la liturgia también tiene que hacerlo si su fuerza ha de influenciar la vida de los creyentes más allá de los confines de los templos. Así que debemos prestar atención al rito, al símbolo, la imagen y el ambiente y a todos aquellos elementos relacionados con ellos, así como lo hacen las prácticas de religiosidad popular. Esto es parte del puente que se puede tender entre ellas.

La declaración pastoral *Encuentro y Misión* afirma que los obispos ven la religiosidad popular como un elemento clave para la inculturación de la liturgia, la cual es culmen y fuente de la vida cristiana. Para que esto ocurra, los obispos insisten en que «[t]odos están invitados a compartir formas de oración que reflejen sus diversos valores culturales y tradiciones y a recibir gustosos sus talentos» (*Encuentro y Misión*, n. 34). Una manera de hacer esto es aceptar la liturgia

---

40 Sin embargo, Eduardo Fernández, miembro del grupo de estudio reflexionando sobre la relación entre el ministerio hispano, la liturgia y la espiritualidad en el Simposio Nacional del 2009 en Boston College, advirtió que también es importante ser conscientes del lado oscuro del catolicismo popular como por ejemplo su abuela culpando a san Lorenzo por haber quemado la granja de la familia porque no se había cumplido una promesa. Con todo, Robert Hurteau, otro miembro del grupo, señaló que tal observación apunta a las dimensiones éticas del catolicismo popular.

como lo que es: la oración oficial de la Iglesia. Una máxima importante en este sentido es *lex orandi, lex credendi*, o sea, oramos lo que creemos[41]. Lo que creemos como Iglesia también está constituido en parte por lo que creemos como individuos; aspectos de ambas fuentes pueden ser distinguidas en el catolicismo popular. La teóloga católica Cecilia González-Andrieu acertadamente indica que la religión popular hace visible una sed profunda de más participación en la vida oficial de la Iglesia y podemos ver esto en la apropiación de símbolos provenientes de la liturgia[42]. Las normas en las instrucciones generales que se encuentran en los libros litúrgicos y las «rúbricas» conceden suficiente espacio para incorporar elementos que ayuden a establecer un puente entre la fe individual y la comunitaria al igual que entre la fe privada y la pública expresadas tanto en la liturgia como en la religiosidad popular. Estas normas proporcionan pistas que ayudan a enfocar la liturgia como una estructura que hay que revestir a través de opciones, acciones, símbolos y el uso de expresiones culturales de espiritualidad como nuestra mística[43]. Esto significa que hay que eliminar las barreras del paternalismo que han impedido a los fieles tomar un papel más activo y pleno en la liturgia.

3) *Identificar y capacitar a los líderes de la comunidad.* Ésta es la principal manera para vencer el paternalismo. El PPNMH ofrece nueve orientaciones pastorales tomadas del Tercer Encuentro (Cfr. n. 16). En particular el objetivo «B. Evangelización» identifica a los líderes pastorales como puentes entre los «marginados y la Iglesia» apreciando el valor de la religiosidad popular[44]. Allí ya se nota un cambio significativo en el mismo objetivo, el cual invita a adquirir «conocimientos básicos sobre la liturgia y su relación a la oración privada»[45]. Esto es reiterado aún más en el objetivo «D. Formación», el cual recomienda que se ofrez-

---

41 Esta máxima es la forma abreviada de la expresión de Próspero de Aquitania (m. 460): *legem credendi lex statuat supplicandi.*

42 Respuesta personal de Cecilia González-Andrieu a este ensayo en comunicación con el autor.

43 Orientaciones, sugerencias y principios para adaptar la liturgia se encuentran en CONGREGACIÓN PARA EL CULTO DIVINO Y LA DISCIPLINA DE LOS SACRAMENTOS, *Directorio sobre la piedad popular y la liturgia*; FRANCIS M.R., *Multicultural Celebrations/Celebraciones Multiculturales*, Federation of Diocesan Liturgical Commissions Publications, Washington, D.C. 2000; SOSA J.J. *One Voice, Many Rhythms*, Oregon Catholic Press, Portland, OR 2009; idem, *Manual para entender y participar en la misa*, Liguori Publications, Liguori, MO 2009. Aún más, *Sacrosanctum Concilium*, n. 37 afirma que: «La Iglesia no pretende imponer una rígida uniformidad en aquello que no afecta a la fe o al bien de toda la comunidad, ni siquiera en la Liturgia: por el contrario, respeta y promueve el genio y las cualidades peculiares de las distintas razas y pueblos».

44 Véase PPNMH, n. 48 (4), en UNITED STATES CONFERENCE OF CATHOLIC BISHOPS, *Ministerio Hispano*, 78.

45 PPNMH, n. 48 (4), en UNITED STATES CONFERENCE OF CATHOLIC BISHOPS, *Ministerio Hispano*, 78.

can «seminarios o encuentros de reflexión de pastoralistas en los diferentes campos de liturgia, catequesis, teología y evangelización»[46]. Notemos, sin embargo, que esta recomendación se dirige a los «especialistas pastorales» y no a los fieles en general. Aún así, una mejor comprensión del papel que juega la sacramentalidad tanto en la liturgia como en la religiosidad popular puede ayudar a que ambas sean percibidas como un encuentro más profundo con Cristo. Esto debe hacerse por medio de la catequesis y la predicación así como en seminarios y sesiones de estudio para todos los interesados, no sólo con los especialistas. Es urgente que identifiquemos a los líderes naturales en la parroquia, entremos en diálogo con ellos, pidamos su consejo y lo usemos, les motivemos para que integren la mística hispana en la liturgia, y así hagan de esta dinámica una fuerza mucho más poderosa para el ministerio pastoral hispano con todas las generaciones.

Se pueden encontrar líderes en movimientos como el Cursillo de Cristiandad y la Renovación Carismática, entre otros, y asociaciones vibrantes como la National Catholic Network de Pastoral Juvenil Hispana —La Red. Al establecer puentes entre estos movimientos y sus líderes se podrá fortalecer mejor el vínculo con la liturgia. Para lograr esto es importante recordar lo que ya se ha hecho para que los nuevos líderes se enriquezcan con la memoria histórica, la entiendan y la usen como base de sus proyectos[47]. También, al considerar la liturgia como algo más amplio que la celebración eucarística, por ejemplo incluyendo la Liturgia de las Horas y las Bendiciones, un gran número de mujeres que tienen funciones de liderazgo en estos movimientos se pueden preparar para presidir como lo contemplan las normas litúrgicas para estos tipos de celebraciones. Al asumir papeles de liderazgo litúrgico, los laicos que guían estas celebraciones llegan a conocer a Cristo de un modo distinto que los motiva a invitar a la comunidad al encuentro que conduce a vivir más plenamente en la presencia de Dios y en la evangelización del mundo a la que todos los cristianos estamos llamados como discípulos. Es más, esto resaltaría la eclesiología que los hispanos ofrecemos a la Iglesia, marcada por un espíritu de hospitalidad y lucha por la justicia así como una pastoral y una teología en conjunto en sus distintas formas como fue enfatizado por distintas voces que participaron en el Simposio

---

46 *PPNMH*, n. 71 (2), en UNITED STATES CONFERENCE OF CATHOLIC BISHOPS, *Ministerio Hispano*, 83.

47 Alejandro López-Cardinale, miembro del grupo de estudio reflexionando sobre la relación entre el ministerio hispano, la liturgia, y la espiritualidad en el Simposio Nacional del 2009 en Boston College, señaló la importancia de no perder la memoria de lo que se ha logrado para que los nuevos líderes y los recién llegados vean las bases que han llevado a la situación actual y puedan construir sobre ellas para avanzar hacia adelante en lo que se ha logrado y dejar atrás lo que ya no se necesita.

Nacional sobre el Presente y Futuro del Ministerio Católico Hispano en los Estados Unidos celebrado en Boston College en el año 2009.

4) *Hacer conexiones explícitas entre la mística hispana y la experiencia litúrgica y espiritual dominante en la Iglesia Católica en los Estados Unidos.* Es posible que porque todos los días hay celebraciones litúrgicas no les pongamos mucha atención. Cecilia González-Andrieu sugiere que una teoría estética coherente podría ser útil para tomar lo que es familiar, hacerlo poco familiar y luego traerlo de regreso para una mejor apreciación de lo que ocurre en el catolicismo popular, y así hacer las conexiones apropiadas con la liturgia. Los hispanos también tenemos que tender puentes hacia otros católicos y sus expresiones de fe. Una manera de hacer esto es entrar en diálogo con lo que Andrew Greeley llama la «imaginación católica»[48]. Es interesante leer la portada de su libro declarando que: «Los católicos viven en un mundo encantado: un mundo de estatuas y agua bendita, vidrieras y velas votivas, santos y medallas religiosas, rosarios y estampas. Pero esta parafernalia católica es simplemente un signo de una sensibilidad más profunda y prevalente que lleva a los católicos a ver lo Sagrado como algo escondido en toda la creación. El mundo del católico está cautivado por un sentido de que los objetos, los eventos y las personas de la vida diaria son revelaciones de la gracia». Claramente expresiones tales como «escondido» y «cautivado» son términos de mercadeo cuya meta es crear interés en el tema, pero revelan cierto prejuicio presente en la cultura dominante de los Estados Unidos en contra de lo misterioso o lo religioso[49].

La tendencia a privatizar la fe ha impactado de gran manera a los hijos de los católicos de todos los grupos inmigrantes durante varias generaciones. Dicha tendencia se expresa por medio de la resistencia a demostraciones de fe públicas y por medio de un énfasis en la salvación individual[50]. Por un lado, se espera que los católicos hispanos adopten la gran variedad de expresiones de espiritualidad del resto de los católicos estadounidenses. Por otro lado, la espiritualidad católica hispana nos recuerda que la fe también es comunitaria y pública.

48 GREELEY A., *The Catholic Imagination*, University of California Press, Berkeley, CA 2000.

49 Aunque ésta ciertamente no es la visión personal de Greeley, a menudo los medios de comunicación dominantes transmiten dicha perspectiva.

50 Algunas encuestas demuestran cómo un número ascendente de personas que se llaman cristianos y se identifican ya sea como evangélicos o simplemente cristianos tienden a exhibir una fe individualista o privatizada. Véase por ejemplo *American Religious Identification Survey* (ARIS 2008) publicado en marzo del 2009, http://www.americanreligionsurvey-aris.org/2009/03/catholics_on_the_move_non-religious_on_the_rise.html, disponible en inglés (página visitada el 3 de enero del 2010).

De hecho, parte de esta influencia hispana se puede notar en las prácticas religiosas emergentes que miembros de la cultura dominante están adoptando como las ofrendas (altares en día de los muertos) y descansos (cruces en los caminos que recuerdan accidentes de tránsito donde mueren seres queridos). Estas prácticas demuestran que a pesar de la tendencia a querer privatizar la fe, la imaginación hispana católica se puede adaptar y compartir con otros. En gran parte la razón de esta actitud es que para los católicos hispanos el mundo ciertamente está «encantado», en cuanto que es percibido como un lugar maravilloso y sorprendente lleno de signos de la presencia y la gracia de Dios. Tan maravilloso es esto que inspira admiración y humildad en lugar del temor y la incertidumbre que pueden provocar palabras tales como «escondido» y «cautivado». La sacramentalidad a la latina no está llena de sentimientos atormentados o de miedo, extrañeza o rareza, sino de consolación, paz y bienestar, realidades que al mismo tiempo son familiares y reconocibles, misteriosas pero descifrables, memorables aunque efímeras. Para muchos hispanos Dios es un miembro de la familia: el Padre es «Tata Dios» (Abuelo Dios); Jesús, claramente Señor y Salvador, es «el niño Dios» inocente que inspira cariño o el «Nazareno» (o Señor sufriente) quien evoca un sentimiento de dolor e inquietud. Ambos aspectos de Jesús mueven a las personas a salir de sí mismas para responder al que está necesitado. El Espíritu, lejos de ser un fantasma, es Santo y dador de vida, capaz de consolar, confortar, alegrar y guiar en buenos y malos tiempos. Es por ello que los hispanos buscan modos de cultivar su «imaginación sacramental» y entran y prolongan la sensibilidad religiosa que es sacramentalidad, la cual arraiga su mística tanto en expresiones de religiosidad popular como en la liturgia. La primera generación de inmigrantes hispanos trae consigo mucho de esto innatamente; nuestro desafío es transmitir dicha sensibilidad a las siguientes generaciones y compartirla con el resto de nuestros hermanos y hermanas católicos de los Estados Unidos. Estoy de acuerdo con Cecilia González-Andrieu quien señala que la religiosidad popular hispana como receptora de la sabiduría de la comunidad «en algunos momentos… puede que haya salvaguardado la imaginación sacramental de la Iglesia, protegiéndola de las fuerzas que la pudieran haber silenciado radicalmente. Esto es importante porque permite la continuidad y la comunicación inteligible con previas generaciones de católicos (y de hecho con toda la historia de la Iglesia) y también tiene el potencial de establecer puentes con otras comunidades católicas profundamente imaginativas, particularmente las de África y Asia»[51].

51 Respuesta personal de Cecilia González-Andrieu a este ensayo.

6

Conclusión

Aquí estamos a comienzos de la segunda década del siglo XXI considerando el presente y el futuro del ministerio hispano en los Estados Unidos. Muchas oficinas de ministerio hispano se han cerrado o se han combinado con otras oficinas de ministerios étnicos. El Secretariado para Asuntos Hispanos de la Conferencia de Obispos Católicos ha cerrado sus puertas. Muchos institutos dedicados a la formación de liderazgo para el ministerio hispano luchan por sobrevivir económicamente. En términos del presente y futuro del ministerio hispano, la liturgia y la espiritualidad en los Estados Unidos, el Instituto Nacional Hispano de Liturgia —el único instituto dedicado a la formación y promoción de buenas celebraciones litúrgicas entre las diversas comunidades hispanas en el país— está en peligro de desaparecer completamente debido a la falta de recursos[52]. ¿Qué nos ayudará a seguir adelante?

La experiencia de los Andrade es instructiva. El presente y el futuro dependen de personas como ellos que están encontrando maneras relacionar la liturgia y la religiosidad popular y están asumiendo la tarea pastoral de la Iglesia. Ellos también dependen de nosotros, personas dedicadas a la reflexión sobre la realidad hispana, para ayudarles a nombrar, guiar y articular lo que está ocurriendo. Quizás la fe hispana, la cual ya era vibrante en esta tierra antes de que se convirtiera en los Estados Unidos de América, pueda ahora convertirse en una fuerza para ayudar a revitalizar, transformar y completar los muchos y variados rostros de los Estados Unidos para que podamos dar mejor testimonio de ser el Pueblo de Dios, el Cuerpo de Cristo y el Templo del Espíritu Santo, invitados por nuestros sacramentos celebrados en la liturgia. Para hacerlo, nuestra mística debe estar articulada teológicamente de una manera que quizás sólo los hispanos en los Estados Unidos podemos hacer. Partiendo de la riqueza de las relaciones que fomentamos a través de la familia, la comunidad, el mestizaje, la teología en conjunto, etc., podemos sacramentalizar no solo la mezcla del agua y el vino en la Eucaristía, sino también las corrientes étnicas, políticas y teológicas de agua y vino ofrecidas por mujeres y hombres llenos de fe para que todos podamos llegar a celebrar y vivir verdaderamente la Eucaristía juntos y así compartir en la divinidad de Cristo que encontramos allí.

52 Véase *Amén*, Boletín del Instituto Nacional Hispano de Liturgia, primavera 2008: «What About the Instituto?» en la sección de noticias , http://liturgia.cua.edu/newsletter/Amen Spring 2008.pdf (página visitada el 5 de enero del 2010).

El ministerio hispano y la justicia social

Arturo Chávez

«La bendición del Padre, la bendición del Hijo, la bendición del Espíritu Santo… y la mía que te acompañe». Con esta bendición me despedía mi abuelita cuando yo salía a mis viajes tanto cerca como lejos de casa. Mucho después de que el calor de su abrazo se disipara yo seguía sintiendo su amor y sus oraciones —su acompañamiento— al encontrarme con las alegrías y los dolores de mis caminos. En su manera sencilla de expresar amor, mi abuela me transmitió una profunda fe en el Dios trinitario cuya esencia íntima es ser relación de amor. De igual manera, los pioneros del ministerio hispano han bendecido a la Iglesia con una memoria histórica que narra las luchas buscando justicia en nuestra sociedad y un lugar de pertenencia en la Iglesia. Este testimonio ha sido preservado oralmente y en varios documentos que fueron escritos entre los años setentas y ochentas sobre los históricos Encuentros Nacionales, culminando en 1987 con el *Plan Pastoral Nacional para el Ministerio Hispano*. El *Plan* fue adoptado unánimemente por la Conferencia Nacional de Obispos Católicos (NCCB, sigla en inglés) llamando a los católicos a:

> vivir y promover… mediante una pastoral de conjunto un modelo de Iglesia que sea: comunitaria, evangelizadora y misionera, encarnada en la realidad del pueblo hispano y abierta a la diversidad de culturas, promotora y ejemplo de justicia… que desarrolle liderazgo por medio de la educación integral… que sea fermento del Reino de Dios en la sociedad[1].

Esta declaración de la misión para el ministerio hispano, impregnada con un significado teológico profundo, inspiró muchos años de reflexión activa, debates vibrantes y nuevos trabajos académicos que dieron luz a lo que ahora llamamos teología y espiritualidad latina contextual[2]. En general, este discurso no sólo dio frutos en círculos académicos, sino que sirvió como justificación para establecer oficinas diocesanas de ministerio hispano en todo el país y para educar a un nuevo liderazgo eclesial: obispos, sacerdotes, religiosos y ministros laicos hispanos. La declaración de la misión también sirvió como impulso para la acción social, especialmente a nivel parroquial, usando los principios de la

---

1 NATIONAL CONFERENCE OF CATHOLIC BISHOPS, *Plan Pastoral Nacional para el Ministerio Hispano*, USCC, Washington, D.C. 1988, n. 71, en UNITED STATES CONFERENCE OF CATHOLIC BISHOPS, *Ministerio Hispano: Tres Documentos Importantes*, USCCB, Washington, D.C. 1995.

2 Un análisis general de las contribuciones hispanas a la teología se encuentra en FERNÁNDEZ E., *La Cosecha: Harvesting Contemporary United States Hispanic Theology 1972-1998*, Liturgical Press, Collegeville 2000.

Doctrina Social de la Iglesia y las tácticas y redes organizacionales del momento[3]. Así, el ministerio hispano se afirmó como una realidad inseparable de la justicia social, firmemente establecida en muchas diócesis y parroquias.

Sin embargo, un proceso consistente de implementación del *Plan Pastoral Nacional* en todo el país no tuvo lugar. En lugar de constituir una red nacional fuerte, en los años noventas el ministerio hispano se dividió en diversos grupos de interés, compitiendo por los mismos recursos limitados en una comunidad eclesial que enfrentaba múltiples desafíos[4]. Externamente, los acontecimientos trágicos del 11 de septiembre del 2001, la guerra en Irak, el creciente sentimiento anti-inmigratorio y la crisis económica global han empeorado las condiciones para poner en marcha el *Plan Pastoral Nacional para el Ministerio Hispano*, a pesar de que la USCCB lo reafirmó en su documento *Encuentro y Misión* en el año 2002. Mientras que el cuidado pastoral continúa en muchas de nuestras diócesis, las metas más importantes tales como educación integral, formación para el liderazgo, justicia social y cambio sistémico, las cuales lastimosamente no son consideradas como prioridades por muchos, en varios lugares se han dejado de lado. Nos sentimos desorientados, tanto en la Iglesia como en la sociedad, incluso cuando volvemos a los mapas que un día guiaron e inspiraron nuestro camino. Las bendiciones invaluables que recibimos de nuestros pioneros aún nos acompañan, pero el sendero es ahora una autopista de ocho carriles, con muchos puentes y túneles, y en medio de gran tráfico vehicular. Las señales están bien marcadas e incluso tenemos nuestros sofisticados sistemas de posicionamiento global (GPS) y nuestros «teléfonos inteligentes», pero nos movemos demasiado deprisa y estamos demasiado aislados en nuestros vehículos particulares como para ver con claridad los cambios evidentes a nuestro alrededor y por consiguiente ajustar nuestra visión.

---

3 Muchos de los pioneros del ministerio hispano también habían estado involucrados en las luchas por los derechos civiles, el «Movimiento por un Mundo Mejor», las organizaciones sindicales, la reforma migratoria y el movimiento de santuario.

4 CHAVEZ A., «Diversity: Barriers Blown Away» en *CHURCH Magazine* 24, n. 8 (2008).

1
Sin una visión, el pueblo perece

En su reciente encíclica *Caritas in Veritate* el Papa Benedicto XVI afirma que toda la Iglesia se encuentra en una encrucijada. Las nuevas complejidades y desafíos del siglo XXI —culminando en la crisis económica global— son los nuevos «signos de los tiempos» que deben ser interpretados a través del lente de nuestros valores católicos fundamentales. El Papa nos llama a una renovación cultural profunda sostenida por una esperanza confiada y atenuada por medio de una actitud realista[5]. Esta exhortación se identifica en particular con nuestros esfuerzos de promocionar la justicia social en el ministerio hispano. Al escuchar esta llamada, debemos «replantear nuestro viaje» proponiendo un nuevo curso de acción que afirme todas las experiencias positivas y refute todas las negativas que nos han desviado en nuestro camino. El Santo Padre nos asegura que sólo entonces la crisis podrá convertirse en «...*una oportunidad para el discernimiento, sobre la cual modelar una nueva visión para el futuro*»[6].

Una visión para el ministerio hispano en el siglo XXI debe ser realista, aunque lo suficientemente motivadora, para inspirar un compromiso renovado con la pastoral de conjunto. El término pastoral de conjunto, imbuido por una teología profunda, no sólo describe las dimensiones prácticas de un ministerio colaborativo —comunicación, consenso, planificación conjunta— sino también el espíritu de armonía entre diversos instrumentos que se complementan, en lugar de competir entre ellos, para lograr el bien común. La pastoral de conjunto nos llama a orar juntos y a compartir nuestros recursos. La comunión en la misión requiere una inversión sostenida de recursos espirituales, económicos, institucionales y humanos. Esto es ciertamente un desafío cuando tantas oficinas diocesanas de ministerio hispano se están cerrando, fusionándose con otros ministerios o haciendo mucho más cada vez con menos recursos.

Las cifras demográficas son bien claras; el futuro de la Iglesia Católica en los Estados Unidos está íntimamente relacionado con la manera como nuestra institución responda de manera eficaz a las necesidades espirituales, educativas y

---

5 BENEDICTO XVI, *Caritas in Veritate*, n. 21.
6 BENEDICTO XVI, *Caritas in Veritate*, n. 21, énfasis original.

sociales de los hispanos hoy en día[7]. Debemos, por consiguiente, ser más astutos y creativos. No lo podemos hacer todo. Sin embargo debemos establecer prioridades en nuestra agenda y hacer lo que nos corresponde con la esperanza de que nuestro entusiasmo por el futuro contagie a toda la Iglesia y a los nuevos protagonistas: profesionales, intelectuales, políticos, negociantes, un electorado activo, artistas, filántropos y particularmente nuestros jóvenes hispanos. Estos protagonistas son en su mayoría católicos pero no han sido parte de nuestro caminar hasta ahora. A menudo son abandonados o alienados dentro de la Iglesia pero aún así buscan sentido espiritual para sus vidas. Tienen pasión por la justicia social y quieren invertir en un futuro mejor para los hispanos y para todo el país.

2

Aprovechar las oportunidades al máximo

El establecer prioridades implica discernimiento. En nuestra búsqueda de estructuras de justicia social es esencial distinguir entre un problema social y un asunto particular. Aunque ciertamente están interrelacionados, no se podrá progresar en la lucha contra la pobreza, el racismo, el sexismo, la violencia o cualquier otro problema social sin discernir cuidadosamente los asuntos interrelacionados que estos problemas generan. Por ejemplo, la persistencia de la pobreza entre los niños hispanos se relaciona directamente con los asuntos específicos a los que se enfrentan: acceso limitado a una educación de calidad, violencia familiar, servicios de salud restringidos, etc. Sin embargo, después de un discernimiento cuidadoso de los problemas sociales y los asuntos particulares relacionados con ellos, establecer una lista de prioridades entre los asuntos que se pueden «ganar» dentro del ambiente político cambiante en el que vivimos puede ser aún más desafiante. Cuando se trata de asuntos políticos hay que saber cuál es el mejor momento, pues no hay aliados o enemigos permanentes. Como católicos, nuestros principios de acción social van más allá de la política y de ideologías particulares; sin embargo, nuestras estrategias exigen trabajar y negociar con los «poderes reinantes» en un momento dado sin comprometer la integridad tanto de los fines como de los medios de nuestra acción.

7   Un análisis de los cambios dramáticos en la población hispana se encuentra en THE PEW FORUM ON RELIGION AND PUBLIC LIFE, *Changing Faiths: Latinos and the Transformation of American Religion*, Pew Hispanic Center, Washington, D.C. 2007, http://pewforum.org/newassets/surveys/hispanic/hispanics-religion-07-final-mar08.pdf (página visitada el 4 de enero del 2010).

El electorado hispano en las últimas dos elecciones presidenciales han demostrado su creciente poder político. No es sorprendente que el Presidente Barack Obama haya nombrado más latinos para trabajar en su administración durante sus primeros cinco meses de su presidencia que cualquiera de sus predecesores, incluyendo nombramientos en altos cargos como el de Sonia Sotomayor a la Corte Suprema de Justicia y del teólogo Miguel H. Díaz como nuevo embajador de los Estados Unidos ante la Santa Sede. ¿Cuáles son las oportunidades y los desafíos de este momento histórico? ¿Cómo podemos aprovechar las oportunidades de este nuevo nivel de participación en el poder sin comprometer nuestros valores? Para mí, personalmente, esto ya no es un debate abstracto sino un examen de conciencia diario. A comienzos de febrero del 2009 sorpresivamente la administración del Presidente Obama me contactó para indagar sobre mi interés en servir como miembro del Consejo Asesor de Alianzas Religiosas y Comunitarias de la Casa Blanca. Después de consultar con mis propios consejeros espirituales, acepté servir como una manera de llevar las preocupaciones y los valores de la Iglesia Católica y las necesidades urgentes de las comunidades hispanas para hacerlas parte de la agenda de la nueva administración.

Desde entonces, he estado trabajando con otros 24 líderes de diversas tradiciones religiosas y culturales para aconsejar a la Casa Blanca sobre estrategias eficaces para que el gobierno colabore con comunidades de fe y organizaciones sin ánimo de lucro en las siguientes áreas: la restauración de la economía de nuestro país; la respuesta eficaz a las necesidades básicas de los pobres, especialmente mujeres y niños que se encuentran entre los más vulnerables en nuestra sociedad; la prevención de embarazos entre adolescentes y la reducción del número de abortos; la promoción de la paternidad responsable y de familias estables; y la promoción de un diálogo interreligioso en todo el mundo como medio para construir la paz y la cooperación global. Esto es ciertamente una agenda ambiciosa en la que debemos involucrarnos con lo mejor de nuestras capacidades y recursos.

Siguiendo el ejemplo de nuestros obispos[8], debemos trabajar con la nueva administración para implementar políticas sociales justas que respondan a las necesidades de los más vulnerables y débiles. Podemos trabajar juntos para sa-

---

8 En una carta de felicitación fechada el 4 de noviembre del 2008 dirigida al Presidente electo Barack Obama, el Cardenal Francis George de Chicago, presidente de la Conferencia Episcopal Estadounidense (USCCB, sigla en inglés), ofreció el apoyo y las oraciones de los obispos mientras que le desafió a proteger el aspecto central de la Doctrina Social Católica: la defensa y apoyo de la vida y dignidad de todo ser humano. Más recientemente, el 17 de septiembre del 2009, el Arzobispo José Gómez de San Antonio encabezó una delegación de obispos hispanos para una

nar las divisiones en nuestro país y en nuestro mundo buscando áreas de interés común en lugar de acrecentar polarizaciones. Sobre todo, debemos mantenernos unidos a nuestros obispos en la defensa y el apoyo de la vida y la dignidad de toda persona humana, desde la concepción hasta la muerte natural. Ellos han dado la pauta a seguir al oponerse enérgicamente a las posiciones de la Administración Obama con relación a la investigación con células madre y al aborto. Al mismo tiempo, han afirmado las posiciones de la administración que son coherentes con la Doctrina Social de la Iglesia y su enseñanza moral, como por ejemplo la prohibición del uso de la tortura, la terminación de la guerra en Irak de manera responsable, el cuidado del medio ambiente, el desarme nuclear, la solución de dos estados en Tierra Santa y muchas de las iniciativas incluidas en el Plan de Recuperación (*Recovery Act*) que beneficiarían directamente a los más pobres y vulnerables. La Conferencia de Obispos Católicos también se ha comprometido activamente a afirmar nuestra Doctrina Social Católica mientras que se intensifican los debates sobre la reforma del sistema de salud y la reforma migratoria. Si queremos llevar los principios de la Doctrina Social de la Iglesia a la mesa de toma de decisiones, es esencial que hagamos un discernimiento cuidadoso y aprovechemos al máximo las oportunidades que se presenten en los próximos años.

3

Discernimiento pastoral permanente

En el ministerio hispano el método *ver, juzgar y actuar* ha servido para movilizar a nuestra gente «de los asientos a los caminos»[9], a través de una acción social eficaz guiada por la luz del Evangelio y por nuestro «secreto escondido»[10]: el amplio número de documentos, encíclicas y cartas pastorales del Magisterio sobre la Doctrina Social de la Iglesia. A lo largo de varias décadas, hemos incor-

reunión con legisladores demócratas y republicanos sobre cuatro áreas de profunda preocupación: una política de inmigración quebrantada, la falta de acceso a educación de calidad, servicio médico adecuado y oportunidades económicas. Véase www.usccb.org para obtener más información actualizada sobre las posiciones de los obispos sobre diversos temas sociales.

9 NATIONAL CONFERENCE OF CATHOLIC BISHOPS, *Plan Pastoral Nacional para el Ministerio Hispano*, dimensión C, 79.

10 DEBERRI E.P., HUG J.E., con HENRIOT P.J. y SCHULTEIS M.J., *Catholic Social Teaching: Our Best Kept Secret*, cuarta edición revisada y expandida, Orbis Books, New York, NY 2003.

porado al método los siguientes pasos: *celebrar* nuestros logros y *evaluar* su impacto. El singular enfoque pedagógico del Instituto Fe y Vida también ha introducido la dimensión de «*ser*» al círculo hermenéutico para subrayar que la educación y la llamada a la justicia son intrínsecos a la naturaleza humana.

Más recientemente, la exhortación apostólica postsinodal *Ecclesia in America* y las declaraciones del Papa Benedicto xvi durante la v Conferencia General del Episcopado Latinoamericano y del Caribe en Aparecida, Brasil invitan a toda la Iglesia a contextualizar el discernimiento para la acción social dentro de la llamada al discipulado que brota del encuentro con Jesucristo, el Señor resucitado. Esto nos lleva a una conversión más profunda, una comunión más íntima y un compromiso valiente en solidaridad con aquellos que son pobres y los que sufren. El Espíritu Santo sigue guiando nuestros planes de acción social abriendo nuestros ojos para ver con los ojos de Jesús y para juzgar estas realidades con la mente de Cristo. Esto, por supuesto, no es nuevo para el ministerio hispano. Sin embargo, la suposición implícita de este elemento indispensable para un verdadero discernimiento puede que haya abierto las puertas a ideologías y métodos de análisis social que son incompatibles con el Evangelio. El error fundamental del materialismo marxista es solamente un ejemplo y quizás el más fácil de refutar. Los errores fatales del capitalismo, el reduccionismo y el relativismo de la postmodernidad son más cercanos a nuestra experiencia y por consiguiente más amenazadores.

Por lo tanto, la razón más importante para comenzar nuestro análisis de temas sociales con el momento llamado «creer» es porque hemos de tener en cuenta una nueva generación de latinos que nunca han recibido una catequesis sistemática sobre los elementos fundamentales de nuestra fe, ni han experimentado la riqueza de nuestra cultura católica. Nos corresponde como líderes en el ministerio hispano fundamentar explícitamente los procesos comunitarios y los métodos para discernir, planear e implementar la acción social en la dignidad ontológica de la persona humana (*ser*) y la llamada primordial a la santidad por la fe (*creer*). De esta manera podremos asegurar que los siguientes cinco momentos del discernimiento pastoral estarán arraigados en una comprensión integral y en la fidelidad al rico depósito de nuestra fe apostólica:

«*Ciclo de discernimiento pastoral*»

Junto con este método familiar de discernimiento tenemos que tener claridad sobre los principios fundamentales que deberán guiar las metas y estrategias de nuestra acción social. El resto de este ensayo delineará algunos de los temas centrales de la Doctrina Social de la Iglesia junto con unas cuantas sugerencias para la acción que son centrales para el ministerio hispano:

3.1. EL DERECHO A LA VIDA

Al fondo de la Doctrina Social de la Iglesia se halla un respeto profundo e inmutable por la vida. El Papa Benedicto XVI expresa este punto con extrema claridad al exhortar a los católicos a tener claras nuestras prioridades[11]. No podemos planear una agenda de justicia social pasando por alto o teniendo un conocimiento fragmentado de las enseñanzas de la Iglesia. Más bien, comenzamos nuestro discernimiento y planificamos nuestra acción social desde esta verdad fundamental para asegurarnos de que estamos salvaguardando fielmente la enseñanza sólida de la Iglesia sobre la dignidad de la vida humana. Esto incluye las enseñanzas contraculturales de la Iglesia sobre sexualidad y la santidad del matrimonio como la unión entre un hombre y una mujer.

Existe una gran desconexión, sin embargo, entre la claridad de las enseñanzas de la Iglesia y la actitud ambigua de muchos católicos sobre los métodos artificiales de control natal y el aborto. Entre los hispanos ésta es una preocupación creciente en cuanto que actitudes culturales hacia la vida sexual y ciertas conductas como el machismo hacen que el problema sea más complejo. Estadísti-

---

11 *Caritatis in Veritate*, n. 67.

cas recientes indican que aproximadamente el 53 por ciento de jóvenes latinas quedan embarazadas en algún momento entre los 15 y los 19 años, casi el doble del promedio nacional[12]. Más del 40 por ciento de esos embarazos no son planeados. La tasa de aborto entre mujeres hispanas, particularmente adolescentes, está creciendo y las latinas tienen más posibilidades de contraer enfermedades de transmisión sexual, incluyendo el SIDA. A menudo sus decisiones son fuertemente restringidas por esposos abusivos y parejas con quienes tienen una vida sexual activa, los cuales poco respetan su dignidad y su salud.

¿Cómo podemos responder a estos temas de vida o muerte en el lenguaje diario de los hispanos, especialmente cuando se trata de nuestros adolescentes y preadolescentes abrumados por mensajes sexuales en los medios de comunicación? Esto es particularmente nocivo en los medios de comunicación en español tales como la televisión, la radio, la música y el cine. La razón por la cual muchos programas de educación sexual que hacen énfasis «sólo en la abstinencia» no funcionan es porque no proporcionan a los adolescentes alternativas viables que sean bien comunicadas a las que ellos puedan responder positivamente. ¿Cómo podemos elaborar materiales educativos que enseñen la teología católica sobre el cuerpo de manera accesible a personas que no son expertas en teología? ¿Cómo hacemos para que la educación sexual sea relevante a la cultura de nuestro pueblo aunque reteniendo su carácter contracultural? ¿Cómo podemos reducir el número de abortos valiéndonos de estructuras de participación política y al mismo tiempo mantenernos fieles a la enseñanza de la Iglesia?[13]

3.2. EL SISTEMA ECONÓMICO

Los sistemas sociales son un elemento necesario para nuestra convivencia como seres humanos. Los sistemas políticos, económicos, educativos y otros sistemas sociales pueden traer orden y estabilidad a la sociedad. Sin embargo, la Doctrina Social de la Iglesia nos recuerda que no existe un sistema perfecto. Los cristianos y las personas de buena voluntad deben trabajar juntos para asegurarse de que los sistemas sean justos y respondan a las necesidades de todos los seres humanos sin discriminación alguna. El principio de subsidiariedad garantiza que los sistemas nunca deben crecer demasiado porque esto inevitablemente con-

---

12 BASU M., «Survey delves into high birth rate for young Latinas» en *CCNHealth.com*, 19 de mayo del 2009, http://www.cnn.com/2009/HEALTH/05/19/latinas.pregnancy.rate/index.html (página visitada el 4 de enero del 2010).

13 Véase JUAN PABLO II, *Evangelium Vitae*, n. 73.

duce a respuestas inadecuadas a las «necesidades reales» de la gente. Se responde mejor a las necesidades de los seres humanos por medio de sistemas funcionado en su expresión más simple.

Una gran preocupación en la mente de muchas personas durante estos días es la crisis económica. La corrupción reinante y la ambición escandalosa del sistema económico global han salido a la luz del día. El obispo Michael Pfeifer de San Angelo, Texas expresó con claridad en un artículo reciente que: «No se trata sólo de que los balances bancarios están en rojo; no se trata sólo de que el sistema económico global se haya tambaleando; nuestro equilibrio religioso y nuestra dirección moral también se han salido de control»[14]. Nos encontramos en un estado de pánico al ver cómo se nos escapan los recursos materiales que nos daban seguridad. Millones de personas han perdido sus trabajos, sus casas, sus ahorros y, según advierten los expertos, esto es sólo el principio.

¿Cómo afecta esto al ministerio hispano? Sin duda alguna, la tasa de pobreza entre los hispanos, calculada en el 23.2 por ciento, continuará creciendo especialmente entre las mujeres, los niños y los ancianos. En diciembre del 2009 el Departamento de Trabajo de los Estados Unidos reportó que la tasa de desempleo en el país se mantenía en 10 por ciento, pero para los hispanos era del 12.9 por ciento[15]. Evidentemente esto no incluye el gran número de jornaleros y trabajadores indocumentados que ya no pueden encontrar trabajo. Con el desempleo viene la pérdida de beneficios tales como los seguros de salud y las casas en donde viven nuestras familias, los cuales son importantes para lograr el «sueño americano». El 30.7 por ciento de los hispanos en los Estados Unidos no tienen seguro médico[16]. Aunque los reportes estadísticos nacionales relacionados con embargos de vivienda no están especificados según la etnicidad o la raza, existe amplia evidencia de que los propietarios de vivienda hispanos se han visto desproporcionadamente afectados por la ola reciente de embargos, especialmente en California, Nevada y Florida. El Centro de Investigaciones Pew descubrió que casi uno de cada 10 hispanos (9 por ciento) que están pagando sus vivien-

---

14 BISHOP MICHAEL PFEIFER, OMI, «Economic Crisis Fueled by Greed» en *West Texas Angelus*, 39, n. 5 (2009) 17, http://www.talleypress.com/angelus/wta0509.pdf (página visitada el 8 de enero del 2010).

15 U.S. DEPARTMENT OF LABOR, «The Employment Situation — December 2009», nota de prensa, 8 de enero del 2010, http://www.bls.gov/news.release/pdf/empsit.pdf (página visitada el 8 de enero del 2010).

16 U.S. CENSUS BUREAU, «Income, Poverty, and Health Insurance Coverage in the United States: 2008», reporte publicado en septiembre del 2009, http://www.census.gov/prod/2009pubs/p60-236.pdf (página visitada el 8 de enero del 2010).

das dicen que no han hecho un pago mensual de sus hipotecas en el último año y el 3 por ciento ha recibido notificaciones de embargo. Tristemente, más de un tercio de los latinos (36 por ciento) que están pagando sus viviendas temen que probablemente se verán involucrados en un proceso de embargo en los próximos doce meses[17].

Nuestra agenda para la acción social en el área de la economía debe responder a las preguntas profundas que propusieron los obispos de los Estados Unidos en su profética carta pastoral *Justicia económica para todos:*

> Cualquier perspectiva humana, moral y cristiana sobre la vida económica necesariamente se configura a partir de tres preguntas: ¿Qué hace la economía *por* el pueblo? ¿Cómo afecta la economía *al* pueblo? y ¿Cómo *participa* el pueblo en ella?[18].

Éstas no son preguntas fáciles de responder, especialmente sabiendo que los sistemas económicos de nuestro tiempo están inseparablemente unidos a otros sistemas sociales poderosos, principalmente de carácter político, los cuales proporcionan privilegios a algunos grupos e individuos mientras que otros son excluidos.

3.3. **POBREZA Y EDUCACIÓN**

Aunque es difícil determinar los datos con exactitud, las tasas de deserción escolar entre los jóvenes hispanos son consistentemente más altas que las de los jóvenes blancos y en muchos estados esta tasa es el doble. Esto tiene implicaciones serias cuando se habla de educación superior. Un informe de actualización del Censo del 2000 indica que sólo un 13 por ciento de los hispanos tienen un título profesional universitario, comparado con un 19 por ciento de los afroamericanos y 32 por ciento de los blancos. Incluso nuestro sistema educativo católico ha fracasado en el intento de proveer acceso a una educación de calidad a los latinos. En la actualidad sólo un 3 por ciento de los niños latinos en edad escolar va a escuelas católicas en los Estados Unidos[19]. Esto es particularmente

17 KOCHHAR R., GONZÁLEZ-BARRERA A., y DOCKTERMAN D., «Through Boom and Bust: Minorities, Immigrants and Homeownership» en *Pew Research Center Publications*, 13 de mayo del 2009, recurso electrónico, http://pewresearch.org/pubs/1220/home-ownership-trends-blacks-hispanics (página visitada el 8 de enero del 2010).

18 NATIONAL CONFERENCE OF CATHOLIC BISHOPS, *Justicia económica para todos: carta pastoral sobre la enseñanza social católica y la economía de los E.U.A.*, USCC, Washington, D.C. 1987 (publicada en inglés en 1986), n. 1.

19 Cfr. EL EQUIPO DE TRABAJO DE LA UNIVERSIDAD DE NOTRE DAME RESPECTO A LA PARTICIPACIÓN DE LOS NIÑOS Y FAMILIAS LATINAS EN ESCUELA CATÓLICAS, *Para alentar el espíritu de una nación:*

alarmante porque los latinos ya constituyen la mayoría de los católicos menores de 18 años en los Estados Unidos y tienen más probabilidades de permanecer católicos que los jóvenes blancos[20].

Las escuelas católicas educan estudiantes de familias de bajos ingresos, especialmente latinos, de manera mucho más eficaz que las escuelas públicas. Los estudiantes hispanos en escuelas secundarias católicas tienen un 42 por ciento más de oportunidades de graduarse, y dos veces y media más probabilidades de ir a la universidad que los estudiantes hispanos en las escuelas públicas[21]. Las escuelas católicas siguen siendo el medio más eficaz de transmitir la fe de la Iglesia en los Estados Unidos tal como lo demuestran muchos estudios. A pesar de que ésta parece ser una propuesta atractiva para las familias latinas, el porcentaje de niños hispanos en escuelas católicas es excesivamente bajo como ya vimos. Es esencial preguntarse por qué el número de niños hispanos en nuestras escuelas católicas no es más alto. Un argumento frecuente es que la educación católica es demasiado costosa para las familias latinas, quienes están desproporcionalmente representadas entre los trabajadores pobres y no la pueden pagar. Sin embargo, trabajos investigativos parecen indicar que el dinero no es la única barrera[22]. Así que debemos preguntarnos: ¿cuáles son las barreras sistémicas y las razones culturales que no permiten una mayor presencia de niños latinos en nuestras escuelas católicas?

El informe del Equipo de Trabajo de la Universidad de Notre Dame respecto a la participación de los niños y familias latinas en escuelas católicas propone una estrategia nacional para fomentar participación y un mayor sentido de pertenencia en las escuelas católicas entre los latinos en toda la nación. El informe es una invitación a hacer las escuelas católicas más acogedoras y accesibles para los niños y las familias hispanas y a mejorar su capacidad para servir eficientemente a los niños latinos. El Equipo de Trabajo ha propuesto la mera ambiciosa, aunque realista en cierta manera, de doblar el porcentaje de niños hispanos matriculados en escuelas católicas para el año 2020. A la luz del crecimiento pobla-

---

familias latinas, escuelas católicas y oportunidades educativas, University of Notre Dame, 12 de diciembre del 2009, http://catholicschooladvantage.nd.edu/assets/19177/nd_ltf_report_final_spanish_12.2.pdf (página visitada el 8 de enero del 2010).

20 Véase el ensayo de Ken Johnson-Mondragón sobre el ministerio hispano y la pastoral juvenil hispana en este libro.

21 Cfr. EL EQUIPO DE TRABAJO DE LA UNIVERSIDAD DE NOTRE DAME RESPECTO A LA PARTICIPACIÓN DE LOS NIÑOS Y FAMILIAS LATINAS EN ESCUELA CATÓLICAS, *Para alentar el espíritu de una nación*.

22 Cfr. EL EQUIPO DE TRABAJO DE LA UNIVERSIDAD DE NOTRE DAME RESPECTO A LA PARTICIPACIÓN DE LOS NIÑOS Y FAMILIAS LATINAS EN ESCUELA CATÓLICAS, *Para alentar el espíritu de una nación*.

cional proyectado, esto significa que habrá que aumentar el número de niños hispanos en escuelas católicas de 290.000 en la actualidad a más de 1 millón para el año 2020[23]. Los líderes comprometidos con el ministerio hispano debemos dar prioridad a este tema en nuestra agenda de justicia social. Esto verdaderamente tendrá un impacto profundo en la comunidad hispana de los Estados Unidos.

3.4. LA OPCIÓN POR LOS POBRES: CARIDAD Y JUSTICIA

La opción preferencial por personas que son pobres es una de las piedras angulares de la Doctrina Social de la Iglesia y una convicción central para el ministerio hispano. La fuerza de una sociedad se mide según la manera ésta trata a sus miembros más vulnerables. La opción de la Iglesia por los pobres no pretende crear divisiones entre las clases sociales; más bien, se basa en el mandato de las Sagradas Escrituras de preguntar siempre cómo las políticas sociales afectan a los más pobres entre los hijos de Dios. Toda persona es preciosa ante Dios y merece justa participación en los bienes del mundo. La opción preferencial de la Iglesia por los pobres va más allá de las fronteras nacionales y requiere una solidaridad global para acabar con el hambre y la pobreza en el mundo, causadas por el abuso de los recursos naturales y un desarrollo irresponsable.

¿Qué significa la opción por los pobres hoy en día cuando el número de personas que viven en la pobreza aumenta dramáticamente en este país y en todo el mundo? Ciertamente significa una mayor generosidad en nuestras ofrendas y el aumento de los servicios caritativos y los esfuerzos de asistencia por parte de la Iglesia. Esto incluye el fortalecimiento y la expansión de las redes de seguridad para personas que son pobres con el fin de proporcionar servicios tales como vivienda transicional para el número ascendente de personas sin hogar, expansión del cuidado de salud para los niños, ofrecer alimentación que responda a las necesidades nutricionales de las familias a través de programas escolares y otros programas para proveer servicios directos y recursos a los que las personas puedan acceder de manera eficaz: de persona a persona, una familia a la vez, un niño o una niña la vez.

La Doctrina Social Católica enseña claramente que también debemos esforzarnos por discernir las raíces de la pobreza y trabajar con valentía hacia un cambio sistémico junto con las personas que son pobres de manera que verda-

---

23 Cfr. EL EQUIPO DE TRABAJO DE LA UNIVERSIDAD DE NOTRE DAME RESPECTO A LA PARTICIPACIÓN DE LOS NIÑOS Y FAMILIAS LATINAS EN ESCUELA CATÓLICAS, *Para alentar el espíritu de una nación.*

deramente les favorezca. Dada la realidad actual como resultado del deterioro del sistema económico, nuestra agenda para la acción social y la defensa de los intereses de los más pobres debe incluir enfoques creativos para confrontar las raíces de la pobreza, especialmente tratando de entender la relación entre los procesos de educación formal y las oportunidades económicas equitativas. Esta agenda debe incluir: inversión continua en nuestras ciudades, especialmente en los barrios marginados, a través de fondos para el desarrollo comunitario; integridad fiscal en todos los niveles del gobierno y en las corporaciones públicas; acceso a préstamos y finca raíz; acceso a educación temprana y continuada, especialmente por medio de programas bilingües y biculturales; e, idealmente, educación católica que las familias pobres puedan costear. Esto puede ocurrir por medio de iniciativas tales como las de la aprobación de programas de cupones para la educación (*vouchers*, en inglés) que proporcionarían a los padres opciones viables para la educación de sus hijos. Una educación accesible y asequible también se debe considerar como un derecho básico para toda persona en el competitivo mercado de trabajo actual. Parte de la ecuación para el éxito de cualquier programa de justicia social, especialmente entre los hispanos, tiene que ser la existencia de programas de capacitación laboral que sean eficaces y el cuidado de niños para los padres de familia solteros.

3.5. INMIGRACIÓN, RACISMO Y TRABAJO

La Iglesia Católica cuenta con una larga tradición de defender el derecho fundamental a formas de trabajo que conduzcan a la realización personal en medio de condiciones seguras y que respeten la dignidad de la persona humana. Los trabajadores tienen el derecho a un salario justo y a pertenecer a sindicatos[24]. En general, la Iglesia defiende los derechos de las personas a tener propiedad privada y a ejercer libre iniciativa económica. Estos derechos, sin embargo, se deben balancear con un entendimiento apropiado de los principios relacionados con la justicia, el bien común y una administración cuidadosa de la creación de Dios. Los sistemas económicos existen para servir a la gente y no al contrario. Estas enseñanzas son importantes para los trabajadores hispanos en los Estados Unidos, especialmente porque la mayoría trabajan en el sector obrero y el de servicios generales. El paso de leyes laborales justas y el derecho a pertenecer a sindicatos son preocupaciones esenciales para los trabajadores hispanos.

---

24 LEÓN XIII, *Rerum Novarum*, n. 49.

Para los hispanos, los temas relacionados con los derechos de los trabajadores están vinculados en gran medida a las políticas de inmigración. Desafortunadamente, muchas de estas políticas son reflejo de males intrínsecos como el racismo que aún persisten en el tejido social de los Estados Unidos y de los países latinoamericanos de donde la mayoría de los trabajadores inmigrantes provienen. A pesar de que la migración es motivada principalmente por dinámicas económicas, los gobiernos se han rehusado consistentemente a tener una conversación seria sobre este asunto cuando negocian tratados y acuerdos comerciales como el Tratado de Libre Comercio de América del Norte (NAFTA, sigla en inglés). En gran parte, estos pactos abren las puertas al movimiento sin restricciones de capital, materiales y productos más allá de las fronteras nacionales. Las corporaciones multinacionales ahora tienen más poder político que naciones enteras y constantemente se reinventan a través de entidades subsidiarias en países donde la gente es desesperadamente pobre y está dispuesta a trabajar por salarios miserables. Dichas corporaciones operan fuera de las leyes del estado debilitando su poder político y eventualmente erosionando todos los aspectos de sus sociedades civiles. Éste es el nuevo colonialismo que continúa privando de sus productos básicos a los países en desarrollo al igual que de sus ciudadanos más brillantes y decididos[25]. Este «Nuevo Orden Mundial», recientemente cuestionado por el Papa Benedicto XVI, impone pactos legalmente vinculantes entre naciones cuyas estructuras gubernamentales son débiles para asegurar el movimiento de capital y de productos y al mismo tiempo restringir el movimiento de trabajadores de esos países empobrecidos. Cuando el dinero y las cosas materiales tienen más derechos que las personas humanas podemos decir verdaderamente que «¡esto no es católico!»

Estos acuerdos de libre comercio, las exenciones de impuestos a las corporaciones y las políticas económicas han generado una gran riqueza que beneficia a menos de un cuarto de la población mundial. Los otros tres cuartos de la población mundial, sin embargo, sufren por causa de los «derechos» económicos ilimitados de las corporaciones, por un lado, y los derechos severamente restringidos de los trabajadores que se ven forzados a ser parte de migraciones masivas, por el otro. Por cada persona que se beneficia del orden económico y político actual, miles y miles se ven forzadas a elegir entre la pobreza en sus patrias o la posibilidad de una mejor vida para sí mismas y sus familias en otro lugar. La migración es un derecho fundamental y la Doctrina Social Católica así lo afirma.

25 *Caritatis in Veritate*, n. 32-33.

A través de su reciente carta pastoral *Juntos en el Camino de la Esperanza: Ya No Somos Extranjeros*[26] y de la campaña *Justicia para los Inmigrantes*[27], los obispos de los Estados Unidos han buscado valerosamente defender los derechos humanos básicos de los migrantes y han llamado a los católicos a acoger activamente al «extranjero entre nosotros» al igual que a trabajar por una reforma migratoria integral. Recientemente los obispos ofrecieron una serie de soluciones prácticas a la administración del Presidente Barack Obama, presentando argumentos morales convincentes para sacar de las sombras a más o menos 12 millones de inmigrantes indocumentados en los Estados Unidos. Obispos hispanos y no hispanos están dialogando con el Congreso para reparar nuestro deteriorado sistema migratorio y denunciar la creciente ola de retórica deshumanizadora que demoniza a los inmigrantes. La visión católica para una reforma migratoria humanitaria no sólo se fundamenta en argumentos legales y morales. La Iglesia también se vale de argumentos prácticos. Durante las últimas dos décadas el gobierno federal ha asignado cerca de diez mil millones de dólares para reforzar la seguridad a lo largo de la frontera entre los Estados Unidos y México. La respuesta de los inmigrantes ha sido encontrar nuevas rutas de entrada a los Estados Unidos, aunque más peligrosas. No hay muro que sea lo suficientemente alto como para detener los sueños de quienes buscan una vida mejor.

Detener el motor socioeconómico de la migración y las consecuencias negativas para las personas reales cuyas vidas son afectadas negativamente por causa de políticas imperfectas exigen más que palabras duras por parte de los políticos que se acusan unos a otros o de prácticas pendencieras por parte de agentes del orden público a nivel local. Se requiere una respuesta organizada que ponga en evidencia las alternativas falsas. Podemos proteger nuestras fronteras y al mismo tiempo defender la dignidad humana. Una reforma migratoria integral debe incluir un camino para obtener la ciudadanía, protecciones apropiadas para los trabajadores y políticas que eviten que las familias se separen. No es una amnistía ni un regalo; es una solución sensata a un sistema en el que empresarios y consumidores estadounidenses ya se benefician del trabajo de trabajadores indocumentados mientras que al mismo tiempo millones de inmigrantes no gozan de protección contra la explotación laboral. La inhabilidad

26 UNITED STATES CONFERENCE OF CATHOLIC BISHOPS, *Juntos en el camino de la esperanza, ya no somos extranjeros: carta pastoral de los obispos católicos de los Estados Unidos y México sobre la migración*, USCCB, Washington, D.C. 2003, http://www.usccb.org/mrs/strangersp.shtml.

27 http://www.justiceforimmigrants.org/

del Congreso de pasar una reforma migratoria ha forzado a los distintos gobiernos estatales a adoptar una mezcla extraña de normas punitivas a nivel local. El Consejo Nacional de la Raza y el Instituto Urbano (*Urban Institute*) reportaron que dos tercios de los niños separados de sus padres durante las redadas de inmigración son ciudadanos de los Estados Unidos. Esto es vergonzoso. Si queremos pasar de las soluciones simplistas y de la retórica de odio que están marcando nuestro polarizado debate sobre inmigración, tenemos que tener conversaciones más substanciales y un liderazgo hispano más activo tanto en la Iglesia como en la sociedad.

Quienes trabajamos en el ministerio hispano tenemos que apoyar a nuestros obispos a medida que ellos hacen oír sus voces y abogan a favor de este tema vital. Tenemos una oportunidad, quizás antes de lo que pensábamos posible, para ejercer influencia en la aprobación de leyes que comiencen a reformar el sistema migratorio actual, el cual está deteriorado y es racista. Como constructores de puentes, más importante aún es la tarea de «re-articular» el discurso polarizador sobre una reforma migratoria en nuestro país pasando del debate al diálogo, del problema a la oportunidad, de los síntomas a las causas y de la acción unilateral a una colaboración renovada y multinacional. No podemos hacer esto solos o exclusivamente a nivel parroquial; debemos darle vida nueva a nuestras redes nacionales e internacionales. La migración es un fenómeno global que exige solidaridad global. El Cardenal Óscar Andrés Rodríguez Madariaga de Honduras nos recuerda: «…la manera principal de de globalizar la solidaridad es globalizar el respeto por la vida… todas las vidas»[28].

Como mínimo, el liderazgo en el ministerio hispano debe trabajar unido para abogar por lo siguiente:

1) Medidas para asegurar que los inmigrantes recién llegados se integren, se eduquen, se mantengan con salud, conozcan y respeten la ley, tengan permiso para conducir y seguro de automóvil, tengan buen acceso a créditos, a servicios bancarios y la educación;

2) Mejor manejo de la administración fronteriza para proteger a las personas más afectadas por la violencia y el tráfico de drogas en lugar de construir muros costosos e ineficaces;

---

28 RODRÍGUEZ MADARIAGA O.A., «The Catholic Church and the Globalization of Solidarity» en *Caritas.org*, July 7, 2003, http://www.caritas.org/activities/economic_justice/the_catholic_church_and_the_globalization_of_solidarity.html (página visitada el 8 de enero del 2010).

3) Cooperación bilateral sobre temas económicos, laborales, de salud, de educación, sociales, del medio ambiente y de infraestructura;

4) Un programa de trabajadores temporales que se centre en el bienestar de los trabajadores y sea supervisado por ellos mismos, sus empleadores y organizaciones independientes de derechos humanos u organizaciones no gubernamentales;

5) Un proceso razonable para que aquellos inmigrantes que quieran ser parte de la sociedad estadounidense puedan obtener la ciudadanía;

6) Protección y asistencia para los más vulnerables: mujeres, niños, ancianos y quienes están enfermos o tienen limitaciones físicas; y,

7) Leyes y políticas que fortalezcan y reúnan a las familias inmigrantes.

Finalmente, tenemos que trabajar juntos para hacer que la universidad sea posible para los jóvenes inmigrantes latinos que, sin tener culpa alguna, carecen de la documentación adecuada para acceder a oportunidades de educación superior. Éste es el momento en el que el paso de actos legislativos como el DREAM Act se puede hacer realidad.

4

Conclusión

Este ensayo es un llamado a los líderes en el ministerio hispano a unir fuerzas para proponer una visión renovada que responda colaborativamente a los signos críticos de nuestro tiempo con creatividad y a trabajar en conjunto con los nuevos protagonistas en búsqueda de justicia. Las reflexiones anteriores son sugerencias que afirman el método de discernimiento pastoral *ver, juzgar* y *actuar,* con énfasis en *creer.* Lo que es más urgente, este ensayo ha identificado elementos claves dentro de una agenda de justicia social para un plan nacional unificado de acción que tenga en cuenta la gran gama de asuntos que afectan nuestras vidas. Entre estos asuntos tenemos: una sexualidad responsable y la defensa de la santidad del matrimonio y la familia; justicia económica que nace de una opción preferencial por los pobres; acceso equitativo a la educación y especialmente una educación católica; y un resumen de lo que una reforma migratoria integral deberá incluir para beneficiar realmente a los trabajadores hispanos. Más importante aún, este ensayo es un llamado a todos los líderes en el ministerio hispano a que renovemos nuestro compromiso a ser instrumentos de paz.

Hemos experimentado la Buena Nueva del Evangelio y hemos preservado las bendiciones de nuestros pioneros en el ministerio hispano. Por medio de sus luchas buscando justicia en nuestra sociedad y un lugar de pertenencia en la Iglesia, creemos que tenemos un don singular de liderazgo para ofrecer a la comunidad mundial, especialmente a los pobres y los que sufren. Nos regocijamos en nuestra cultura y en nuestra fe católica, la cual fue proclamada por primera vez en este hemisferio por nuestros antepasados. Buscamos compartir esta fe respondiendo generosamente a la llamada de la Nueva Evangelización dirigida especialmente a las personas que están desheredadas, sin educación, enfermas y sufrientes y a todos los que desean conocer a Jesús. En nuestras redes nacionales hemos prometido crecer en la fe y el conocimiento. Trabajamos para comunicar nueva vida en esas organizaciones nacionales a través de un plan de acción común impulsado por una visión que se hace más clara cada vez que nos reunimos para escuchar y para hablar según nos guía el Espíritu Santo. Nos acompañamos unos a otros a medida que aprendemos a confiar de nuevo, nos arriesgamos de nuevo, avistamos sin temor nuevos sueños para nuestro mundo de hoy y confiadamente reclamamos la promesa de nuestro Dios amoroso: «Porque yo sé muy bien lo que haré por ustedes; les quiero dar… un porvenir lleno de esperanza» (Jr 29,11).

El ministerio hispano y la formación para el liderazgo

HOSFFMAN OSPINO *y* ELSIE MIRANDA

Nosotros, como pueblo hispano, nos comprometemos a participar en la planificación, toma de decisiones y posiciones de responsabilidad en la Iglesia a todos los niveles (nacional, regional, diocesano, parroquial)[1].

Los católicos hispanos en los Estados Unidos durante varias décadas se han comprometido a establecer estructuras sólidas de liderazgo ministerial. Dicho compromiso nace de la convicción de que las voces y las perspectivas latinas son parte integral de la vida de la Iglesia en los Estados Unidos, especialmente en el contexto culturalmente diverso en el que vivimos y celebramos nuestra fe. Al comenzar la segunda década del siglo XXI, en un momento en el que los católicos hispanos constituimos el 40 por ciento de la población católica estadounidense, este compromiso adquiere vida nueva. Como teólogos que hemos tenido el privilegio de participar en varias conversaciones sobre el ministerio hispano, nuestra convicción es que se necesita reflexionar con gran claridad sobre la formación para el liderazgo pastoral para así fortalecer el trabajo de evangelización entre los latinos en los Estados Unidos. A esta tarea nos dedicamos en las siguientes páginas.

En este ensayo exploramos el presente y el futuro de la formación para el liderazgo pastoral en el ministerio hispano. Esta reflexión está basada en nuestra experiencia personal, el estudio de esta realidad dentro de la vida de la Iglesia y en gran parte en las ideas valiosas que emergieron durante el Simposio Nacional sobre el Presente y Futuro del Ministerio Católico Hispano en los Estados Unidos celebrado en Boston College en el año 2009. Teniendo en cuenta que existe una gran abundancia de recursos en esta área, decidimos limitar nuestro análisis a aquellos procesos y conversaciones claves que tuvieron lugar durante la primera década del siglo XXI, teniendo como perspectiva el futuro inmediato. Sin embargo, es necesario notar que cualquier reflexión sobre el ministerio hispano tiene que hacer honor a la memoria histórica, es decir las ideas, los movimientos y los logros de los católicos latinos en los Estados Unidos durante las décadas anteriores. Estos eventos sin lugar a duda permitieron el crecimiento de las distintas estructuras sobre las cuales se sostiene el ministerio hispano hoy en día. A pesar de que ya existen trabajos que nos acercan a distintos aspectos de

---

1 *Voces Proféticas: El Documento del Proceso del III Encuentro Nacional Hispano de Pastoral*, n. 40, en UNITED STATES CONFERENCE OF CATHOLIC BISHOPS, *Ministerio Hispano: Tres Documentos Importantes*, USCCB, Washington, D.C. 1995, 43.

esta memoria histórica[2], hacemos eco a la llamada de varios líderes hispanos para que esta tradición siga siendo interpretada y compartida[3].

Los Encuentros Nacionales Hispanos de Pastoral (1972, 1977, 1985) han sido quizás los espacios más importantes en la historia del catolicismo estadounidense en los cuales los líderes católicos hispanos articularon sus ideas sobre la importancia de la presencia hispana en la vida de la Iglesia en los Estados Unidos y ofrecieron su visión sobre la clase de liderazgo que se necesita para afirmar dicha presencia[4]. Las voces proféticas y comunitarias de los líderes latinos han llamado a reflexionar sobre lo que significa ser un líder pastoral en una Iglesia en la cual los hispanos estamos presentes en grandes números, muchas veces como mayoría numérica todavía percibida como «minoría» sociopolítica, y así proponer estrategias apropiadas para formar líderes que puedan responder a las necesidades espirituales y a las expectativas de la Iglesia *aquí* y *ahora*. Los ecos de esas voces llegan a nosotros por medio de las notas tomadas durante los Encuentros, varios simposios, convocaciones de líderes, reuniones sobre el ministerio hispano y declaraciones de la Conferencia de Obispos Católicos de Estados Unidos (USCCB, sigla en inglés) sobre la experiencia católica hispana[5].

2 Cfr. DOLAN J.P. Y FIGUEROA-DECK A. (eds.), *Hispanic Catholic Culture in the U.S.: Issues and Concerns*, University of Notre Dame Press, Notre Dame, IN 1994; MATOVINA T. Y POYO G.E. (eds.), *Presente!: U.S. Latino Catholics from Colonial Origins to the Present*, Orbis Books, Maryknoll, NY 2000; SANDOVAL M., *On the Move: A History of the Hispanic Church in the United States*, segunda edición revisada, Orbis Books, Maryknoll, NY 2006.

3 Los miembros del grupo de estudio que reflexionaron sobre la relación entre el ministerio hispano y la formación para el liderazgo durante el simposio en Boston College invitaron a elaborar más recursos e iniciativas investigativas que exploren las contribuciones de los líderes latinos católicos durante el siglo XX. Es urgente que las nuevas generaciones de líderes hispanos y de otras tradiciones culturales consideren como objeto de estudio y fuente de inspiración las experiencias de los muchos católicos latinos y nuestros movimientos, los cuales establecieron mejores estructuras para el liderazgo pastoral en la Iglesia y en el resto de la sociedad. La memoria histórica de los católicos latinos en los Estados Unidos debe estar disponible a todas las personas trabajando como agentes pastorales en la Iglesia y debe ser nombrada como una contribución central a la experiencia histórica del catolicismo estadounidense.

4 Véase NATIONAL CONFERENCE OF CATHOLIC BISHOPS, *Conclusiones: Primer Encuentro Nacional Hispano de Pastoral*, USCC, Washington, D.C. 1972; GASTÓN M.L. (ed.), *Proceedings of the II Encuentro Nacional Hispano de Pastoral*, NATIONAL CONFERENCE OF CATHOLIC BISHOPS, SECRETARIADO PARA ASUNTOS HISPANOS, USCC, Washington, D.C. 1978; *Voces Proféticas: El Documento del Proceso del III Encuentro Nacional Hispano de Pastoral*.

5 Es urgente que estos documentos se compilen sistemáticamente, se organicen y se pongan a disposición de las nuevas generaciones de líderes en la Iglesia, especialmente en formato electrónico.

Los católicos hispanos le dimos la bienvenida al siglo XXI con esperanza renovada aunque conscientes de los muchos retos que la Iglesia enfrenta hoy en día en los Estados Unidos. Dentro de estos retos resaltamos la creciente diversidad en las comunidades parroquiales y diocesanas, la «hispanización» de grandes regiones geográficas y eclesiásticas alrededor del país, el número elevado de sacerdotes y religiosos ancianos, la carencia de vocaciones para reemplazarles, el número limitado de sacerdotes preparados adecuadamente para trabajar con los católicos hispanos y un proceso constante de reurbanización del catolicismo. Aún más, en el nuevo siglo otros dos retos han llevado a los católicos estadounidenses a reconsiderar ciertas actitudes y prácticas: los escándalos relacionados con el abuso sexual de niños en la Iglesia y la reciente recesión económica. Ambas realidades han provocado grandes procesos de reorganización institucional y redistribución de recursos en la Iglesia. Conscientes de todos los retos anteriores y el impacto de estos en el ministerio hispano, los líderes pastorales latinos estamos comprometidos a ser parte de las iniciativas colaborativas que conduzcan a una respuesta adecuada. Creemos que este siglo es un momento privilegiado para que los católicos hispanos sigamos compartiendo nuestros dones pastorales, nuestra imaginación y nuestra participación plena con el resto de la Iglesia y asumir creativamente el liderazgo en la siguiente fase de la historia de la experiencia católica estadounidense.

En la década anterior, líderes pastorales latinos y de otras tradiciones culturales nos reunimos en distintas ocasiones para ser parte de varias conversaciones sobre el trabajo pastoral y la formación para el liderazgo pastoral en el contexto del ministerio hispano. Estas reuniones destacaron muchas de las preocupaciones y esperanzas que ya se habían identificado en la segunda parte del siglo XX. Al mismo tiempo, se dieron pasos hacia adelante en el proceso de crear una mayor conciencia a nivel nacional sobre estas áreas. Ninguna conversación contemporánea sobre la vida de la Iglesia en este país tendrá suficiente credibilidad si ignora la realidad del catolicismo hispano estadounidense. Casi toda conversación sobre el ministerio eclesial laico, pastoral juvenil, reconfiguración de parroquias, nombramientos episcopales, formación para el sacerdocio y el diaconado, educación teológica, etc., ha requerido reflexión sobre la creciente presencia de los católicos hispanos en la Iglesia en los Estados Unidos y los asuntos relacionados con dicha presencia. Sin embargo, para responder adecuadamente a la relación entre el ministerio hispano y la formación para el liderazgo pastoral en la Iglesia, *todos* los líderes pastorales tenemos que comprometernos honestamente a adoptar prácticas de inclusión y colaboración. Sabiendo que ésta es verdaderamente una tarea vasta y compleja, proponemos enfocarnos en dos áreas centrales: el liderazgo efectivo y las estructuras de apoyo para el ministerio hispano y la formación para el liderazgo.

1

Liderazgo efectivo

La efectividad de las iniciativas pastorales en las comunidades hispanas depende y dependerá en gran parte de la calidad de los líderes que las adelanten. Es importante aclarar que cuando se habla de liderazgo en el ministerio hispano no nos referimos exclusivamente al trabajo pastoral de quienes son latinos ni sólo a las preocupaciones de los católicos de cultura latina. La complejidad de la experiencia católica en los Estados Unidos es ante todo una invitación a los líderes de todas las etnicidades y tradiciones culturales a servir y trabajar en favor de las necesidades de una población diversa en general y a participar en la riqueza de la experiencia católica hispana en particular.

1.1. LA VISIÓN

En el año 2002 los obispos católicos de los Estados Unidos presentaron su declaración pastoral *Encuentro y Misión* a todos los católicos del país. El documento fue escrito para afirmar «especialmente aquellos esfuerzos pastorales en el ministerio hispano que fomentan el objetivo general y las dimensiones específicas del Plan Pastoral Nacional para el Ministerio Hispano» y proveer «principios pastorales básicos, prioridades, y acciones sugeridas para continuar esfuerzos en el ministerio hispano a la vez que fortalece la unidad de la Iglesia en Estados Unidos»[6]. *Encuentro y Misión* es un marco pastoral que ofrece una visión convincente para el ministerio católico en el nuevo siglo prestando atención especial a la experiencia hispana. El documento es un buen recurso que recoge el espíritu de reflexiones previas sobre el catolicismo hispano proponiendo una visión sobre la clase de liderazgo que la Iglesia en los Estados Unidos necesita en este momento histórico. Podemos identificar en el documento cuatro temas cen-

---

6 UNITED STATES CONFERENCE OF CATHOLIC BISHOPS, *Encuentro y Misión: Un Marco Pastoral Renovado para el Ministerio Hispano*, USCCB, Washington, D.C. 2002, n. 1, http://www.usccb.org/hispanicaffairs/encuentromissionsp.shtml.

trales que iluminan la conversación sobre un liderazgo efectivo: la Nueva Evangelización, pastoral de conjunto, líderes que sean gente puente y la centralidad de la justicia social.

Primero, *Encuentro y Misión* claramente propuso que la Nueva Evangelización es el lente por medio de cual se ha de interpretar y avanzar el ministerio en el nuevo siglo[7]. Los líderes del ministerio hispano tenemos que ser verdaderos testigos del encuentro con Cristo vivo, constructores de la comunidad eclesial y participantes activos en la misión de la Iglesia[8]. Todas nuestras acciones pastorales tienen que reflejar esta triple relación con Cristo, la Iglesia y la evangelización.

Segundo, la Iglesia necesita mujeres y hombres que entiendan y estén dispuestos a hacer suyo el modelo de pastoral de conjunto (comunión en misión)[9], el cual, considerando las circunstancias particulares de nuestro contexto eclesial, demanda «una colaboración estrecha en el ministerio entre todos los grupos étnicos y culturales»[10]. Dicho modelo de liderazgo, arraigado en la sabiduría compartida de los líderes hispanos en Latinoamérica y los Estados Unidos, exige que se adopten procesos de participación y consulta, especialmente al nivel de la base, en «colaboración con el clero, religiosos, religiosas y laicos»[11]. Tal fue el espíritu de los procesos de Encuentro que llevó a proponer prácticas pastorales y planeación realizadas «con el pueblo, no para el pueblo»[12].

Tercero, existe una necesidad urgente de líderes que sean gente-puente[13]. La complejidad de nuestras comunidades puede parecer abrumadora a los ojos de cualquier persona haciendo trabajo pastoral en el contexto pluralista estadounidense. Con frecuencia dicha complejidad se acentúa gracias a varios de los factores que coinciden en las vidas de los latinos. Por ejemplo, multiplicidad de generaciones, distintos lugares de procedencia, vivencias históricas diferentes, muchos idiomas, variedad de condiciones sociales e incluso diversidad de interpretaciones de la experiencia católica. Sería ingenuo esperar que todos los líderes respondieran a todas las dimensiones de la vida y de la fe de nuestras comunidades y ser todo para todos. Sin embargo, *Encuentro y Misión* sugiere que los líderes pastorales deben ser gente-puente, o al menos aspirar a serlo, mujeres y

---

7 Cfr. UNITED STATES CONFERENCE OF CATHOLIC BISHOPS, *Encuentro y Misión*, n. 27.
8 Cfr. UNITED STATES CONFERENCE OF CATHOLIC BISHOPS, *Encuentro y Misión*, n. 25-29.
9 Cfr. UNITED STATES CONFERENCE OF CATHOLIC BISHOPS, *Encuentro y Misión*, n. 19.
10 UNITED STATES CONFERENCE OF CATHOLIC BISHOPS, *Encuentro y Misión*, n. 33.
11 UNITED STATES CONFERENCE OF CATHOLIC BISHOPS, *Encuentro y Misión*, n. 44.
12 UNITED STATES CONFERENCE OF CATHOLIC BISHOPS, *Encuentro y Misión*, n. 44.
13 Cfr. UNITED STATES CONFERENCE OF CATHOLIC BISHOPS, *Encuentro y Misión*, n. 46.

hombres que tengan apertura a «recibir gustosos a personas de diferentes culturas, flexibilidad para trabajar y caminar con ellas, y un buen entendimiento de la Iglesia universal… [con un] compromiso para servir a todos los católicos. Los líderes deben saber escuchar bien y tener gran sensibilidad por la vida de las personas, interesarse en ellas, en sus necesidades, en sus aspiraciones e ideas. Necesitan también creer y ser modelos de servicio, con un compromiso profundo de solidaridad con los más necesitados… [y ser] pioneros que abren puertas para ellos y para los demás»[14].

Cuarto, *Encuentro y Misión* hizo un llamado a los líderes pastorales en los Estados Unidos, especialmente a quienes están trabajando en el ministerio hispano, a comprometerse sinceramente en asuntos de justicia social. La experiencia católica hispana en los Estados Unidos tiene lugar en medio de circunstancias desafiantes tales como la pobreza y los prejuicios sociales entre los cuales podemos resaltar el racismo, el clasismo, la homofobia y el sexismo deshumanizador que afecta particularmente a las latinas. A esto hemos de añadir la pobre atención a los jóvenes hispanos en todo nivel. No es suficiente nombrar estas realidades y hacer poco para cambiarlas. Tampoco es suficiente simplemente esperar lo mejor en medio de las adversidades. Los líderes pastorales de todas las etnicidades trabajando en el ministerio hispano tenemos que hacer todo lo posible para «educar a católicos hispanos sobre asuntos y procesos socio-políticos y legislativos y sobre las habilidades básicas necesarias para la organización comunitaria»[15] que lleven a la transformación de la comunidad. Las actuales conversaciones sobre reforma migratoria, el acceso adecuado al sistema de salud, la calidad de la educación y los derechos de los trabajadores, entre otros, exige la contribución de líderes pastorales que sean conocedores de las enseñanzas de la Iglesia sobre estos asuntos, denunciando con voz profética lo que es injusto y guiando la reflexión sobre estos asuntos en sus comunidades. Las aflicciones de los latinos y las latinas en los Estados Unidos son las aflicciones de todo el cuerpo eclesial. Tenemos que ofrecer el bálsamo de la acción compasiva y cuidadosa a quienes llevan estas cargas, tal como lo hizo Jesús en su vida y ministerio.

14 UNITED STATES CONFERENCE OF CATHOLIC BISHOPS, *Encuentro y Misión*, n. 46.
15 UNITED STATES CONFERENCE OF CATHOLIC BISHOPS, *Encuentro y Misión*, n. 57.4.c.

1.2. RETOS

Un estudio realizado en 1999 sobre liderazgo pastoral entre los latinos viviendo en cinco estados con altas concentraciones de población hispana reveló que aproximadamente el 70 por ciento de las latinas y los latinos trabajando activamente en contextos pastorales eran inmigrantes[16]. Este número contrasta significativamente con el hecho de que la mayoría de los latinos viviendo en los Estados Unidos, tanto en aquel entonces como ahora, nacieron en el país. La contribución de los líderes hispanos de primera generación al ministerio pastoral es un signo importante que refleja su celo y su deseo de servir en nuestras comunidades diversas, muchas de las cuales son sostenidas primordialmente por estas mujeres y hombres. Sin embargo, algunas limitaciones de estos líderes con frecuencia restringen su servicio pastoral: muchos de ellos sólo hablan español y, sin la intención de hacerlo, perpetúan la segregación de sus comunidades, particularmente en parroquias en donde se habla más de un idioma. Muchos no saben cómo funciona «el sistema» y carecen del conocimiento básico para valerse de las conexiones y oportunidades de apoyo en sus diócesis, parroquias y otras organizaciones eclesiales. Aunque la mayoría esperan con buena intención que modelos pastorales que funcionaban bien en sus países de origen también funcionen en los Estados Unidos, con frecuencia son víctimas de la frustración porque dichos modelos «no funcionan» en los Estados Unidos. Aún más, muchos desconocen la memoria histórica de la comunidad católica hispana en los Estados Unidos y continuamente caen en la tentación de comenzar de cero. Algunos de los ensayos en este libro resaltan el hecho de que muchos de estos líderes de primera generación son sacerdotes latinoamericanos[17] quienes por su condición de ordenados reciben la responsabilidad de dirigir comunidades enteras casi inmediatamente después de llegar al país. El impacto de su acción ministerial en estas comunidades ciertamente es de bastante valor. Sin embargo, estas comunidades tienen el potencial de fortalecerse o

---

16 Cfr. DAVIS K.G., HERNÁNDEZ A. y LAMPE P.E., «Hispanic Catholic Leadership: Key to the Future» en HERNÁNDEZ E.I., PEÑA M., DAVIS K., y STATION E. (eds.), *Emerging Voices, Urgent Choices: Essays on Latino/a Religious Leadership*, Brill, Boston, MA 2006, 55. La estadística se basa en los resultados del estudio hecho en 1999 por la National Community on Latino/a Leadership (NCLL) en California, Texas, New York, Florida e Illinois, comisionado por el Consejo Nacional Católico para el Ministerio Hispano (NCCHM).

17 Aproximadamente el 83 por ciento de los sacerdotes latinos sirviendo en los Estados Unidos nacieron fuera del país. Cfr. INSTITUTO FE Y VIDA, «Pastoral Juvenil Hispana: Datos recientes» en *Perspectives on Hispanic Youth and Young Adult Ministry* 4, Instituto Fe y Vida Stockton, CA 2007, 8, recurso electrónico, http://www.feyvida.org/research/researchpubs.html.

debilitarse dependiendo de la manera como estos líderes ordenados respondan a los asuntos que acabamos de señalar y de su capacidad de trabajar colaborativamente con los líderes laicos que ya están allí en lugar de aislarlos. Esta realidad exige también una reflexión seria sobre la generación «omitida» (el término que proponemos en inglés es *skipped generation*) de posibles líderes de entre la segunda y tercera generaciones de latinos, especialmente hijos de inmigrantes que se están integrando rápidamente en la cultura dominante pero no se sienten atraídos a servir en sus comunidades eclesiales. Su ausencia ha creado un vacío inmenso que está afectando profundamente el trabajo pastoral entre los latinos en los Estados unidos. La inhabilidad de comprometer estas generaciones de hispanos con frecuencia refleja la ambigüedad en cuanto a ciertos asuntos al interior de la Iglesia tales como la necesidad de salarios justos para los trabajadores laicos, sexismo institucional, ausencia de un liderazgo efectivo e inclusivo y oportunidades limitadas de colaboración. La ironía es que muchos de estos latinos y latinas sirven efectivamente como líderes biculturales y bilingües en contextos que no tienen relación con la Iglesia. ¿Qué tiene que hacer la Iglesia para ofrecerles un hogar y una alternativa viable para satisfacer su deseo de servir?

Un segundo reto importante al que los latinos tenemos que responder con frecuencia es el nivel educativo de nuestros líderes. Actualmente la mayoría de los latinos en los Estados Unidos posee niveles muy bajos de educación formal. Esta situación pone a la comunidad latina en posiciones de desventaja extrema dentro de un ambiente en el que la educación es símbolo de status social. En general la educación formal es el factor más significativo que facilita la movilidad social y los latinos en los Estados Unidos están rezagados en este sentido con relación a otros grupos[18]. Dicha situación es particularmente preocupante cuando reflexionamos sobre asuntos de liderazgo pastoral dentro de la Iglesia. La acción pastoral en los Estados Unidos con frecuencia se define en términos de profesionalismo, no sólo en el caso del clero, los religiosos y las religiosas, sino también en el de los miles de hombres y mujeres que sirven como ministros eclesiales laicos alrededor del país. Con niveles bajos de educación y con menos del 15 por ciento de nuestros adultos habiendo obtenido un título profesional (*bachelor's degree*, en inglés), el número de latinos y latinas que pueden responden a la llamada al ministerio eclesial en las estructuras eclesiales actuales y de

---

18 Véase el ensayo de Hosffman Ospino en este libro sobre el ministerio hispano, la evangelización y la formación en la fe.

hecho sobresalir es muy pequeño. En el año 2005 los obispos de los Estados Unidos indicaron en un documento sobre el ministerio eclesial laico, *Colaboradores en la Viña del Señor*, que «[u]na formación inadecuada y defectuosa perjudica a la Iglesia, en lugar de ayudarla. Generalmente, es preferible un grado de maestría, o por lo menos de bachiller universitario, en un campo de estudios apropiado»[19]. Por un lado, estamos completamente de acuerdo con esta recomendación y pensamos que la esperanza de hacerla realidad es una meta que requiere que toda la Iglesia valore e invierta en la educación y formación de sus líderes eclesiales laicos al igual que valora e invierte en la educación y formación de quienes aspiran a los ministerios ordenados. Por otro lado, exigir un título universitario como requisito para servir como ministros eclesiales laicos bajo las circunstancias actuales requeriría excluir del servicio pastoral a muchos latinos y latinas y agudizar el vacío que existe en cuanto al liderazgo eclesial[20]. No obstante, es importante observar que el hecho de que la mayoría de los latinos carezcan de títulos académicos a nivel universitario y de seminario no es necesariamente un indicador de ausencia de liderazgo. Miles de latinos y latinas sirven pastoralmente de distintas maneras en la vida de la Iglesia, muchos de ellos como voluntarios asumiendo responsabilidades que son similares a las de los ministros pastorales asalariados. En algunos casos estas responsabilidades son más complejas y exigen mucho más tiempo. Dicha situación revela dos anomalías. Primero, el trabajo pastoral de muchos latinos y latinas no es completamente reconocido ni adecuadamente remunerado bajo el pretexto de que carecen de credenciales educativas. Con ello se ha creado una subclase de ministros eclesiales a los cuales no cobijan los estándares establecidos para reglamentar esta actividad en la Iglesia. Cuando esto se convierte en una práctica deliberada, es necesario que el asunto se mire a la luz de los derechos legales de los

---

19 UNITED STATES CONFERENCE OF CATHOLIC BISHOPS, *Colaboradores en la viña del Señor: un recurso para guiar el desarrollo del ministerio eclesial laico*, USCCB, Washington, D.C. 2005, 31, también disponible electrónicamente en http://www.usccb.org/laity/laymin/CoworkersSpanish.pdf. El documento ofrece algunas estadísticas importantes que indican el alto nivel educativo de los ministros eclesiales laicos en los Estados Unidos: «En 2005, el 48,1% de los ministros eclesiales laicos contaba con un grado de maestría o superior, el 51,4% de éstos fue obtenido en un área pastoral o teológica. Más de la mitad de los ministros eclesiales laicos empleados por parroquias han completado un programa de formación para el ministerio, 64,3% de los cuales fueron patrocinados por la diócesis».

20 Cfr. 2007 National Symposium on Lay Ecclesial Ministry: *Resumen Ejecutivo*, 6, http://www1.csbsju.edu/sot/Symposium/documents/ExecutiveSummary-Spanish.pdf (página visitada el 19 de marzo del 2010).

trabajadores y las convicciones básicas de la moralidad cristiana[21]. Segundo, las latinas y los latinos están implementando modelos de liderazgo creativo en sus comunidades como parte de su compromiso con movimientos eclesiales y pequeñas comunidades eclesiales que necesitan ser estudiados y reconocidos como formas de ministerio eclesial laico. Esto ha de hacerse aún cuando el resultado de dicho análisis confronte convicciones dominantes relacionadas con el profesionalismo del trabajo pastoral. Por ello debemos preguntar: ¿estamos todos los miembros de la Iglesia dispuestos y queremos tener una conversación abierta, honesta y verdaderamente inclusiva sobre la educación y la formación de los ministros eclesiales laicos latinos?[22].

Un último reto que enfrenta la Iglesia católica en los Estados Unidos con relación a la preparación de líderes pastorales es el paso rezagado por medio del cual los programas de formación ministerial están integrando estrategias para preparar mujeres y hombres que puedan servir de manera pastoralmente efectiva a los latinos y a otras comunidades católicas que no son dominantes. En muchas instituciones de formación ministerial estos programas ni siquiera existen aún cuando en las áreas geográficas que supuestamente sirven viven grandes porcentajes de latinos. *Encuentro y Misión* hace un buen trabajo esquematizando las esperanzas más importantes para la formación que los líderes hispanos han articulado a través de varios procesos de deliberación:

- «Desarrollar y apoyar programas que ayuden a las personas hispanas laicas a obtener grados universitarios para el ministerio eclesial»[23]
- Establecer mecanismos de colaboración entre las estructuras eclesiales y universidades, seminarios e institutos[24]
- Afirmar el valor de los programas de certificación[25]

---

21 Un recurso de gran ayuda en este sentido es la declaración escrita por la Asociación Nacional para el Ministerio Laico (NALM, sigla en inglés) en el 2007, «Working in the Vineyard: A Position Statement on Employment Practices for Lay Ecclesial Ministers» (Trabajar en la viña: declaración sobre las prácticas de empleo para los ministros eclesiales laicos). El documento se encuentra disponible en inglés en forma electrónica en http://www.nalm.org/mc/page.do?sitePageId= 45861&orgId=nalm (página visitada el 16 de marzo del 2010).

22 Cfr. BURGALETA C., «A Latino/a Perspective on Co-Workers» (ensayo sin publicar). Estamos agradecidos al Rev. Claudio Burgaleta, S.J. por compartir con nosotros este ensayo, el cual fue presentado inicialmente como parte de una conferencia sobre el ministerio eclesial laico en Fordham University el 25 de septiembre del 2009.

23 UNITED STATES CONFERENCE OF CATHOLIC BISHOPS, *Encuentro y Misión*, n. 55.1.a.

24 Cfr. UNITED STATES CONFERENCE OF CATHOLIC BISHOPS, *Encuentro y Misión*, n. 55.1.a.

25 Cfr. UNITED STATES CONFERENCE OF CATHOLIC BISHOPS, *Encuentro y Misión*, n. 55.1.c.

- Establecer mecanismos de colaboración entre las oficinas de ministerio hispano y los programas de formación para los ministros ordenados, religiosos, religiosas y ministros eclesiales laicos[26]
- «Incorporar el ministerio y la cultura hispana en los programas de formación de las oficinas de evangelización, formación religiosa y formación, y en los seminarios»[27]
- Formar ministros que sean capaces de servir en contextos culturalmente diversos[28]
- «Apoyar a jóvenes hispanos en sus esfuerzos para mejorar su educación académica, su formación catequética y su desarrollo humano y de liderazgo»[29]
- «Desarrollar líderes hispanos capaces de hacer su ministerio en el contexto de una sociedad culturalmente diversa y pluralista a la vez que se les refuerza su identidad cultural y ministerial hispana»[30]
- «Fomentar la participación de profesionales hispanos en la iglesia como líderes y expertos en diversas disciplinas y ministerios, y no sólo en asuntos que traten con el ministerio hispano»[31].

La mayoría de estos puntos fueron parte de la conversación del grupo de estudio que exploró la relación entre el ministerio hispano y la formación para el liderazgo pastoral en el Simposio Nacional del 2009. Ciertamente se necesita más que un ensayo para reflexionar adecuadamente sobre cada uno de ellos. Sin embargo, creemos que es urgente que cualquier conversación sobre la formación de agentes pastorales preparándose para servir en comunidades eclesiales en los Estados Unidos, especialmente en contextos en donde los latinos estamos presentes, tiene que comenzar por estudiar atentamente los anteriores puntos e integrarlos en sus guías, decisiones curriculares y programas de formación pastoral. Resaltamos el trabajo de las universidades, seminarios, institutos pastorales y programas diocesanos que ya incorporan estos puntos en sus prácticas educativas. Sin embargo, estas pocas instituciones siguen siendo la excepción. La efectividad del ministerio pastoral en el siglo XXI dependerá en gran medida de la habilidad de las instituciones eclesiales y académicas de ofrecer formación ministerial y teológica no sólo que atraiga a los latinos sino que inten-

---

26 Cfr. UNITED STATES CONFERENCE OF CATHOLIC BISHOPS, *Encuentro y Misión*, n. 55.2.a.
27 UNITED STATES CONFERENCE OF CATHOLIC BISHOPS, *Encuentro y Misión*, n. 55.2.c.
28 Cfr. UNITED STATES CONFERENCE OF CATHOLIC BISHOPS, *Encuentro y Misión*, n. 55.3.b.
29 UNITED STATES CONFERENCE OF CATHOLIC BISHOPS, *Encuentro y Misión*, n. 55.4.a.
30 UNITED STATES CONFERENCE OF CATHOLIC BISHOPS, *Encuentro y Misión*, n. 57.4.a.
31 UNITED STATES CONFERENCE OF CATHOLIC BISHOPS, *Encuentro y Misión*, n. 57.4.b.

cionalmente haga suyas las preocupaciones de las distintas comunidades culturales que constituyen la Iglesia. ¿De qué manera las instituciones de formación ministerial harán intencionalmente suyo el compromiso con la actual pluralidad cultural y considerarán las implicaciones de la diversidad en sus programas? ¿Qué tanta apertura hacia las voces poco dominantes tendrán los distintos sectores de la Iglesia que actualmente tienen en sus manos el poder de decisión? ¿Qué tanto acceso se dará a los líderes hispanos que han sido pioneros en sus iniciativas curriculares, metodológicas y programáticas?

2

Estructuras de apoyo para el ministerio hispano y la formación para el liderazgo

406   La misión evangelizadora de la Iglesia también requiere de estructuras y recursos adecuados para que sea efectiva. Sin estas estructuras y recursos los resultados de la misión serán limitados. Es muy claro que la misión evangelizadora entre los católicos latinos en los Estados Unidos se ha beneficiado de la creación de oficinas, redes y movimientos a distintos niveles: nacional, regional, diocesano y parroquial. Estas estructuras han jugado un papel muy importante en el proceso de abogar en favor de asuntos relacionados con la realidad de los latinos en este país, tanto en la Iglesia como en el resto de la sociedad. Aunque muchas de estas oficinas, organizaciones y movimientos siguen contribuyendo a la reflexión sobre lo que significa ser hispano y católico en los Estados Unidos, parece que para algunos de ellos es momento de dar paso a nuevos esfuerzos e iniciativas[32]. El presente y el futuro del ministerio hispano y cualquier otra iniciativa relacionada con la formación para el liderazgo entre los católicos hispanos dependerán del fortalecimiento o la desaparición de estas estructuras.

2.1.   LA VISIÓN

La primera década del siglo XXI fue un momento clave para que los líderes católicos latinos nos reuniéramos varias veces a reflexionar sobre temas importantes sobre el ministerio hispano y la formación ministerial. Estos momentos de auto-reflexión fueron oportunidades para evaluar el trabajo hecho hasta ahora

---

32   Véase el ensayo de Timothy Matovina en este libro sobre el ministerio hispano y el catolicismo en los Estados Unidos.

e imaginar posibles cambios que habrán de implementarse en distintos niveles de la vida de la Iglesia.

La historia del catolicismo hispano en los Estados Unidos atestigua el poder de los movimientos, convocaciones y reuniones del ministerio hispano que han formado la imaginación de varias generaciones de líderes latinos en distintos momentos. Cada serie de eventos ha contribuido al desarrollo de un lenguaje común, visiones y modelos pastorales que han influenciado las direcciones en las cuales se ha movido el ministerio hispano durante el último medio siglo. Estos eventos respondieron a la particularidad de las circunstancias históricas dentro de las cuales tuvieron lugar. Hoy en día tenemos que discernir qué clase de iniciativas serán más efectivas para convocar a los líderes católicos hispanos, qué preguntas habrán de discutirse y bajo qué circunstancias necesitamos reunirnos. Por ejemplo, el proceso que condujo al Primer Encuentro Nacional de Pastoral Juvenil Hispana en el año 2006 movilizó más de 40.000 jóvenes latinos alrededor del país. Este proceso sirvió al mismo tiempo como una oportunidad para formar jóvenes latinos para el liderazgo pastoral, un esfuerzo que ya está dando frutos en diócesis y parroquias en todas partes, y proveer al ministerio hispano con una nueva generación de aliados y recursos. La novedad de este Encuentro Nacional está en la clase de líderes que convocó, las metas específicas que se propuso lograr y el momento histórico en el que ocurrió cuando el 50 por ciento de todos los católicos estadounidenses menores de 18 años son hispanos[33].

Hace sólo cuarenta años el Centro Cultural México Americano (MACC, sigla en inglés, el cual ahora se llama Colegio Católico México Americano) era prácticamente el único instituto pastoral formando líderes pastorales de todas las culturas para servir en comunidades latinas en los Estados Unidos. Hoy en día cerca de veinte institutos pastorales asociados por medio de la Federación de Institutos Pastorales (FIP) trabajan en el proceso de formación ministerial de líderes de habla hispana junto con docenas de institutos pastorales diocesanos de formación para el liderazgo, institutos bíblicos y programas de formación en línea en español[34]. Un número creciente de universidades y seminarios están

---

33 Véase el ensayo de Ken Johnson-Mondragón en este libro sobre el ministerio hispano y la pastoral juvenil hispana. También Cfr. NATIONAL CATHOLIC NETWORK DE PASTORAL JUVENIL HISPANA —LA RED, *Conclusiones: Primer Encuentro Nacional de Pastoral Juvenil Hispana*, PENPJH, USCCB, Washington, D.C. 2008.

34 Cfr. CENTER FOR APPLIED RESEARCH IN THE APOSTOLATE (CARA), *Catholic Ministry Formation Enrollments: Statistical Overview for 2008–2009*, Washington, D.C. 2009, 30, http://cara.georgetown.edu/pubs/Overview200809.pdf (página visitada el 19 de marzo del 2010). Véase también http://www.fipusa.com/.

estableciendo programas académicos que integran cursos e iniciativas en teología y ministerio hispano, algunos de ellos en español. La quinta edición del *Programa de Formación Sacerdotal* (2006) propuesto por los obispos católicos estadounidenses recomienda repetidamente que los seminaristas aprendan español (u otro idioma dependiendo de las necesidades pastorales de las comunidades locales en donde los futuros sacerdotes servirán) y se familiaricen con las culturas hispanas[35]. Como afirma *Encuentro y Misión*, «[e]sto ya no es una opción —es una necesidad»[36]. La formación de organizaciones nacionales como el Consejo Nacional Católico para el Ministerio Hispano (NCCHM, sigla en inglés), la Asociación Nacional Católica de Directores Diocesanos para el Ministerio Hispano (NCADDHM, sigla en inglés), la Academia de Teólogos Católicos Hispanos de los Estados Unidos (ACHTUS, sigla en inglés), la Asociación Nacional de Sacerdotes Hispanos (ANSH) y la National Catholic Network de Pastoral Juvenil Hispana –La Red fue vital para reunir las voces de líderes latinos de distintas partes del país y así planear grandes iniciativas con una visión común[37]. El crecimiento de las estructuras organizacionales entre los católicos hispanos en la segunda parte del siglo XX fue ciertamente impresionante.

Conscientes de dicho crecimiento, diversidad y potencial para la formación de líderes para el ministerio hispano, *Encuentro y Misión* recomendó la afirmación y fortalecimiento de estas organizaciones e instituciones. El documento invitó a estas estructuras a establecer lazos de colaboración mutua y a trabajar de cerca con otras estructuras eclesiales en distintos niveles[38]. Es urgente que estas organizaciones propongan estrategias para que los latinos avancen de niveles básicos de liderazgo pastoral en sus parroquias y movimientos eclesiales a programas de nivel educativo superior en institutos, universidades y seminarios[39]. Estas estructuras tienen que aprovechar su posición privilegiada para incorporar la teología, la cultura, el idioma y el ministerio hispano en todas las

35 Cfr. UNITED STATES CONFERENCE OF CATHOLIC BISHOPS, *Program of Priestly Formation*, quinta edición, USCCB, Washington, D.C. 2006, n. 162, 172, 182, 228 (disponible sólo en inglés).
36 UNITED STATES CONFERENCE OF CATHOLIC BISHOPS, *Encuentro y Misión*, n. 55.2.c.
37 NCCHM ha organizado con éxito tres convocaciones de líderes católicos hispanos de todo el país bajo el título *Raíces y Alas* (1992, 1996, 2003) para discutir y reflexionar sobre temas urgentes relacionados con el ministerio hispano en los Estados Unidos. Una cuarta reunión está en el proceso de planeación para el año 2010. Cada año ACHTUS reúne docenas de teólogos católicos latinos en los Estados Unidos para su coloquio anual. En el año 2006 la National Catholic Network de Pastoral Juvenil Hispana –La Red organizó el Primer Encuentro Nacional de Pastoral Juvenil Hispana.
38 Cfr. UNITED STATES CONFERENCE OF CATHOLIC BISHOPS, *Encuentro y Misión*, n. 48.
39 Cfr. UNITED STATES CONFERENCE OF CATHOLIC BISHOPS, *Encuentro y Misión*, n. 55.1.a.

instancias de formación para el liderazgo en la vida de la Iglesia[40]. Al hacer esto llevan a cabo la doble responsabilidad de formar latinos y latinas para trabajar con todos los miembros de la Iglesia y formar líderes que no son hispanos para que sean más efectivos en contextos eclesiales latinos[41]. Estas son las organizaciones e instituciones que los profesionales católicos hispanos buscarán como guía para poner sus dones al servicio de la Iglesia[42]. Con perspectiva profética, *Encuentro y Misión* claramente indicó que organizaciones e instituciones eclesiales que trabajan colaborativamente en la formación de ministros que sirven en contextos hispanos tienen que asumir la responsabilidad de ofrecer educación y formación que sean atentas al pluralismo cultural.

De entre las distintas estructuras de apoyo con las que cuentan los líderes pastorales en los Estados Unidos, la oficina diocesana de ministerio hispano, cuando existe y tiene recursos adecuados, sigue siendo uno de los instrumentos más efectivos para avanzar la misión evangelizadora de la Iglesia con los católicos latinos. La oficina diocesana de ministerio hispano tiene que existir en la iglesia local para

- «servir de recurso a parroquias y a otros ministerios»[43]
- «colaborar con escuelas, escuelas superiores y universidades así como con seminarios»[44]
- asistir en la elaboración de «programas de formación catequética, pastoral y teológica diseñados para hispanos»[45]
- fortalecer las iniciativas relacionadas con la pastoral juvenil[46]
- «promover leyes que apoyen oportunidades educacionales para la juventud en riesgo y programas de apoyo para llegar a los nuevos inmigrantes»[47]
- facilitar conversaciones relacionadas con áreas del ministerio tales como «jóvenes, familia, educación religiosa, catequesis, liturgia y abogacía»[48]
- «educar a católicos hispanos sobre asuntos y procesos socio-políticos y legislativos y sobre las habilidades básicas necesarias para la organización comunitaria... [y] promover acciones legislativas políticas sobre asuntos que

40 Cfr. UNITED STATES CONFERENCE OF CATHOLIC BISHOPS, *Encuentro y Misión*, n. 55.2.c.
41 Cfr. UNITED STATES CONFERENCE OF CATHOLIC BISHOPS, *Encuentro y Misión*, n. 55.2.c.
42 Cfr. UNITED STATES CONFERENCE OF CATHOLIC BISHOPS, *Encuentro y Misión*, n. 56.3.c.
43 UNITED STATES CONFERENCE OF CATHOLIC BISHOPS, *Encuentro y Misión*, n. 57.2.a.
44 UNITED STATES CONFERENCE OF CATHOLIC BISHOPS, *Encuentro y Misión*, n. 55.2.a.
45 UNITED STATES CONFERENCE OF CATHOLIC BISHOPS, *Encuentro y Misión*, n. 55.3.a.
46 Cfr. UNITED STATES CONFERENCE OF CATHOLIC BISHOPS, *Encuentro y Misión*, 56.2.a.
47 UNITED STATES CONFERENCE OF CATHOLIC BISHOPS, *Encuentro y Misión*, n. 56.3.a.
48 UNITED STATES CONFERENCE OF CATHOLIC BISHOPS, *Encuentro y Misión*, n. 57.3.a.

afecten a los hispanos y a otros católicos, tales como inmigración, derechos

afecten a los hispanos y a otros católicos, tales como inmigración, derechos humanos y educación»[49], y

- participar activamente en conversaciones sobre la vida litúrgica en contextos en donde los latinos y las latinas celebramos nuestra fe[50].

Un estudio reciente sobre buenas prácticas en el ministerio hispano a nivel diocesano concluyó que una «oficina de ministerio hispano bien establecida cuenta con un/a director/a y personal asistente competentes, con acceso directo al ordinario local quien es en cierta medida bilingüe. En diócesis y arquidiócesis en donde el ministerio hispano es más organizado, la oficina de ministerio hispano está bajo la supervisión directa del ordinario local o un miembro de la curia»[51]. Aún más, una buena práctica «implica el liderazgo compartido en el cual los hispanos y otros líderes bilingües son miembros del equipo administrativo central de la estructura diocesana o arquidiocesana y otros organismos que son clave en la toma de decisiones, y las distintas oficinas pastorales tienen una persona directamente responsable de desarrollar el ministerio entre los hispanos»[52]. Este modelo de liderazgo requiere el compromiso por parte de los obispos y los líderes diocesanos para hacer que las oficinas de ministerio hispano sean parte integral de sus estructuras pastorales en las cuales la colaboración con los líderes latinos realmente se valore y afirme. El que la Iglesia haga de estas «buenas prácticas» modelos permanentes o no será la medida de su efectividad institucional.

2.2. RETOS

En décadas anteriores los líderes latinos concentraron su atención en retos tales como marginalización, escasez de recursos, acceso limitado a la educación, estructuras inadecuadas de formación para el liderazgo y espacio para reunirse. Dichos retos exigieron respuestas específicas señalando que el tiempo era propio para el nacimiento de estructuras que hicieran posible la organización del ministerio hispano como lo conocemos actualmente. Aunque dichas situaciones siguen presentes en muchas partes, quienes trabajamos en el ministerio his-

---

49 UNITED STATES CONFERENCE OF CATHOLIC BISHOPS, *Encuentro y Misión*, n. 57.4.c.

50 Cfr. UNITED STATES CONFERENCE OF CATHOLIC BISHOPS, *Encuentro y Misión*, n. 58.3.a.

51 UNITED STATES CONFERENCE OF CATHOLIC BISHOPS, COMITÉ EPISCOPAL PARA ASUNTOS HISPANOS, *Study On Best Practices for Diocesan Ministry among Hispanics/Latinos*, USCCB, Washington, D.C. 2006, 3, 5, 8. Recurso electrónico, http://www.usccb.org/hispanicaffairs/BestPractices2.pdf (página visitada el 26 de marzo del 2010).

52 UNITED STATES CONFERENCE OF CATHOLIC BISHOPS, *Encuentro y Misión*, n. 9.

pano hoy en día también vemos una nueva serie de retos indicándonos que el tiempo es propicio una vez más para renovar creativamente las estructuras actuales y permitir el nacimiento de otras nuevas que ayuden a fortalecer el ministerio hispano y los procesos de formación para el liderazgo pastoral. Veamos tres de estos retos.

Primero, tal como mencionamos anteriormente, en los primeros años del siglo XXI los católicos en los Estados Unidos fuimos testigos de la restructuración de varias organizaciones eclesiales, la redefinición de las metas e identidad de otras y la desaparición de unas cuantas. Los procesos de restructuración han ocurrido en todos los niveles: la conferencia episcopal, las diócesis, las parroquias y las redes de apoyo ministerial. En este ambiente las estructuras sosteniendo el ministerio hispano y los programas de formación para el liderazgo han sido severamente afectados. Algunas diócesis y parroquias han cerrado o reconfigurado oficinas de ministerio hispano, algunas veces haciéndolas parte de oficinas encargadas de muchos ministerios, con presupuestos reducidos y un sentido poco claro de su misión. Los asuntos económicos siguen afectando directamente al ministerio hispano y nuestros programas de formación para el liderazgo. Algunas estructuras han desaparecido (por ejemplo, la Organización Nacional de Catequesis Hispana, NOCH). Algunas oficinas regionales para el ministerio hispano han cerrado y otras han perdido fuentes importantes de apoyo económico. Un número considerable de líderes pastorales han perdido sus trabajos y muchas mujeres y hombres con credenciales académicas no ven claramente la posibilidad de seguridad laboral en la Iglesia, por lo cual deciden trabajar en el sector público o en otras instituciones privadas. A pesar de estos cambios, la Iglesia católica sigue creciendo en gran parte gracias a los millones de inmigrantes católicos que llegan primordialmente de países de habla hispana y ahora viven en los Estados Unidos. La Iglesia tiene que continuar su misión evangelizadora sirviéndole a varios millones más de personas pero con presupuestos más reducidos, menos personal y con recursos limitados para apoyar el trabajo de los líderes pastorales. Las estructuras de apoyo en toda institución requieren cambios y adaptaciones. Sin embargo, tenemos que preguntar, ¿cuál será el método operativo para definir el proceso de restructuración, las voces que se incluirán, los idiomas que se considerarán y las metas esperadas? ¿Será la Iglesia un ejemplo profético en este sentido?

El segundo reto está relacionado con el debilitamiento de las estructuras de apoyo del ministerio hispano creadas en las últimas décadas y su impacto sobre el liderazgo y la formación de líderes. Teniendo en cuenta la información obtenida en un reciente análisis de veinte iniciativas organizacionales para el ministerio hispano católico a nivel nacional y regional, el cual fue comisionado por el P. Allan Figueroa-Deck[53] en el año 2009, es evidente que la reducción de recursos en las oficinas diocesanas y parroquiales que trabajan directamente con los latinos tiene un efecto adverso sobre las redes de apoyo del ministerio hispano y por consiguiente las instituciones asociadas con ellas. El estudio reveló que la mayoría de estas organizaciones tienen menos de cinco personas en posiciones de liderazgo dentro de la misma organización[54]; la mayoría se enfoca en asuntos generales relacionados con el ministerio hispano y sólo unas cuantas se especializan en un área específica dentro de este ministerio[55]; la mayoría de personas que se benefician directamente de los servicios ofrecidos por estas organizaciones son mujeres laicas, luego jóvenes y jóvenes adultos, sacerdotes, religiosas y diáconos[56]; el 58 por ciento de estas organizaciones tienen un presupuesto anual de menos de US$50.000[57]; las personas que dirigen la mitad de estas organizaciones son empleados con un salario y quienes dirigen la otra mitad son voluntarios[58]. Entre las situaciones que más preocupan a estas organizaciones se encuentran la falta de líderes preparados adecuadamente, la necesidad de tener que reinventarse cada vez que hay cambio de liderazgo[59] y el hecho de que las diócesis no reconozcan sus servicios como una prioridad[60]. El debilitamiento de estas estructuras organizacionales sin duda alguna afectan negativamente las iniciativas de formación para el liderazgo entre los católicos hispanos. Cuando las oficinas de ministerio hispano a nivel diocesano y parroquial cierran sus puertas o se convierten en algo más, las estructuras y redes que apoyan el ministerio hispano pierden miembros, recursos económicos y los beneficiaros de sus servicios.

---

53 El P. Allan Figueroa-Deck, SJ es el primer Director Ejecutivo del nuevo Secretariado de Diversidad Cultural en la Iglesia en la Conferencia de Obispos Católicos de Estados Unidos.

54 Cfr. DINGES W.D., *National and Regional Hispanic Catholic Ministry Organizational Initiatives: An Assessment*, Life Cycle Institute, Catholic University of America, Washington, D.C. 2009, 5.

55 Cfr. DINGES W.D., *National and Regional Hispanic Catholic Ministry Organizational Initiatives*, 6.

56 Cfr. DINGES W.D., *National and Regional Hispanic Catholic Ministry Organizational Initiatives*, 9.

57 Cfr. DINGES W.D., *National and Regional Hispanic Catholic Ministry Organizational Initiatives*, 12.

58 Cfr. DINGES W.D., *National and Regional Hispanic Catholic Ministry Organizational Initiatives*, 12.

59 Cfr. DINGES W.D., *National and Regional Hispanic Catholic Ministry Organizational Initiatives*, 16.

60 Cfr. DINGES W.D., *National and Regional Hispanic Catholic Ministry Organizational Initiatives*, 17.

El tercer reto tiene que ver con la redefinición de las identidades de las estructuras que apoyan el ministerio hispano. Este reto en gran parte es otro resultado inmediato de la debilitación de redes de apoyo del ministerio hispano y oficinas especializadas que sirven a los católicos hispanos. La disminución de recursos ha llevado a tres situaciones particulares: algunas de las estructuras de apoyo del ministerio hispano han desaparecido (ej. oficinas diocesanas, redes nacionales), otras se han adaptado a un estilo de sobrevivencia y otras están buscando nuevas asociaciones con redes nacionales de apoyo ministerial que no son hispanas (un proceso que es necesario según algunos líderes, problemático según otros). Los líderes hispanos estamos bien familiarizados con las primeras dos situaciones. La tercera exige más análisis. Gracias al número creciente de hispanos alrededor del país, las organizaciones de apoyo ministerial más grandes han incrementado sus estrategias para invitar más líderes hispanos a ser parte de sus membrecías. Al mismo tiempo muchos líderes hispanos han llegado a la conclusión de que en una Iglesia en donde los latinos constituimos cerca de la mitad de la población católica, una estrategia sabia consiste en unir nuestros esfuerzos a las organizaciones que tienen una voz más fuerte y más recursos. En esto percibimos un sentido de mutualidad intencional inspirada en una misión común. Sin embargo, al nivel de la práctica todavía hay muchos asuntos que necesitamos resolver si queremos ver los frutos de tal colaboración. En general las organizaciones ministeriales dominantes se han tardado demasiado en abordar de lleno la complejidad de la experiencia hispana católica estadounidense y ajustar sus agendas para reflejar las preocupaciones y las inquietudes de una Iglesia culturalmente diversa. Muchas veces simplemente se espera que los latinos —y cualquier otro grupo que no es considerado parte del sector dominante— se ajusten al «orden establecido» y «aprendan cómo se hacen las cosas». Dicha actitud se refleja en iniciativas ministeriales en las cuales los líderes latinos no están presentes como agentes creativos desde un principio y sólo son parte de consultas aisladas o se les pide que ofrezcan una «perspectiva hispana». Nuevas alianzas exigen la apertura a nuevas voces, nuevas maneras de ver las cosas e incluso nuevas maneras de proceder. La inhabilidad de integrar el liderazgo hispano *ahora*, teniendo en cuenta el rápido crecimiento de los latinos en la Iglesia, afectará negativamente los buenos esfuerzos de apoyo ministerial de estas organizaciones. Al mismo tiempo los líderes hispanos tenemos la obligación de revisar continuamente nuestras estrategias y compromisos. Muchos de nosotros necesitamos ampliar la visión de lo que es el ministerio hispano y verlo como algo que incluye trabajar con inmigrantes de habla hispana pero no se puede quedar allí porque la experiencia hispana en los Estados Unidos es mucho más amplia y compleja. También tenemos que superar sentimientos de desconfianza hacia aquellas personas o grupos que no comparten nuestras preocupaciones más inmediatas. Es urgente que más líderes latinos se unan a las redes dominantes de apoyo ministerial que ya existen y participen activamente en ellas. Las organizaciones hispanas de apoyo ministerial pueden y tienen que existir en este contexto para articular mejor las perspectivas hispanas. Sin embargo, la afirmación del trabajo de estas organizaciones no excluye la colaboración con las redes de apoyo ministerial más grandes o dominantes. A medida que la población católica en los Estados Unidos en el siglo XXI se hace más hispana habrán más latinas y latinos dirigiendo las estructuras, redes y organizaciones actuales, y los temas de reflexión serán determinados de acuerdo a la realidad de nuestras comunidades de fe en lugar de seguir agendas predefinidas. Estas alianzas nos tienen que llevar a proponer visiones renovadas para la formación de líderes pastorales.

3
Conclusión

Como teólogos católicos ofrecemos las reflexiones anteriores sobre el ministerio y la formación para el liderazgo dentro del contexto de la experiencia hispana estadounidense como punto de partida para continuar la conversación. El Simposio Nacional sobre el Presente y Futuro del Ministerio Católico Hispano en los Estados Unidos celebrado en Boston College en el año 2009 realmente fue una oportunidad para identificar algunas de las preocupaciones más urgentes de los líderes católicos hispanos hoy en día. Las dos áreas que decidimos explorar en este ensayo (el liderazgo efectivo y las estructuras de apoyo para el ministerio hispano y la formación para el liderazgo) examinan varias de estas preocupaciones. Tenemos la responsabilidad de seguir reflexionando, afirmando la sabiduría que es fruto de décadas de memoria histórica, conversando con distintas voces en la Iglesia y mirando al futuro con esperanza renovada. Invitamos a los líderes eclesiales y a los teólogos a unirse a la conversación sobre procesos de formación para el liderazgo pastoral con atención especial a la experiencia católica hispana en los Estados Unidos. Dicha conversación exige una colaboración auténtica entre líderes laicos y ordenados en las comunidades eclesiales culturalmente diversas en las cuales compartimos nuestra fe e imaginamos modelos creativos de formación para el liderazgo en la Iglesia.

Invitamos a los líderes eclesiales a permanecer atentos a la manera como esta conversación avanza en los siguientes foros: 1) la Federación of Institutos Pastorales; 2) las iniciativas nacionales para articular teologías y estándares para el ministerio eclesial laico; 3) la Academia de Teólogos Católicos Hispanos de los Estados Unidos (ACHTUS) y otras organizaciones de teólogos católicos estadounidenses; 4) el trabajo de las universidades católicas que están estableciendo programas de teología y ministerio hispano; 5) el trabajo de las redes nacionales de apoyo ministerial; 6) las redes nacionales de apoyo al ministerio hispano; y 7) las iniciativas patrocinadas por el nuevo Secretariado de Diversidad Cultural en la Iglesia de la Conferencia de Obispos Católicos de Estados Unidos. Nuestra esperanza es que todos estos grupos y voces encuentren maneras para unir esfuerzos, reflexionar en conjunto y proponer juntos una visión que haga de la Iglesia una presencia más fuerte en nuestra sociedad para que más mujeres y hombres se encuentren con Jesucristo.

EXCURSUS DEL CAPÍTULO 7
Sobre la necesidad de una reflexión teológica más inclusiva sobre el ministerio y la formación para el liderazgo

La creatividad de los católicos estadounidenses se ha expresado de manera especial en las distintas reflexiones teológicas sobre el ministerio y el liderazgo pastoral especialmente en las décadas que le han seguido al Concilio Vaticano II. Sin duda alguna estas reflexiones, articuladas simultáneamente en contextos académicos y pastorales, han influenciado profundamente muchos de los documentos eclesiales sobre el ministerio laico y ordenado. Los católicos hispanos en los Estados Unidos no hemos estado ausentes en este reflexionar teológico. Quizás nuestra contribución más notable como teólogos y agentes pastorales es la convicción de partir preferencialmente de la experiencia vivida de los latinos en la Iglesia y en la sociedad para nuestra reflexión sobre el ministerio y el liderazgo pastoral. Al hacer esto, nuestras reflexiones teológicas privilegian las experiencias particulares de las latinas y los latinos en la inmediatez de nuestras realidades eclesiales teniendo en cuenta la naturaleza culturalmente diversa del contexto eclesial en el que vivimos.

1
Contextos, temas, fuentes

De entre los varios ejercicios contemporáneos de reflexión sobre el ministerio y la formación para el liderazgo en nuestro país, los católicos hispanos estamos particularmente interesados en aquellas conversaciones relacionadas con el ministerio eclesial laico[61], estándares para el ministerio[62] y modelos de ministerio pastoral en una Iglesia diversa[63]. La participación de los latinos en estas conversaciones es fundamental para poder afirmar las ideas descubiertas y profundizadas en procesos tales como los Encuentros, documentos generales sobre el catolicismo hispano en los Estados Unidos y las contribuciones de los miembros de la Academia de Teólogos Católicos Hispanos de los Estados Unidos (ACHTUS).

No existe una sola perspectiva que describa de lleno la complejidad de la experiencia católica hispana en los Estados Unidos. Sin embargo, es posible identificar varios elementos dentro de nuestra experiencia compartida que pueden enriquecer nuestras conversaciones sobre el ministerio y la formación para el liderazgo. Los católicos hispanos en los Estados Unidos partimos de categorías

---

61 Especialmente la revisión de documentos tales como *Colaboradores en la Viña del Señor* y el desarrollo de teologías de ministerio eclesial laico en contextos culturalmente diversos.

62 La Federación de Institutos Pastorales (FIP) es una organización que reúne a institutos nacionales, regionales, diocesanos y locales comprometidos con la formación y enriquecimiento del pueblo hispano a todos los niveles, en su contexto histórico y cultural. Actualmente la FIP está trabajando en la actualización de su manual de acreditación de liderazgo pastoral y las guías que seguirán las instituciones que son miembros para optimizar la formación de este tipo de liderazgo entre los católicos latinos que son parte de sus programas. Varios miembros de la FIP participaron activamente en la conversación sobre la relación entre el ministerio hispano y la formación para el liderazgo en el simposio nacional en el año 2009. Para obtener más información sobre la FIP se puede visitar su página electrónica http://www.fipusa.com/.

63 Véase por ejemplo los enfoques en el ministerio hispano que propone Timothy Matovina en su ensayo en este libro. El Dr. Matovina ofrecerá una versión ligeramente revisada de estos enfoques en un libro que publicará más adelante sobre el catolicismo hispano. Agradecemos al Dr. Matovina por compartir los borradores de varios capítulos que serán parte de dicha obra. Véase también FIGUEROA-DECK A., «Models» en FIGUEROA-DECK A., TARANGO Y., y MATOVINA T. (eds.), *Perspectivas: Hispanic Ministry*, Sheed & Ward, Kansas City, MO 1995; JOHNSON-MONDRAGÓN K., «Ministry in Multicultural and National/Ethnic Parishes: Evaluating the Findings of the Emerging Models of Pastoral Leadership Project», Emerging Models of Pastoral Leadership Project, 2008, http://www.emergingmodels.org/doc/Multicultural%20Report%20%282%29.pdf (página visitada el 15 de abril de 2010).

teológicas profundas y un modelo de teología de conjunto que constituyen una rica tradición que informa muchas de nuestras conversaciones. De la experiencia eclesial latinoamericana hemos heredado categorías teológicas tales como la opción preferencial por los pobres, el poder de las pequeñas comunidades eclesiales y el carácter misionero de la acción pastoral en todas sus dimensiones. Inmersos en nuestra realidad como católicos hispanos en los Estados Unidos continuamos nuestra reflexión sobre lo que significa servir pastoralmente en contextos marcados por experiencias como el mestizaje, el exilio y la marginalización social. Algunos pensadores católicos hispanos están haciendo exploraciones ecuménicas valiosas a partir de la particularidad de la experiencia latina en los Estados Unidos. Otros están avanzando reflexiones usando perspectivas interculturales para hablar de teología y ministerio. De estas conversaciones emergen ideas claves que los católicos latinos ofrecemos para avanzar las conversaciones sobre el ministerio y la formación para el liderazgo pastoral. En el contexto pluralista en el que los católicos estadounidenses compartimos nuestra fe, es urgente que las reflexiones sobre el ministerio eclesial incorporen las contribuciones teológicas de los latinos.

La tarea de poner atención a los aportes teológicos hispanos sobre el ministerio y la formación para el liderazgo es un proceso que tiene dos momentos. Por un lado, es necesario repasar la memoria histórica de la comunidad católica latina en los Estados Unidos para poder entender el origen y contexto de las categorías que permean nuestro lenguaje y nuestras reflexiones[64]. Por otro lado, los teólogos y los líderes pastorales latinos tenemos que seguir creando nuevas categorías y modelos para contribuir profundamente a la formación de ministros laicos y ordenados en el contexto culturalmente diverso en el que está insertada la Iglesia en los Estados Unidos. Muchas de estas categorías y modelos deben ser explorados en conversación con las distintas voces que constituyen nuestras comunidades eclesiales alrededor del país. Por consiguiente, las contribuciones de los líderes hispanos serán el resultado de un estudio consciente de la memoria histórica de las distintas comunidades hispanas en la Iglesia en los Estados Unidos y de la propuesta creativa de categorías que respondan a las preocupaciones más urgentes dentro de nuestra realidad actual. Este proceso de reflexión es ciertamente una invita

---

64 Por ejemplo el ensayo de Jorge Presmaness y Alicia Marill en este libro resalta ciertas categorías eclesiológicas que surgieron en los procesos de Encuentro, las cuales han servido para interpretar el liderazgo pastoral en muchos sectores del ministerio hispano.

ción a ir más allá de la idea de añadir una « perspectiva hispana» a nociones preconcebidas para hablar del ministerio y la formación para el liderazgo pastoral.

2

Consideraciones importantes

Como católicos en los Estados Unidos somos parte de un nuevo momento en nuestra historia común y por consiguiente tenemos que trabajar juntos para responder a los retos que el siglo XXI nos ha traído con relación a la formación para el liderazgo ministerial. Porque los católicos hispanos nos hemos comprometido a compartir nuestras contribuciones y nuestras preocupaciones con el resto de la comunidad católica estadounidense y así responder a estos retos, es

apropiado que formulemos algunas preguntas importantes.

a) Las definiciones predominantes del ministerio eclesial en los Estados, tanto teológica como organizacionalmente, con frecuencia reflejan perspectivas que muchas veces no tienen en cuenta las voces de los grupos que todavía son considerados como minorías, aún cuando estos grupos en conjunto constituyen la mayoría de los católicos en el país. Por consiguiente hacemos las siguientes preguntas: ¿qué es lo que exactamente tenemos en mente cuando hablamos ministerio eclesial? ¿Para qué clase de ministerio eclesial estamos formando a nuestros líderes? ¿De qué manera nuestras reflexiones teológicas sobre la formación para el ministerio eclesial tienen en cuenta las preguntas que emergen en todos los sectores de la Iglesia, especialmente los grupos marginalizados? ¿Qué hacemos para que miembros de todas las comunidades participen cuando nos proponemos responder a dichas preguntas? Estos puntos exigen que hagamos opciones preferenciales en nuestras reflexiones y en la manera como formamos a nuestros líderes pastorales en la Iglesia.

b) Los ministros eclesiales laicos son el grupo de mujeres y hombres en posiciones de servicio pastoral que más rápido está creciendo en la Iglesia en los Estados Unidos[65]. Su trabajo y su formación son tema constante de conversaciones sobre estándares profesionales que buscan garantizar niveles de calidad y efectividad. El esfuerzo colaborativo de tres organizaciones naciona-

---

65 Cfr. DeLAMBO D., *Lay Parish Ministers: A Study of Emerging Leadership*, National Pastoral Life Center, New York 2005, 44.

les de apoyo ministerial[66] dio lugar en el año 2003 a la publicación de un conjunto de estándares comunes de certificación para los ministros eclesiales laicos que son parte de sus membrecías. En el año 2006 se publicó una edición ampliada de los estándares con la contribución de la Asociación Nacional de Músicos Pastorales (NPM, sigla en inglés). Ambas ediciones fueron aprobadas por la Comisión de Certificación y Acreditación de la Conferencia de Obispos Católicos de Estados Unidos. Al tiempo de escribir este ensayo existe una nueva iniciativa para revisar los estándares actuales y se ha creado una nueva alianza nacional de organizaciones de apoyo ministerial que asumió la responsabilidad de guiar dicho proceso[67]. Aunque las organizaciones de apoyo al ministerio hispano generalmente conocen los estándares y muchas los usan en sus programas de formación, es inquietante que entre los miembros de la nueva alianza no se encuentre ni una sola organización hispana como parte del equipo de liderazgo avanzando esta iniciativa. ¿Cómo influenciarán las perspectivas hispanas los borradores centrales del nuevo documento? Es cierto que las organizaciones dominantes cuentan con miembros latinos, pero en la mayoría de los casos estas personas son muy pocas. ¿Es suficiente limitarse a consultas aisladas con algunos líderes hispanos cuando dichos estándares aspiran a regular la práctica ministerial de miles de líderes pastorales en una Iglesia en donde los latinos pronto constituirán el 50 por ciento de la población católica? ¿Qué clase de eclesiología se asume cuando grandes organizaciones de apoyo ministerial avanzan proyectos de esta magnitud sin afirmar las iniciativas de liderazgo de los católicos latinos y nuestras organizaciones? El hecho de que el liderazgo hispano no participe de una manera más significativa en estos procesos es una oportunidad perdida en el contexto culturalmente diverso en el que vivimos.

c) En muchos sectores de la Iglesia en los Estados unidos con frecuencia se asume que el eje del liderazgo ministerial es la oficina diocesana o parroquial. Aunque estas oficinas son importantes en muchas maneras, los cató-

---

66 Las tres organizaciones son: National Association for Lay Ministry (NALM) / *Asociación Nacional para el Ministerio Laico*, National Conference for Catechetical Leadership (NCCL) / *Conferencia Nacional de Líderes Catequéticos*, y National Federation for Catholic Youth Ministry (NFCYM) / *Federación Nacional de Pastoral Juvenil Católica*.

67 Las organizaciones que son miembros de la nueva alianza son: Federation of Diocesan Liturgical Commissions / *Federación de Comisiones Litúrgicas Diocesanas*, National Association for Lay Ministry / *Asociación Nacional para el Ministerio Laico*, National Association of Pastoral Musicians / *Asociación Nacional de Músicos Pastorales*, National Conference for Catechetical Leadership / *Conferencia Nacional de Líderes Catequéticos*, and National Federation for Catholic Youth Ministry / *Federación Nacional de Pastoral Juvenil Católica*.

licos latinos en los Estados Unidos estamos atentos al hecho de que muchos de nuestros líderes se forman y se sostienen en el contexto de los movimientos eclesiales (ej. la Renovación Carismática, el Cursillo de Cristiandad, las pequeñas comunidades eclesiales) y muchos de nuestros líderes más efectivos evangelizan en sus hogares y barrios. ¿Qué debemos hacer para integrar estas contribuciones y espiritualidades en las reflexiones teológicas contemporáneas sobre el ministerio?

d) El grupo más grande de católicos hispanos en los Estados Unidos es el de los jóvenes. Por varias décadas los líderes latinos han invitado a poner atención renovada a los jóvenes puesto que ellos son el presente y el futuro de la Iglesia en este país[68]. ¿Qué preguntas teológicas hacen nuestros jóvenes? ¿De qué manera la comunidad latina joven reta la manera en que los católicos estadounidenses entendemos nuestra relación con el Dios de la vida por medio de Jesucristo en la Iglesia? Gracias al trabajo excelente de organizaciones como el Instituto Fe y Vida, el Instituto Pastoral del Sureste (SEPI, sigla en inglés) y la red de liderazgo que hizo posible la organización del Primer Encuentro Nacional de Pastoral Juvenil Hispana, las reflexiones teológicas sobre el liderazgo ministerial se han enriquecido con preguntas claves que los jóvenes proponen a la toda la Iglesia en los Estados Unidos[69]. Algunas de estas preguntas se encuentran formuladas de distintas maneras en las conclusiones del Primer Encuentro Nacional de Pastoral Juvenil Hispana. Por ejemplo, los jóvenes latinos afirman:

- «[Necesitamos] personal capacitado en PJH [Pastoral Juvenil Hispana], en las oficinas diocesanas y en las parroquias; y mayor apertura y atención de los agentes de pastoral parroquiales, que se traduzca en más participación de los jóvenes en la misión de la Iglesia».

- Hay necesidad de fomentar «la creación de pequeñas comunidades cristianas en la Pastoral Juvenil, con apertura a personas de otras culturas e igualdad de derechos en las distintas actividades de la Iglesia»[70].

---

[68] Cfr. *Voces Proféticas: El Documento del Proceso del III Encuentro Nacional Hispano de Pastoral*, n. 40-42, en UNITED STATES CONFERENCE OF CATHOLIC BISHOPS, *Ministerio Hispano: Tres Documentos Importantes*, USCCB, Washington, D.C. 1995; *Plan Pastoral Nacional para el Ministerio Hispano*, USCC, Washington, D.C. 1987, n. 64-66, en UNITED STATES CONFERENCE OF CATHOLIC BISHOPS, *Ministerio Hispano; Encuentro y Misión*, n. 55.2.a.b.;70.

[69] NATIONAL CATHOLIC NETWORK DE PASTORAL JUVENIL HISPANA —LA RED, *Conclusiones: Primer Encuentro Nacional de Pastoral Juvenil Hispana*, PENPJH, USCCB, Washington, D.C. 2008.

[70] NATIONAL CATHOLIC NETWORK DE PASTORAL JUVENIL HISPANA —LA RED, *Conclusiones: Primer Encuentro Nacional de Pastoral Juvenil Hispana*, J0-16, p. 50.

¿Preparan nuestros programas de formación para el liderazgo ministros eclesiales que efectivamente acojan y respondan a la realidad diaria de la juventud hispana estadounidense? ¿De qué manera facilitamos que la juventud hispana participe en la misión de la Iglesia? ¿Afirma nuestra manera de hacer pastoral las contribuciones de las pequeñas comunidades cristianas a la experiencia católica en los Estados Unidos? ¿De qué manera los líderes de la Iglesia afirman sinceramente el don de la diversidad cultural? ¿Qué circunstancias en la Iglesia y en el resto de la sociedad limitan la participación plena de la juventud hispana? No podemos darnos el lujo de ignorar estas preguntas ni en nuestras reflexiones teológicas ni en nuestros programas de formación para el liderazgo pastoral.

e) Para los católicos latinos en los Estados Unidos la relación entre fe y cultura ha permanecido constantemente al centro de nuestras reflexiones. La manera como vivimos nuestra fe está profundamente marcada por la forma como vivimos en lo cotidiano, nuestras costumbres, idiomas, tradiciones y prácticas. Al mismo tiempo, la manera como interpretamos nuestra latinidad está influenciada profundamente por nuestro catolicismo. La formación para el liderazgo ministerial en contextos hispanos no puede ignorar el papel central de las culturas latinas. Porque los latinos vivimos nuestra fe en un contexto culturalmente diverso, es urgente que se sigan proponiendo teologías, metodologías, y modelos de formación ministerial interculturales que reconozcan con respeto la particularidad de las experiencias hispanas. Sin embargo, tenemos que interpretar estas experiencias en diálogo con las de mujeres y hombres de otros grupos étnicos y culturales con quienes compartimos y celebramos nuestra identidad católica. Los teólogos católicos hispanos de los Estados Unidos como comunidad de reflexión estamos trabajando para proponer fundamentos de lo que se considera una teología intercultural[71]. Dicha teología, de acuerdo con la teóloga católica María Pilar Aquino, confronta todas las condiciones de opresión y conduce a una liberación integral, construye sobre la plataforma de la solidaridad, entra en diálogo con la dimensión pluralista de la realidad, afirma la diferencia y seriamente tiene en cuenta la experiencia histó-

---

71 Cfr. AQUINO M.P., «Theological Method in U.S. Latino/a Theology: Toward an Intercultural Theology for the Third Millennium» en ESPÍN O. y DÍAZ M. (eds.), *From the Heart of Our People: Latino/a Explorations in Catholic Systematic Theology*, Orbis, Maryknoll, NY 1999, 6-48; ESPÍN O., «Toward the Construction of an Intercultural Theology of (Catholic) Tradition» en ESPÍN O., *Grace and Humanness: Theological Reflections Because of Culture*, Orbis Books, Maryknoll, NY 2007, 1-50; OSPINO H., «Foundations for an Intercultural Philosophy of Christian Education» en *Religious Education* 104, n. 3 (2009) 303-314.

rica y cultural del pueblo en sus comunidades[72]. Esto es teología católica en su mejor expresión. Por lo tanto, es urgente que estas contribuciones sean integradas en los procesos de reflexión sobre el ministerio y la formación para el liderazgo pastoral en nuestras comunidades.

f) Finalmente, la dinámica diaria del trabajo pastoral con los latinos se avanza normalmente en la particularidad de las parroquias en donde líderes laicos y ordenados de distintas generaciones y culturas traen consigo una variedad de perspectivas ministeriales que coexisten en tensión. El encuentro de estas perspectivas en la vida de la parroquia se puede interpretar como el encuentro de diversas teologías del ministerio eclesial forjadas en medio de experiencias socioculturales particulares. Preguntamos entonces, ¿es posible hablar de una teología del ministerio eclesial dentro de un marco eclesiológico que afirme la particularidad de cada una de estas perspectivas, facilite una tensión saludable entre ellas y conduzca a formas creativas de ministerio pastoral? ¿Qué hemos de hacer para integrar dichas perspectivas teológicas en procesos de formación ministerial, desde los seminarios y las universidades hasta los programas de liderazgo a nivel diocesano y parroquial? Estas preguntas exigen la atención de teólogos y agentes pastorales trabajando en conjunto.

Las anteriores preguntas no son las únicas que preocupan a los teólogos y líderes católicos latinos en los Estados Unidos comprometidos en la reflexión sobre el ministerio hispano y la formación para el liderazgo pastoral. No obstante, estas son algunas de las preocupaciones que exigen nuestra atención inmediata en este momento histórico. Es urgente que líderes pastorales y teólogos, hispanos y de otras tradiciones culturales, nos pongamos de acuerdo para responder a estas preguntas en nuestros trabajos, nuestras reuniones periódicas, conferencias e investigaciones para así encontrar el lenguaje más apropiado y las direcciones que necesitamos para articular nuestras perspectivas como una sola comunidad de discurso compartiendo una fe común. Al hacer esto estaremos mejor posicionados para entrar en conversaciones más amplias sobre el ministerio eclesial y la formación para el liderazgo pastoral en el contexto culturalmente diverso en el que vivimos nuestra fe hoy en día[73].

---

72 Cfr. AQUINO M.P., «Theological Method in U.S. Latino/a Theology: Toward an Intercultural Theology for the Third Millennium», 19-20.

73 Un buen ejemplo de la reflexión sobre lo que significa ser católico en una Iglesia culturalmente diversa es el proceso y las conclusiones del Encuentro 2000, http://www.usccb.org/hispanic affairs/encuentrosp.shtml. Véanse también los recursos que emergieron de las distintas conversaciones durante la Convocatoria de la Red Católica de Diversidad Cultural organizada por el Secretariado de Diversidad Cultural en la Iglesia de la Conferencia de Obispos Católicos de Estados Unidos la cual tuvo lugar en mayo del año 2010, http://usccb.org/ccdnc/.

Discurso inaugural durante el simposio nacional sobre el presente y el futuro del ministerio hispano católico en los Estados Unidos

Excelentísimo Monseñor JOSÉ H. GÓMEZ, S.T.D. *Arzobispo coadjutor de Los Ángeles,*

*Director del Comité sobre Diversidad Cultural en la Iglesia (*USCCB*) en el año 2009*

Junio 8 del 2009

Boston College

(A la fecha del simposio, Monseñor Gómez
era el arzobispo de San Antonio, TX)

¡Un saludo cordial muy queridos hermanos y hermanas! Es un gusto estar con ustedes, mis amigos. Me honra el haber sido invitado a compartir mis ideas con un grupo tan distinguido.

Mi amigo, Hosffman Ospino, me ha pedido que hable sobre tres asuntos: primero, los retos más urgentes a los que se enfrentan los católicos hispanos; segundo, los caminos que como líderes debemos tomar para responder a estos retos; y finalmente, algunas ideas sobre qué iniciativas podemos avanzar en este momento histórico en el que nuestro pueblo está a punto de convertirse en una «mayoría numérica» en los Estados Unidos.

Con gusto trataré de decir algo sobre estos temas. Pero quiero comenzar con algunas noticias recientes. Como usted saben, el Presidente Obama hace poco nominó dos hispanos para servir en posiciones muy importantes: el teólogo católico cubanoamericano, Dr. Miguel Díaz, para ser embajador ante el Vaticano, y la juez puertorriqueña Sonia Sotomayor, quien creció como católica, para servir en la Corte Suprema de Justicia.

No conozco personalmente a ninguno de los dos nominados. Sin embargo, al leer sus biografías en la prensa, encuentro sus vidas bastante inspiradoras. Y al pensar sobre lo que diría hoy, se me ocurrió que sus historias dicen mucho sobre nuestra gente y sus experiencias durante las últimas generaciones en este país.

El Dr. Díaz nació en la Habana y es el hijo de un mesero. Él fue la primera persona de su familia en ir a la universidad y se ha convertido en un teólogo respetado. Su relación con la Iglesia es bastante activa y es el padre de cuatro hijos.

La juez Sotomayor tiene una historia aún más dramática. Creció en el Bronx y su padre murió cuando ella tenía apenas nueve años. Su madre trabajó arduamente y se sacrificó para enviarla a ella y a su hermano a una escuela católica hasta que terminaron la preparatoria. Según la Casa Blanca y otras personas que le conocen, la juez Sotomayor ya no practica su fe católica ni ninguna otra religión.

Ahora bien, permítanme hacer una aclaración. La razón por la cual menciono al profesor Díaz y a la juez Sotomayor nada tiene que ver con intenciones políticas. No estoy interesado en pasar juicio sobre su fe o sus perspectivas políticas o sus cualificaciones para las posiciones para las que han sido nominados. Menciono sus nombres porque pienso que sus trayectorias dicen mucho cuando consideramos el futuro de nuestro ministerio con nuestro pueblo hispano.

Permítanme explicar.

Tenemos ante nosotros dos líderes hispanos. Ambos han logrado en una generación, viniendo de hogares en donde sus padres tenían niveles de educación muy limitados y con pocos recursos económicos, ubicarse con éxito en los puestos más altos de sus respectivas profesiones. Ambos se encuentran ahora listos para asumir posiciones prominentes en el gobierno de este país. Cada uno es una «historia de triunfo» dentro de la inmigración hispana; él sigue practicando la fe católica en la que creció y ella no lo hace.

En estos dos líderes tenemos una sinopsis de las tendencias más grandes con relación a la práctica de la fe y la afiliación religiosa de nuestra población hispana. El sondeo general del Foro Pew Religión y Vida Pública dado a conocer el año pasado y el sondeo sobre identificación religiosa en los Estados Unidos conducido por Trinity College, el cual se publicó hace un mes, coinciden en sus conclusiones sobre la fe de nuestra gente. Cerca del 58 por ciento de los hispanos se identifican como católicos; cerca de un 25 por ciento se identifican como miembros de algún grupo protestante; y entre el 10 y el 12 por ciento se autodescriben como personas sin religión.

Estos porcentajes representan un gran cambio al compararlos con los de hace veinte años e incluso los de hace diez años. El número de hispanos que se identificaban como católicos ha declinado de casi 100 por ciento hace sólo dos décadas, mientras que quienes se describen como protestantes casi se ha duplicado y el de los que dicen «no tener religión» también se ha duplicado.

No creo mucho en estos sondeos sobre convicciones y prácticas religiosas. Pero en este caso los sondeos reflejan la experiencia en nuestras propias comunidades y nos ofrecen medidas gráficas de lo que creo que será el reto más grande que enfrentarán los católicos hispanos en los próximos años.

Permítanme formular el reto abiertamente y luego explicar lo que quiero decir. Lo pondré en términos de la pregunta que Jesús hizo una vez: «Pero, cuando el Hijo del hombre venga, ¿encontrará fe sobre la tierra?» (Lc 18,8).

Ése es el reto, mis amigos. A medida que los hispanos logran más éxitos, mientras más y más se asimilan a la cultura dominante estadounidense, ¿mantendrán la fe? ¿Qué camino seguirán? ¿Se mantendrán católicos o se alejarán hacia… las denominaciones protestantes, aquellos grupos con una espiritualidad difícil de definir, o dejarán la religión por completo?

¿Cuál será su relación con la Iglesia Católica? ¿Vivirán según las enseñanzas de la Iglesia y promoverán esas enseñanzas en las arenas públicas? ¿Se convertirá su catolicismo en alguna clase de experiencia «cultural», una característica más de su personalidad, una dimensión de su infancia que informa sus perspectivas sobre la vida pero que no necesariamente les invita a mantenerse fieles o devotos a la Iglesia?

Todas éstas son preguntas abiertas que debemos tener en cuenta al movernos durante los primeros años del siglo xxi. El desafío es bien grande, amigos. Porque hablando históricamente, los hispanos siempre han sido más que un grupo étnico. Ser hispano siempre ha significado ser católico.

Hay muchos factores presentes en este asunto. Tenemos la realidad básica de nuestra cultura consumista inexorable. «Comprar y comprar» (*shopping around*, en inglés) es más que una metáfora para los estadounidenses; es un estilo de vida. Las personas salen a buscar iglesias y religiones como si estuvieran en el centro comercial, y los hispanos en este país no son nada diferentes. También es verdad que los cristianos protestantes que hacen proselitismo han tenido éxito al valerse de la pobreza y la inseguridad de nuestra gente, especialmente predicando el «evangelio de la prosperidad».

Otro factor: no podemos desestimar el impacto del racismo, y hay que ser francos en este sentido, tanto en la sociedad estadounidense como en la Iglesia, desafortunadamente. El debate sombrío, poco productivo y sin término sobre asuntos de inmigración ha revelado esta realidad. Si nuestra gente se siente victimizada en la sociedad y marginada en la vida de la Iglesia, es natural que comiencen a buscar otro lugar que les dé la bienvenida y les trate con la dignidad que se merecen. Desafortunadamente, muchas de estas personas terminan rechazando el cristianismo porque se dan cuenta de que muchos de quienes se identifican como cristianos les tratan de una manera que poco refleja la fe cristiana.

Estos son problemas serios. Pero creo que el problema más serio que tenemos no viene tanto de estos factores sino de la cultura dominante en los Estados Unidos, la cual es agresiva e incluso militantemente secularizada. Este es un tema que desafortunadamente no se discute mucho en las discusiones sobre el futuro del ministerio hispano. Es tiempo de cambiar eso.

De hecho, a no ser que nosotros como líderes hispanos diseñemos una estrategia para entender y confrontar la cultura secular, nuestros planes y programas pastorales nunca serán tan efectivos como esperamos.

Los retos de una cultura secular

Permítanme clarificar lo que tengo en mente al hablar de una cultura secularizada. Existe una teoría sociológica que afirma que la secularización es inevitable, casi el resultado más natural del proceso de modernización. En otras palabras, la fe religiosa está supuesta a perder importancia y eventualmente a desaparecer a medida que la sociedad avanza tecnológicamente, accede a educación y es más sofisticada. Esa teoría puede ser una buena explicación del tipo de secularización que ocurrió en Europa. Pero aquí en los Estados Unidos la secularización se ha servido de una estrategia deliberada de «descristianización» llevada a cabo por élites culturales durante muchos años.

Existe un buen libro académico sobre este tema, el cual se titula «The Secular Revolution» (La revolución secular) editado por Christian Smith de la Universidad de Carolina del Norte. Smith y sus colegas demuestran cómo el fenómeno de la secularización ha sido avanzado por grupos poderosos sirviendo intereses especiales en los mundos del derecho y la política, la educación y los medios de comunicación.

El resultado es que lo que llamo «ateísmo práctico» de hecho se ha convertido en la religión establecida en los Estados Unidos. El precio a pagar por participar en nuestra vida económica, política y social es que esencialmente tenemos que aprender a vivir como si Dios no existiera. No podemos hablar de religión o fe en los lugares de trabajo o públicamente. Con seguridad la gente lo hace, pero aquellas personas son consideradas como fanáticas o miembros de la «derecha cristiana».

Todo esto es muy extraño en un país que fue fundado por cristianos; de hecho, por católicos hispanos. Ciertamente, de donde vengo, en San Antonio, el Evangelio ya se predicaba en español y los hispanos celebraban misa antes de que George Washington naciera; antes de que hubiera un Congreso; antes de que hubiera Wall Street.

Pero hoy en día la religión en los Estados Unidos ha sido reducida a un área de devoción privada y emoción personal. La religión es algo que hacemos los domingos o en nuestros hogares, pero no se considera como algo que ha de influenciar lo que hacemos el resto de la semana en nuestro trabajo y nuestra vida civil. Esta separación entre la religión y la vida pública ha provocado muchos otros problemas en nuestro país. Ha contribuido al incremento de un relativismo moral, es decir la idea de que no hay verdades en el orden moral, sólo opiniones diferentes y puntos de vista.

Más en línea con mi argumento, la secularización tiene un «efecto alarmante» en la vivencia de la fe de todas las personas. Vemos esto en el aumento del número de personas que dicen que no practican ninguna religión. Nunca antes en la historia de nuestro país habían vivido tantas personas sin estar conscientes día a día de la presencia de Dios. Estas personas no odian a Dios como los ateos. Simplemente han olvidado quién es Dios.

Estas fuerzas secularizadoras ponen aún más presión sobre los hispanos y otros grupos inmigrantes. ¿Por qué? Porque los inmigrantes son constantemente forzados a «acomodarse», a desestimar sus diferencias culturales y religiosas, y también a demostrar que son «verdaderos» estadounidenses o americanos. Hace una generación era difícil imaginar a un hispano diciendo que «no tenía religión», pero el número se ha duplicado en los últimos años.

Mis amigos, creo que necesitamos pensar críticamente sobre la realidad de nuestra cultura. Los primeros misioneros en este país estudiaron las culturas indígenas para luego evangelizarlas. Necesitamos hacer lo mismo. Necesitamos estrategias para confrontar la cultura que vayan más allá de simplemente servir a los hispanos a nivel pastoral. Definitivamente necesitamos fomentar la formación de líderes católicos hispanos y necesitamos un plan pastoral para educar a los hispanos en la fe y sostenerlos con los sacramentos. Pero esto tiene que ser parte de una amplia estrategia evangélica. Necesitamos comprometernos una vez más con la misión de re-evangelización, de predicar el Evangelio una vez más a los Estados Unidos.

Quiero decir más sobre esto en un minuto.

2

El reto de la pobreza: material y espiritual

Pero antes de hacer esto, quiero mencionar un segundo reto urgente que creo que enfrentamos como líderes hispanos. Llamaré este segundo reto: «pobreza: material y espiritual».

En términos generales, los hispanos en este país están siguiendo el modelo inmigrante tradicional. La segunda y tercera generación de hispanos son mucho más educados, hablan mejor el idioma dominante y están mejor posicionados económicamente que la primera generación.

Pero lo preocupante es que cerca del 25 por ciento de todos los hispanos, sin importar su generación, viven por debajo del nivel de pobreza y ese número no mejora mucho después de varias generaciones. Unido a esto tenemos una tasa de deserción escolar de cerca del 22 por ciento entre jóvenes en la preparatoria y el incremento dramático de niños hispanos creciendo en hogares con sólo un padre de familia. Ambas situaciones son indicadores indiscutibles de futura pobreza. Me preocupa que podemos estar sirviendo pastoralmente a una subclase hispana permanente.

Tenemos problemas morales y sociales también. Nuestro pueblo tiene una de las tasas más altas de embarazo entre adolescentes, aborto y niños nacidos fuera del matrimonio en comparación con otros grupos étnicos en el país. Estos son asuntos de los cuales no hablamos lo suficiente. No podemos ignorarlos simplemente como «asuntos conservadores».

La verdad es que muchos de nuestros jóvenes están tomando decisiones morales erróneas que tienen consecuencias enormes y permanentes, no sólo para ellos sino también para nuestra sociedad y para el futuro de la cultura hispana en los Estados Unidos. Desde mi perspectiva, estos son asuntos serios que tienen que ver con «justicia». Si queremos justicia para nuestros jóvenes, si queremos lo que Dios quiere para ellos —vidas que manifiesten su gran dignidad de hijos e hijas de Dios— entonces necesitamos encontrar maneras de enseñar a nuestros jóvenes sobre virtudes, autodisciplina y responsabilidad personal. Cualquier valoración del futuro de nuestro ministerio tiene que contemplar estos asuntos. Cualquier plan pastoral con sentido tiene que responder a este reto.

3

El único camino para el liderazgo: Jesucristo

Muy bien. Hasta ahora he respondido a la primera pregunta de Hosffman, los retos que creo que enfrenta nuestro pueblo hispano. En general, he identificado estos retos como la cultura secular agresiva en los Estados Unidos y las realidades de pobreza material y espiritual entre nuestra gente.

Ahora miremos a la segunda pregunta de Hosffman: qué caminos debemos tomar para responder a estos retos.

Mi respuesta a esta pregunta es corta; una palabra: Jesucristo.

Jesucristo tiene que ser nuestro camino, nuestra verdad y nuestra vida, tanto para cada uno de nosotros a nivel personal como para nuestro ministerio en general. No puede haber otro camino ni otro paradigma o modelo para el ministerio hispano.

La única «razón» para la cual existe el ministerio hispano es para llevar a cabo la llamada de Cristo, la misión que le dio a su Iglesia: predicar el arrepentimiento y el perdón de los pecados en su nombre a todas las naciones, bautizar y hacer discípulos, y dar a conocer sus enseñanzas.

El ministerio hispano debe significar sólo una cosa: llevar al pueblo hispano al encuentro con Jesucristo en su Iglesia. Con frecuencia, debemos decir, perdemos de vista esta dimensión. Nos ocupamos pensando en nuestros planes y programas, quién tiene el control, qué es lo que ocurre en la burocracia. Nuestras intenciones siempre son buenas. Queremos buscar la mejor manera de ayudar a nuestro pueblo. Sin embargo, me preocupa que nos concentremos tanto en los «medios» que podemos terminar confundiéndolos con el fin.

Todos nuestros planes y programas pastorales asumen que estamos tratando de servir a Cristo y su Evangelio. Pero mis hermanos y hermanos, no podemos seguir simplemente asumiendo a Cristo. Necesitamos asegurarnos que lo estamos proclamando.

La proclamación de Jesucristo tiene que ser el criterio por medio del cual medimos todo lo que hacemos en el ministerio hispano. ¿Estamos haciendo discípulos nuevos? ¿Estamos fortaleciendo la fe de quienes ya son discípulos? ¿El conocimiento y el amor de Cristo son dados a conocer por medio de nuestro trabajo?

La misión que Cristo le dio a su Iglesia se puede resumir en dos palabras: la predicación y la enseñanza. Proclamar la Buena Nueva de la salvación y enseñar a mujeres y hombres a vivir según lo que Cristo nos dejó. Ésta es una buena manera de pensar y organizar nuestra respuesta pastoral a los retos que he identificado. La predicación y la enseñanza.

La predicación y la enseñanza

Primero, necesitamos predicar el Evangelio. «La Nueva Evangelización» se ha convertido en una frase común en la Iglesia. Esto está bien. Ahora debe convertirse en un estilo de vida, una forma de discipulado, la clave básica para toda nuestra acción pastoral.

En nuestros ministerios hispanos tenemos que entender que predicamos la Buena Nueva a los pobres. Ésta es la realidad, mis amigos. Mucha de nuestra gente es pobre ahora y será pobre por muchos años. Nuestra gente sufre discriminación y explotación por causa de su pobreza y su raza. Millones de ellos tienen que vivir forzadamente en la sombras porque nuestros legisladores no tienen el suficiente valor de arreglar nuestro deteriorado sistema de inmigración.

Necesitamos predicar la Buena Nueva de Cristo a ellos. Pero también necesitamos mostrarles esa buena noticia en la acción. Cada vez estoy más convencido que tenemos que responder a los asuntos relacionados con la pobreza hispana con un énfasis intencional y práctico en la educación: educación en general y educación en la fe.

Todo experto sobre el tema de la pobreza nos dice que la educación es la clave esencial para salir de ésta. Eso significa, en primer lugar, que necesitamos reducir las tasas de deserción escolar entre los hispanos. Para ello tenemos que buscar nuevas maneras de mantener a nuestros niños castos y en la escuela y ayudarles a apreciar el valor de la educación. Necesitamos abogar en favor de cambios reales en la educación pública y del apoyo público a la educación privada, especialmente en nuestros distritos escolares más pobres. Y necesitamos reunir todos los recursos de nuestra propia red de escuelas católicas para responder a este reto.

Educar a nuestra gente en la fe también debe ser una prioridad urgente. Necesitamos encontrar caminos para enseñar la fe de tal manera que nuestra gente «la entienda»; no sólo el contenido intelectual de la fe sino el poder verdadero y transformador del encuentro con Jesucristo.

Necesitamos mostrarles que nuestra fe católica es una forma de vida hermosa y completa, la cual trae gozo y paz y nos ofrece respuestas verdaderas a los problemas de la vida diaria. Necesitamos enseñar la fe de manera que mujeres y hombres no sólo la quieran vivir sino que sean inspirados para defenderla y compartirla con otros, en sus hogares, en sus comunidades y en sus lugares de trabajo.

Mis hermanos y hermanas, es esencial que nuestro pueblo conozca su propia historia, nuestra historia, la gran historia del catolicismo hispano en las Américas.

¿Sabe nuestro pueblo que el Evangelio era predicado en español y que los hispanos celebran la santa misa en nuestro país en hacia el año 1560, más de 200 años antes de la declaración de independencia? ¿Conocen ellos los nombres y las vidas de los admirables sacerdotes y misioneros laicos, los santos y los mártires que trajeron la fe a esta tierra?

¿Saben ellos sobre la más reciente «memoria histórica» del ministerio hispano? ¿Los Encuentros, incluyendo el «Encuentro 2000», el cual fue la única celebración oficial del año jubilar a nivel nacional? ¿Conocen los documentos de la Conferencia de Obispos Católicos sobre el ministerio hispano?

¿Cómo va a conocer nuestra gente todas estas cosas a no ser que nosotros seamos quienes se las compartamos? Como líderes, nosotros mismos tenemos que aprender esta gran historia y promover maneras creativas para compartirla con nuestro pueblo. Necesitamos motivar la devoción a nuestros santos locales, especialmente nuestros santos y beatos hispanos y latinoamericanos. Nuestra gente necesita conocer a estas mujeres y hombres santos que compartieron su fe y reconocer el valor de sus luchas en contra del pecado, la injusticia y la opresión.

Nuestro pueblo también necesita saber sobre las mujeres y los hombres que han dedicado sus vidas en los últimos años al servicio de la Iglesia en el ministerio hispano.

También necesitamos concentrarnos en animar nuevos líderes. Todavía no tenemos suficientes latinos preparados asumiendo posiciones de liderazgo en la Iglesia y en nuestras comunidades. Hay muchas razones para ello. Las mujeres y los hombres latinos que son profesionales todavía luchan fuertemente para establecerse en sus campos. Todavía enfrentan mucho racismo y obstáculos institucionales para triunfar, lo cual les toma gran parte de su energía y su tiempo. Por consiguiente, no les queda mucho para «dar» a la comunidad, a la Iglesia.

Necesitamos encontrar maneras para ayudarles y motivarles a compartir su tiempo, talento y tesoro sirviendo a nuestra gente. Tenemos que encontrar una mejor manera de promover nuestras organizaciones y facilitar la participación de los latinos exitosos en nuestros ministerios y actividades.

Pero lo que realmente tenemos que hacer es promover el sentido de discipulado entre toda nuestra gente. Necesitamos recordarles que todos los católicos están llamados a ser misioneros y líderes proclamando la fe y predicando el Evangelio con nuestras vidas.

Esto aplica a nosotros también, mis amigos. La mayoría de nosotros aquí reunidos somos «católicos profesionales». Digo esto con respeto profundo y agradecimiento por su servicio a Cristo y a su Iglesia. Pero ustedes deben recordar que su trabajo por la Iglesia —en oficinas diocesanas y parroquias, en salones de clase, en todos sus distintos ministerios— no agota sus responsabilidades como discípulos. Su discipulado tiene que actualizarse en toda área de sus vidas.

Estamos llamados a convertirnos en mejores ejemplos del Evangelio que se nos invita a proclamar. Si ustedes guían el camino, mis amigos, otros seguirán. Tengan la seguridad.

5
¡Somos Católicos!

Ya me queda poco tiempo. Déjenme contemplar la tercera pregunta de Hosffman: ¿Cómo podemos aprovechar este momento histórico?

Primero, pienso que necesitamos considerar lo que está en juego. Escucho en estos días bastante conversación sobre lo que se conoce como «catolicismo cultural» al hablar de los hispanos. Ésta es una categoría que se supone describe a personas que han crecido como católicos. Se asume que estas personas tienen una dedicación especial al trabajo por la justicia social que se mantiene con ellos aún cuando muchos ya no practican su fe. Se asume que el «catolicismo cultural» es algo bueno, un signo de que los valores cristianos han penetrado profundamente en el carácter de una persona y la manera como ésta ve la vida.

Sin embargo, recuerdo las palabras que una vez habló el Señor: «¿De qué le servirá al hombre ganar el mundo entero, si pierde su vida?» (Mc 8,36).

¿De qué le servirá a nuestro pueblo convertirse en una mayoría en los Estados Unidos si abandonamos nuestra fe católica en el proceso, si perdemos nuestra vida? Jesús no vino a sufrir y morir para que pudiéramos ser «católicos culturales».

El Evangelio no es una actitud o una filosofía de vida. Es una relación con el Dios de la vida, una relación que Cristo mismo quiso que fuera profundamente eclesial; es decir, una relación que vivimos por él, con él y en él, en su Iglesia.

Necesitamos abstenernos de toda simplificación, de cualquier intento de reducir el Evangelio a un mínimo común denominador. Los principios católicos pueden hacer de la sociedad un mejor lugar para vivir, pero sólo la plenitud del Evangelio puede llevar a mujeres y hombres a la vida eterna.

Para aprovechar este momento necesitamos asumir nuestra identidad como católicos.

¡Somos Católicos! Esto significa que aceptamos la plenitud de nuestra herencia como católicos hispanos.

Carlos Fuentes, nuestro gran escritor mexicano, ha dicho: «no hay futuro vivo con un pasado muerto». Él tiene la razón. El camino hacia el futuro consiste en siempre nutrirnos del pasado, no sólo de las palabras en las Escrituras sino también de la gran comunión de los santos.

En ese espíritu quiero dejarlos esta tarde con las reflexiones de dos personajes de nuestra historia católica hispana.

El primero es Bartolomé de Las Casas, el gran evangelista dominico y campeón de los derechos humanos. Todos conocemos su historia. De hecho, hace poco estaba releyendo su defensa de la dignidad de los indígenas y pensaba que cada palabra pudiera aplicarse a nuestros debates actuales sobre el aborto.

Lo que lo hace que Bartolomé de Las casas sea relevante para nosotros es que sus ideas sobre la evangelización de la cultura fueron simples pero efectivas. De su obra clásica, «Del único modo de atraer a todos los pueblos a la verdadera religión», ofrezco dos puntos:

Primero, Fray Bartolomé dice que Cristo y los apóstoles evangelizaron (a) ganándo la mente de las personas con argumentos razonables; y (b) atrayendo sus corazones con invitaciones amables y motivos convincentes.

Esa es una buena manera para que nosotros pensemos nuestros ministerios también. Necesitamos una estrategia para evangelizar nuestra cultura que sea intelectualmente rigurosa e insertada en un amor profundo por nuestros hermanos y hermanas y un deseo de que conozcan a Cristo.

Segundo, Fray Bartolomé nos recuerda algo que acabo de mencionar: que nuestra misión es profundamente eclesial. Él nos dice que tenemos una «triple responsabilidad: primero, predicar la fe. Segundo, alimentar a los creyentes con los sacramentos. Tercero, enseñar a los creyentes que han sido alimentados con los sacramentos a mantener los sacramentos y vivir una vida buena».

Una vez más, éste es un camino claro y simple a seguir. Evangelizamos, educamos y traemos hombres y mujeres a la vida de la Iglesia, los alimentamos con el Pan de Vida y les ayudamos a vivir según las enseñanzas de Cristo.

Finalmente, quiero proponer que reflexionemos sobre el trabajo del Beato misionero Miguel Pro, el gran mártir jesuita durante la persecución mexicana en la década de 1920.

Pienso que todos conocen su historia, también. Lo que necesitamos es su convicción de que sólo Cristo puede salvarnos. En un momento en el que practicar la fe era considerado un pecado que merecía el máximo castigo, su convicción le llevó a arriesgar su vida todos los días al llevar a la gente a Cristo en la Eucaristía y en el sacramento de la Penitencia.

Necesitamos su creatividad, valor y osadía para encontrar caminos nuevos para llevar a nuestros hermanos y hermanas hacia Cristo.

Mis amigos, en el futuro debemos predicar con la confianza de aquellos que conocen la esperanza de la resurrección. Si el Dios que resucitó a Jesús de entre los muertos está con nosotros, ¿qué podemos temer?

Gracias por su atención esta tarde. Agradezco la oportunidad de acompañarles en esta discusión tan importante.

Permítanme dejarlos con las últimas palabras del Beato Miguel: «¡Viva Cristo Rey!»

Y oro para que Nuestra Señora de Guadalupe, nuestra madre, nos proteja y nos guíe en nuestro servicio a su Hijo, especialmente en los próximos días en que reflexionaremos sobre el presente y el futuro del ministerio católico hispano en los Estados Unidos.

Gracias.

Participantes en el simposio por grupos de estudio

1

El ministerio hispano y el catolicismo en los Estados Unidos

1. Carmen Aguinaco
   Presidenta del Consejo Nacional Católico para el Ministerio Hispano (NCCHM)
2. Alejandro Aguilera-Titus
   Director asistente del Secretariado de Diversidad Cultural en la Iglesia, USCCB
3. Rev. Richard Clifford, SJ
   Decano de la Escuela de Teología y Ministerio (STM) de Boston College
4. Rev. Allan Deck, SJ
   Director ejecutivo del Secretariado de Diversidad Cultural en la Iglesia, USCCB
5. Mons. Ricardo García
   Obispo de Monterey, CA; Director del Subcomité de Asuntos Hispanos, USCCB
6. Mons. José H. Gómez
   Arzobispo coadjutor de Los Ángeles; Director del Comité sobre Diversidad Cultural en la Iglesia, USCCB, en el año 2009
7. Dr. Timothy Matovina
   Profesor de teología, Director del Centro Cushwa para el estudio del catolicismo estadounidense, University of Notre Dame
8. Mario Paredes
   Presidente de la Asociación de Líderes Católicos Latinos (CALL); Sociedad Bíblica de América
9. Dra. Milagros Peña
   Profesora de sociología y decana asociada de ciencias sociales y del comportamiento, University of Miami
10. Enid Román
    Presidenta de la Asociación Nacional Católica de Directores Diocesanos para el Ministerio Hispano (NCADDHM)

2

El ministerio hispano y la reflexión teológica

1. Dra. María Pilar Aquino
   Profesora de teología y estudios religiosos, University of San Diego

2. **Dra. Shawn Copeland**
Profesora asociada de teología, Boston College

3. **Dr. Roberto Goizueta**
Profesor de teología, Boston College

4. **Rev. Rafael Luévano**
Profesor asociado de estudios religiosos, Chapman University

5. **Dra. Alicia Marill**
*Profesora asociada y directora del programa de doctorado en ministerio en Barry University,
Barry University*

6. **Dra. Carmen Nanko**
*Profesora asistente de ministerio pastoral, directora del programa doctorado ecuménico en
ministerio, directora del certificado en estudios pastorales, Catholic Theological Union*

7. **Rev. Jorge Presmanes, o.p.**
*Profesor asistente de teología y director del Instituto para la Teología y el Ministerio
Hispano/Latino en Barry University*

8. **Dra. Nancy Pineda-Madrid**
Profesora asistente de teología y ministerio hispano, Boston College

9. **Rev. Mark Wedig, o.p.**
*professor de teología litúrgica, decano asociado de estudios de postgrado en el colegio de
ciencias y artes, director del departamento de teología y filosofía, Barry University*

3

El ministerio hispano, la evangelización y la formación en la fe

1. **Carlos Aedo**
Director de educación religiosa para hispanos, Arquidiócesis de Hartford

2. **Santiago Cortés-Sjoberg**
Loyola Press

3. **William S. Dinger**
Presidente de William H. Sadlier, Inc.

4. **Dr. Thomas Groome**
Profesor de teología y educación religiosa, Boston College

5. **Dulce Jiménez**
William H. Sadlier, Inc.

6. Dr. Hosffman Ospino

   Profesor asistente de ministerio hispano y educación religiosa, director de programas de postgrado en ministerio hispano, Boston College

7. Jo Ann Paradise

   Harcout Religion Publishers

8. Jo Rotunno

   RCL Benziger

9. Dra. Maruja Sedano

   Directora de la oficina de educación religiosa, Arquidiócesis de Chicago

10. Thomas McGrath

    Loyola Press

11. Daniel Mulhall

    RCL Benziger

4

El ministerio hispano, la liturgia y la espiritualidad

1. Rev. Eduardo Fernández, SJ

   Profesor asociado de teología pastoral y ministerio, Escuela Jesuita de Teología de Santa Clara

2. Rev. Raúl Gómez-Ruíz, S.D.S.

   Profesor y vicepresidente de asuntos académicos en la Escuela de Teología del Sagrado Corazón en Hales Corners, WI

3. Dra. Cecilia González-Andrieu

   Profesora asistente de estudios teológicos, Loyola Marymount University

4. Dr. Robert Hurteau

   Director del Centro para la Religión y la Espiritualidad, Loyola Marymount University

5. Rev. Alejandro López-Cardinale

   Renew International

6. Pedro Rubalcava

   Oregon Catholic Press

7. Rev. Juan Sosa

   Presidente del Instituto Nacional Hispano de Liturgia

5

El ministerio hispano y la Pastoral Juvenil Hispana

1. Rev. José Burgués, Sch. P.

   Director del Instituto Pastoral del Sureste (SEPI)

2. Liliana Flores

   National Catholic Network de Pastoral Juvenil Hispana, La Red

3. Reinardo Malavé

   Director del Primer Encuentro Nacional de Pastoral Juvenil Hispana (2006)

4. Rev. Michael G. Lee, SJ

   Professor asistente de studios teológicos, Loyola Marymount University

5. Walter Mena

   Director de programas de formación, Instituto Fe y Vida

6. Ken Johnson-Mondragón

   Director de investigación y publicaciones, Instituto Fe y Vida

7. Guadalupe Ospino

   Apostolado hispano, parroquia de San Patricio en Lawrence, MA

8. Sean Reynolds

   National Federation for Catholic Youth Ministry (NFCYM)

9. Víctor Valenzuela

   William H. Sadlier, Inc.

442

6

El ministerio hispano y la justicia social

1. Hna. Sonia Avi, IHM

   Oficina del ministerio hispano, Diócesis de Candem, NJ

2. Dr. Arturo Chávez

   Presidente y director ejecutivo del Colegio Católico México Americano (MACC)

3. Rev. Ken Davis, OFM, Conv

   Seminario San José, Saint Benedict, LA

4. Hna. Hilda Mateo, MGSpS

   Misioneras Guadalupanas del Espíritu Santo

5. Rev. Bill Rickle, sj
Director del Instituto para la Migración, la Cultura y el Ministerio

6. Mons. Jaime Soto
Director del Comité sobre Diversidad Cultural en la Iglesia, usccb, en el año 2010

7. Hope Villella
National Pastoral Life Center

7
El ministerio hispano y la formación para el liderazgo

1. Hna. Ruth Bolarte, ihm
Presidenta de la Federación de Institutos Pastorales

2. Rev. Wayne Cavalier, o.p.
Director del Congar Institute for Ministry Development

3. Paulina Espinosa
Directora del Instituto Hispano, Escuela Jesuita de Teología de Santa Clara

4. Rev. Tom Florek, sj
Director del Instituto Cultural de Liderazgo en el Medio Oeste (iclm)

5. Dra. Elsie M. Miranda
Profesora asistente de teología práctica, directora de la maestría en teología práctica y directora de formación ministerial, Barry University

6. Dra. Ana María Pineda
Profesora asociada de estudios religiosos, Santa Clara University

7. Luis Soto
Director ejecutivo del Centro San Juan Diego, Denver, co

8. Rudy Vargas
Director ejecutivo del Centro Pastoral Hispano del Nordeste

9. Rev. Richard Vega
Presidente de la Federación Nacional de Consejos Presbiterales (nfpc)

Autores

Arturo Chávez, Ph.D. es presidente y director ejecutivo del Colegio Católico México Americano en San Antonio, TX.

Raúl Gómez-Ruíz, S.D.S., Ph.D. es profesor y vicepresidente de asuntos académicos en la Escuela de Teología del Sagrado Corazón en Hales Corners, WI.

Ken Johnson-Mondragón, candidato al D.Min. es director de investigación y publicaciones del Instituto Fe y Vida en Stockton, CA.

Alicia Marill, D.Min. es profesora asociada y directora del programa de doctorado en ministerio en Barry University, Miami, FL.

Timothy Matovina, Ph.D. is profesor de teología y el director del Centro Cushwa de la Universidad de Notre Dame para el estudio del catolicismo estadounidense, South Bend, IN.

Elsie M. Miranda, D.Min. es profesora asistente de teología práctica, directora de la maestría en teología práctica y directora de formación ministerial en Barry University, Miami, FL.

Hosffman Ospino, Ph.D. is profesor asistente de ministerio hispano y educación religiosa; director de programas de postgrado en ministerio hispano en la Escuela de Teología y Ministerio de Boston College, Boston, MA.

Jorge Presmanes, O.P., D.Min. es profesor asistente de teología y director del Instituto para la Teología y el Ministerio Hispano/Latino en Barry University, Miami, FL.

Is Life in society possible without Morality?

Sergio Bastianel answers the question by addressing the responsibility of Christians to confront issues of justice within society in ways that promote the common good. The author, who views one's relationship with the «other» as foundational to the moral experience, places a priority on human relationships based on sharing and solidarity. He emphasizes the interconnections between personal morals and social justice and raises fundamental questions about such issues as political life and economics, about hunger and development, and about the true meaning of «charity», all of which are relevant issues in our contemporary societies.

Sergio Bastianel s.J. is currently professor of moral theology at the Pontifical Gregorian University in Rome and also serves as its academic vice-rector. He spent his early years teaching and lecturing at the Pontifical Theological Faculty of San Luigi in Naples, Italy, and in later years he served as dean of the theological faculty of the Pontifical Gregorian University.

Expressing Christian Faith in ways that are meaningful to the Latino/Hispanic Community

In this work Goizueta challenges both traditional European and American theologies. Although Goizueta recognizes that «Hispanic» and «Latino» might be artificially imposed labels, he finds a common link in the Spanish language and a shared culture. He describes the Latino/Hispanic experience using the Biblical language of people in exile who are living on the margins of society and who are seeking ways to rediscover their identity. Faith is central to their experience, and the author suggests ways in which these communities can embrace and follow the presence of Jesus. The author offers examples of discipleship that will have universal significance both for Christians and for all who are working for a better world.

The Cuban-American Roberto Goizueta is presently a noted professor in the theology department at Boston College. He is past-president of the Society of Catholic Theology in the United States and of the Academy of Hispanic Catholic Theologians of the United States. This book has received an award from the Association of Catholic Press. This work and the content of his unique Hispano/Latino theology are presented for the first time to the Spanish speaking world.

BUY IT AT:

www.conviviumpress.com

Caminemos con Jesús.
Hacia una teología
del acompañamiento
ROBERTO S. GOIZUETA
ISBN: 978-1-934996-10-2
Spanish Language
320 Pages
Series Hispania

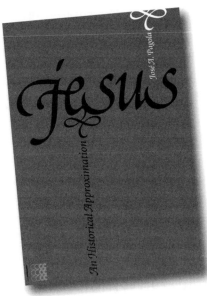

Rediscover the significance of the Doctrine of the Trinity for the Christian Faith

A book for students and professors in the field of Theology and Religious Studies. The Christian church affirms that the Trinity —one God in three persons, Father, Son, and Holy Spirit— is the central mystery of the Christian faith. This book documents the historical development of the doctrine of the Trinity and its significance. In a broad and systematic way, Ladaria traces the debates within the early Christian church as the concept of the Trinity developed. He also reflects on the great masters of church tradition, and is in dialogue with various contemporary theologians. This book has been written as an aid in grasping the Trinitarian formulation both historically and theologically.

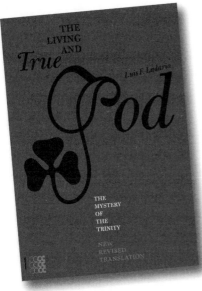

Archbishop Luis F. Ladaria, a Jesuit theologian who is currently the Secretary of the *Congregation for the Doctrine of the Faith*, has been a professor of theology at the Pontifical Gregorian University of Rome since 1984, teaching Christology, Trinity and Anthropology. Since 2004 he has been the general secretary of the International Theological Commission.

Hispanic Ministry in the 21st Century: Present and Future

El ministerio hispano en el siglo XXI: presente y futuro

This book was printed on *thin opaque smooth white Bible paper*, using the *Minion* and *Type Embellishments One* font families.
This edition was printed in D'VINNI, S.A., in Bogotá, Colombia, during the last weeks of the ninth month of year two thousand ten.

Ad publicam lucem datus mense septembre in nativitate Sancte Marie